soup

photography by Battman

recipes by 108 chefs
from the simple to the complex

Distributed in the United States by Battman Studios
New York, New York

Published by Battman Studios
Text and Photographs © 2008 by Battman
All rights reserved. Printed in China.

ISBN 0-933477-29-5

www.battmanstudios.com

Editor: Stephanie R. Mercurio
Book Design: enmoda design, New York
Recipe Editor: Mark R. Vogel, foodforthoughtonline.net

Food Styling: Kersti Bowser, gourmetbutterfly.com / page 20, 42, 154, 184
Bowls provided by: jonopandolfi.com / page 18, 58, 86, 158, 176, 194, front cover
nytogei.com / page 26, 132, 138 — Tadashi Ono, Matsuri / page 114

Front Cover Photograph: Michael Anthony, Gramercy Tavern
Back Cover Photograph: Derrick VanDuzer, District
Cover Photography: Battman

Restaurants and Chefs

Restaurant	Chef	Page
21 Club	John Greeley	48
Allen & Delancey	Neil G. Ferguson	12
Annisa	Anita Lo	14
Aquavit	Johan Svensson	18
Aureole	Tony Aiazzi	16
B. Smith's	Barbara Smith	20
Barbounia	Efi Naon	98
Blackbird	Paul Kahan	22
BLT Fish	Amy Louise Eubanks	24
BLT Market	David Malbequi	152
BLT Steak	Laurent Tourondel	34
Blue Smoke	Kenny Callaghan	26
Brasserie 8½	Julian Alonzo	28
Brio	Massimo Carbone	30
Butter	Alexandra Guarnaschelli	32
Café Boulud	Gavin Kaysen	36
Cafe Centro	Franck Deletrain	38
Casa Mono	Andy Nusser	40
Chanterelle	David Waltuck	136
Charlie Trotter's	Charlie Trotter	200
Chez Jean Pierre	Jean Pierre Leverier	196
Craft	Karen DeMasco	44
Crave Ceviche Bar	Todd Mitgang	46
Daniel	Dominique Ansel	82
Daniel	Daniel Boulud	70
Daniel	Jean François Bruel	94
David Burke & Donatella	Eric Hara	50
David Burke Las Vegas	David Burke	92
DB Bistro Moderne	Olivier Muller	52
District	Derrick VanDuzer	54
District	Patricia Williams	6
Dos Caminos	Ivy Stark	76
Dovetail	John Fraser	56
Dry Creek Kitchen	Charlie Palmer	74
Eighty One	Ed Brown	10
Eleven Madison Park	Daniel Humm	8
Emporium Brasil	Samire Soares	78
Fleur de Sel	Cyril Renaud	80
Food Network	Susan Stockton	84
Gilt	Christopher Lee	4
Gramercy Tavern	Michael Anthony	86
Havana Blue	Jose "Pepe" Rodriguez	60
Ilili	Philippe Massoud	72
Izakaya	Michael Schulson	88
Jean-Georges	Greg Brainin	66
Kyotofu	Pauline Balboa	102
Landmarc	Marc Murphy	106
Landmarc	Frank Proto	106
L'Atelier	Joël Robuchon	104
L'Atelier	Yosuke Suga	96
Le Bernardin	Michael Laiskonis	108
Le Bernardin	Eric Ripert	62
Le Petit Chateau	Scott Cutaneo	110
Mandarin Oriental	Toni Robertson	112
Matsuhisa	Nobu Matsuhisa	138
Matsuri	Tadashi Ono	114
Merkato Fifty Five	Marcus Samuelsson	198
Mozzarelli's	Ron Malina	116
Mr. K's	Cheng-Hua Yang	118
Negril Village	Marva Layne	120
Nobu	Ricky Estrellado	122
Nobu	Toshio Tomita	128
Norma's	Emile Castillo	124
Olana	Albert DiMeglio	126
P*ong	Pichet Ong	142
Park Avenue Spring	Craig Koketsu	130
Pearl Oyster Bar	Rebecca Charles	132
Peri Ela	Yasin Varol	134
Perry St	Erik Battes	68
Rickshaw Dumpling Bar	Anita Lo	144
RM Seafood Las Vegas	Rick Moonen	146
Rock Center Café	Antonio Prontelli	148
Rocking Horse Cafe	Jan Mendelson	150
Shanghai Cuisine	Hongfu Feng	160
Shanghai Cuisine	Jijie Hong	160
Sueños	Sue Torres	156
Sushi Samba	Michael Cressotti	162
Table 10	Emeril Lagasse	58
Table fifty-two	Art Smith	164
Tamarind	Gary Walia	168
Telepan	Bill Telepan	166
Terrace in the Sky	Jason Potanovich	170
Thai Market	Tanaporn Tangwibulchai	172
The Four Seasons	Christian Albin	190
The Four Seasons	Fred Mero	190
The Four Seasons	Peco Zantilaveevan	190
The Harrison	Amanda Freitag	174
The Harrison	Paul Lefebvre	174
The Institute of Culinary Education	Andrew Gold	90
The Modern	Gabriel Kreuther	176
The River Café	Brad Steelman	140
The Russian Tea Room	Peter Moldovan	158
The Russian Tea Room	Marc Taxiera	158
The Waverly Inn	John DeLucie	188
Tropic Spice	Kenneth W. Collins	182
Trump Grill	Armando Carbone	180
Union Square Cafe	Carmen Quagliata	186
Vong	Pierré Schutz	64
Vong	Jean-Georges Vongerichten	64
WD~50	Wylie Dufresne	202
Woo Lae Oak	Harold Soo Hyung Kim	192
Yonah Shimmel Knishes	Alex Volfman	194

Chefs / Authors

	Chef	Page
	Cat Cora	42
	Tyler Florence	184
	Joanna Pruess	100
	Timothy Reardon	178
	David Rosengarten	154

Bread Pairing

For decades now I've been on a mission. As a baker who is obsessed with his occupation, I've been spending my life baking bread and trying to get people to appreciate it more than I think most do. One problem is that the people eating bread just don't think much about it. They'll slap some meat between a couple of slices: A convenient way to eat the meat isn't it? Or they'll slather it with something and then admire the slatherings…"Wonderful olive oil, my dear." Or "Did you ever taste such good butter?" They're not doing what they would if it were wine. They're not savoring it.

But just as with wine, the first taste can be heaven. You drink wine with your eyes, inhale it, sip it, notice the nuances of flavor. Now, I'm pleading with you, do something just like that with bread. Don't munch on it mindlessly, don't wolf it down, don't take it for granted. Instead, start by looking at it. If it happens to be the species of bread I'm so wild about, the traditional Italian rustic loaf, notice the dark, handsome crust, notice the interior's complexly beautiful honeycomb structure formed by bubbles – or "eyes" – ranging from about a dime to a nickel in size. Smell the pleasantly mellow/acrid aroma (a result of fermentation, just as with wine, beer and cheese). Bite into it and chew slowly. There should be almost a meatiness to it as you break through the crust to the soft but resiliently alive "crumb" inside. There should be a maltiness (think beer again) and a hint of agriculture, by which I mean that if you think about it you know it came from wheat, from the field.

But what about the essence of this book, SOUP – and beyond that, soup paired with bread? In the Renaissance, the French formally married the two. At first a food called "sop" – liquid or semi-liquid nourishment meant to be sopped up with bread – was sold by street vendors as a remedy for exhaustion, as a restorative, a restaurer. And eventually it appeared in the shops that would become the restaurants of today. The truth is, I think any good bread is going to go well with any good soup. But you can improve on the randomness, immeasurably.

In my new book, My Bread, which describes my simple no-knead, long-fermentation technique for baking rustic Italian loaves, I start with a simple round loaf, or boule, and then I keep manipulating its personality – in traditional ways (with olives, say, or pancetta) and adventurous ways like corn juice, or beer or peanut butter. When I thought about pairing my breads with soups, sometimes I was looking for counterpoint – a smooth, soft soup joined by an assertively flavored bread; other times I had in mind a combination where the bread ingredients and the soups were similar so the bread seemed almost an extension of the soup. That's why you'll find corn bread with corn and shrimp chowder. But sometimes, getting back to the very beginnings of this gustatory marriage, I just thought one bread or another would be particularly wonderful for sopping up the soup. And then the two, the soup and the bread, become one.

Jim Lahey,
Sullivan St Bakery

The soups within this book are paired with breads from Sullivan St Bakery, sullivanstreetbakery.com. Pairings with an asterisk are from Jim Lahey's forthcoming book, My Bread.

The wine pairings were provided by David Bowler Wine, bowlerwine.com

Never was the phrase "devoured with the eyes" more aptly applied than to the luscious food books of Battman. Photographer extraordinaire, Alan Batt, a.k.a. Battman, creates his own kind of aesthetic fusion, marrying intelligence, imagination, technical superiority and the appetite of a true sensualist to the inspired culinary gifts of some of the world's greatest chefs. In this book, the results are glamorous, tantalizing and – yes – sexy portraits of astonishing soups along with detailed recipes for making them.

Many of those creating these globally-influenced dishes are so famous as to require but a single name – such as Emeril, Cat, Daniel, Eric, Jean Georges, Laurent, Joel, Tyler, Tadashi. There are also beloved soups from the very old guard (Yonah Shimmel) and up-and-coming stars that soon may be able to drop their last names, too. All are unified by a passion to stimulate, satisfy and nourish with soup.

In SOUP, an ever-growing number of innovative minds produce a dazzling array of potages, purées and soulful spoonfuls. Battman is more than up to the challenge of faithfully capturing them in glorious color and complexity. This book shows that every cuisine has its own unique soups. The combinations seem endless but universally they all somehow manage to afford sustenance and satisfaction.

In researching cookbooks and food books over the years, I discovered that soups

are good for every body, as well as everyone. Whether you're lean or hoping to lose extra pounds, a child or in your ninth decade, a vegetarian or meat lover, rich or poor, there's ample room in your diet for soups.

A perfect fit for our contemporary lifestyle, soups find favor in today's world because, simply put, they make us feel so good. They are the quintessential comfort foods we all seek. We eat them for lunch, late at night, for dinner and even, by some, for breakfast. Soup is wonderfully versatile as well as, in many cases, easy to make.

When we have little time to enjoy the pleasures of cooking, there is soup. With a few chops of a knife or pulses of a food processor, a little of this and that along with some liquid, and a tasty, rewarding meal emerges.

Novice and accomplished cooks alike can find soup-making easy. It's also unique in the food repertoire. Few dishes can claim to be elegant and rustic, hearty and delicate, delicious when served hot and cold as a first course, a whole meal and even dessert. Winter or summer, any season of the year is soup time.

In this stylish collection of soups, your taste buds and aesthetic senses will be more than satisfied.

Joanna Pruess,
Author
Soup for Every Body

executive chef
Christopher Lee

Swiss Ale Cheese Soup

Yields four six-ounce portions / Requires advance preparation

Ingredients

2 ounces vegetable oil

½ cup onion, cut into small dice

6 garlic cloves

½ cup celery, cut into small dice

¼ cup parsnip, peeled, cut into small dice

1 cup cauliflower, small dice

4 cups chicken or vegetable stock

4 thyme sprigs

2 bay leaves

½ cup heavy cream

½ pound Râclette cheese

¼ cup Swiss ale

Salt and pepper, to taste

½ pound sautéed sweetbreads (recipe follows)

24 Muscat grapes, cut in half

Dijon mustard oil (recipe follows)

4 brussels sprouts, leaves only (recipe follows)

4 pieces soft pretzel (recipe follows)

Sweetbreads

½ pound cleaned sweetbreads

2 cups milk

2 cups water

Salt and pepper, to taste

Flour, as needed

3 ounces vegetable oil

Dijon Mustard Oil

1 tablespoon Dijon mustard

3 sprigs chervil, minced

2 tablespoons extra virgin olive oil

Pretzel

1 full teaspoon fresh yeast (or one-half teaspoon each fresh yeast and water)

1 teaspoon glucose

1¾ cups flour

¼ cup whole wheat flour

1 tablespoon kosher salt

½ cup baking soda

Pretzel salt, as needed

Soup Base   Heat a large pot over medium heat, add the vegetable oil and sweat the onions, garlic, and celery until tender but not browned. Add the parsnip, cauliflower, stock, thyme, and bay leaves and cook for 25 minutes. Add the heavy cream and cook for five minutes. Remove the thyme and bay leaf and blend until smooth. Strain the soup through a fine sieve and put into a large pot and bring to a simmer. Add the cheese and ale, remove from heat and allow the cheese to melt, about five minutes. Blend soup again until smooth. Adjust seasoning with salt and pepper and reserve until serving.

Sweetbreads   Prepare the sweetbreads a day before serving by soaking in the milk and water for 24 hours. After soaking, remove and rinse well. Then dry them off and tear them into small bite size pieces. Heat a fry pan over high heat, and then season with salt, pepper, and toss in a little flour. When pan is hot, add the cooking oil and sauté until golden brown. Remove and reserve until serving.

Dijon Mustard Oil   In a small bowl, add all the ingredients. Mix well and reserve until serving.

Brussels Sprouts   Heat a medium size pot of salted water over high heat. When the water starts to boil, add the brussel sprout leaves and blanch for one minute. Remove and shock in an ice bath. Dry the leaves and reserve until serving.

To Serve   Reheat the soup base over low heat and whisk to prevent burning. In four bowls, evenly place the sweetbreads in the middle and garnish the rest of the bowl with about eight halves of Muscat grapes. Ladle about six ounces of soup into each bowl and garnish with the Dijon mustard oil and brussels sprouts leaves. Serve the pretzel on the side.

Recipe continues on page 204

RECOMMENDED PAIRINGS

Sullivan St Bakery — Pizza Bianca

Chandon de Briailles Pernand Vergelesses Blanc "Ile des Vergelesses" 2006

executive chef
Patricia Williams

Celery Root and Asian Pear Soup

Yields six servings

Soup

4 teaspoons butter

1 onion, diced

3 cloves garlic, sliced

2 quarts chicken stock

14 ounces Asian pear, peeled and diced

11 ounces celery root, peeled and diced

2 tablespoons honey

1 teaspoon curry powder

2 tablespoons salt

Black pepper, to taste

Green Papaya Chutney

1 green papaya peeled, seeds removed and chopped

1 jalapeño, seeded and diced

¼ cup cilantro leaves

1 tablespoon lime juice

4 teaspoons sugar

Salt and pepper, to taste

Roast Cod Cakes

1 pound cod

2 cloves garlic

Thyme, chopped as needed

Salt and pepper, to taste

½ cup olive oil to sauté the cod cakes plus extra as needed for roasting cod

½ pound potatoes

1 cup wondra flour

Green Papaya Salad

(ingredients are per serving)

¼ cup green papaya, julienned

1 sliced scallion

2 tablespoons cilantro, sliced

2 tablespoons green papaya chutney

Soup In a saucepan, melt the butter and add the onions and garlic. Sauté until translucent. Add the chicken stock, pears, celery root, and cook until tender. Purée in a blender and add the honey, curry powder, two tablespoons salt, or to taste, and several generous turns of the pepper mill. This is served with cod cakes, green papaya chutney and a salad of green papaya with cilantro and scallions.

Green Papaya Chutney Combine all of the ingredients in a blender and purée.

Roast Cod Cakes Roast the cod in 325°F oven for 20 minutes covered with garlic, thyme, salt, pepper and olive oil. Cool slightly and flake the fish with your hands. Cook potatoes and dry in oven. Mash the potatoes and add to the flaked fish. Season with salt and pepper and form into a cake. Dust the cakes with wondra flour and sauté in the olive oil.

Green Papaya Salad Combine all of the ingredients in a bowl.

To Serve Ladle the soup in a bowl and top with drops of the chutney. Serve the cod cake on the side and top with the green papaya salad.

It can also be served with the cod cake placed in the center of the bowl, then ladle in the soup and top with the salad and drops of the chutney.

RECOMMENDED PAIRINGS

Sullivan St Bakery — Ciabatta

Albert Mann Crémant d'Alsace NV

Velouté of Celery Root with Black Truffles

Yields four servings

Velouté of Celery Root

16 ounces celery root

1 tablespoon butter

3 ounces white wine

1¾ pints water

1 ounce crème fraîche

Salt, to taste

Cayenne pepper, to taste

Garnish

2 ounces celery root, small diced

2 ounces black truffles, divided

1 tablespoon butter

Salt, to taste

12 celery leaves

1 ounce olive oil from the Provence

Velouté of Celery Root Peel the celery root and cut into medium dice. Sweat the celery in the butter without colorization. Deglaze with white wine and add the water. Bring to boil a and simmer until celery is tender. Blend in a blender until smooth consistency. Finish with crème fraîche and season to taste with salt and cayenne pepper.

Garnish Chop the celery root and one ounce of the black truffles into small dice. Sweat the celery root slowly in the butter without colorization. When tender, add the diced truffles and season with salt.

To Serve Shave the remaining ounce of truffles. Place garnish into warm bowls. Ladle the soup on top and garnish with shavings of truffles, celery leaves and drizzle with olive oil.

RECOMMENDED PAIRINGS

Sullivan St Bakery — Casa Reccio

Domaine Gauby Cotes du Roussillon Blanc "Vieilles Vignes" 2005

eighty one

chef / owner
Ed Brown

Fennel & Parsley Soup with Frog's Legs and Sweet Garlic Espuma

Yields four servings

Fennel Parsley Soup

2 fennel bulbs, roughly chopped
1 head garlic, cut in half
5 dry fennel sticks
1 ounce extra virgin olive oil
1 ounce butter
1 ounce frog leg broth (recipe follows)
1 bunch parsley
½ bunch tarragon
½ bunch chervil
1 ounce spinach
1 ounce romaine lettuce, roughly torn
8 ounces light chicken stock

Frog Leg Broth

12 frog's legs, trimming and bones
(reserve meat for fricassee)
1 teaspoon butter
1 teaspoon extra virgin olive oil
1 fennel bulb, roughly sliced
1 shallot, sliced
1 head garlic, roughly chopped
1 stick celery, roughly chopped
1 sprig thyme
8 ounces white wine
½ quart light chicken stock

Tempura Frog Legs

16 ounces club soda
1 egg yolk
12 ounces tempura flour, plus extra for dusting
12 frog leg lollipop (see procedure)
Salt, to taste
Espellete pepper, to taste
Canola oil, as needed for frying

Frog Leg Fricassee

Meat from the 12 frog's legs
Wondra flour, for dredging
Extra virgin olive oil, as needed for frying
2 ounces wild mushrooms, cut to medium dice
½ ounce shallot, minced
Butter, to taste
¼ bunch parsley, chopped

Sweet Garlic Espuma

1 quart chicken stock, reduce to two ounces
1 quart heavy cream
2 heads roasted garlic
Thyme, chopped, as needed
Parsley, chopped, as needed

Fennel Parsley Soup In a medium sized soup pot on medium heat, sweat the fennel, garlic, and fennel sticks in oil and butter. Add the frog leg broth and simmer for 30 minutes. Remove the garlic and fennel sticks, add the herbs and greens, and then blend adding chicken stock if needed. Strain and chill as quick as possible.

Frog Leg Broth Roast the trimmings and bones from the 12 frog's legs with butter and oil until light golden brown. Add the vegetables and thyme and sweat for ten minutes. Add the wine and reduce completely. Add the stock and cook for one hour. Strain and chill.

Tempura Frog's Legs Mix the soda and egg yolk. Add to flour until a light cream consistency is achieved. Pull the meat down from the drumstick until it resembles a lollipop. Season legs with salt and espellete, then dust legs in flour, then dip in batter and fry in canola oil at 375°F until browned.

Frog Leg Fricassee Dredge frog leg meat in wondra, shake off excess and cook in oil until light golden brown, add mushrooms and shallot. Cook until lightly browned. Finish with butter and parsley.

Sweet Garlic Espuma Simmer the chicken stock, heavy cream and garlic until reduced by half. Infuse with the herbs for ten minutes and strain. Place in a siphon with two chargers.

To Serve In a bowl, place the frog leg fricassee topped with the sweet garlic espuma. Pour the soup around the fricassee and espuma tableside. Serve the tempura on the side.

RECOMMENDED PAIRINGS

Sullivan St Bakery — Stecca

Domaine Servin Chablis "Les Pargues" 2006

Beef Consommé, Chou Farci, Braised Flatiron and Bone Marrow

Yields eight servings / Requires advance preparation

Braised Beef Blade

1 pound beef blade (flatiron)

Salt and pepper, to taste

1 carrot

½ onion

½ celery stalk

½ a leek

3 mushrooms

1 tomato

Vegetable oil, as needed

10 black peppercorns

10 coriander seeds

1 ounce thyme

Half a bay leaf

1 sprig parsley + 1 tablespoon chopped parsley

1 head garlic

4 ounces port

8 ounces red wine

½ quart beef stock

½ quart veal stock

1 tablespoon shallot confit

8 savoy cabbage leaves

Beef Consommé

2 pounds oxtail

1 pound brisket

3 pounds beef shins

1½ pounds beef chuck

Vegetable oil, as needed

1 onion

2 carrots

5 mushrooms

2 celery stalks

1 leek

2 tomatoes

2 ounces thyme

1 bay leaf

1 head garlic

2 ounces flat parsley

15 black peppercorns

1 star anise

1 clove

½ teaspoon fennel seed

Garnish (per serving)

1 cabbage ball

1 thumbelina carrot

1 radish

1 one-inch slice celery, trim and cut on the bias

1 slice of salsify

1 celery root wedge

1 square bone marrow

Olive oil, as needed

Flour, as needed

3 to 4 sprigs chervil

3 to 4 tarragon leaves

3 to 4 chive batons

1 pinch maldon sea salt

Braised Beef Blade Cut the beef blade into large pieces and season with salt and pepper. In a frying pan, sear the beef in hot oil. In a large casserole, toss the carrots, onions, celery, leeks, mushrooms, and tomato with some oil and roast to a golden brown. Then add the black peppercorns, coriander, thyme, bay leaf, sprig of parsley, and garlic. Cook for another two to three minutes. Add port and reduce to a syrup followed by red wine and again reduce to a syrup. Place beef into pan, add stocks, bring to a simmer and cover. Transfer to a 350°F oven and braise for approximately three hours until completely tender. Remove beef from pan to cool, strain braising liquid and reduce in a clean pan, skimming as required. Once cool enough to handle, break the beef down into small strands, place in a bowl and add shallot confit, parsley and the heavily reduced liquid. Season with salt and ground pepper.

Blanch the cabbage leaves in salted boiling water until tender, refresh in ice water then drain. Cut the central vein from the leaves, lightly press to flatten the remaining veins with a rolling pin and pat dry on paper towels. Roll out a square of plastic wrap and place a large leaf of cabbage, overlapped by smaller ones. Place a two-ounce scoop of the meat in the middle of the cabbage. Roll the leaves around it, into a ball and secure with plastic wrap. To heat, place in boiling water for a minimum five minutes, then cut with scissors to release the plastic wrap.

Beef Consommé Cut the meat into large pieces. Soak in cold water for 2 hours. Drain the oxtail, pat dry, then sear in hot oil, until well colored. Reserve in a colander. Place all the meat in a large pot and fill with water to 90% of its capacity. Bring to a boil. Chop the onions and caramelize to a dark brown color in vegetable oil. Caramelize carrots in hot oil, add remaining ingredients, caramelize and reserve. Skim the surface constantly as it comes to a boil, reduce to a simmer for a few minutes, then add the reserved vegetables and reduce to a simmer, skimming the surface regularly. Allow to cook 3 to 4 hours, adding water as needed to keep everything submerged and simmer for another 18 hours. Drain the consommé through a cheesecloth into another pan and reduce slowly, if required. Cool. Refrigerate until ready to use.

Recipe continues on page 204

RECOMMENDED PAIRINGS

Sullivan St Bakery — Filone

La Bastide Blanche Bandol Rouge "Estagnol" 2004

a n n i s a

chef/co-owner

Anita Lo

Slow Cooked Egg with Parsnips in a Truffled Broth

Yields eight servings

Ingredients

8 soft-poached eggs

White vinegar, as needed

1 cup Madeira wine

2 large cloves garlic, smashed

1 shallot, sliced

½ cup black truffle juice

2 quarts chicken stock

1½-inch square piece parmesan rind

Salt and pepper, to taste

Garnish (per serving)

3 peelings of parsnip

Vegetable oil, as needed

Salt, to taste

1 pinch of nutmeg

3 tablespoons parsnips, cubed and blanched

1 pinch black truffle breakings

1 pinch pink salt

3 sprigs chervil

1 small pinch lemon zest

A few drops black truffle oil

Procedure Heat a large pot of water seasoned with salt and a splash of white vinegar to a poaching temperature (160-185°). In two batches, poach the eggs to the soft-cooked stage, about 3 to 3 ½ minutes. Hold in warm water until ready to use. Reduce the Madeira with the garlic and shallot until almost dry. Add truffle juice and reduce by half. Add chicken stock and parmesan rind and simmer, skimming occasionally until well flavored, about 30 to 45 minutes. Strain and season to taste with salt and pepper.

Garnish Deep fry the parsnip peelings in vegetable oil. Season with salt and nutmeg and reserve.

To Serve Heat the stock with the parsnip cubes and truffle breakings. Place in a bowl and add a soft-poached egg. Season the egg with the pink salt and garnish with the chervil, zest, truffle oil and fried parsnip peelings.

RECOMMENDED PAIRINGS

Sullivan St Bakery — Brioche

Domaine Charvin Cotes du Rhone "Les Poutet" 2006

AUREOLE

executive chef
Tony Aiazzi

Mushroom Dashi Broth with Lobster Tortellini, Crab and Monkfish

Yields six servings as an appetizer

Mushroom Dashi

10-inch kombu (dried kelp)

6 cups water

3 ounces bonito flakes

Lobster Tortellini

3 U-10 scallops

Salt and white pepper, to taste

1¼ cups lobster knuckles, chopped

2 tablespoons chives, chopped

18 squares fresh pasta

Garnish

6 ounces honsemiji mushrooms

6 ounces hen of the wood mushrooms

8 ounces monkfish, diced

Butter, as needed

1 cup picked dungeness crab meat

½ cup tomato concassé (peeled, seeded and diced tomatoes)

3 scallion greens, cut on the long thin bias

1½ tablespoons spicy lobster oil

1½ tablespoons chive oil

Mushroom Dashi Wipe the kombu with clean cloth. Put water in a deep pot and soak the kombu for ten minutes. Then place the pot on low heat and remove the kombu just before the water boils. When boiling, add the dried bonito flakes. Remove any foam that rises to the surface, and turn off heat. Let set until the bonito flakes sink. Strain the stock and reserve.

Lobster Tortellini Purée the scallops with an ice cube or two, until smooth. Season with salt and fresh ground white pepper. Fold in the chopped lobster and chives. Form into tortellini using the fresh pasta and place on a well floured tray until ready to cook.

To Serve Cook the tortellini in boiling, salted water for about two minutes.

Sauté the mushrooms and monkfish in whole butter, toss in the crab, tomato, and scallions just at the end to heat through.

Assemble the garnishes into bowls, drizzle with the oils. Pour the dashi broth over the garnish tableside.

RECOMMENDED PAIRINGS

Sullivan St Bakery — Semi di Sesamo

David Clark Bourgogne Rouge "Au Pelson" 2005

Nettle Soup with Carabinero Shrimp

Yields 15 servings

Poached Eggs

15 eggs, cracked

1 cup Swedish vinegar

Salt, to taste

Soup Base

2 pounds cauliflower, green stems removed, roughly chopped

½ pound parsnips, peeled and roughly chopped

3 gallons chicken stock

Salt and white pepper, to taste

3 quarts heavy cream

Nettle Purée

2 pounds nettles, leaves only

4 cups chicken stock

Salt and pepper, to taste

Chive Oil

4 ounces chives

½ cup canola oil

Carabinero Shrimp

15 Carabinero Spanish shrimp

¼ teaspoon olive oil

1 teaspoon garlic, minced

1 tablespoon whole butter

Brioche Crouton

Brioche bread, as needed

Poached Eggs Combine eggs with vinegar gently and let sit for 45 minutes. Pour the salted water into a hotel pan with a perforated pan inside of it. Gently add the eggs into water and poach until just set. Lift perforated pan from water, let cool in refrigerator. Store for later use.

Soup Base Combine the cauliflower, parsnips and chicken stock, in a pot, season lightly with salt and pepper, and simmer until completely tender. Blend well with an immersion blender. Add heavy cream and adjust seasoning.

Nettle Purée Bring a large pot of salted water to a boil. Blanch the nettle leaves for 30 seconds. Cool down in ice water. Drain the leaves and mix with just enough chicken stock to purée easily in a blender. Season lightly and strain. Rapidly cool down.

Chive Oil Blanch chives quickly in boiling water and then cool down in ice water. Finely chop the chives and dry well with paper towels; squeezing out excess water. Combine chives with canola oil in blender and blend in intervals of ten seconds, cooling down blender top in ice between intervals. Repeat process three to four times until very smooth. Allow to drip through coffee filter in refrigerator.

Carabinero Shrimp Peel the shrimp leaving head and tail on. Remove intestinal tract. Heat olive oil in pan, add shrimps and sear on one side. Add the minced garlic and butter and sauté on opposite side until just cooked through.

Brioche Crouton Cut the brioche into three by half-inch rectangle. Toast under salamander or broiler until golden and crisp.

To Serve Bring plenty of salted water to a simmer in a wide, shallow pot. Carefully add the poached eggs. Warm the eggs in the water, drain on paper towels, and place in soup bowl. Combine the soup base with nettle purée and bring to a boil. Foam the soup with an immersion blender and ladle around the eggs. Garnish with chive oil, shrimp and crouton.

RECOMMENDED PAIRINGS

Sullivan St Bakery — Brioche

Joel Falmet Champagne Brut Rosé NV

chef / owner
Barbara Smith

Roasted Plum Tomato Soup with Chèvre Croutons

Yields six servings

Roasted Plum Tomato Soup

2 tablespoons olive oil

½ cup onion, finely diced

½ cup turnip, finely diced

½ cup carrot, finely diced

2 teaspoons garlic, minced

4 cups vegetable or chicken stock (homemade or store-bought)

¼ cup tomato paste

3 cups roasted plum tomatoes with their cooking juices (recipe follows)

¼ cup fresh, firmly packed basil leaves, divided

¼ cup fresh parsley plus extra for garnish

3 tablespoons mascarpone cheese

3 tablespoons chèvre cheese

12 slices French bread

Roasted Plum Tomatoes

(yields about 3 cups)

24 large ripe plum tomatoes

2 tablespoons olive oil

1 tablespoon fresh chopped basil

1 teaspoon fresh chopped oregano

Roasted Plum Tomato Soup Heat the oil in a large saucepan over a medium to high heat, and sauté the onion, turnip, carrot, and garlic until softened. Stir in the stock, tomato paste and roasted tomatoes together with any cooking juices. Cover and bring to a boil. Reduce the heat and simmer for 30 minutes.

Meanwhile, finely chop one tablespoon of the basil leaves. In a small bowl, combine the chopped basil and one tablespoon of the parsley with the mascarpone and chèvre. Blend thoroughly. Preheat the broiler and grill the slices of French bread until light golden brown. Spread the cheese mixture over the toasted bread.

Coarsely chop the remaining basil leaves, and stir the basil and the remaining parsley into the soup. Divide the soup among six soup bowls and top each with two cheese croutons. Garnish with extra parsley leaves, if desired.

Roasted Plum Tomatoes Preheat oven to 325°F. Cut the tomatoes in half crosswise, and place into a large roasting pan. Drizzle with olive oil and sprinkle chopped basil and oregano over the top. Roast for 45 minutes. Let the tomatoes cool slightly. Then remove the skins and cores, and coarsely chop the flesh.

RECOMMENDED PAIRINGS

Sullivan St Bakery — Stirato

Le Cecche Dolcetto "Sori le Cecche" 2004

Blackbird

chef / owner
Paul Kahan

Braised Pork Potée

Yields eight servings / Requires advance preparation

Braised Pork

2 pounds fresh pork shoulder or butt

3 cloves garlic

1 teaspoon chopped parsley

1 teaspoon chopped thyme

3 tablespoons extra virgin olive oil, plus extra as needed

Vegetable oil, as needed

Salt and pepper, to taste

1 cup white wine

1 small carrot, diced

1 small onion, diced

1 rib celery, diced

4 cup chicken stock

Vegetables

½ pound slab bacon, cut into ½-inch square pieces

Extra virgin olive oil, as needed

½ pound baby carrots, cut into ¼-inch pieces

½ pound baby turnips, cut into ¼-inch pieces

¼ pound green cabbage, sliced thinly

1 bay leaf, preferably fresh

Salt and pepper, to taste

1 medium leek, white only, cut into 2-inch lengths, julienned as finely as possible

1 teaspoon extra virgin olive oil

Final Assembly

1–1¼ pounds pork tenderloins, cleared of fat and silverskin

Vegetable oil, as needed

Extra virgin olive oil, as needed

Shoulder meat, shredded into one-inch chunks, discard fatty pieces

Pork braised liquid, with fat skimmed off

Shaved black truffles, as needed

Braised Pork Begin by marinating the pork shoulder with the garlic, parsley, thyme, and extra virgin olive oil. Refrigerate for three hours or overnight. Remove pork from marinade and wipe off any solids. Coat a heavy-bottomed pan with vegetable oil for searing. Season the shoulder well with salt and pepper. Brown evenly. Deglaze pan with white wine and pour over shoulder in an ovenproof braiser of suitable size. Add a little extra virgin olive oil to the pan and sauté the onions, carrots and celery. Pour over the shoulder and finish with the chicken stock. The liquid should only cover the bottom half of the shoulder. Bring entire contents to a boil, cover and braise in a 325°F oven for 2 ½ hours. When done the meat should be easily pierced with a small knife. Carefully remove the shoulder from the liquid, strain liquid through a mesh strainer, discarding any solids. Refrigerate broth and pork shoulder for later.

Vegetables In a four-five quart heavy-bottomed pan, over medium heat, render bacon with extra virgin olive oil until just starting to crisp. Add the carrots, turnips, cabbage and bay leaf. Season with salt and pepper and cook until vegetables just start to soften. Add the leeks and cook for another three minutes. Cool vegetables on a plate or tray. Drain off excess bacon fat.

Final Assembly Preheat oven to 425°F. Season tenderloin and brown in vegetable oil in an oven-proof skillet. Finish tenderloin in oven until desired degree of doneness. Cool on wire rack until ready to serve. In a four to five quart pot, heat extra virgin olive oil to just smoking. Add the shredded pork, crisp well, moving meat only when crisp on first side. Check salt and pepper, adjust and add vegetables, pork braising liquid and bring to a simmer.

To Serve Spoon a hearty portion of veggies and meat into each bowl and top with a few think slices of pork tenderloin. Shave some black truffles over the top.

RECOMMENDED PAIRINGS

Sullivan St Bakery — Stecca

Porter Creek Pinot Noir "Russian River" 2005

Red Curry Spiced Shrimp Bisque

Yields six servings

Shrimp Bisque

2 tablespoons canola oil

3 pounds red Maine shrimp, rinsed and left whole

1 knob of ginger, peeled and sliced

1 stalk lemongrass, chopped

1 small carrot, sliced

5 shallots, sliced

1 tablespoon red curry paste

2 quarts heavy cream

3 Kaffir lime leaves

2 tablespoons fish sauce

Garnish

2 cups plus 2 tablespoons canola oil

2 shallots, thinly sliced

1 tablespoon Wondra flour

1 small carrot, cut into half-inch dice

1 Yukon gold potato, cut into half-inch dice

18 pieces tiger shrimp, shelled and veined

Salt and pepper, to taste

12 sprigs of cilantro

12 sprigs of micro pea leaves, optional

Shrimp Bisque In a large, heavy-bottomed pot, heat two tablespoons of canola oil. Add the whole red Maine shrimp and sauté for five minutes until the shrimp are cooked through. Add the ginger, lemongrass, carrot, and shallots and sauté for an additional five minutes, until the vegetables are tender. Add the curry paste and stir to coat the shrimp and vegetables. Pour in the heavy cream and bring to a boil. Remove from heat, add the lime leaves, cover with a lid and let steep for one hour. After the bisque has steeped, strain through a fine mesh strainer and add the fish sauce to taste. Reserve the soup until ready to serve.

Garnish In a medium pot, heat the two cups of canola oil to 300°F. Lightly coat the shallot slices in Wondra flour and fry the shallots in the oil. Using a small strainer, remove the shallots from the oil and dry them on a plate lined with a paper towel. Set the shallots aside.

Place the carrots in a small pot, cover with salted water and bring to a boil. Cook the carrots until tender, about five minutes. Strain and set aside. Repeat the same process with the diced potatoes and set aside.

To Serve Heat a large frying pan to high heat and add two tablespoons canola oil. Season the tiger shrimp with salt and pepper. Place shrimp in frying pan, searing each side for two minutes, then add the cooked potatoes and carrots to the pan and return to heat. Meanwhile, bring the shrimp bisque to a boil. Divide the shrimp, potatoes and carrots evenly between six bowls. Garnish with shrimp, cilantro sprigs, pea leaves and fried shallots. Pour the bisque into each bowl and serve immediately.

RECOMMENDED PAIRINGS

Sullivan St Bakery — Stecca

Cold Heaven Viognier "Le Bon Climat" 2006 (California)

executive chef / partner
Kenny Callaghan

Seafood and Chorizo Chowder

Yields four 10-ounce servings

Ingredients

2 Idaho potatoes, small dice

12 ounces dry sherry, divided

24 ounces water

Kosher salt, to taste

6 ounces butter

6 ounces all-purpose flour

Extra virgin olive oil, as needed

1 Spanish onion, small dice

1 celery root (about 1¼ pounds)

1 leek, white part only, small dice

2 links dried chorizo, brunoise (very small dice)

1 ounce thyme, stemmed and chopped fine

½ ounce rosemary, stemmed and chopped fine

3 cloves of garlic, minced

2 bay leaves

6 ounces Chardonnay wine

12 ounces lobster stock

12 ounces milk

8 ounces heavy cream

Ground white pepper, to taste

8 to 10 pieces gulf shrimp, peeled and deveined, cut in 4 pieces each

16 to 20 pieces sweet bay scallops

8 pieces manila clams

4 pieces baby squid, cleaned and sliced

2 ounces of chives, sliced fine

Procedure

In a saucepot, place the diced potatoes, ten ounces of dry sherry wine, the water, and kosher salt. Allow the potatoes to simmer for about seven to eight minutes until partially cooked. Drain the potatoes and place on a half-sheet pan lined with parchment paper and allow to cool. In a small sauce pot, melt the butter, add flour and cook for about 20 minutes, constantly stirring. Set aside until needed. Place a soup pot on high heat and add extra virgin olive oil to cover the bottom of the pot. Add the onions, celery root, leeks, and sweat until translucent in appearance. Add the chorizo, thyme, rosemary, garlic, and bay leaves and allow to cook. Deglaze the mixture with the Chardonnay wine and reduce by half. Add the lobster stock and milk and simmer for 15 minutes. Add the heavy cream and simmer for an additional five minutes. Add the potatoes to the liquid. Season the soup with salt and fresh ground white pepper. In a stainless steel bowl take the butter and flour mixture and gently whisk 10 ounces of the liquid into the mixture until slightly thick. Return the thickened liquid to the pot and allow the soup to boil for 10 minutes. Add the remaining two ounces of sherry. The consistency of soup should coat the back of a spoon. Add all of the seafood and continue to cook for two additional minutes. Finish with the chives and serve in a bowl.

RECOMMENDED PAIRINGS

Sullivan St Bakery — Corn Bread*

Herederos de Arguero Manzanilla NV

Bouillabaisse

Yields four to six servings

Bouillabaisse

1 tablespoon ginger, chopped

1 teaspoon garlic, chopped

1 tablespoon lemongrass, chopped

1 tablespoon shallots, chopped

2 tablespoon red curry paste

1 tablespoon canola oil

2 quarts chicken stock

8 ounces Thai coconut milk

2 sprigs Thai basil

1 tablespoon fish sauce

1 tablespoon lime juice

Salt and white pepper, to taste

From the Sea

1 large red snapper fillet, cut to 1 oz cubes

6 little neck clams

6 razor clams

6 mussels

6 squid bodies, sliced open and scored

Saffron Rouille

2 pinches saffron

2 ounces white wine

2 egg yolks

1 teaspoon water

1 roasted garlic clove, smashed

7 ounces blended oil (50% grapeseed oil and 50% olive oil)

Salt and white pepper, to taste

Garnish

Cheese sticks, as needed

Lotus root chips, as needed (see recipe)

Vegetable oil for frying

Salt, to taste

Bouillabaisse

Sweat the ginger, garlic, lemongrass, shallots, and curry paste in canola oil until aromatic, approximately five minutes. Add the chicken stock and coconut milk. Simmer for 20 minutes. Remove from heat and add the basil sprigs. Let steep for five minutes. Strain broth through a chinoise. Add fish sauce and lime juice. Add salt and white pepper to taste.

From the Sea

Steam the snapper cubes in a bamboo steamer, approximately two to three minutes. Add little neck clams, razor clams, and mussels into the simmering bouillabaisse until they open. Add the squid for 45 seconds. Then add the snapper cubes to the bouillabaisse.

Saffron Rouille

In a pot, add the saffron to white wine until reduced 75%. Whisk the eggs yolks and water over a double boiler until stiff peaks form. Remove from heat. Whisk in the saffron/wine reduction and roasted garlic. Gradually add the oil in a slow stream, whisking continuously. Add salt and white pepper to taste.

Lotus Root Chips

Peel the lotus roots and slice very thin, then fry at 350°F until golden, approximately one minute. Transfer chips from fryer to a dry towel and season with salt.

To Serve

Place a sheet of fata paper* in soup bowl and then add bouillabaisse. Place a few cheese sticks in the soup. On another plate arrange the seafood, add the rouille either on the side or drizzled over the seafood. Garnish with the lotus root chips.

*Fata Paper: professional cooking foil that can be purchased at kitchen supply stores. Allows cooking temperatures up to 440°F. Beneficial because it seals in all natural juices.

RECOMMENDED PAIRINGS

Sullivan St Bakery — Ficelle

Ployez-Jacquemart Champagne "Brut" NV

Brio

executive chef
Massimo Carbone

Chill Vellutata Brio Style

Yields one serving

Ingredients

½ onion, sliced

1 can San Marzano tomatoes

1 ounce basil

2 tablespoons extra virgin olive oil, plus extra for drizzling

Salt and pepper, to taste

2 sea scallops with roe

1 tablespoon butter

2 slices prosciutto di Parma

2 breadsticks

1 ounce micro greens

Procedure In a medium pot, sauté the onions with the San Marzano plum tomatoes. Add the basil and two tablespoons of olive oil. Purée the mixture in a blender and chill. Add salt and pepper. Sauté the sea scallops with butter in a medium sauté pan. Cook for approximately five minutes. Wrap the prosciutto around the breadsticks. Then skewer the scallops with the prosciutto-wrapped breadsticks.

To Serve Pour the soup into a bowl. Straddle the side of the bowl with the breadsticks. Sprinkle the micro greens on top of soup. Finish by drizzling the soup with some extra virgin olive oil.

RECOMMENDED PAIRINGS

Sullivan St Bakery — Stecca

Tour de Bon Bandol Rouge 2005

BUTTER

executive chef
Alexandra Guarnaschelli

Roasted Butternut Squash Soup

Yields four to six servings / Requires advance preparation

Ingredients

6 pounds butternut squash, split lengthwise, seeds removed

10 ounces butter

2 tablespoons dark brown sugar

3 tablespoons molasses

Kosher salt, to taste

Freshly ground white pepper, to taste

1 teaspoon ground ginger

1 knob fresh ginger, peeled and finely grated

1 teaspoon ground cinnamon

¼ teaspoon ground cloves

Zest of one orange (keep an extra orange on hand in case more is needed)

Juice from one orange

2 tablespoons Worcestershire sauce

1 tablespoon garlic oil

2 cups skim milk

1 cup heavy cream

1 to 2 cups water

Fresh pea shoots, as needed for garnish

Procedure Preheat oven to 375°F. Place the squash, skin side down, in a single layer in two baking dishes. In a small saucepan, melt the butter completely over medium heat until it starts to turn a light brown color. Remove from the heat and immediately drizzle six ounces into the cavities of the squash (reserve remaining four ounces brown butter). Sprinkle with the brown sugar, molasses, salt and pepper. Finish by covering with the ground (dry) ginger, fresh ginger and the ground cloves.

Fill the bottom of the dishes with one-inch of water to create steam while the squash bakes in the oven. Cover with aluminum foil and seal the edges tightly and place in the oven to bake, undisturbed, for two hours. Check for doneness by piercing the flesh of the squash with the tip of a knife. If there is any firmness, continue to bake for an additional 30 to 45 minutes, or until soft. Remove from the oven. Carefully peel back the foil and let squash cool.

Using a large spoon, scoop the flesh from the squash into a food processor in small batches. Do this carefully, retaining the liquid inside the squash, as this will add flavor to the soup. Be careful not to take any skin with it as the skin can give a bitter flavor. Blend in small batches and place puréed squash into a large pot. Turn heat on low. Add orange zest, orange juice, Worcestershire sauce, garlic oil and two ounces (half) of the remaining brown butter. Stir to blend and taste for seasoning. If the squash lacks sweetness, add a little molasses; if it lacks salt, add a little salt or Worcestershire sauce.

In a separate pot, heat the skim milk, cream and one cup of water over medium heat. Season the liquid with salt and pepper and bring to a simmer. Add the squash and remaining brown butter and stir to combine. Once the mixture has returned to a simmer, taste for seasoning. Purée the soup in batches in the blender. Note: If the soup needs more flavor, adjust with salt, orange zest or pepper to taste. It if is too thick, add additional water.

To Serve Ladle soup into bowls. Top with fresh pea shoots. Serve.

RECOMMENDED PAIRINGS

Sullivan St Bakery — Carrot Currant Bread*

Kurt Angerer Gruner Veltliner "Kies" 2006

Mushroom Velouté with Truffle Sabayon

Yields six servings / Requires advance preparation

Ingredients

2 tablespoons unsalted butter

4 small shallots, peeled and thinly sliced

2 cloves garlic, peeled and chopped

1 bay leaf

1 sprig thyme

12 ounces white mushrooms, cleaned and chopped

1½ cups water

1 cup plus 2 tablespoons heavy cream

Fine sea salt, to taste

Freshly ground black pepper, to taste

2 egg yolks

½ teaspoon white truffle oil

6 slices black truffle, optional

Mushroom Velouté Put the butter in a large, heavy-bottomed pot set over medium heat. When the butter has melted, add the shallots, garlic, bay leaf, and thyme, and sauté until the shallots are translucent, approximately three minutes. Add the mushrooms, lower the heat and sauté for three minutes. Add 1½ cups of water, raise the heat to high, bring the water to a boil, and boil until the mushrooms are tender, approximately five minutes. Pour mixture into a blender or the bowl of a food processor fitted with the metal blade and blend until smooth. Pour the velouté back into pot, stir in the cream, and season with salt and pepper. Cover and set aside. The velouté can be made to this point, cooled, covered, and refrigerated overnight in an airtight container in the refrigerator. Let come to room temperature before proceeding.

Sabayon Put the egg yolks and two tablespoons of water in a stainless-steel bowl set over a double boiler, and beat them with a whisk until the yolk has a foamy but stable consistency. Remove the bowl from the boiler, stir in the truffle oil, and season with salt and pepper.

To Serve Gently reheat the velouté if necessary and divide it among six warm soup bowls. Spoon a generous tablespoon of sabayon into the center of each serving and place one slice of black truffle, if using, atop the sabayon. Serve immediately.

RECOMMENDED PAIRINGS

Sullivan St Bakery — Casa Reccio

Chandon de Briailles Savigny Les Beaune 2006 (Burgundy)

34

SOUPS

Broccoli Velouté with Black Truffles

SOUPS

36

Yields four to six servings

Ingredients

4 heads of broccoli, divided
2 tablespoons butter
2 tablespoons olive oil
1 large white onion, chopped
1 leek, chopped

2 tablespoons garlic, chopped
Salt and pepper, to taste
1 gallon chicken stock
2 cups heavy cream
4 cups baby spinach, cleaned
Shaved black truffle (optional)

Procedure Bring a large pot of salted water to a boil and set a bowl of ice water on the side. Separate the broccoli florets from one head of broccoli and cut into equal size pieces. Boil the florets for about 45 seconds, and then chill immediately in the ice water; pat dry and set aside. Roughly chop the remaining stem and broccoli heads.

In a large pot over medium heat, melt the butter with the olive oil. Add the onions, leek, garlic, and a pinch of salt, and cook, stirring, until they become tender and translucent. Add the chopped broccoli and continue to cook, stirring occasionally, until tender.

Add the chicken stock, bring to a boil and simmer for 40 minutes. Remove from the heat, and stir in the heavy cream.

Carefully transfer the soup to a blender (you may have to do this in batches depending on the size of blender) and purée, adding one cup of spinach at a time. Strain through a fine mesh sieve. Season with salt and pepper and keep warm.

To Serve When you are ready to serve, ladle the soup into pre-warmed bowls. Reheat the broccoli florets and sprinkle on top as garnish. If using, thinly shave the black truffle over top.

RECOMMENDED PAIRINGS

Sullivan St Bakery — Integrale

Tabatau "Genevieve Blanc" Vin de Pays 2006

Onion Soup Gratinée

Yields eight servings

Onion Soup Base

2 tablespoons sweet butter

4 cloves of garlic, finely chopped

8 large Spanish onions, peeled and sliced about a half-inch wide.

2 Granny smith apples, peeled and cut to a fine julienne

1 large Idaho potato, peeled and cut to a fine julienne

2 ounces of Calvados liquor

8 ounces of dry white wine

4 quarts of beef stock

Salt and black pepper, to taste

1 sprig of thyme

1 bay leaf

Garnish

16 French baguette toasts, cut lengthwise to fit in soup tureen, about ¼- inch thick.

8 slices of aged gruyère cheese

8 ounces shredded Emmenthaler cheese

Onion Soup Base In a large pot on medium flame place the butter, add the garlic and sweat for three minutes. Add the onions and cook slowly, stirring continuously, until the onions are well caramelized. Add the apples and potatoes, combine well, deglaze with the Calvados, then the white wine. Let evaporate and add the hot beef stock. Bring the soup to a boil, reduce to simmer and skim the soup as needed. Season with salt and pepper, thyme and the bay leaf and cook for 1½ hours on a low simmer. Set aside.

To Serve Preheat the oven's broiler. Reheat the soup. Fill eight soup tureens to almost the rim. Place the croutons on top, covering the surface evenly and completely so cheese doesn't sink into the soup when melting. Place the gruyère cheese on top of the croutons followed by the Emmenthaler cheese. Place in the broiler until the cheese is melted and browns. Serve.

RECOMMENDED PAIRINGS

Sullivan St Bakery — Stirato

Schoffit Chasselas Vieilles Vignes 2006

Dorada with Artichokes and Gazpacho Verde

Yields six servings

Ingredients

12 small artichokes, trimmed and halved

3 lemons, divided

3 tablespoons salt plus extra as needed

1 small baguette

1 cup olive oil, plus extra as needed

½ pound fresh fava beans

3 green tomatoes, chopped

1 bulb fennel, chopped

2 cucumbers; 1 chopped, 1 peeled and diced

1 jalepeño, chopped

1 bunch parsley; half blanched and shocked in ice water, the other half picked leaves

Black pepper, to taste

6 fillets of dorada with skin

Procedure

Trim and halve the artichokes. Boil in medium sized pot of water with the juice of two lemons and three tablespoons of salt. Strain and cool when the artichokes are tender and reserve. Remove crust from the bread and cut into small dices. Lay croutons on a sheet tray, drizzle with olive oil and salt. Bake at 300°F for ten minutes. Remove and cool. Peel, blanch and shock the fava beans. Blend the green tomatoes, fennel, chopped cucumber, jalapeño and blanched parsley in a blender. Emulsify with the one cup olive oil, salt and the juice of the remaining lemon. In a bowl combine the croutons and diced cucumber, dress with olive oil, salt and pepper. Place this mixture in the center of the serving bowls. Pour gazpacho around it. Place the artichokes on top of the gazpacho. Season fish with salt and pepper and sauté in a hot pan with olive oil. Place the fish on top of the artichokes. Garnish with fava beans and parsley leaves.

RECOMMENDED PAIRINGS

Sullivan St Bakery — Stirato

Pedralonga Albariño (Rias Biaxas) 2006

Cat Cora
chef / author

North African Fish Stew

Yields four to six servings

Ingredients

2 tablespoons olive oil, divided

2 red onions, sliced into thin rings, divided

2 tablespoons raisins

3 tablespoons salted, roasted cashew nuts

1 red bell pepper, seeded and sliced into thick rings

1 yellow bell pepper, seeded and sliced into thick rings

1 green bell pepper, seeded and sliced into thick rings

4 fresh, firm, ripe tomatoes, blanched, peeled, seeded, and sliced into thick rounds

1½ cups fish or vegetable stock, or ¾ cup fortified wine (sweet sherry or Madeira) mixed with ¾ cup water

1½ pounds swordfish fillets, cut into 1¼ inch cubes

Salt and pepper, to taste

1 tablespoon fresh parsley, chopped

Couscous

2 cups quick-cooking couscous

2 cups vegetable stock or water, boiling

2 to 3 teaspoons butter

¼ cup diced carrots

¼ cup pine nuts

¼ cup dried currants

1 to 2 scallions, finely chopped

½ teaspoon salt (optional)

Procedure

Heat half of the oil in a large heavy-based skillet and sauté half of the onions on medium to high heat for six to eight minutes, or until very dark golden, stirring all the time. Using a slotted spoon, remove the fried onions from the oil, place them on paper towels, and set aside. Fry the raisins in the same hot oil until they plump. Remove with the slotted spoon and add to the fried onions. Fry the cashews for about one minute. Remove and add to the raisin-and-onion mix.

Add the remaining oil to the skillet and fry the other half of the onions until golden. Add the bell peppers and continue cooking for about ten minutes, or until the peppers are soft. Add the tomatoes and the stock, partially cover and cook for about ten minutes on medium to low heat.

Stir the fish through the onion and pepper mixture. Taste and season with salt and pepper. Continue simmering for ten minutes, or until the fish is tender. Do not forget to stir periodically to prevent sticking.

To make the couscous, place the couscous grains in a large, deep dish with a lid. Pour in the boiling stock and stir in the butter, carrots, pine nuts, dried currants, scallions, and salt. Cover and set aside to keep warm for about 15 minutes so the couscous can absorb the liquid and swell up.

Carefully pour the fish mixture over the couscous and gently fold it through to mix thoroughly into a colorful presentation. Sprinkle with onion rings, raisins, cashew nuts, and the parsley. Serve hot immediately.

RECOMMENDED PAIRINGS

Sullivan St Bakery — Pizza Bianc

Peique "Seleccion Familiar" Red (Bierzo, Spain)

craft

pastry chef
Karen DeMasco

Chocolate Consommé with Toasted Meringue and Cacao Nib Brittle

Yields six to eight servings, depending on the size of bowl

Chocolate Consommé

1 quart water

¼ teaspoon kosher salt

⅓ ounce cocoa powder

6 ounces chocolate, 70%

3½ ounces egg whites

⅓ ounce cacao nibs

Meringues

¾ cup sugar, divided

4 egg whites

½ teaspoon kosher salt

½ teaspoon vanilla paste

Cacao Nib Brittle

2 ounces unsalted butter

2 tablespoons corn syrup

½ teaspoon baking soda

2 teaspoons kosher salt

4 ounces cacao nibs

Chocolate Consommé Bring the water, salt and cocoa powder to a boil and then reduce to a simmer. Whisk in the chocolate one piece at a time as it melts. Maintain a simmer. Whisk the egg whites until they are frothy, quickly fold in the cacao nibs and pour onto the top of the soup. Let this simmer for about two hours. Skim off the egg whites and strain the consommé through cheesecloth and chill.

Meringues Cook a half-cup sugar in a saucepot to the soft ball stage. On a tabletop mixer with the whisk attachment, whisk the egg whites until frothy. Add the remaining sugar. Slowly pour the cooked sugar into the egg whites while they are mixing. Turn mixer to medium-high and let mix until they form a shiny meringue. Add the salt and vanilla. When the meringue is cool, remove the bowl from the mixer.

Spoon the meringue onto a sheet pan in the desired size and shape. Brûlée the meringues with a propane torch on low flame. When they are cool, move them into the soup bowl.

Cacao Nib Brittle In a small saucepot, cook the sugar, butter, corn syrup, and water to a golden caramel color. Remove the pot from heat and whisk in the baking soda and then salt (in this order). Switch to a spatula and fold in the cacao nibs. Pour the brittle onto a sheet pan with parchment and roll the brittle out with a rolling pin. When the brittle is cool, break it into pieces. Store the brittle in an airtight container.

To Serve Pour the chocolate consommé over the meringues. Garnish with a piece of the cacao nib brittle.

RECOMMENDED PAIRINGS

Sullivan St Bakery — Brioche

Albani "Deibes Rosso" NV (Italian red sweet wine)

Little Neck Clam Ceviche

Yields six servings / Requires advance preparation

Clam Ceviche

24 little neck clams, washed and scrubbed

1 cup of fresh lemon juice

1 shallot, sliced

1 clove of crushed garlic

1 teaspoon roasted crushed red pepper flake

Clam Broth

12 chowder clams, washed and scrubbed

1 cup white wine

1 cup of San Marzano whole peeled tomatoes

4 sprigs of lemon thyme

1 fresh bay leaf

1 teaspoon whole black peppercorns

Kosher salt, to taste

Garnish

12 thin slices of duck prosciutto
(recipe follows)

6 whole leaves of escarole, washed,
blanched and julienned

1 tablespoon of golden raisins

1 lemon confit, julienned (recipe follows)

Basil leaves, as needed

1 tablespoon basil oil (recipe follows)

20 pieces of brioche, cubed and toasted

Clam Ceviche Using a clam knife, open your clams keeping the meat attached to the shell (reserve the clam juice). Place clams open side down in a shallow container. Pour lemon juice and reserved clam juice over the clams to cover. Sprinkle with the sliced shallot, garlic and crushed red pepper flakes. Refrigerate until ready to use, at least four hours.

Clam Broth Add all of the ingredients to a covered stock pot. Use medium heat until your chowder clams open. Remove each clam, making sure all of the clam juice is left in your pot. Strain the contents over another pot using a fine mesh strainer. Taste and add salt if needed.

Duck Prosciutto Place duck breasts in a shallow container. Cover with kosher salt, and any aromatic you'd like. After two days check your duck for moisture. When the salt has cured the duck breast, remove from salt, brush off, and wrap in cheesecloth. When wrapped, hang in a refrigerator for at least one month until your duck breast has dried nicely. Slice and enjoy.

Lemon Confit Cut the lemon lengthwise in quarters leaving one end intact. Pack as many lemons as you'd like in kosher salt using aromatics of your choice. Allow to cure for at least one month. When ready wipe off the salt, and use only the outer skin. Slice and enjoy.

Basil Oil Blanch two cups of whole basil leaves. Once cool, place in a high speed blender. Cover with a half cup each of canola oil and extra virgin olive oil. Purée until smooth. Let sit one hour. Strain through a fine mesh strainer lined with a cheesecloth. Store in refrigerator.

To Serve Place four clams open side up in a bowl. Lace with two slices of duck prosciutto, two leaves of escarole, a couple of raisins, a sprinkle of lemon confit, a couple of leaves of basil, and a spoonful of basil oil. Place charred brioche in a decorative manner atop your clams. To the side, pour your seasoned clam broth in a teapot or a gravy bowl. When your ready to eat, pour your hot broth over the contents of the bowl.

RECOMMENDED PAIRINGS

Sullivan St Bakery — Carta

Perez Barquero (Montilla Morilles) Grand Barquero Oloros NV

Tortilla Corn Soup with Crispy Foie Gras and Chicken Flauta

Yields 4 one-cup servings

Tortilla Corn Soup

1 tablespoon butter

1 teaspoon minced garlic

1 Vidalia onion, small dice

4 ears sweet corn, with kernels removed

1 quart white chicken stock

1 kafir lime leaf, minced

Juice of one lime

Tomato chili oil (recipe follows), as needed

Micro cilantro, as needed

Corn kernels, as needed

Tomato Chili Oil   (yields one cup)

1 tablespoon tomato powder (sold as dry powder)

1 tablespoon smoked paprika

1 teaspoon ancho chili powder

1 teaspoon cayenne pepper

1 cup canola oil

Foie Gras and Chicken Flauta

2 cups masa harina flour

8 ounces chicken

One-half egg, beaten, plus extra as needed for brushing dough

4 ounces foie gras

1 tablespoon chilled chicken stock

1 teaspoon salt

½ teaspoon smoked serrano pepper powder

Canola oil, as needed for frying

Tortilla Corn Soup In a non-reactive saucepot melt the butter, then add the onion and garlic, and sweat until translucent. Add corn kernels, cobs and stock and let simmer for 30 minutes. Remove the cobs and transfer to a high powered blender and purée until super silky smooth. Strain the soup through a fine chinoise and keep warm. Finish soup with minced kafir lime leaf and lime juice. Garnish with tomato chili oil, micro cilantro, corn kernels.

Tomato Chili Oil In a non-stick fry pan, toast the spices on medium heat, stir occasionally, being careful not to burn them. Take off heat and let cool to room temperature and add oil. Place on a low flame and warm until the oil just starts to bubble then turn off the heat and let sit for one hour. Strain through a coffee filter and reserve in a plastic squeeze bottle for use.

Foie Gras and Chicken Flauta Mix the masa harina with cold water to form a pliable paste and roll out on wax paper until a $\frac{1}{16}$-inch thick long rectangle. In food processor, purée the chicken, egg, foie gras, chilled chicken stock, salt, and smoked serrano pepper until smooth.

Fill a pastry bag with small ¼-inch round tip with the chicken purée. Cut a rectangle from the dough approximately 3-inches wide by 11-inches long, brush with a lightly beaten egg. Pipe a strip of the purée along the long edge of the rectangle. Gently roll the masa harina around the purée and seal with your fingers. The flauta should look like a long thin flute or cylinder. Fry in canola oil until crispy. Cut and serve.

To Serve Pour the soup into bowls, drizzle some tomato chili oil on top, followed by the micro cilantro and corn kernels. Finally, cut the flauta into pieces and insert one piece into each bowl.

RECOMMENDED PAIRINGS

Sullivan St Bakery — Corn Bread*

Espadana Verdejo 2006 (Rueda, Spain)

davidburke & donatella

executive chef
Eric Hara

Sea Urchin & Cauliflower Chowder with Shark's Fin

Yields four servings

Chowder

1 head cauliflower, chopped

1 medium onion, chopped

2 tablespoons chopped garlic

1 leek, chopped

2 celery stalks, chopped

¼ cup bacon pieces

1 tablespoon fennel seed

2 tablespoons butter

¼ cup dry vermouth

1 quart chicken stock

½ cup heavy cream

10 live sea urchins plus extra for garnishing

Garnish

1 cup potatoes, diced and blanched

½ cup pearl onions, chopped

2 tablespoons butter

Shark's Fin

1 onion, chopped

2 shallots, chopped

1 tablespoon ginger, chopped

1 tablespoon lemon grass, chopped

2 celery stalks, chopped

2 tablespoons garlic, sliced

Vegetable oil, as needed

Cooking wine, as needed

2 tablespoons soy sauce

1 quart chicken stock

1 shark fin

Chowder Sauté cauliflower, onion, garlic, leek, celery, bacon, and fennel seed in the butter. Deglaze with the vermouth and reduce it by half. Add chicken stock add cream. Simmer until vegetables are tender. Purée in a blender. Add ten tongues of sea urchin and purée again.

Garnish Sauté the potatoes and onions in butter until tender.

Shark's Fin Sauté onion, shallots, ginger, lemon grass, celery and garlic in oil. Deglaze with cooking wine. Add soy and chicken stock. Add shark fin. Simmer for two hours until shark is tender. Strain, cool, pick and clean.

To Serve Pictured is a whole sea urchin hollowed out. If you can not find a whole sea urchin use a regular soup bowl. Pour the chowder in first, then the garnish. On the top place the shark's fin and some of the extra tongues of sea urchin.

RECOMMENDED PAIRINGS

Sullivan St Bakery — Semi di Sesamo

Schafer-Fröhlich Bockenaur Felseneck Spätlese (Germany)

Bouillabaisse Moderne

Yields ten servings

Bouillabaisse

½ cup olive oil

1 head of fennel, cut in half-inch pieces

1 large onion, cut in half-inch pieces

6 cloves of garlic

1 teaspoon saffron threads

5 plum tomatoes, quartered

1 cup Pernod

2 to 3 liters chicken stock

Salt and pepper, to taste

2 pounds Idaho potatoes, peeled and cut in half-inch pieces

8 pounds of assorted, firm-textured whitefish and shellfish such as: Loup de Mer

Red Snapper	Mussels
Baby Squid	Shrimp
Red Mullet	Monkfish

Rouille

1 egg yolk

¼ teaspoon saffron threads

2 cloves garlic

½ cup cooked potato

1 cup olive oil

1 baguette, cut in half-inch pieces, drizzled with olive oil, and toasted

Bouillabaisse In a pot large enough to hold all of the fish, heat ½-cup olive oil, and add the fennel, onion, and garlic. Cook slowly, stirring often, until the vegetables are tender and almost translucent. Add the saffron threads and stir briefly, then add the tomatoes. Continue cooking until tomatoes become tender, about three minutes, then add the Pernod. When the Pernod has evaporated, add the chicken stock and bring to a simmer. Season the broth with salt and pepper, then add the potatoes. Cook for five minutes, then add the fish and shellfish.

Simmer the fish until all the pieces are just cooked through, and shellfish such as mussels or clams have all opened. Remove the seafood and transfer to a warm platter. With a hand-held immersion blender, puree the remaining soup until smooth and creamy.

Rouille Combine the yolk, saffron, garlic, and potato in the container of a high-speed blender. Turn the blender to a low speed, and slowly drizzle in the olive oil, until you have a thick, pale, red colored emulsion. Add a little water if the mixture becomes too thick to purée.

To Serve Divide the puréed soup equally between ten warmed bowls. Add the cooked fish, and top with the toasted croutons. Serve the rouille on the side. Alternately, serve the soup as a first course with the croutons and rouille, and the cooked fish as a separate, second course.

RECOMMENDED PAIRINGS

Sullivan St Bakery — Ficelle

Mourges de Gres Rose "Fleur d'Eglantine" 2007 (France)

chef
Derrick VanDuzer

Parsley Root Soup with Bay Scallops

Yields four servings

Bay Scallops

10 bay scallops

Salt, to taste

Parsley Root Soup

1 onion, diced

5 cloves garlic, chopped

3 tablespoons butter

10 bunches medium size parsley root

4 quarts chicken stock

2 cups of sour cream

Sea salt and white pepper, to taste

Cilantro Purée

2 cups packed cilantro

6 tablespoons grapeseed oil

Salt, to taste

Vadouvan Air

1 quart chicken stock

2 tablespoons soy lecithin (can be purchased in your local GNC or vitamin shop)

2 tablespoons of butter

4 tablespoons of vadouvan

Bay Scallops Season the bay scallops with salt to taste and place in a preheated oven until just warmed through.

Parsley Root Soup Sweat the onions and garlic in butter. Do not brown. Add the chicken stock and the parsley root. Cook until tender, adding water as necessary to maintain fluid level. Purée soup in the blender on high adding the sour cream, salt and white pepper, and then strain

Cilantro Purée Combine all of the ingredients in a blender and purée.

Vadouvan Air Warm all of the ingredients together. Tilt your heating vessel and incorporate using a hand blender.

To Serve Place the barely warmed bay scallops in the bottom of your bowl. Drizzle cilantro purée over the scallops, than pour your soup on top. Garnish with a spoonful of vadouvan air.

RECOMMENDED PAIRINGS

Sullivan St Bakery — Carta

Freeman Vineyard Chardonnay "Ryo-Fu" 2006 (Sonoma, CA)

Clam Chowder
smoked potatoes, chorizo and black pepper croissants

Yields four servings of chowder

Ingredients

24 Manila clams

½ cup salt

½ cup apple wood chips

2 potatoes, sliced half-inch thick

1 cup white wine

1 sachet d'epices:
  2 sprigs thyme, 1 bay leaf, 2 white peppercorns, wrapped, tied in cheesecloth

1 carrot, large dice

3 stalks celery, large dice

1 onion, large dice

1 leek, white part only, sliced

¼ pound butter

1 cup flour

2 cups cream

2 cups milk

Juice of one lemon

Salt and black pepper, to taste

Garnish

4 tablespoons Spanish hard chorizo, diced

Black Pepper Croissants

4 cups + 3 tablespoons AP flour, divided

3 sticks (¾ lb) of butter, equally divided, softened at room temperature

2 teaspoon salt

2 tablespoons sugar

2 packages dry yeast

¼ cup warm water

1½ cups milk, warmed to 80°F to 90°F

½ cup half-and-half, warmed

1 egg

1 tablespoon water

Black pepper, as needed

Procedure

Place the clams in cold water to cover and add the salt. Let sit for thirty minutes to purge them of their grit.

Light the wood chips in a small grill. Let them burn till the flames subside, about five minutes.

Blanch the potatoes in salted water until tender. While still hot, place on the grill and cover for ten minutes with the lid. The potatoes will slightly brown. Once cool, dice them in square half-inch pieces and reserve for garnish.

Place the clams, white wine, and sachet d'epices in a heavy-bottom saucepot and cover with a lid. Boil until the clams open and immediately remove them. Place them in a bowl and cool in the fridge. When cool, strain the cooking liquid and reserve two cups. Clean the clams from their shells and reserve.

Sweat the carrot, celery, onion, and leek in the butter until soft. Add the flour and cook until a blonde roux forms. Add the cream and milk and bring to a boil. Skim, reduce to a simmer and cook for thirty minutes. Add the reserved clam and lemon juice. Season with salt and pepper.

To Serve

Heat the soup and ladle it into the bowls. Garnish with the smoked potatoes and chorizo. Serve with two black pepper croissants per person on the side.

Recipe continues on page 204

RECOMMENDED PAIRING

Freeman Chardonay "Ryo-Fu" 2006

chef / owner
Emeril Lagasse

Classic Seafood Gumbo

Yields six servings

Ingredients

¾ cup vegetable oil

1 cup all-purpose flour

1½ cups onions, finely chopped

¾ cup green bell peppers, finely chopped

¾ cup celery, finely chopped

2 tablespoons minced garlic

One 12-ounce bottle amber beer

6 cups shrimp stock (recipe follows)

¼ teaspoon dried thyme

2 bay leaves

½ pound gumbo crabs, split in half (about 2), or more to taste

2 teaspoons Worcestershire sauce

1 tablespoon salt

½ teaspoon cayenne pepper

1 pound medium shrimp, peeled, deveined

1 pound white fish fillets, such as catfish snapper, or sole, cut into large chunks

1 tablespoon Emeril's Original Essence (recipe follows)

2 cups shucked oysters with their liquor

¼ cup fresh parsley, chopped

½ cup tender green onion tops, chopped

Cooked white rice, for serving

Shrimp Stock

1 pound (about 8 cups) shrimp shells and heads

1 cup yellow onions, coarsely chopped

½ cup celery, coarsely chopped

½ cup carrots, coarsely chopped

3 garlic cloves, smashed

3 bay leaves

1 teaspoon black peppercorns

1 teaspoon dried thyme

2 teaspoons salt

Emeril's Essence Creole Seasoning

2½ tablespoons paprika

2 tablespoons salt

2 tablespoons garlic powder

1 tablespoon black pepper

1 tablespoon onion powder

1 tablespoon cayenne

1 tablespoon dried oregano

1 tablespoon dried thyme

Procedure Place an eight-quart stockpot over medium heat, and add the oil. Allow the oil to heat for about five minutes, then add the flour to the pot. Stir the oil and flour together with a wooden spoon to form a roux. Continue to stir the roux for 20 to 25 minutes, or until the color of milk chocolate. Add the onions, bell peppers, and celery to the roux. Stir to blend. Stir the vegetables for five minutes, then add the garlic. Cook the garlic for 30 seconds before adding the beer and shrimp stock to the pot. Season the gumbo with thyme, bay leaves, gumbo crabs, salt, cayenne and Worcestershire. Bring the gumbo to a boil and lower the heat to a simmer. Continue to simmer the gumbo for one hour, skimming the foam and any oil that rises to the surface.

Season the shrimp and the fish with 1½ teaspoons Essence. Stir the shrimp and fish into the gumbo and cook for two minutes. Add the oysters to the pot and cook, stirring often, for an additional five minutes. Taste the gumbo and season if necessary.

Garnish with the parsley and green onions and serve in shallow bowls over white rice.

Shrimp Stock Place the shrimp shells and heads in a large colander and rinse under cold running water. Place all the ingredients in a heavy six-quart stockpot, add four quarts of water, and bring to a boil over high heat, skimming to remove any foam that rises to the surface. Reduce the heat to medium-low and simmer, uncovered, for 45 minutes, skimming occasionally. Remove the stock from heat. Strain through a fine-mesh sieve into a clean container; let cool completely. Refrigerate for up to three days or freeze in airtight containers for up to two months.

Emeril's Essence Creole Seasoning In a small bowl combine all the ingredients thoroughly. Store in an airtight container.

RECOMMENDED PAIRINGS

Sullivan St Bakery — Guinness Bread*

Dogfish Head Beer 60 minute IPA

chef de cuisine

Jose "Pepe" Rodriguez

Cold Avocado Soup with Chorizo Carpachio

Yields four servings

Avocado Soup

8 fresh avocados

3 cups chicken stock

1 tablespoon garlic, chopped

2 tablespoons fresh cilantro

2 ounces lime juice

1 cup heavy cream

1 fresh yellow onion

1 red pepper

1 ounce celery

¼ tablespoon garlic powder

½ tablespoon onion powder

½ teaspoon Tabasco

Chorizo Oil

3 ounces chorizo citterio

3 cups vegetable oil

Garnish

Gaspachio, as needed

Avocado Soup Mix all ingredients for the avocado soup together in a blender, until smooth. Add salt and pepper to taste.

Chorizo Oil Place the chorizo in a hot pan with the vegetable oil for five minutes. Drain and reserve the oil.

To Serve Pour soup into a bowl. Drizzle a few drops of the chorizo oil on top and finish with the gaspachio.

RECOMMENDED PAIRINGS

Sullivan St Bakery — Pancetta Bread*

Mourgues de Gres Rosé "Fleur d'Eglantine" 2007

Le Bernardin

executive chef
Eric Ripert

Risotto Soup with Perigord Truffles

Yields four servings

Rice Crispies requires advance preparation

Risotto Soup

2 tablespoons olive oil

3 tablespoon unsalted butter, divided

1 small onion, minced

2 cloves garlic, minced

8 cups chicken stock

1½ cup Arborio rice

½ cup white wine

Fine sea salt, to taste

Freshly ground white pepper, to taste

4 ounces freshly grated parmesan cheese

Perigord truffles, sliced, as needed

Spiced Rice Crispies

¼ cup sushi rice

¾ cup water

2 tablespoons rice wine vinegar

Fine sea salt, to taste

Freshly ground white pepper, to taste

Espelette pepper, to taste

Canola oil, as needed for frying

Risotto Soup Heat olive oil over medium heat in heavy-bottomed saucepan. When the oil is hot, add one tablespoon of the butter, onion and garlic and cook, stirring often, until softened but not colored, about eight minutes.

While the onion and garlic are cooking, bring the chicken stock to a boil and leave to simmer over very low heat.

Stir the rice into the onion and garlic and continue cooking until the rice turns opaque, about three minutes. Add the wine and reduce until almost dry.

Ladle about eight ounces of chicken stock over the rice and cook, stirring constantly until the stock is absorbed. Repeat this four times, making sure the liquid is absorbed completely each time until the rice is tender and creamy. At this time add twelve ounces of chicken stock and bring to a simmer. Remove the pan from heat. Season with salt and pepper and stir in the remaining butter and grated parmesan.

Spiced Rice Crispies Preheat oven to 375°F. Soak the rice in cold water for 30 minutes. Drain and place the rice in a small casserole, add the water and rice wine vinegar and season with salt, pepper and espelette. Cover the casserole and cook the rice in oven for 25 minutes; there should be some water left. Spoon the rice, in an even layer, onto a Silpat lined baking sheet. Place rice in an oven, or a very dry place for two days. The rice should be completely dry and brittle. Prior to serving, heat the canola oil in a small deep pot to 400°F. Fry the dried rice in batches, until it puffs and turns golden brown. Drain rice on a paper towel-lined plate. When cool, break the rice up into 20 smaller pieces.

To Serve Ladle soup into four bowls and garnish with a slice of truffle and rice crispies.

RECOMMENDED PAIRINGS

Sullivan St Bakery — Filone

Tour de Bon Bandol Blanc 2007

chef / owner Jean-Georges Vongerichten
chef de cuisine Pierré Schutz

Chicken and Coconut Milk Soup with Lemongrass and Galangal

Yields six servings

Broth

Half an onion, sliced

Pinch of sliced galangal

7 ounces red curry paste

1 ounce butter

1 sachet (recipe follows)

1 quart chicken stock

Sachet

1 lime leaf

⅓ bunch cilantro stems

1 cloves garlic

1 Thai chili, smashed

1 stalk lemongrass, smashed

4 ounces chicken wings or carcass

Garnish

36 ounces coconut milk

Chicken breast cubed, as needed

6 shiitake mushrooms, sliced

Lime juice, to taste

Fish sauce, to taste

6 lime leaves

Scallions sliced, as needed

Cilantro leaves, julienne, as needed

Procedure Melt the butter In a saucepan, add the onion, galangal and red curry and sweat slowly until translucent, about 20 minutes. Add the sachet and chicken stock and simmer for 30 to 40 minutes. Chill and reserve.

To Serve For each portion; heat four ounces broth and six ounces coconut milk. Add four cubes chicken breast and some shiitake. Simmer until chicken is cooked. Season with lime juice and fish sauce. Garnish with lime leaf, scallion and cilantro.

RECOMMENDED PAIRINGS

Sullivan St Bakery — Semi di Sesamo

Schoffit Pinot Gris "Cuvee Tradition" 2005 (Alsace, France)

chef / owner Jean-Georges Vongerichten
creative director Greg Brainin

Cream of Tomato Soup with Grilled Sourdough

Yields four servings

Soup

Half a small onion, sliced

Olive oil, as needed

Salt, to taste

3 pounds canned plum tomatoes, puréed

3 ounces cream

Grilled Sourdough

Sourdough, cut 4-inch long by 3-inch wide

Olive oil, as needed

Salt and ground white pepper, to taste

Cumin Oil

½ teaspoon cumin seed, toasted, ground fine

1 pinch of salt

3 tablespoons olive oil

Garnish

6 ounces soup

Olive oil, as needed

Basil, chiffonade, as needed

Grated cheddar cheese, as needed

Soup Sweat the onion in olive oil and salt until tender. Add tomatoes and simmer slowly for 40 minutes. Add the cream and return to simmer, then immediately remove from heat. Purée in vita prep until smooth and strain through a chinios.

Grilled Sourdough Drizzle bread with olive oil and season gently with salt and white pepper. Grill until crispy.

Cumin Oil Combine toasted, ground cumin, salt and olive oil. Bring to a gentle simmer and remove from heat. Cool to room temperature.

To Serve Heat soup, aerate with a few drops of olive oil. Top the grilled bread with grated cheddar, then plenty of basil. Balance on the rim of the bowl. Drizzle a few drops of the cumin oil on the bottom of the bowl. Serve soup on the side to be poured tableside.

RECOMMENDED PAIRINGS

Sullivan St Bakery — Casa Reccio

Capella S. Andrea Vernaccia 2007

PerrySt

chef / owner Jean-Georges Vongerichten

chef de cuisine Erik Battes

Sweet Pea Soup with Parmesan Foam

Yields six servings

Sweet Pea Soup

1 tablespoon olive oil

4 ounces onion, small dice

1 garlic clove, sliced thin

Salt, to taste

28 ounces water

9 ounces frozen peas

Parmesan Foam

4 ounces heavy cream

1½ ounces parmesan, chopped small in a Cusinart

Pinch of Thai chile pepper. chopped

2 sprigs thyme, tied with string

Salt, to taste

Sweet Pea Soup In a rondeau, combine the oil, onions, garlic, and salt and sweat, covered, until totally soft. Add the water and bring to a boil. Let boil for one minute, then cool over ice until very cold. Purée until totally smooth with the peas, adding additional salt if needed. Strain through a chinois.

Parmesan Foam Combine all the ingredients in a pot and bring to a simmer. Remove from heat, and let steep for fifteen minutes. Remove the thyme and purée cream in a blender until smooth. Pass through a chinois. Let cool to room temperature. Load into whipping gun with two cartridges, if cold, warm until just above body temperature before loading. The parmesan foam must be served warm.

To Serve Pour the soup into a bowl and top with some of the parmesan foam.

RECOMMENDED PAIRINGS

Sullivan St Bakery — Pizza Bianca

Vinicola Resta Gelsomoro Rosso 2004

Chilled Spring Pea Soup

Yields six servings

Soup

1 ounce slab bacon, cut in half; or 4 slices of bacon

1 tablespoon extra virgin olive oil

2 stalks celery, peeled, trimmed and thinly sliced

1 small onion, peeled, trimmed and thinly sliced

1 leek, white part only, thinly sliced

Salt and freshly ground white pepper, to taste

5 cups unsalted chicken stock or store-bought low-sodium broth

1 sprig rosemary

6 cups fresh peas, preferably assorted, such as 1½ pounds English sweet peas, shelled; ¾ pound fava beans, shelled; ¼ pound snap peas thinly sliced; and ¼ pound snow peas, thinly sliced

1 bunch Italian parsley, leaves only

The Cream

1 cup heavy cream

1 sprig rosemary

1 clove garlic, peeled, split and germ removed

Salt and freshly ground white pepper, to taste

5 slices bacon

Soup Heat a medium casserole over medium heat and toss in the bacon. Brown the bacon very well, then pour off all of the rendered fat. Add the olive oil to the pot and warm it, then add the celery, onion, leek and a little pepper. Lower the heat and cook the vegetables, stirring, until they soften but do not brown, about 15 minutes.

Add the chicken stock and sprig of rosemary. Bring to a boil, lower the heat and simmer the soup for 15 minutes. Spoon out and discard the bacon and rosemary. Pour the soup into the container of a blender and purée until smooth. (You may have to do this is batches.) Set the soup aside to cool.

Bring a large pot of salted water to a boil. Toss the sugar snap and snow peas into the pot and cook for three minutes. Add the sweet peas and cook for another three minutes. Put the fava beans in a colander and plunge the colander into the pot so that the beans can boil for one minute. Toss the parsley into the colander and cook everything a final minute. Remove the colander, leaving the fava beans and parsley in it, return the other peas into a strainer, and run all of the ingredients under cold water to cool them down quickly and to set their colors; drain again. Pop the fava beans out of their skins by pressing each bean between your thumb and index finger. (You may have to pinch the skin of some of the favas open with your fingernail.) Dry the parsley leaves by squeezing them between your palms.

Put the peas, fava beans, parsley and a little of the soup into the container of a blender and blend until vegetables are smooth. (You may have to add more soup to keep things moving.) Add the remainder of the soup, in batches, and blend until you have a smooth mixture. Push the soup through a fine mesh strainer to make certain it is smooth and free of small pieces of pea skin, then taste for salt and pepper. Pour soup into a container and refrigerate until cold.

Recipe continues on page 205

RECOMMENDED PAIRINGS

Sullivan St Bakery — Pizza Bianca

Albert Mann Riesling "Cuveé Albert" 2007

ILILI RESTAURANT

chef / owner
Philippe Massoud

Kibbeh Yogurt Soup

Yields four servings

Kibbeh Dumplings

¾ pound ground beef, refrigerated until partially frozen

½ pound fine bulgur

¼ pound onion, finely chopped

1 teaspoon all spice

1 teaspoon black pepper

Salt, to taste

Extra virgin olive oil, as needed

Yogurt Soup

½ cup cilantro leaves, chopped

4 garlic cloves, minced

Vegetable oil, as needed

8 cups fresh, natural yogurt, such as Dannon or Stoneyfield, divided

2 teaspoons corn starch

1 minced garlic clove

¼ cup julienned mint leaves

4 teaspoons Aleppo red pepper

Kibbeh Dumplings Combine all of the ingredients, except the olive oil and process in a food processor until mixture is homogenous. Remove from mixer and knead like bread dough for ten minutes. Portion into 1½ ounce balls. Place one ball in your left hand. Using your right hand index finger, poke the kibbeh ball and gently rotate the kibbeh around your wet index finger while applying pressure to almost create a conic shape. Once formed, close the open end to form a symmetrical shape.

Preheat oven to 350°. Brush the kibbeh dumplings with olive oil and bake for twenty minutes; ten minutes for each side.

Yogurt Soup Sauté the julienne of cilantro with the four cloves of garlic in oil until the cilantro is wilted. Reserve for serving time. In a bowl, mix half a cup of yogurt with corn starch until fully incorporated. Place the remaining yogurt in saucepan on medium heat with one clove of minced garlic and gently whisk as frequently as possible. Once yogurt reaches boiling point, add the yogurt/cornstarch mixture, mix well, remove from heat and drop the kibbeh dumplings into the mixture and let sit for four minutes.

To Serve In each bowl, place four kibbeh balls along with eight ounces of the yogurt soup. Garnish with one-third teaspoon each of the cilantro, garlic mixture, julienne mint, and the Aleppo pepper.

RECOMMENDED PAIRINGS

Sullivan St Bakery — Carta

Eric/Kent Pinot Noir Russian River "Stiling Vineyard" 2006

Roasted Sunchoke Chowder

Yields six servings as an appetizer

Clams

2 tablespoons butter

2 shallots, peeled and sliced

2 cloves garlic, peeled and smashed

6 sprigs thyme

1 pinch crushed red chili flakes

1 cup white wine

18 cherry stone clams, purged

Sunchoke Soup

2 pounds large sunchokes

½ cup butter

1 onion, peeled and chopped

3 garlic cloves, peeled and smashed

½ bunch thyme

1 fresh bay leaf

Salt and freshly ground white pepper, to taste

8 cups chicken stock

2 tablespoons crème fraîche

Additional Garnishes

½ cup carrot, diced and blanched

½ cup celery, peeled, diced, and blanched

½ cup turnip, diced and blanched

¼ cup canned truffle, diced

Butter, as needed

2 cups picked braised ham hock

Sunchoke chips, as needed

Clams Melt the butter in a large sauté pan (large enough to accommodate all of the clams in a single layer) and add the shallot, garlic, thyme and chili flakes. Sweat for three minutes over medium heat and then add the white wine and cook for an additional three minutes. Add the clams and cover the pan with aluminum foil to steam the clams. Cook until all of them open, checking occasionaly, to remove the open ones with tongs. After all the clams have opened, allow to cool until able to handle, then gently remove with a spoon to keep them from getting damaged. Pass the cooking liquid through a fine sieve and store the clams in it.

Sunchoke Soup Preheat oven to 350°F. Thoroughly scrub the sunchokes. Add to a roasting pan with the butter and roast on the stove top until the butter is frothy, Add the onion, garlic, thyme and bay leaf with a good pinch of salt and some freshly ground white pepper and stir to incorporate. Cover loosely with aluminum foil and transfer to the oven.

Roast for approximately 25 minutes, stirring occasionally, or until sunchokes are just tender. Remove the foil and add the chicken stock. Continue to cook in the oven for 15 minutes or until the sunchokes are very tender. Remove the thyme and bay leaf and purée all ingredients until smooth, adjust seasoning and fold in the crème fraîche.

To Serve Heat the clams, vegetables, and truffle together with a knob of butter in the clam braising liquid. Add the ham hock to mix right before serving, to keep it from breaking up. Arrange the garnish in heated soup plates, top with sunchoke chips. Pour the soup tableside.

RECOMMENDED PAIRINGS

Sullivan St Bakery — Brioche

Domaine Les Grand Bois Cotes du Rhone Rosé 2007

Tortilla Soup with Grilled Chicken, Avocado and Queso Fresco

Yields eight servings

Tortilla Soup

4 quarts rich, dark chicken stock

12 plum tomatoes, roasted until charred and peeled

3 cloves roasted garlic

½ bunch clean cilantro stems

¼ cup chopped epazote

½ cup heavy cream

¼ pound tortilla chips

3 pasilla negro chilies, cleaned and toasted

1 chipotle morita, cleaned and toasted

Garnish

2 eight-ounce boneless, skinless, chicken breast, grilled

8 ounces avocado, diced

8 ounces queso fresco, diced

4 ounces fried tortilla strips

Tortilla Soup Bring all of the ingredients to a boil in a stock pot. Blend until smooth. Strain. Return to heat and bring to a slow simmer for 45 minutes to one hour, until reduced by half, skimming fat from the top. Add the heavy cream and season with salt to taste.

To Serve For each serving, place two ounces of grilled chicken breast, one ounce of diced avocado, one ounce queso fresco, and one-half ounce fried tortilla strips in a warm soup bowl. Ladle the hot soup on top and serve.

RECOMMENDED PAIRINGS

Sullivan St Bakery — Corn Bread*

Durigutti Malbec 2006 (Argentina)

Langoustine and Hearts of Palm Soup

Yields four servings

Ingredients

2 pounds langoustines

3 tablespoons olive oil

3 cloves garlic, chopped

Salt and pepper, to taste

8 ounces butter

1 tablespoon shallots

2 tablespoons flour

1 teaspoon nutmeg

3 cups milk

16 ounces hearts of palm
(reserve the juice)

Dill, as needed for garnishing

Procedure Cut the langoustines open and sauté over medium heat with olive oil, garlic, salt, and pepper for five minutes. Set aside.

In a large pan, melt the butter over a medium flame add the shallots, flour, nutmeg, salt, and pepper. Sauté while stirring continuously. Combine the milk and the reserved hearts of palm juice to pan, mixing to obtain a desired creamy texture. Bring to a boil. Add the hearts of palm and let cook for five minutes. Purée in a blender. Serve with a langoustine and a touch of dill to garnish.

RECOMMENDED PAIRINGS

Sullivan St Bakery — Brioche

Tour de Bon Bandol Blanc 2006

Steamed Parsnip Emulsion
roasted chestnuts, white truffle oil and lobster reduction

Yields four servings

Vegetable Stock

1 carrot

1 onion

1 celery stalk

2 sprigs of thyme

2 quarts water

Parsnip Emulsion

2 pounds parsnips

Salt and pepper, to taste

1½ quarts vegetable stock (see recipe)

Lobster Reduction

2 lobsters

Salt and pepper, to taste

Butter, as needed

1 tablespoon tomato paste

1 tablespoon armagnac

1 cup vegetable stock

Roasted Chestnut

1 tablespoon olive oil

1 pound chestnuts (can be frozen)

Pinch of sugar

Butter, as needed

Vegetable stock, as needed

For Assembly / Garnish

1 tablespoon crème fraiche

White truffle oil, as needed

4 sprigs of chives

Vegetable Stock Boil all of the ingredients together for 15 minutes. Then strain.

Parsnip Emulsion Season the parsnips with salt and pepper and steam. Blend the parsnips with the vegetable stock, one cup at time until a smooth soup-like consistency is achieved. Taste for additional salt and pepper and reserve.

Lobster Reduction Break down the lobsters by separating the head, tail, claw, and heads. Steam the claws and tails for seven minutes, allow to cool, clean, slice and reserve. Split the lobster heads in two, lengthwise, season with salt and pepper and pan-sear with a touch of butter and the tomato paste. Cook for a few minutes, deglaze with the armagnac, add one cup of vegetable stock and let simmer for five minutes. Pass through a chinoise and reserve.

Roasted Chestnuts In a casserole, heat the olive oil then add the chestnuts, toss in a pan with sugar and butter. Cook slowly until lightly browned. Add a little vegetable stock, cover and steam for a few minutes until soft.

To Serve Emulsify the parsnip emulsion and the crème fraîche with a hand blender. Place pieces of sliced lobster and chestnuts in the bottom of four soup bowls, add a tablespoon of lobster reduction then equally divide the parsnip emulsion amongst the four bowls. Drizzle the truffle oil into each bowl and decorate with a sprig of chive.

RECOMMENDED PAIRINGS

Sullivan St Bakery — Brioche

Raymond Usseglio Chateauneuf du Pape Blanc "Roussane Pure" 2007

Pineapple Coconut Soup with Mango Pearls

Yields six servings / Requires advance preparation

Pineapple Gelée

6 ounces pineapple purée
⅔ ounce sugar
Zest of half a lime
½ sheet gelatin

Mango Pearls

3 ounces mango purée
3 ounces mango juice
1 ounce sugar
Tiny pinch agar-agar
1 cup canola oil, very cold

Poached Pineapple

½ ounce rum
½ ounce pineapple purée
⅓ ounce sugar
5⅓ ounces pineapple, quarter-inch dice

Coconut-Lime Foam

6¾ ounces coconut purée
2¾ ounces milk
⅔ ounce cream
⅛ ounce sugar
½ vanilla bean, scraped
Tiny pinch lime zest
½ sheet gelatin

Coconut Soup

4½ ounces whole milk
1 ounce cream
¾ ounce sugar
Zest of half a lime
Small piece of lemongrass, chopped fine
4½ ounces coconut milk

Garnish

6 stalks lemongrass
6 sugar tuile

Pineapple Gelée Bring the pineapple purée to a boil. Add the sugar and boil for another two minutes. Soak gelatin in cold water for ten minutes. Remove from the heat, add the lime zest and gelatin sheet, stirring to dissolve. Chill to set. Once set, transfer gelée to a piping bag.

Mango Pearls Bring the mango purée and mango juice to a boil. Add the sugar and agar and boil for three more minutes. Allow the mixture to cool to 140°F, and immediately transfer to a syringe or eyedropper into the cold oil, forming pearls. Rest the pearls in the oil for two minutes, then remove with a strainer. Rinse very gently with cold water.

Poached Pineapple Combine all ingredients in a small pan and simmer until the pineapple is tender. Let chill.

Coconut-Lime Foam Requires a two-day preparation. The day before, bring the purée, milk, cream, and sugar to a boil. Remove from heat, add the vanilla beans along with the pod and lime zest; infuse for 15 minutes and strain. Soak gelatin in cold water for ten minutes. Add the softened gelatin to the purée, stirring until dissolved. Store in the refrigerator overnight. The next day: Transfer to a foam canister that is charged twice with CO_2.

Coconut Soup Bring the whole milk, cream and sugar to a boil. Remove from heat and add the zest and chopped lemongrass. Infuse for 15 minutes, then strain over the coconut milk.

To Serve Cut the lemongrass stalk to six-inches with a slice removed lengthwise to make a flat side. Pipe the pineapple gelée on top of the flat side of each lemongrass stalk. Place the mango pearls, poached pineapple and a bit of coconut lime foam into six chilled bowls. Garnish with sugar tuiles and lemongrass stalks with gelée. Pour the soup into bowls tableside.

RECOMMENDED PAIRINGS

Sullivan St Bakery — Osso di Morti

Schoffit Pinot Gris "Vendange Tardive" 2001

food network kitchen
Susan Stockton

White Grape Gazpacho

Yields 2⅓ cups

Gazpacho

3 cups green grapes

Juice of one lime

1 stalk celery

½ cucumber

1 clove garlic

2 slices country white
bread, crusts removed

½ cup Marcona almonds, lightly toasted

½ teaspoon sherry vinegar

Garnish

Chopped grapes

Almonds

Plain yogurt

Chives

Gazpacho Place grapes, lime juice, celery and cucumber in a blender and liquefy. Add garlic, bread and almonds. Blend until very smooth. Strain mixture into a clean bowl and add vinegar. Chill thoroughly.

Assembly Place the chopped grapes and almonds in each bowl and cover with gazpacho. Top with a dollop of yogurt and chives.

RECOMMENDED PAIRINGS

Sullivan St Bakery — Almond Bread*

Capella S Andrea Vernaccia 2007

Snow Crab Soup

Yields eight servings

Ingredients

3 whole snow crabs

2 tablespoons olive oil

1 onion, peeled and minced

3 shallots, peeled and minced

3 cloves garlic, peeled and minced

1 carrot, peeled and minced

1 celery stalk, minced

½ bulb fennel, minced

½ ounce Pernod

½ ounce Lillet

1 pinch saffron

3 quarts fish stock

½ bunch basil, crushed

6 cups water

1 tablespoon salt

Lemon juice, to taste (about half a lemon)

Riviera olive oil, to taste

Garnish

1 watermelon radish, peeled and thinly sliced

1 small bunch mizuna

4 grams (a pinch) paddlefish roe

Procedure   Separate the crab legs from the bodies and split the bodies into four pieces. Sauté the body pieces lightly in olive oil. Add onions, shallots, garlic, carrot, celery and fennel and sweat without browning. Deglaze with Pernod and Lillet and reduce until dry. Add saffron and fish stock. Let simmer for approximately 30 minutes. Remove from heat and infuse with crushed basil. While the basil is infusing the soup, in a separate pot bring the water to a boil, add salt and cook the crab legs for three minutes. Immediately shock in an ice water bath.

Remove crab leg meat from shells and reserve for the garnish. Remove crab bodies form the soup and discard. Strain the soup and finish with the lemon juice and Riviera olive oil to taste.

To Serve   Garnish the soup with crab leg meat, radish, mizuna, and paddlefish roe.

RECOMMENDED PAIRINGS

Sullivan St Bakery — Stirato

Pedralonga Albarino 2006 (Rias Baixas, Spain)

izakaya
modern japanese pub

chef / partner
Michael Schulson

Miso Soup
with scallion foam and tofu custard

Yields eight servings

Miso Soup

1 quart cold water
1 ounce konbu
10 ounces dried bonito flakes
6 scallops
6 mussels
6 clams
3 crab claws
4 shrimp
4 tablespoons miso

Tofu Custard

1 quart soymilk
7 eggs
1 teaspoon salt

Scallion Foam

1 bunch scallions
6 grams (pinch) Versa Whip
1 gram (tiny pinch) xanthan gum

Garnish

Nori, as needed

Miso Soup Fill a pot with the water, add the konbu and bring to a boil. Before the water boils remove the konbu and shut the flame off. Add the bonito flakes and let sit for ten minutes.

Add the seafood and let steep for ten minutes off the heat. Strain the liquid. Add the miso to the liquid.

Tofu Custard In a large bowl, mix all of the ingredients. Steam the custard, in the bowl that you will be serving it in, for 40 minutes. To steam, place the bowl inside a bamboo steamer over boiling water.

Scallion Foam Blanch the scallions in boiling water for 30 seconds and then shock in cold water. Purée the scallions in a blender with 1 to 1½ cups of the water you blanched them in. Strain and reserve 7 ounces of the purée. Add the remaining ingredients and whip until the mixture foams. Blend them with a small amount of water.

Assembly Spoon some of the tofu custard into a bowl; pour some miso broth over the custard. Top with the scallion foam and a piece of nori. Garnish the plate with the seafood.

RECOMMENDED PAIRINGS

Sullivan St Bakery — Semi di Sesamo

J. J. Prum Riesling "Spätlese" 2005

The Institute
of Culinary Education

Director of Student Affairs
Andrew Gold

Black Tea and Mint Broth

Yields four servings

Black Tea and Mint Broth

1 quart clear brown lamb broth (chicken or beef broth can be substituted)

2 tablespoons Lapsang Souchong (smoked black tea)

4 sprigs fresh mint

Salt and pepper, to taste

Braised Lamb Shank

4 pieces of lamb shanks (see procedure for details)

1 tablespoon canola oil

1 cup black tea and mint broth (see recipe above)

1 sachet d'epices (see procedure for contents)

Salt and black pepper, to taste

Beggar's Purse of Ground Lamb with Harissa

2 ounces ground lamb

½ teaspoon harissa

1 tablespoon sliced chives

Salt and pepper, to taste

4 summer roll skins, reconstituted in cold water

4 whole chives, blanched and refreshed for tying around purse

Caramelized Tomato and Feta Flan

1 teaspoon butter, plus extra as needed for ramekins

Flour, as needed

1 teaspoon minced garlic

1 teaspoon minced shallots

3 tablespoons tomato paste

2 eggs

3 ounces heavy cream

1 ounce feta cheese

1 pinch ground nutmeg

Salt and black pepper, to taste

Petite White Asparagus

2 ounces petite white asparagus

Honshemeji Mushrooms

4 ounces Honshemeji mushrooms, broken into one-ounce clusters

Fried Phyllo

1 cup grape seed oil

1 ounce phyllo dough, cut thinly in a chiffonade

Fine sea salt, to taste

Garnish

8 nasturtium buds

8 sprigs micro mint (or 4 sprigs regular mint tops)

Black Tea and Mint Broth Place broth, tea and mint in a saucepot. Gently bring to a simmer. Turn off heat and let steep for ten minutes. Strain through a fine mesh strainer. Season with salt and pepper and reserve to bring back to a boil before serving.

Braised Lamb Shank Purchase 4 pieces of lamb shanks with 1-inch of meat around a 4 inch high bone scraped clean (about 3 to 4 ounces of meat on the bone).

Sachet d'epices: 1 bay leaf, 2 parsley stems, 1 small sprig of thyme, and 5 black peppercorns, tied in a bundle of cheesecloth

Pre-heat a small saucepot large enough to accommodate the 4 lamb shanks. Add the oil. Let smoke for 10 seconds. Place the seasoned lamb shanks, meat side down and caramelize the meat. Remove from pot. Remove the grease and place the lamb shanks bone side up / meat side down in the pot. Add the cup of the black tea broth and the sachet and bring to a simmer. Cover and let braise about 2 hours until tender and the meat is flaking off the bone. Reserve both the shanks and the 1 cup of broth until ready to serve.

Beggar's Purse of Ground Lamb with Harissa Mix the ground lamb with the harissa and thinly sliced chives and season with salt and pepper. Remove summer roll wrappers from water and lay out side by side. Place ¼ of the lamb mixture in a ball in the center of the moist wrapper. Gather the edges of the wrapper in pleats, twist and gently tie with the blanched whole chive. Cut excess wrapper about ½-inch above the tied chive to make a neat bundle. Cover and refrigerate until serving.

Recipe continues on page 205

RECOMMENDED PAIRINGS

Sullivan St Bakery — Pane Pugliese

Nalle Zinfandel "Dry Creek Valley" 2005

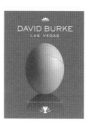

chef / owner
David Burke

Duck, Duck, Prawn Soup

Yields four servings

Ingredients

3 cups fresh corn kernels

1 cup onions, chopped

½ cup leeks, sliced

½ cup fennel, chopped

¼ cup celery, chopped

2 tablespoons chopped shallots

½ teaspoon chopped garlic

3 tablespoons vegetable oil

1 cup chardonnay

4 cups chicken stock

1 cup heavy cream

2 tablespoons salt

1 teaspoon white pepper

½ cup bacon fat

1 teaspoon chopped thyme

Bacon Wrapped Duck & Prawn

4 skinless duck breast

¼ cup pistachios

4 U-10 prawns with the head on

1 lettuce leaf, chopped, blanched

20 slices bacon

Duck Wings

4 duck wings

¼ cup chopped lobster meat

Foie Gras

1 ounce foie gras

Procedure Sweat the corn, onions, leeks, fennel, celery, shallots, and garlic with vegetable oil in a heavy-bottom pot for approximately ten minutes. Add the wine and reduce by half. Add chicken stock, heavy cream, salt and pepper and cook for approximately 15 minutes. Blend in a food processor with the bacon fat. Strain though a chinos and chill in ice bath.

Bacon Wrapped Duck & Prawn Butterfly duck breast. Layer the pistachios, prawns, and lettuce in the middle and then fold the breast back together. Wrap each breast with five slices of bacon. Pan sear over medium heat until crispy. Finish in oven at 400°F, four to five minutes for medium rare.

Duck Wings Remove one bone from duck wing and stuff with chopped lobster. Deep fry at 350°F until crispy.

Foie Gras Pan sear the foie gras over high heat on both sides for approximately two minutes or until golden brown.

To Serve Ladle soup into the bowl. Slice duck breasts into roulade, approximately one-inch thick. Place one roulade, one duck wing and one piece of foie gras into each bowl of soup.

RECOMMENDED PAIRINGS

Sullivan St Bakery — Brioche

Pfeffingen "Ungsteiner Herrenberg" Scheurebe Spatlese 2006

DANIEL

executive chef

Jean François Bruel

Pot Pie of Florida Frog's Legs Velouté

Yields eight servings

Pot Pie

4 pounds fresh frog's legs, divided

½ large onion, coarsely chopped

Bouquet garni (1 bay leaf, 1 sprig flat-leaf parsley, 1 sprig thyme, wrapped in a leek green and tied)

1 medium leek, white and light green part only, chopped and rinsed

½ cup Sauvignon Blanc, or other dry white wine

4 cups unsalted chicken stock or low sodium broth

¼ cup extra-virgin olive oil, divided

½ large onion, thinly sliced

5 garlic cloves, peeled and halved

2 ½ Yukon gold potatoes, peeled and cut into quarter-inch dice

½ cup crème fraîche

Salt and freshly ground white pepper, to taste

Grated nutmeg, to taste

Lemon juice, to taste

1 shallot, finely chopped

1 garlic clove, finely chopped

Sherry vinegar, as needed

2 tablespoons finely chopped flat-leaf parsley

2 sheets frozen puff pastry

2 egg yolks

1 tablespoon of cream

Garnish

16 one-inch strips of crisped bacon

Glazed Mushroom and Onion

2 tablespoons butter

1 pound pearl onions, peeled

1 pound button mushrooms, trimmed and rinsed

¼ cup bordelaise sauce or demi-glace

Fried Frog Leg Lollipops

½ cup all-purpose flour

1 pinch espellette pepper

2 eggs

½ cup fine bread crumbs

3 cups vegetable oil

Parsley Cream

1 bunch parsley, leaves only

1 cup heavy cream

Pot Pie Pick out one pound of the meatiest looking frog's legs, set aside. Remove the meat from the bones of the remaining three pounds of frog's legs, reserving separately. In a large casserole or Dutch oven, over medium heat, add the frog's legs bones, the coarsely chopped onion, bouquet garni and leek. Cook, stirring for five minutes. Add the white wine and chicken stock and bring to a boil. Reduce the heat and simmer for 35 minutes, skimming off the fat, solids or foam that rises to the surface. Strain through a large colander. Discard the bones, onions, bouquet garni, and leek. Set broth aside. Rinse out pot and warm half of the olive oil over medium-high heat. Add the thinly sliced onion and the five cloves of halved garlic and cook, stirring, for five minutes. Add the potato and cook, stirring, for another two minutes. Add the reserved frog's legs broth and bring to a boil. Reduce heat and simmer until the potatoes are tender, about 20 minutes. Stir in the crème fraîche. Carefully transfer to the container of a blender. (You may have to do this in batches.) Purée the soup until smooth, then push it through a fine mesh sieve. Season to taste with salt, pepper, nutmeg, and lemon juice.

Warm the remaining olive oil in a large sauté pan over medium-high heat. Add the reserved frog's legs meat with a pinch of salt and cook, stirring, until light golden brown, four to five minutes. Remove the meat and reserve. In the same pan, add the shallot and the remaining clove of garlic and cook, stirring, until tender, two to three minutes. Add back the frog's legs meat, a few drops of sherry vinegar and the parsley and toss to combine. Season to taste with salt and pepper. Combine the meat with the soup. Chill.

Slightly defrost the puff pastry and roll out to ⅟₁₆-inch thickness; then refreeze. Using the soup bowls that you will be serving in as a guide, trim circles out of the puff pastry about ½-inch in diameter wider than the rims. Whip together the yolks, cream, and a pinch of salt to combine, and brush on top of the puff pastry circles. Then, using a fork, lightly press a cross-hatch design on top of each circle. Divide the soup into bowls, place the pastry circles on top and when they have thawed slightly, mold around the edges of bowls to seal. Keep chilled until ready to serve.

Recipe continues on page 205

RECOMMENDED PAIRINGS

Sullivan St Bakery — Pane Pugliese

Dupont Fahn Puligny Montrachet "Les Charmes" 2006

La Soupe Chaude de Palourde à La Mimolette
clam soup with mimolette cheese

Yields 20 servings

Soup

21 ounces clam juice

1 quart chicken stock

7 ounces Mimolette cheese, grated

12 ⅔ ounces créme fraîche

Soup Garnish

60 Clams (three per serving)

Chopped chives, as needed

Mimolette cheese, cut into curls, as needed

Whipped cream, as needed

Soup Base Bring the clam juice and chicken stock to a boil. Add grated Mimolette cheese and mix with a hand held mixer until smooth. Add créme fraîche and blend again until smooth.

To Serve Poach the clams in water until cooked three-quarters of the way. Add three pieces of clam per plate and top with soup, chopped chives, Mimolette curls and a dollop of freshly whipped cream.

RECOMMENDED PAIRINGS

Sullivan St Bakery — Casa Reccio

Robert Niero Condrieu "Les Ravines" 2005 (Rhone, France)

Harira Soup

Yields six servings / Requires advance preparation

Ingredients

1 pound fresh veal cheeks

Salt and black pepper, to taste

4 tablespoons vegetable oil, divided

4 yellow onions medium size, cut into small cubes

8 plum tomatoes, peeled and cut into small cubes

5 liters chicken stock

1 pint chickpeas, soaked overnight in cold water

1 pint French lentils, soaked in cold water for two hours

5 bunches of cilantro, chopped

1 cup jasmine rice

1 tablespoon cumin

1 tablespoon turmeric

1 tablespoon spicy paprika

1 cinnamon stick

1 tablespoon salt

1 pint lemon juice

Procedure Clean the veal cheeks of any fat. Cut in half. Season with salt and black pepper. Sauté the veal in a heavy pan with two tablespoons of vegetable oil, until each side is lightly browned. Sauté the onions and tomatoes in a large pot with the remaining two tablespoons of vegetable oil for five minutes. Add the sautéed veal cheeks, top with cold chicken stock, and add the chickpeas. Bring to a boil. Skim the surface of any fat. Reduce to a simmer and add the lentils. Cook for 30 minutes more and add the rice, cilantro, spices and lemon juice. Let cook for ten more minutes. Add more salt if needed.

RECOMMENDED PAIRINGS

Sullivan St Bakery — Stecca ai Pomodori

Yann Chave Crozes Hermitage "La Rouvre" 2006

Joanna Pruess
chef / author

Corn and Shrimp Chowder

Yields four to six servings; makes six cups

Ingredients

3 cups defrosted frozen or fresh corn kernels, divided

2 tablespoons unsalted butter or olive oil

1 cup chopped onion

2 cups fish stock or bottled clam broth

1 cup light cream or half-and-half

2 teaspoons sugar

½ each medium green and red bell pepper, seeds and membranes removed, and finely chopped

¾ pound fresh or frozen medium shrimp, peeled, deveined, and cut into ¾-inch slices

⅓ cup chopped cilantro leaves, plus extra leaves to garnish

Salt and freshly ground black pepper, to taste

Procedure Purée two cups of the corn in a food processor until smooth. Set aside.

Heat the butter or olive oil in a medium-sized heavy saucepan over medium-high heat. Add the chopped onion and sauté until wilted, three to four minutes. Stir in the puréed corn, fish stock, light cream, and sugar, and simmer for two to three minutes.

Stir in the remaining corn, bell peppers, shrimp, one-third cup cilantro, salt and pepper. Gently simmer until the shrimp are just cooked through.

To Serve Ladle into heated bowls, garnish with the remaining cilantro leaves, and serve.

RECOMMENDED PAIRINGS

Sullivan St Bakery — Corn Bread*

Edmund St. John Pinot Gris 2003 (California)

chef
Pauline Balboa

Kabocha and Roasted Chestnut Soup

Yields eight servings

Advance preparation suggested for soup

SOUP

Ingredients

21 ounces kabocha (fresh or frozen)

10½ ounces carrots, peeled and chopped

5⅓ ounces daikon, peeled and chopped

7 ounces chestnuts, roasted and peeled

3 sticks kombu (Japanese kelp for broth)

½ cup miso

17⅔ ounces water

½ cup soy milk

¼ cup heavy cream

¼ cup chopped naganegi onion
(can be substituted with scallion)

Procedure Preheat oven to 400°F. Roast the kabocha for 20 minutes or until golden brown.

Chop the carrots and daikon into small chunks. Combine roasted kabocha, roasted chestnuts, carrots, daikon, kombu sticks, miso, and water in a large pot. Simmer about one hour or until tender. Remove kombu, strain, and mix with a hand mixer until smooth. If mixture is too thick, add kombu stock until desired consistency is reached. Let cool. It's best if it sits overnight in the refrigerator.

When reheating, finish with soymilk and heavy cream before serving. Add naganegi garnish.

RECOMMENDED PAIRINGS

Sullivan St Bakery — Semi di Sesamo

Chateau Franchaie Savennieres 2004

La Crème Légère De Haricots Cocos Au Lard
white tarbais bean soup with bacon and black truffle

Yields four servings

Requires advance preparation

Bean Soup Base

5 ½ ounces Tarbais beans

½ carrot

½ onion studded with 2 pieces of clove

1 garlic clove

1 small bouquet garni (parsley, thyme, celery, and bay leaf tied together)

1¾ ounces bacon skin

9 ounces chicken stock

Pinch of garlic purée

1 ounce butter

Garnish

1¾ ounces bacon

Vegetable oil, as needed

1 dollop of fresh whipped cream

¾ ounce truffle chopped, plus extra as needed

Bean Soup Base
Soak the beans in water overnight. In a large pot add the beans, carrot, onion, garlic, bouquet garni, bacon skin, and enough water to cover. Bring to a boil and let simmer for two hours until the beans are tender. Drain the beans and discard the vegetables, bacon and bouquet garni. Blend the beans in a blender and thin with the chicken stock. Pass through a chinois (fine mesh sieve). Pour the mixture into a pot and bring to a boil then add garlic purée and butter.

To Serve
Cut the bacon into small batons. Sauté bacon in vegetable oil in a pot until crispy. Add chopped truffle and sweat for one minute. Add bean soup, cook until hot and then fold in whipped cream. Pour the soup into a bowl and garnish with more chopped truffle.

RECOMMENDED PAIRINGS

Sullivan St Bakery — Rye Bread*

Yann Chave Crozes Hermitage Blanc 2006 (Rhone, France)

Oxtail Soup

Yields 6 to 8 servings

Ingredients

3 tablespoons olive oil

5 pounds oxtail, cut into two-inch pieces

Salt and black pepper, to taste

2 large white onions, medium dice

3 cloves garlic, sliced

2 large carrots, medium dice

3 ribs celery, medium dice

4 sprigs fresh thyme

1 strip of orange rind

1 bay leaf

4 cups beef stock or broth

2 cups water

½ pound fregola, cooked

1 large beefsteak tomato, diced

Procedure

Heat a large pot on high and add the oil. Season the oxtail with salt and pepper and sear in the hot oil on all sides until brown. Remove the oxtail and reserve. Add the onions and garlic. Sauté until lightly caramelized. Add the carrots, celery, thyme, orange rind, and bay leaf and cook for five minutes. Add the oxtail back to the pot and add the stock and water. Season with salt and pepper and let cook for 1½ to 2 hours covered on a low simmer. Remove oxtail, pick the meat off the bones and add it back to the soup. Add the fregola and tomatoes and serve.

RECOMMENDED PAIRINGS

Sullivan St Bakery — Filone

Bucklin Cabernet Sauvignon "Old Hill Ranch" 2005 (Sonoma, CA)

Strawberry Consommé

Yields eight servings
Requires advance preparation

Tapioca
39 ½ ounces water, divided
1 ounce large pearl tapioca
3 ½ ounces granulated sugar

Basil Seed Film
⅓ ounce basil seeds
9 ¾ ounces water, divided
4 grams (two sheets) gelatin
1 gram (tiny pinch) agar-agar
3 ½ ounces sugar

Strawberry Consommé
35 ounces strawberries, hulled, coarsely chopped
9 ounces granulated sugar
1 ½ ounces lemon juice
2 ounces orange juice
Zest of two lemons
Zest of one orange

Garnish
Strawberries, as needed
Micro basil, as needed

Tapioca In a medium saucepan, bring 35 ounces of water to a boil. Stir in tapioca, reduce heat to a low simmer, and cook for approximately 50 minutes, stirring occasionally to prevent the tapioca pearls from sticking to the bottom of the pan or each other. The tapioca is done just when they appear translucent in the center. In a second saucepan, combine the sugar and remaining water. Bring to a boil and allow to cool. Drain the tapioca and rinse with cold water. Reserve in the cooled syrup and chill.

Basil Seed Film Soak basil seeds in three-quarter ounce of water and allow to hydrate for two hours. Bloom gelatin in two ounces of water. Combine agar-agar with sugar. Disperse into the remaining seven ounces of water. Gently bring to a boil; reduce heat while maintaining a simmer for two to three minutes. Remove from heat and whisk in bloomed gelatin and basil seeds. Allow to cool slightly for a few moments and transfer to a flat plastic lined half-sheet pan. Chill and allow to set. Cut into small squares.

Strawberry Consommé Combine all of the ingredients in a large bowl. Coarsely pulse with immersion blender. Cover and place in warm area and allow to stand six hours. Transfer to the refrigerator and allow to chill at least four hours, or overnight. Strain as necessary, decant, and adjust balance of sweetness and/or acidity with additional sugar or lemon juice as needed.

To Serve Using a small melon baller, roughly the same size as the cooked tapioca pearls, prepare several strawberry balls for each portion of soup. Combine the balls with the drained tapioca and pile into each bowl. Drape each mound of strawberry and tapioca with a sheet of the basil seed film and garnish with micro basil. Pour the consommé into the bowl at tableside.

RECOMMENDED PAIRINGS

Sullivan St Bakery — Brioche
Fritz Haag Brauneberger Juffer Auslese 2004

Potato Leek Soup

Yields four servings

Ingredients

Peanut oil, as needed

1 medium size Idaho potato, sliced into ⅛-inch thick disks

Salt and pepper, to taste

2 leeks, white stalks

4 ounces butter

Pinch of fresh nutmeg

1 large potato, peeled and cut

Garnish

Frisée

Micro greens

Julienned leeks, fried

Sliced radishes

Chives

Procedure Heat the peanut oil in a 1½ quart pot to 325°F. Add the sliced potato disks into the oil and deep fry until golden brown. Remove onto a plate lined with paper towel to absorb excess oil. Season immediately with salt and pepper. Set aside for assembly.

Cut the whites of the leeks lengthwise, and then into one-inch pieces. Put into a bowl with some water and rinse three times to remove any sand. Drain. In a large saucepot, melt the butter; add leeks, season with salt and pepper, and a pinch of nutmeg.

Cover with paper and put into 355°F oven until tender. (Making sure to periodically toss the leeks to ensure even cooking.) When finished, remove leeks from the oven and cool at room temperature. Boil the potato in salted water until tender. Drain. Place the leeks and potatoes in a blender and purée. Place back into saucepot, heat and season to taste.

To Serve Stack the fried potato slices with the frisée, sliced radishes, and micro greens in-between. Top with the fried julienned leeks. Put soup into a saucer and serve at the table when presented to guests (French Service). Pour the soup into the bowl around the potato stack. Garnish the soup with the sliced radishes and chives.

RECOMMENDED PAIRINGS

Sullivan St Bakery — Foccacia

Gunderloch Riesling Kabinet "Jean Baptiste" 2007

Truffle Chowder

Yields six servings

Soup

2 quarts mushroom stock
2 cups roasted shallots
1 can black truffle
1 (8-ounce) can truffle juice
2 tablespoon butter
Salt and pepper, to taste

Vegetable Garnish

1 cup purple potato, diced small
½ cup barley, cooked
1 cup rutabaga, diced
½ cup diakon, diced small
½ cup fennel, diced small
1 cup Tuscan kale, chopped
½ cup white mushroom, thinly sliced
1 tablespoon butter
½ cup white wine
Salt and pepper, to taste
Rye bread croutons, as needed

Soup Combine all the ingredients together in a high-speed blender and purée until smooth. Heat the soup to boil. Season to taste with additional salt and pepper if necessary.

Vegetable Garnish Sauté all of the vegetables in butter and then deglaze pan with the white wine and simmer until the vegetables are cooked. Season with salt and pepper to taste.

To Serve Place a healthy amount of vegetable garnish in the middle of a medium size bowl and gently pour in the hot truffle soup. Garnish with rye bread croutons.

RECOMMENDED PAIRINGS

Sullivan St Bakery — Rye Bread*

di Ciacci Rosso di Montalcino 2005 (Tuscany, Italy)

MATSURI

executive chef
Tadashi Ono

Red Miso Soup with Lobster

Yields four servings

Ingredients

2 one-pound live lobsters

1 quart cold water

2 four-inch square pieces kombu seaweed

½ ounce bonito flakes

1 tablespoon mirin

2 tablespoons hatcho-miso (dark soy bean paste)

1 ounce shungiku (eatable chrysanthemum leaves)

Garnish

Red chili pepper, as needed (optional)

Grated ginger, as needed (optional)

Procedure Cut lobsters in half vertically. In a soup pot, add the cold water and kombu, let sit for ten minutes. Place the pot over medium heat and bring to a boil. Remove the kombu and add the bonito flakes. Let cook for one minute. Turn off heat and let sit for two minutes. Strain the bonito out from the liquid. Cook the lobsters in the liquid for five minutes. Take out lobsters, remove the shells and reserve the meat and heads. Add the mirin and hatcho miso to the liquid and mix well. Cook the shungiku in the soup for 30 seconds. Set the lobster meat and heads in the bowl.

To Serve Pour the hot soup into the bowl and serve. You can garnish the soup with red chili pepper or grated ginger if you wish.

SOUP

RECOMMENDED PAIRINGS

Sullivan St Bakery — Brioche

Domaine La Monardiere Vacqueyras Rosé 2007 (uRhone, France)

Eggplant Parmesan Soup

Yields six to eight servings

Eggplant

6 to 8 eggplants (depending on size)

¼ cup olive oil

Salt, to taste

2 eggs

2 cups panko bread crumbs

Olive oil, as needed

Soup

5 plum tomatoes

1½ tablespoons olive oil

6 cloves of garlic, sliced thick

2 small shallots, sliced

1 handful of fresh basil leaves

2 (28 ounce) cans whole peeled tomatoes

6 cups chicken stock

1 tablespoon sugar

Salt and pepper, to taste

¼ cup heavy cream

Croutons

1 loaf of day old Italian bread

1 tablespoon extra virgin olive oil

Salt and pepper, to taste

1 teaspoon garlic powder

2 teaspoon parmesan cheese

Garnish

Cooked spaghetti with sauce, as needed

16 ounces mozzarella di bufala, cubed

1 sprig fresh basil leaves

1 teaspoon parsley

2 tablespoon grated parmesan cheese

Eggplant Shell Cut eggplants lengthwise and scoop out the inside. Chop flesh into one-inch cubes. Drizzle with olive oil and salt, then toss to evenly coat. Roast in the oven until golden brown and crispy and reserve. Beat eggs in a bowl. Dip the rim of the eggplant shell into the egg and then into the panko bread crumbs. Heat a sauté pan with olive oil. When the olive oil is hot, immerse only the rim of the eggplant and fry until golden brown.

Soup Slice tomatoes in half and scoop out the flesh. Place on grill and cook until outer skin appears blistery. Cool and remove the skin. Heat olive oil in a pot and add the sliced garlic and shallots. Cook on medium heat until golden brown and soft. Add the fresh basil and stir for an additional minute or two. Add the cans of peeled tomatoes and the peeled grilled tomatoes. Add the chicken stock, sugar, salt and pepper. Simmer for ten minutes. Add the heavy cream. Purée the soup with an immersion blender.

Croutons Preheat the oven to 350ºF. Cut the bread into one-inch cubes. Place in a bowl. Drizzle with olive oil and season with salt, pepper, garlic powder, and parmesan. Toss to coat evenly. Spread on a baking sheet and bake until toasted. When done, remove from the oven and allow to cool.

To Serve Place the roasted eggplant on top a nest of spaghetti. Pour the hot soup into the eggplant shell and top with croutons and mozzarella di bufala. Garnish the soup with a sprig of basil, chopped parsley, and Parmesan cheese around spaghetti and plate edge.

RECOMMENDED PAIRINGS

Sullivan St Bakery — Ciabatta

Fontanelle Porta al Sole-Chianti Superiore 2004

executive chef
Cheng-Hua Yang

Hot and Sour Soup

Yields six servings

Ingredients

6 ounces fresh firm tofu, julienned

3 ounces fresh shiitake mushrooms, julienned

3 ounces fresh enoki mushroom

3 ounces fresh button mushrooms, sliced

3 ounces fresh bamboo shoots, julienne

2 cups chicken stock

2 tablespoons soy sauce

2 tablespoons chinkiang dark vinegar

2 tablespoons white vinegar

½ tablespoon ground white pepper

½ tablespoon corn starch

2 tablespoons water

2 whole eggs, beaten

1 tablespoon sesame oil

Procedure Blanch the tofu, shiitake mushrooms and bamboo shoots and reserve. Bring the chicken stock to a boil, add the blanched ingredients and return to a boil. Meanwhile, mix the soy sauce, chinkiang vinegar, white vinegar, and white pepper together and add to the boiling chicken stock.

Whisk the cornstarch and water together to make a slurry. Thicken the soup by adding the cornstarch and water mixture. Return the soup to a gentle boil, add the eggs, stir slowly, cook for one minute and remove from heat.

To Serve Sprinkle with the sesame oil and serve hot.

RECOMMENDED PAIRINGS

Sullivan St Bakery — Semi di Sesamo

Pfeffingen Ungsteiner Herrenberg Scheurebe Spätlese 2005 (Pfalz, Germany)

Seafood Creole

Yields four servings

Ingredients

4 tablespoons butter

4 tablespoons olive oil

2 onions, chopped

6 scallions, chopped

4 cloves garlic, minced

2 teaspoons fresh thyme leaves

½ teaspoon Scotch bonnet pepper, finely chopped

1 cup white wine

2 cups stock (shrimp, fish, lobster, or chicken) canned or homemade

1 lime, sliced

1 can (16-ounce) plum tomatoes

2 teaspoons old bay seasoning

Salt and pepper, to taste

2 lobster tails, split

8 shrimp

1 pound salmon filet, cut into chunks

1 pound mussels

4 scallops

Cooked rice, as needed for garnish

Procedure Heat the butter and olive oil in saucepan. Add the onion, scallion, garlic, thyme, Scotch bonnet peppers, and cook for ten minutes. Add the wine, stock, lime slices, canned tomatoes, old bay, and salt and pepper to taste. Bring to a boil. Once boiling, add seafood and cook for ten minutes. Serve over rice.

RECOMMENDED PAIRINGS

Sullivan St Bakery — Stirato

Wegeler Riesling Spätlese "Berg Rottland" 2006

Tendon Congee with Chorizo

Yields six to eight servings

Ingredients

1 pound beef tendon

1 quart water

1 quart veal stock

1 pinch saffron

3 cloves garlic, chopped

1 medium onion, chopped

1 tablespoon ginger, chopped

2 tablespoons olive oil

3 cups cooked rice

Salt and pepper, to taste

2 pieces chorizo

Manchego cheese, grated

2 stalks scallions, sliced

Procedure Cook beef tendon in water and veal stock until tender. Strain tendon and steep saffron in cooking liquid. Sauté garlic, onion, and ginger in olive oil until soft, not brown. Add rice and saffron liquid. Season with salt and pepper and simmer until the rice puffs up, then add tendons.

Grill the chorizo and slice. Reserve for garnish.

Cook grated Manchego cheese in a non-stick pan to make crisps.

To Serve Ladle congee in bowls. Top with chorizo and scallions. Serve with Manchego crisp.

RECOMMENDED PAIRINGS

Sullivan St Bakery — Ciabatta

Saxon Brown Syrah "Flora Ranch" 2005 (Sonoma, CA)

Bahamian Conch Chowder

Yields six servings

Ingredients

¼ cup panchetta, diced

2 bay leaves

1 sprig fresh thyme

3 whole allspice berries

6 whole peppercorns

1½ cups onions, chopped

½ cup carrots, diced

½ cup celery, diced

½ cup green peppers, chopped

½ teaspoon hot pepper flakes, or to taste

2 cloves garlic, chopped

4 cups Roma tomatoes, chopped

3 cups chicken broth

3 cups clam juice or fish stock

1½ cups red potatoes, peeled and diced

5 tablespoons tomato paste

2 pounds conch meat, chopped

4 tablespoons fresh parsley, chopped

Procedure In a large pot, cook the diced panchetta over medium heat until browned and the fat has melted. Removed the panchetta pieces and discard. In a six-inch square cheesecloth, add the bay leaves, thyme, allspice, and peppercorns. Close the cheesecloth and tighten with kitchen string to form a bouquet garni.

In the pot with the panchetta fat, sauté the onions, carrots, celery, and green peppers over a medium-high heat for four to five minutes, or until translucent. Add the hot pepper flakes and garlic, sauté for another minute. Add the tomatoes and cook for two to three minutes. Then add the chicken broth, clam juice or fish stock and diced potatoes and bring to a boil. Add the tomato paste and bouquet garni, reduce heat and cook for about half an hour. Add the conch and let simmer until the meat is tender, about 25 to 30 minutes.

To Serve Ladle the soup into bowls and sprinkle with the chopped parsley.

RECOMMENDED PAIRINGS

Sullivan St Bakery — Ficelle

Pelaquie Tavel Rosé 2007

Cauliflower Soup

Yields four to five servings

Cauliflower Soup

1 Vidalia onion, sliced thin

2 cloves garlic, chopped fine

3 tablespoons extra virgin olive oil

3 heads of cauliflower, broken down into small pieces

½ bunch of thyme

½ cup white wine

1 cup of heavy cream

1½ quarts of water

Cheddar Almond Flan

1 ounce toasted almonds

4 ounces milk

4 ounces heavy cream

3 ounces sharp cheddar, shredded

2 egg yolks

2 whole eggs

Spiced Almond Tuile

4 ounces almonds, blanched and sliced

1 egg white

1 tablespoon of sugar

1 teaspoon of Madras curry powder

Garnish

Mushrooms, sautéed with butter and some chopped shallots

Tuile (see recipe)

Micro Cumin

Cauliflower Soup Sweat the onion and garlic in a large saucepot with the oil until soft. Add the cauliflower and thyme and sweat for approximately 5 minutes. Add wine and reduce until almost dry. Add the cream and the water and let simmer for approximately 20 minutes. Let the soup cool slightly and then transfer it to a Vita-Prep blender and purée until smooth.

Cheddar Almond Flan Simmer the almonds with milk and cream in a pan for approximately 15 minutes. Transfer to a Vita-Prep blender and purée until smooth, then strain. Return the liquid back into a pan and bring to boil. Once boiling, take the liquid off the fire and whisk in the cheddar until it is completely melted. Add the cheddar liquid to a bowl and whisk in the yolks and eggs. Add this mixture into four bowls that you wish to serve the soup in and bake slowly in a water bath at 300°F for 15 minutes. Cool the bowls and refrigerate until needed.

Spiced Almond Tuile Mix all of the ingredients together. Spread out on a Silpat or a sheet pan. Cook for 20 minutes at 275°F. Break up the tuile in free-form pieces, reserve for garnish.

To Serve Warm the bowls with the flan in the oven. Have the soup heated and hot. When the bowls are warm, place the sautéed mushrooms in the center of each bowl. Put some of the tuile pieces on top of the mushrooms and scatter the micro cumin over the tuile. Pour the soup around the mushrooms and enjoy.

RECOMMENDED PAIRINGS

Sullivan St Bakery — Almond-Apricot Bread*

Domaine Cassagnoles Gros Manseng Reserve 2007 (Gascogne, France)

executive sushi chef
Toshio Tomita

Lobster Uni Gazpacho

Yields four servings / Requires advance preparation

Gazpacho

60 ounces beefsteak tomatoes, blanched, skin removed

2 to 3 garlic cloves, to taste

1½ ounces red bell pepper, skin removed

1½ ounces yellow bell pepper, roasted, skin removed

1½ ounces green bell pepper, skin removed

2½ ounces onion

5 ounces English cucumber, without seeds

¼ piece jalapeño pepper

6 teaspoons salt, divided

10 teaspoons yuzu juice

1 teaspoon shichimi

1 teaspoon black pepper

3 teaspoons usukuchi soy

For the Pulp

10 teaspoons olive oil

½ teaspoon wasabi-fresh uni

10 ounces lobster meat

2 tablespoons fresh uni

Garnish

Cilantro stems, as needed

Gazpacho Combine the tomatoes, garlic, bell peppers, onion, cucumber, jalapeño, and three teaspoons of the salt in a blender. Pulse the ingredients first then purée on high until all of the ingredients reach a thick consistency. Strain the liquid through a china cap lined with cheesecloth. Reserve the pulp separately. Let the strained liquid rest overnight in the refrigerator.

The following day, add the yuzu juice, shichimi, black pepper, usukuchi soy, and the remaining three teaspoons of salt to the strained liquid.

For the Pulp In a mixing bowl, combine all of the ingredients with the reserved pulp from the gazpacho.

To Serve In a deep bowl place some of the combined pulp. Pour the liquid around the pulp and garnish with cilantro stems.

RECOMMENDED PAIRINGS

Sullivan St Bakery — Jones Beach Bread*

Jager Gruner Veltliner Smaragd "Achleiten" 2006 (Austria)

executive chef
Craig Koketsu

Thai Minestrone Soup

Yields four servings

Hot and Sour Soup

4 cups chicken stock

2 cups pineapple juice

1 cup shrimp shells

Juice of two limes

2 stalks lemongrass, pounded

3 kaffir lime leaves

3 roma tomatoes, split lengthwise

2 cloves garlic, smashed

3 tablespoons fish sauce

3 Thai chili peppers, smashed

2-inch piece of ginger, peeled and smashed

5 sprigs cilantro

5 sprigs Thai basil

2 tablespoons nam prik pao

Vegetables

¼ cup canola oil

¼ cup fresh peas, blanched

¼ cup fresh chickpeas, blanched

¼ cup red bell peppers, diced

¼ cup baby zucchini, cut into rounds

¼ cup baby patty pan squash, sliced thinly

¼ cup large tapioca pearls, cooked

¼ cup Japanese sweet potato, diced and blanched

¼ cup enoki mushrooms, cut into one-inch pieces

¼ cup haricots verts, split, cut into one-inch pieces

Salt, to taste

Green and golden pea tendrils

Hot and Sour Soup Bring all of the ingredients except for cilantro, basil and nam prik pao to a boil. Reduce heat and simmer for twenty minutes. Add cilantro, basil and nam prik pao. Adjust seasoning with additional fish sauce, lime juice and/or sugar if necessary.

Vegetables Heat soup in a pot and keep hot. In a large saute pan, heat oil gently and then add all the ingredients, except for the salt and pea tendrils, and cook. Do not brown. Season lightly with salt and divide equally into four bowls. Garnish with pea tendrils. Pour the hot soup into bowls in front of guests.

RECOMMENDED PAIRINGS

Sullivan St Bakery — Carta

Von Hovel Riesling "Oberemmeler Hütte" Kabinett 2006

chef / owner
Rebecca Charles

Scallop Chowder with Pernod and Thyme

Ingredients

1 large Spanish onion, finely chopped

1 tablespoon butter

2 large white potatoes, cut into half-inch dice

1 pound medium dry sea scallops*, rough chop into different sizes, no larger than the size of a quarter

1 quart heavy cream

¼ cup Pernod

1 teaspoon fresh thyme, chopped

Kosher salt, to taste

Freshly ground black pepper, to taste

Milk, as needed

Chopped chives, as needed

Procedure Sauté the onion over low heat in butter, until translucent. Add the potatoes and stir, cooking for two minutes. Add the scallops and stir another two minutes. Add the heavy cream and simmer over low heat for 35 to 40 minutes. During the last ten minutes of cooking time, add the Pernod and the chopped thyme and season to taste with salt and pepper. If the chowder seems a little too thick for you at this point, thin with a little milk. Ladle into bowls and sprinkle with chopped chives.

*Dry refers to a scallop that has not been soaked in chemicals after harvest.

RECOMMENDED PAIRINGS

Sullivan St Bakery — Brioche

Tour de Bon Bandol Blanc 2007

Chicken Artichoke Soup

Yields four servings

Ingredients

4 artichokes

Juice of two lemons

½ cup extra virgin olive oil

¾ pound boneless, skinless chicken breast cut into small pieces

½ cup flour plus extra for dredging chicken

½ cup diced onion

1 large carrot, peeled and diced

½ cup orzo

2 egg yolks

Salt and fresh ground black pepper, to taste

Fresh dill for garnish, as needed

Procedure

Wash the artichokes thoroughly. Place artichokes in a large pot. Add eight cups of water and the lemon juice and bring to a boil. Reduce the heat, cover, and simmer until the artichokes are tender, about 40 minutes. When the artichokes are done, remove them from the pot, reserving the liquid. Let the artichokes cool. Peel the leaves from the artichokes, and scoop out and discard the fuzzy chokes. Dice the bottoms into small pieces and set aside.

Heat the olive oil in a large soup pot over medium-high heat. Dredge the chicken pieces in the flour and add to the olive oil. Cook until brown. Add the onion and carrots to the chicken, and cook over low heat until soft. Add the orzo and the reserved artichoke cooking liquid to the chicken mixture. Bring to a boil. Reduce heat, cover, and simmer for 20 minutes.

In a mixing bowl, beat the egg yolks with the half-cup flour and slowly add one cup of water to the egg mixture. Gradually add two cups of the soup stock to the egg mixture, beating constantly. Add this mixture back into the soup pot with the chicken. Add the diced artichoke pieces, salt and freshly ground black pepper, and simmer for 15 minutes. Garnish the soup with sprigs of fresh dill.

RECOMMENDED PAIRINGS

Sullivan St Bakery — Ciabatta

Sollner Gruner Veltliner "Wogenrain" 2007

Watercress Soup with Almond Goat Cheese Cream

Yields six servings

Watercress Soup

3 tablespoons butter

½ cup white wine

3 medium Spanish onions, peeled and coarsely chopped

3 large leeks, cut into large chunks

3 quarts chicken stock or water

3 medium Idaho potatoes, peeled and cut into chunks

2 bunches of watercress

Goat Cheese Cream

¼ cup blanched, sliced almonds

3 ounces plain goat cheese

¼ cup cold water

Salt, to taste

Garnish

Lemon juice, to taste

3 tablespoons sliced toasted almonds

Procedure In a heavy, medium saucepot over a medium flame, melt the butter, add the white wine, the onions and leeks. Sweat, stirring occasionally for about 15 minutes, until the onions and leeks are softened and translucent. Do not allow to brown. Add a splash of wine or water, if necessary to inhibit browning.

Add the stock or water and the potatoes and increase the heat to high. Bring to a boil and then reduce heat to medium and simmer for 25 to 30 minutes or until the potatoes are soft. Purée in a blender, return to pot and set aside, or can be refrigerated for two to three days.

In a large pot of boiling water, blanch the watercress for about 20 to 30 seconds until bright green and wilted, drain and shock in an ice bath, drain again. Chop coarsely and purée in a blender. Do not squeeze out the moisture from the watercress, but don't add any water. Set aside. Yields about 1½ cups.

Goat Cheese Almond Cream Purée the sliced blanched almonds in a blender with the goat cheese and cold water. Season with a pinch of salt and set aside.

To Serve Reheat the soup base, whisk in the watercress purée, taste and adjust seasoning with salt and lemon juice. Ladle into bowls, drizzle with the goat cheese cream and sprinkle with the toasted almonds.

RECOMMENDED PAIRINGS

Sullivan St Bakery — Casa Reccio

Aubuisiere Vouvray "Silex" 2007

Cilantro Soup with Monkfish

Yields four servings

Ingredients

2 ¼ cups dashi

2 teaspoons saké

2 teaspoons light soy sauce

¼ teaspoon sea salt, to taste

9 ounces monkfish

Sea salt, to taste

Freshly ground black pepper, to taste

Vegetable oil for deep-frying

Arrowroot starch for dusting

1 teaspoon cilantro leaves, finely chopped

Garnish

Menegi, as needed

Lime, sliced thin, as needed

Procedure Bring the dashi to a boil in a medium saucepan over high heat. Add the saké and light soy sauce, and adjust the flavor with sea salt.

Slice the monkfish into pieces about a half-inch thick, and sprinkle with a little sea salt and black pepper. Bring about three inches of oil in a medium saucepan to 340°- 350°F. Dust the monkfish pieces with arrowroot and deep-fry for three to four minutes until crisp. Drain on paper towels.

To Serve Arrange the monkfish in four soup dishes. Make sure you add the monkfish when it is freshly fried and still hot. Add the cilantro to the soup and pour into dishes. Garnish with menegi and lime. Serve immediately.

RECOMMENDED PAIRINGS

Sullivan St Bakery — Semi di Sesamo

Robert Weil Reisling Spatlese "Estate"

Spring Onion Soup Soufflé

Yields six serving

Ingredients

2 ounces butter (plus additional butter for brushing soufflé molds)

10 spring onions, sliced

¼ cup all-purpose flour (plus additional flour for dusting soufflé molds)

2 cups fresh cream, room temperature

Kosher salt and fresh ground black pepper, to taste

1 ounce dry sherry

1 quart chicken stock

1 quart beef stock

1 bay leaf

1 sprig thyme

6 eggs, separated

¼ teaspoon cream of tartare

8 ounces Gruyère cheese, grated

Procedure

In a sauté pan, over medium heat, add the butter and sliced onions and sauté until golden brown. Remove half of the onions to a saucepot and place over medium heat.

For the onions in the sauté pan: add the flour and allow it to cook for a few minutes to create a roux. Add the cream and season with salt and pepper. The cream will thicken creating a light béchamel sauce. Remove from the heat, check the seasoning, and allow the mixture to cool to room temperature.

For the onions in the saucepot; deglaze with the sherry, add the chicken and beef stock and the herbs. Allow the soup to simmer and reduce slightly. Adjust the seasoning and hold warm.

Butter and flour your soufflé molds and place in the refrigerator. Preheat the oven to 400°F.

Fold the egg yolks into the béchamel. In the bowl of an electric mixer, place the egg whites, the cream of tartare and whip until the whites reach soft peaks. Gently fold into the béchamel half the cheese and only one-third of the whipped whites. Discard the remaining whites.

Fill the soufflé molds three-quarters of the way and top each with the remaining cheese. Place on a baking sheet pan. Bake the soufflés until they are well risen and golden brown.

Serve at once, pouring the soup into the center of the soufflé.

RECOMMENDED PAIRINGS

Sullivan St Bakery — Filone

Chateau de la Greffiere Macon La Roche "Vieilles Vignes" 2007

chef / owner

Pichet Ong

Kabocha and Coconut Soup

Yields sixteen servings / Requires advance preparation

Amaretti Cookies

8 ounces butter

3 ½ ounces walnuts, chopped

½ teaspoon salt

3 ½ ounces ounces brown sugar

1 egg

1 tablespoon amaretto

7 ounces all-purpose flour

5 grams (pinch) of baking powder

5 grams (pinch) of baking soda

Kabocha Coconut Soup

1 medium kabocha (or 3 small ones, 3 pounds)

28 ounces (2 cans) coconut milk

1 tonka bean

1 nutmeg

½ teaspoon Saigon cinnamon powder

Salt and pepper, to taste

Garnish

1 teaspoon chive oil

1 tablespoon amaretti crumbs

Fresh black pepper

Amaretto in spray bottle

Amaretti Cookies Cream the butter, walnut, salt, and sugar to fluffy. Scrape down the bowl, add the egg and amaretto. Add the flour, baking powder, and baking soda, and mix until fully incorporated. Wrap and let chill for at least four hours. Spread batter on baking tray lined with parchment until quarter-inch thick. Bake at 350°F until brown, ten to twelve minutes. Break into smaller pieces and place in a pastry bag. Crush with a wooden pin until crumbly.

Kabocha Coconut Soup Cut the kabocha into quarters and cook in microwave oven until vegetable is tender. Remove seeds and strings and place in a pot. Add two quarts of water, and bring to a simmer. Let cook for about ten minutes, strain, discard the solids, and reserve the liquid. In the meantime, scoop out all the flesh from the kabocha and place in a large pot. Add coconut milk, the reserved liquid, and let cook over low heat for twenty minutes. Blend the soup together with a hand blender. Grate tonka bean and nutmeg into the soup using a microplane and season the soup with cinnamon, salt, and pepper to taste.

To Serve Portion soup into bowl, about six ounces per serving. Drizzle about a teaspoon of chive oil, a tablespoon of amaretti crumbs, and a dash of fresh finely crushed black pepper on soup. Spritz amaretto on top of soup.

RECOMMENDED PAIRINGS

Sullivan St Bakery — Almond Bread*

Schloss Lieser Estate Riesling "Medium Dry" 2006

chef / partner
Anita Lo

Duck Dumplings in Soup

Yields 15 servings / Requires advance preparation

SOUP

Broth

1 roast duck, pre-seasoned with Chinese five spice, salt and pepper

Duck bones from above duck

1 piece dried shitake mushroom

2 slices ginger

1 clove garlic, smashed

5 scallions, white part only, halved

Soy sauce, to taste

Salt and pepper, to taste

Dumplings

Meat from roast duck

Same quantity of duck meat in nappa cabbage, chopped, salted and squeezed dry

1 cup scallions, sliced on a bias

Hoisin, to taste

Black pepper and salt if needed, to taste

1 package dumpling wrappers

Vegetable oil, as needed for pan-frying

Garnish (per serving)

6 ounces cooked noodles

¼ cup julienned cucumber

1 pinch julienned scallion green

Procedure

Pick all the meat off the duck, shred it and reserve for the dumplings. For the broth, place all of the remaining ingredients in a stock pot except for the soy, salt and pepper and bring to a boil. Skim and bring down to a simmer. Cook, skimming occasionally and adding water as necessary to keep ingredients submerged, until well flavored, about 3½ hours. Strain and season to taste with soy, salt and pepper.

To make the dumplings, mix the duck meat and all of the remaining ingredients together in a bowl, except for the wrappers and vegetable oil. Taste and adjust seasonings. Place a heaping tablespoon of the mixture onto the center of each wrapper. Wet the edges and fold into a half moon shape. On the one end of the folded dumpling make a pleat and press to seal. Press your way along the edge of the dumpling, making four more pleats, (a total of five), equidistant across the dumpling until it is completely sealed. Or if you prefer, simply fold the dumpling, (wetting the edge), and press the entire edge closed without making any pleats to seal.

To Serve

Pan fry the dumplings by heating a nonstick pan, adding a little oil and when hot, adding the dumplings, crest sides up so that they are not touching one another. Immediately add water to come halfway up the sides of the dumplings and cover. Cook over high heat until all the water is evaporated and the bottoms are browned and crispy. Reheat ten ounces broth per serving and divide into bowls. Place six ounces hot noodles in each bowl, and top with six dumplings, browned side up so that they remain crispy. Garnish with cucumber and scallions and serve immediately.

RECOMMENDED PAIRINGS

Sullivan St Bakery — Carrot-Currant Bread*

Bucklin Gewurtraminer "Comagni Portis Vineyard" 2006 (Sonoma, CA)

chef / owner
Rick Moonen

White Gazpacho
with crab dumplings, almonds and grapes

Requires advance preparation

SOUP

Gazpacho

¾ cup blanched almonds

2 cloves garlic, peeled

½ teaspoon salt

1 slice stale white bread, crusts removed

4 cups cold sparkling mineral water, divided

6 tablespoons olive oil, plus extra as needed

3 tablespoons white wine vinegar

2 tablespoons sherry vinegar

Salt and white pepper, to taste

Crab Dumpling

1 ripe avocado

1 package clear dumpling skins

Juice of a half lemon, plus extra as needed

Salt and white pepper, to taste

4 ounces jumbo lump crab

1 tablespoon fine herbs: chives, tarragon, and parsley

Garnish

1½ cups seedless grapes, peeled, halved

Chive flowers

Almond oil, as needed

Gazpacho Grind almonds, garlic cloves, and salt to a fine consistency in a food processor. Soak stale bread in one cup of sparkling mineral water and squeeze to exact moisture. Add the bread to food processor then add olive oil and one cup mineral water slowly in a steady stream. Add vinegars and mix on high speed for two minutes. Add one more cup of mineral water and mix two more minutes. Place in a bowl, add remaining mineral water and mix well. Adjust seasonings with salt and vinegar. Chill for six hours. Strain and season to taste.

Crab Dumplings Slice avocado into thin slices, place on clear film that has been rubbed with olive oil and lemon juice. Season with salt and pepper. Mix the crab with the herbs, juice of a half lemon, salt and pepper. Place one spoonful of crab on each slice of avocado, topped by another slice of avocado. Cover with clear film and twist in to a dumpling.

To Serve In a chilled bowl place six to eight halved grapes and three crab dumplings. Pour soup around grapes and dumplings. Finish with chives flowers and toasted almond oil.

RECOMMENDED PAIRINGS

Sullivan St Bakery — Almond Bread*

Domaine des Deux Mondes Viognier "Saints & Sinners" 2006

Watermelon Gazpacho with Lump Crab Meat and Avocado Yogurt

Yields one gallon of soup

Watermelon Gazpacho

½ gallon watermelon juice with pulp
(about one small seedless red watermelon)

6 plum tomatoes

4 celery stalks

1 hot house cucumber, peeled and seeded

1 red pepper, small diced

1 green pepper, small diced

1 red jalapeño pepper, seeded, chopped fine

2 cups tomato juice

Juice of four lime

¼ bunch cilantro, chopped

¼ bunch mint, chopped

3 scallions, sliced

Kosher salt, to taste

Avocado Yogurt

1 ripe avocado, seeded with pulp removed

Juice of one lime

6 sprigs cilantro, chopped

Salt and pepper, to taste

8 ounces low fat yogurt

Garnish

Avocado yogurt (see recipe)

½ pound jumbo lump crab meat

Watermelon Gazpacho Remove the skin from the watermelon and juice it, saving the pulp separately. Split the tomatoes and remove seeds.

Place the tomatoes, celery and cucumber in a food processor and purée until almost smooth. In a large bowl add the watermelon juice, half of the watermelon pulp, the puréed tomatoes, celery and cucumber, diced peppers, tomato juice, lime juice, chopped herbs, scallions, and kosher salt. Mix well, if the soup does not have enough body add more watermelon pulp.

Avocado Yogurt Place avocado pulp, lime juice and cilantro in a food processor and pulse until smooth. Season with salt and pepper. Add yogurt and mix till well combined.

To Serve Ladle the soup into bowls. Place a dollop of the avocado yogurt in the center, surrounded by pieces of the jumbo lump crab meat.

148

SOUP

RECOMMENDED PAIRINGS

Sullivan St Bakery — Carta

Schiavenza Dolcetto d'Alba 2005

Creama de Coliflor
creamy anise scented cauliflower purée

Yields one gallon

Creama de Coliflor

1 head cauliflower
1 tablespoon anise seed
8 cups water
½ cup butter
1 large onion, diced (2 cups)
2 ribs celery, diced (1 cup)
½ cup flour
2 tablespoons salt, or to taste
1 teaspoon white pepper
2 cups heavy cream

Duck Chicharones

1 pound duck skin
1½ teaspoons ancho chile powder
½ teaspoon salt
½ teaspoon black pepper

Ancho Chile Oil

2 cups canola oil
2 ancho chiles

Garnish

Scallions, chopped (1 tablespoon per serving)

Creama de Coliflor Remove the leaves and core from the cauliflower, leaving about eight cups of florets. Combine with anise seed and water, bring to a boil, and simmer ten minutes or until just tender. Melt butter in a large saucepan, and sauté onions and celery until onions are translucent, about five minutes. Stir in flour and cook for two minutes. Add the cauliflower and its cooking water to the onion mixture, stirring to combine. Cook over low heat, stirring occasionally, about ten minutes, or until vegetables are soft and stock has thickened. Add salt, pepper and cream, and purée until smooth.

Duck Chicharones Cut a shallow cross-hatch pattern in the duck skin and place in a shallow roasting pan. Lightly season with ancho chile powder, salt and pepper. Place in a 300°F oven, and bake two to three hours, until fat has rendered and skin is beginning to crisp. Pour off the accumulated fat, return to oven, increase temperature to 350°F and bake for an additional 15 minutes. Cool, and coarsely chop. (If duck skin is unavailable, coarsely chopped crisp bacon can be substituted.) Yields one cup.

Ancho Chile Oil Heat oil to approximately 200°F, remove from heat and add chiles. Bubbles should rise around chilies when added to the oil, and chiles should puff up slowly, but should not become crisp. Leave chiles in oil, and allow to cool. Once cool, purée and strain.

To Serve Ladle soup into bowl and top with one tablespoon duck chicharones, one teaspoon ancho chili oil and one tablespoon scallions.

RECOMMENDED PAIRINGS

Sullivan St Bakery — Foccacia

Ramson Pinot Noir "Barrel Selection" 2005 (Oregon)

Mushroom Velouté

Yields six servings

Ingredients

1 cup shallots, sliced

5 garlic cloves, sliced

1½ leeks, white part only and sliced

4 ounces pound butter

1 pound button mushrooms, sliced

1 quart chicken stock

1 bouquet garni: a few sprigs of fresh parsley, thyme and bay leaves, tied together with string

1 pint heavy cream

Salt and pepper, to taste

Garnish

White button mushroom slices, as needed

Black truffle slices, as needed

Black truffle oil, as needed

Parmesan Ritz crackers, as needed

Procedure Cook the shallots, garlic, and leeks in the butter, until soft. Do not brown. Add the mushroom and sweat until the liquid from the mushroom is released. Add enough chicken stock to cover, add the bouquet garni and simmer for about 20 to 30 minutes. Add the cream and simmer for a few more minutes. Purée the soup in a blender and then strain it through a fine mesh strainer. Finish with salt and pepper.

To Serve Pour the soup into a bowls and top with mushroom and truffle slices. Drizzle with some truffle oil. Serve with the crackers on the side.

RECOMMENDED PAIRINGS

Sullivan St Bakery — Carta

Bruno Pasquero Roero 2005

David Rosengarten
chef / author

Callaloo
west indian vegetable and crab soup with coconut milk

Yields four main-course servings

Ingredients

10 ounces raw spinach

8 okra, cut into half-inch rounds

4 ounces peeled pumpkin, cut into half-inch dice

1 medium onion, coarsely chopped

4 scallions sliced into half-inch rounds

4 ounces salted pork (see note)

2 cups unsweetened coconut milk

4 sprigs fresh thyme

2 cloves

1 Scotch bonnet, habanero or other hot chile

3 pounds crab (either whole live crabs, well-washed or cooked crab claws, defrosted)

1 tablespoon unsalted butter

Procedure Remove any tough stems from spinach. Place in a four-quart saucepan. Add the okra, pumpkin, onion, scallions, pork, coconut milk, and two cups of water.

Place the thyme, cloves and hot chile in a piece of wet cheesecloth. Tie securely and place in the saucepan. Bring to a boil over medium-high heat, then turn the heat to low and simmer, covered, until all the ingredients are soft, about 45 to 60 minutes.

Remove the cheesecloth bag and discard. Remove the pork and discard. Pour half of the remaining contents of the pot into a blender, and purée them. Return purée to the pot and blend well. Add the crab and cook for another ten minutes.

Stir in one tablespoon unsalted butter, or Caribbean margarine, before serving.

Note: The most accessible pork ingredients to use would be either salt pork or bacon. If using either, keep the pork in one chunk. A less accessible but more authentic option would be a salted pig's tail, which you can obtain from a butcher in a Caribbean neighborhood; ask him to cut a four-ounce piece into four chunks. Whichever type of pork you're using, prepare it for the callaloo by placing it in a small saucepan, covering it with water, bringing the water to a boil, then draining the pork in a colander under running tap water.

RECOMMENDED PAIRINGS

Sullivan St Bakery — Palm Bread*

Monchhof Urziger Wurtzgarten Kabinett 2006 (Germany)

chef / owner
Sueños and Los Dados
Sue Torres

Tortilla Soup

Yields four to six servings

Ingredients

2 quarts roasted tomatoes and liquid

1 medium roasted onion

½ cup roasted garlic

6 corn tortillas, fried and crushed in food processor

¾ cup chipotles en adobo

Salt and pepper, to taste

Vegetable oil, as needed

Garnish

1 avocado, ripe, cut into one-inch squares

1 cup queso fresco or queso blanco, cut into one-inch squares

6 corn tortillas, cut into strips and fried, sprinkled with salt

Procedure Purée all of the ingredients, except for the oil, in a blender until smooth. Heat a heavy-bottomed saucepan over high heat. Add enough oil to coat the bottom of the pan. Fry the tomato broth in hot oil. Bring to a boil. Once boiling, reduce to a simmer and cook for 10 to 15 minutes.

To Serve Ladle 12 ounces of the tomato broth into bowl. Place six pieces of avocado and queso fresco around each bowl. Place a handful of tortilla strips in the center of soup. Repeat process with each bowl. Serve immediately.

RECOMMENDED PAIRINGS

Sullivan St Bakery — Stecca al Aglio

Edmunds St. John "Shell & Bone" Red 2003

Borscht

Yields six to eight servings

Ingredients

½ pound bacon, diced

1 tablespoon vegetable oil

1 tablespoon minced garlic

1 cup yellow onions, chopped

1 carrot, peeled and grated

2 quarts beef stock (homemade or a good store brand will do)

3 tablespoons red wine vinegar, or to taste

6 cups shredded green cabbage

1 large russet potato, peeled and diced

1½ pounds red beets, greens tops removed peeled, and grated

Salt and freshly ground black pepper

Garnish

1 cup sour cream

½ cup chopped fresh dill

Procedure

Place the bacon in a Dutch oven or stockpot with one tablespoon of vegetable oil and cook, stirring, over a medium-high heat until the fat begins to render, about three minutes. Add the garlic, onions and carrots and cook until soft, approximately four minutes. Drain the excess fat, add the beef stock and bring to a boil. To the broth, add red wine vinegar, cabbage and potatoes. Simmer over low heat for another 30 minutes. Season with additional red wine vinegar, then add the beets and cook until they are soft, approximately five minutes, add salt and freshly ground black pepper, to taste. If the borscht seems too acidic, add a little sugar to round out the flavor.

To Serve

Ladle the borscht into bowls and garnish with a dollop of sour cream and a pinch of fresh dill.

RECOMMENDED PAIRINGS

Sullivan St Bakery — Rye Bread*

Saxon Brown Zinfandel "Santinamaria" 2003

SHANGHAI CUISINE

co-owner   executive chef
Jijie Hong   Hongfu Feng

Crab Meat Soup Dumpling

Yields 6 to 8 servings

Pork Skin Jelly

1½ pounds fresh pork skin

4 ounces ginger

3 ounces scallion

1 ounce Chinese rice wine

1 teaspoon salt

¼ teaspoon white pepper

Pork Shoulder Filling

1 fresh boneless pork shoulder
(about 3 ½ lbs)

Pork skin jelly (see recipe)

6 ounces ginger juice

1 ounce sesame oil

1 ounce Chinese rice wine

1 ounce soy

2 tablespoons sugar

1 teaspoon salt

¼ teaspoon white pepper

Crab Meat Filling

¼ pound steamed crab meat

1 tablespoon pork fat

1 teaspoon Chinese rice wine

1 teaspoon sugar

1 ounce ginger, grated

½ teaspoon salt

Dumpling Skin

1 pound flour

8 ounces cold water

Pork Skin Jelly Bring a pot of water to a boil and add all of the ingredients. Adjust heat to medium and cook for 30 minutes. Remove the pork skin, ginger, and scallion from the boiling water. Discard the ginger and scallion. Coarsely chop the pork skin and return to the boiling water. Cook until the skin fully softens, remove, cool, and finely chop.

Pork Shoulder Filling Trim the shoulder of the skin and excess fat. Chop the shoulder meat until finely ground. Mix with ground pork skin jelly and remainder of the ingredients.

Crab Meat Filling Coarsely chop the crab meat. Add the pork fat to a very hot wok. Stir-fry the crab quickly with the remaining ingredients.

Dumpling Skin Knead the flour with the water for ten minutes. Roll out the dough to desired thickness and cut out 2½-inch rounds. Mix the pork shoulder and crab meat fillings. Place a dollop of combined filling on a round of dough. Wet the edge of the dough with water and fold it up, crimping and sealing to make a dumpling.

To Serve Place six to eight dumplings in a bamboo steamer. Steam for six to seven minutes. The steaming allows the ingredients within the dumplings to produce their own broth.

RECOMMENDED PAIRINGS

Sullivan St Bakery — Stecca

Aubuisière Vouvray "Silex" 2007

SUSHISAMBA

corporate chef
Michael Cressotti

Seared Gingered Pork Gyoza Soup

Yields four servings

Vegetables

6 pieces baby carrots, blanched and grilled

6 pieces jumbo asparagus, blanched and grilled

1 large elf mushroom, grilled and sliced

Gyozas

4 ounces ground lean pork

1 teaspoon minced ginger

½ teaspoon lite soy sauce

½ teaspoon minced scallions

12 round gyoza skin wrappers

Vegetable oil, as needed

Mushroom Dashi

6 cups dashi (available at Asian markets)

½ cup dried shiitake mushrooms

Garnish

Elf mushrooms, sliced, as needed

Mustard oil

Micro shisho leaf

Shredded nori

Gyozas Combine all of the ingredients, except gyoza skins and oil, and mix well. Refrigerate for one hour. Form gyozas by placing a dollop of the mixture in the center of the wrapper, wet the edges, fold up and crimp to make a sealed package. Steam gyozas for two minutes, then sear in hot oil. Reserve.

Mushroom Dashi Combine the dashi and mushrooms, simmer for 30 minutes and strain.

To Serve Place the carrots and asparagus in the center of a warm soup bowl, top with three gyozas, ladle mushroom dashi over the gyozas. Top the gyozas with a slice of elf mushroom, drizzle with mustard oil and garnish with micro shisho and shredded nori. Serve immediately.

RECOMMENDED PAIRINGS

Sullivan St Bakery — Semi di Sesamo

Bucklin Gewurtraminer "Comagni Porti Vineyard" 2006

Low Country Stew

Ingredients

2 tablespoons extra virgin olive oil

1 pound chicken thighs, cut into pieces

1 pound shrimp, peeled and deveined

1 pound catfish, cut into small pieces

1 pound andouille sausage

1 large onion, chopped

1 bell pepper, chopped

3 cloves garlic, minced

4 celery stalks, chopped

2 tablespoons Creole seasoning

1 (6-ounce) can tomato paste

4 tomatoes, peeled, seeded and chopped

8 cups chicken broth

2 bay leaves

Salt, to taste

8 pieces okra, sliced

½ cup chopped herbs: such as parsley and/or chives

Corn bread, for garnish (optional)

Procedure

Place the olive oil in a large Dutch oven and place over medium heat. When hot, add the chicken, shrimp, fish, sausage, onion, bell pepper, garlic, and celery. Cook until just lightly brown.

Add the Creole seasoning, tomato paste, tomatoes, and chicken broth and bring to a simmer. Add the bay leaves and season with salt. Reduce the heat so that the mixture is at a slow simmer, then cover. Cook until the liquid is reduced by half. Add the okra and cook for five more minutes.

Just before serving, remove the bay leaves and stir in the freshly chopped herbs. Serve with corn bread, if desired.

RECOMMENDED PAIRINGS

Sullivan St Bakery — Pane Pugliese

St Damien Gigondas "Vieilles Vignes" 2006

Telepan

chef / owner
Bill Telepan

Kielbasa and Cabbage Soup

Yields seven cups of soup

Ingredients

4 tablespoons canola oil, divided

6 medium leeks, cut into ⅓-inch dice, divided

1 stalk celery, peeled and cut into ⅓-inch dice

½ onion, peeled and sliced thin

Salt, as needed

1 quart chicken stock or water

1 pound Yukon gold potatoes, peeled and cut into ⅓-inch dice, divided

8 ounces kielbasa, quartered and cut into half-inch dice

3 cups chiffonade white cabbage

3 tablespoons Hungarian paprika

1 teaspoon cayenne

2 tablespoons chopped parsley

Procedure In a pot, heat two tablespoons of the canola oil. Add half the leeks, all the celery and onion, and a pinch of salt. Cover pot and cook over medium-low heat until tender, about 12 minutes. Add the stock and half the potatoes, bring to a boil and simmer until potatoes are tender, about 10 minutes. Purée and pass through a fine strainer, set aside.

In a separate pot, place the remaining canola oil and kielbasa. Render over medium heat for seven minutes until slightly golden brown. Reduce heat to medium-low. Add the cabbage and pinch of salt and cook covered for 12 minutes, stirring occasionally. Add remaining leeks and potatoes and cook, covered, for 12 more minutes, stirring occasionally.

Add paprika and cayenne and cook, covered, for three more minutes. Add puréed vegetables, bring to a boil and simmer for two minutes. Add chopped parsley when ready to serve.

RECOMMENDED PAIRINGS

Sullivan St Bakery — Rye Bread*

Bucklin Zinfandel "Old Hill Ranch" 2005

chef
Gary Walia

Mulligatawny Soup

Yields four servings

SOUP

168

Ingredients

¼ cup red lentils

½ cup yellow lentils

13 ounces water

9 ounces chicken broth

Salt, to taste

1 pinch red pepper powder

½ teaspoon black pepper, crushed

¾ tablespoon fresh apple, chopped

½ baby carrot, chopped

1 tablespoon olive oil

3 curry leaves

1 teaspoon ginger

1 teaspoon garlic paste

1 medium shitake mushroom, chopped

1 tablespoon minced chicken

½ teaspoon chives, chopped

Lemon wedges, as needed

Procedure In a pot, place the red and yellow lentils, water, chicken broth, salt, red pepper, black pepper, apple, and carrot, and bring to a boil. Reduce heat to medium and simmer for 20 minutes stirring occasionally so that the lentils don't stick to the bottom of the pot. Once the lentils are soft, remove from the heat. Let rest for about two minutes and then purée in a blender.

Next, in a frying pan, heat the olive oil and add curry leaves, then the ginger and garlic paste and sear for about 30 seconds. Add the mushrooms and minced chicken and cook for about two minutes. Mix it into the puréed soup. Pour into bowls and garnish with the chives and a lemon wedge.

RECOMMENDED PAIRINGS

Sullivan St Bakery — Pizza Bianca

Sky Zinfandel "Mt. Veeder" 2005

executive chef
Jason Potanovich

Green Spring Garlic Soup
with a ginger carrot foam and crisp frog's legs

Yields four to six servings

Ingredients

¼ pound of butter

1 cup of sweet Vidalia onions, sliced thin

3 pounds of fresh spring garlic with the green tops attached, sliced

½ bulb of celery root, sliced thin

¼ bulb of fennel, sliced thin

1 bay leaf

2 sprigs of thyme

½ cup dry white wine, unoaked

2 Yukon potatoes, peeled and cut into quarter-inch cubes

1½ gallons of chicken stock or water

1½ cups heavy cream

Salt and pepper, to taste

Garnish

2 fresh frog's legs

Salt and pepper, to taste

Juice of one lemon

All-purpose flour for dusting

Olive oil, as needed for sautéing frog's legs plus 2 tablespoons

1 garlic clove, peeled and sliced very thin

Juice of three organic carrots

Juice of one piece of ginger, 2 inches by ½-inch

Procedure

In a heavy-bottomed Dutch oven, melt butter and add the onions, garlic, celery root, and fennel, and sweat without browning for about 12 to15 minutes. Next, add the fresh herbs and mix. Deglaze with the white wine and cook for an additional 10 minutes. Add the potatoes, then the stock, bring to a boil and reduce to a simmer for an additional 30 minutes. Then add the cream, salt and pepper. Warm the soup and purée in a vita blender to achieve a smooth consistency. Pass the soup through a fine meshed sieve to remove any small pieces.

For the Garnish

Scrape the thin part of the frog's leg down with a paring knife to render it more presentable and easier to handle. Season the legs with salt and pepper and lightly dip them into the lemon juice and then the flour. Place the legs into a medium-high heat sauté pan with olive oil and cook on both sides until evenly cooked all the way through, about 1½ to 2 minutes. Remove from heat and set aside to keep warm. In a separate pan, add the two tablespoons of olive oil and the sliced garlic. Sauté at lower heat to prevent burning. Remove the garlic when it has become golden and crispy. Place on a paper towel to remove any excess oil, and season with salt and pepper. For the foam, mix the two juices together and blend with a hand-held blender until a light airy foam has formed on top of the juice.

To Serve

In a small bowl, add the soup and with a spoon just skim off the top of the foam and place a dollop in the center of the soup. Place the garlic chips on top of the foam. Serve.

RECOMMENDED PAIRINGS

Sullivan St Bakery — Fennel-Raisin Bread*

Domaine L'Ecette Rully Blanc "Maizières" 2006 (Burgandy, France)

Tom Yum Goong Soup

Yields six servings

Ingredients

3 stalks lemongrass, green part and root end trimmed, remaining section cut into 3 pieces

5 leaves kaffir lime leaf, break leaf into 4 pieces

2-inches long galanga, slice cross section into six to seven pieces

2 ½ quarts water

1 pound shrimp, medium size, peeled

2 tablespoons tamarind

7-10 tamarind tendril, to taste

3-15 bird's eye chili, crushed, to taste

2 tablespoons nam prig pao (roasted chili paste)

¼ cup white mushroom, sliced

4-8 tablespoons fish sauce, to taste

6-12 tablespoons lime juice, to taste

½ tablespoon sugar

¼ cup cilantro, chopped

Procedure

Add lemongrass, kaffir lime leaf, and galanga to 2 ½ quarts water, bring to a boil and then lower the heat to medium. Add shrimp, tamarind, tamarind tendril, bird's eye chili and nam prig pao. Once the shrimp are cooked, lower flame. Quickly add mushrooms, fish sauce, lime juice and sugar. Garnish with cilantro and serve.

RECOMMENDED PAIRINGS

Sullivan St Bakery — Semi di Sesamo

Weingut George Riesling "Rudesheimer Berg Rottland" 2005

Crawfish Chowder

Ingredients

Olive oil, as needed

1 small Spanish onion, diced

2 garlic cloves, thinly sliced

1 rib of celery, diced

4 medium Yukon gold potatoes, diced, divided

1 quart shrimp stock, divided

1 medium leek, diced

½ cup heavy cream

1 tablespoon Creole spice

Salt and pepper, to taste

Poached crawfish, as needed for garnish

Procedure

In a medium saucepot, heat the olive oil over medium heat. Add the diced onion, garlic, and celery and cook slowly until soft without browning, approximately ten minutes. Then add in half of the diced potatoes and half of the shrimp stock, and cook until the potatoes are tender. In another saucepot, sauté the leeks in olive oil until soft and then add the remaining half of the diced potatoes and the remaining half of the shrimp stock. Cook until the potatoes are soft. Purée the potato, leek, shrimp broth using a hand blender or a Cuisinart. Add this puréed mixture to the first broth, place on low heat and add the heavy cream and Creole spice. Season with salt and pepper and garnish with poached crawfish.

RECOMMENDED PAIRINGS

Sullivan St Bakery — Carta

Aubuisieres Vouvray "Silex" 2007

Green Asparagus Soup
with slow poached farm egg and american caviar

Yields six to eight servings

Soup Base

3 pounds green asparagus, washed and peeled (save the peelings)

1 medium onion, peeled and chopped

1 leek, white part only, washed and chopped

3 garlic cloves, peeled and smashed

1 tablespoon olive oil

1 tablespoon butter

1½ quarts chicken stock

Salt and pepper, to taste

Garnish

6 eggs

White vinegar, as needed to poach eggs

3 tablespoons sour cream

Asparagus tips, blanched

3 ounces of caviar

Soup Base Wash and peel the asparagus, save the peelings and cut into quarter-inch pieces. In a stockpot, sweat the onion, leek and garlic in olive oil and butter until tender, then add the chicken stock and bring to a boil for about five to seven minutes. Add the asparagus peelings and boil until tender. When cooked, blend everything in a blender then strain through a fine chinois. Cool down and reserve until further use.

Asparagus Purée Take the peeled asparagus cut into quarter-inch pieces, reserving the tips for garnish. Blanch in salted water and blend in a blender in order to obtain a smooth purée, then cool in a bowl in an ice-water bath.

Blanch the tips separately and shock them in ice water.

Poached Egg Poach the eggs one by one in boiling water (add three to four tablespoons of white vinegar per quart of water) for about three minutes. Shock in ice water carefully, then place onto a plate of paper towels.

To Serve Bring the soup base to a boil in a stockpot. Once boiling add the asparagus purée, whisk and bring back to a boil then add the sour cream and mix again. Season with salt and pepper to taste and serve with the reheated eggs and blanched asparagus tips and finish with a dollop of caviar. This soup can be served hot or cold.

RECOMMENDED PAIRINGS

Sullivan St Bakery — Stecca ai Carciofi

Jager Gruner Veltliner Smaragd "Achlieten" 2006 (Austria)

Timothy Reardon

chef

Morrocan Mussel and Chickpea Stew with Orzo Salad

Yields ten servings

Mussels

½ cup extra virgin olive oil

1 cup onion, medium dice

½ cup celery, medium dice

½ cup ennel, medium dice

¾ cup leeks, medium dice

1 cup red bell pepper, medium dice

1 tablespoon garlic, minced

3 bay leaves

½ teaspoon chili flakes

Salt and pepper, to taste

5 pounds mussels, cleaned with beards removed

1 quart white wine

Soup Base

¼ cup olive oil

2 tablespoons garlic, minced

1½ tablespoons ginger, minced

1 tablespoon thyme, picked

32 ounces canned tomato (and juice), medium dice

2 ounces tomato paste

1 tablespoon vinegar

1 teaspoon sugar

1 tablespoon harissa*

1 tablespoon pickled lemon*, minced (can substitute lemon zest)

16 ounces canned chickpeas, washed and drained

1 tablespoon lemon juice

Salt and pepper, to taste

1 teaspoon cumin, ground

¼ teaspoon cayenne, ground

1 tablespoon paprika, ground

½ teaspoon cinnamon, ground

*Available at middle eastern markets

Orzo Salad Garnish

1 teaspoon turmeric

½ pound orzo pasta

½ cup fresh cilantro, chopped

1 cup tomatoes, small dice

½ cup scallion, chopped

¼ cup red onion, small dice

1 ounce lemon juice

½ cup olive oil

Salt and pepper, to taste

Mussels Heat a large skillet over medium-high heat and add all ingredients, except mussels and white wine. Sauté until fragrant and translucent, about five minutes. Reserve.

Heat a large heavy-bottomed pot on medium-high heat until very hot. Add the mussels, white wine and the vegetables from the skillet. Season with salt and pepper. Cover and let simmer until most of the mussels have opened, about eight to ten minutes. Using a large colander, strain the contents of the pot, reserving the liquid. When mussels are cool enough to handle, clean the meat from the shells. Discard the shells and any mussels that do not open. Reserve the mussel meat and vegetables.

Soup Base Heat a large heavy-bottomed pot over medium heat. Add the olive oil, garlic, ginger, thyme, and the reserved vegetables. Sauté for a few minutes. Add the rest of the ingredients and the reserved cooking liquid from the mussels. Simmer for 25 to 30 minutes. Add the shelled mussels to the soup and remove from heat.

Orzo Salad Garnish Begin with a medium sized pot of salted water to cook the orzo pasta. Add one teaspoon turmeric to the water before adding pasta. Cook pasta until tender. Strain and rinse under cool running water until just warm.

Toss pasta in a mixing bowl with the cilantro, tomatoes, scallion, red onion, lemon juice, olive oil, salt, and pepper. Mix gently and reserve.

To Serve Ladle stew into a large soup bowl. Place a large mound of orzo salad in the middle.

RECOMMENDED PAIRINGS

Sullivan St Bakery — Semi di Sesamo

Hermanos Pecina Rioja "Crianza" 2000

Lobster Fennel and Corn Chowder

Yields six to eight servings

Ingredients

5 tablespoons unsalted butter

3 medium Spanish onions, cut into brunoise

6 ounces of fresh fennel bulb, cut into brunoise

6 ears of fresh corn, shucked, with kernels removed

2 ounces brandy or cognac

1 tablespoon all-purpose flour

2 quarts lobster stock

1½ cups of heavy cream

Salt and white pepper, to taste

2 sprigs of thyme, chopped, to taste

2 pounds lobster meat, precooked

Procedure In a deep heavy-bottom pot, melt the butter and add the onions, fennel and corn. Add the brandy and cook until it evaporates. Add the flour and stir to thicken. Heat up the lobster stock in a separate pot and the heavy cream in another one. When both become hot, add them to the first mixture. Cook slowly on low heat for one hour, then season to taste with salt, pepper and thyme. Cut the lobster meat into bite size chunks and add at the end.

RECOMMENDED PAIRINGS

Sullivan St Bakery — Filone

Cold Heaven Viognier "Sanford & Benedict" 2006

Curry Duck and Vegetable Consommé

Yields six servings

Duck Stock

1 whole duck, except the breast (reserve breast for garnish)

1 piece fennel

1 onion

2 carrots

8 cloves garlic

8 fresh curry leaves

3 tablespoons curry powder

½ bunch fresh thyme

1cup plum tomatoes, peeled and seeded

1½ gallons water

2 tablespoons kosher salt

½ tablespoon crushed white peppercorns

Duck Breasts

2 duck breasts

Salt and pepper, to taste

Vegetable oil, as needed

Clarification Mise En Place

1 pound ground duck, cold

1 cup mirepoix (onion, celery and carrots)

½ cup mushrooms

7 egg whites, lightly beaten

3 quarts duck stock (see recipe)

4 curry leaves

4 sprigs of thyme

Garnish

Thinly sliced duck breasts (see recipe)

2 carrots and 2 parsnips, parisanne (small round balls)

2 stalks salsify, cut on the bias

6 white asparagus, cut on the bias

1 piece Holland leek, cut on the bias

6 baby corn, split

¼ cup fresh peas, precooked

6 scallions, cut on the bias

12 sprigs cilantro

Duck Stock
Place all of the ingredients in a large stock pot and cook for two hours on low to medium heat. Strain the stock, let cool and reserve.

Duck Breasts
Season the breasts with salt and pepper. Sear on both sides in the oil until medium-rare. Slice thin and reserve.

Clarification Mise En Place
Place duck meat, mirepoix, and mushrooms in food processor and pulse until combined. Place mixture in stock pot and fold in egg whites. Add stock and stir to combine. Heat soup to simmering, stirring until raft starts to form. Add thyme and curry leaves and simmer until desired flavor is achieved. Strain through a cheesecloth.

To Serve
Have garnish standing at room temperature when ready to garnish the soup. Place consommé in clear bowl and add garnish to present soup.

RECOMMENDED PAIRINGS

Sullivan St Bakery — Semi di Sesamo

Fritz Haag Riesling "Estate Kabinett" 2006

Summer Minestrone with Fresh Basil-Mint Pesto

Yields six to eight servings

Ingredients

¼ cup extra virgin olive oil + extra for drizzling

2 garlic cloves, peeled and minced

1 medium yellow onion, diced

3 sprigs fresh marjoram

1 bunch fresh watercress

2 celery ribs, peeled and chopped

½ bunch asparagus, cut into 1-inch pieces

2 cups young green beans, cut into 1-inch pieces

2 cups shelled baby peas (fresh or frozen)

1 bay leaf

Kosher salt, to taste

Freshly ground black pepper, to taste

2 quarts low-sodium chicken stock

½ cup heavy cream

1 cup basil mint pesto (recipe follows)

Fresh basil, for garnish

Basil Mint Pesto

1 cups fresh basil

1 cup fresh mint

1 cup fresh Italian flat-leaf parsley

½ cup Parmigiano Reggiano cheese, shredded

½ cup pine nuts, toasted

4 garlic cloves, roughly chopped

Kosher salt, to taste

Freshly ground black pepper, to taste

½ cup extra-virgin olive oil

Procedure

Take a large, heavy pot and add the extra-virgin olive oil. Add garlic, onion, and marjoram and sauté gently (you don't want any color) until fragrant. Add the vegetables and bay leaf and cook for about five to seven minutes until the vegetables are just tender. Season with salt and pepper. Add the chicken stock then bring to a gentle boil. Reduce the heat and simmer uncovered for ten minutes so the flavors can come together – do not let it boil hard. Using a slotted spoon, scoop approximately half of the vegetables out and purée in a food processor with a bunch of watercress until smooth and creamy. Fold the purée back into pot of soup and continue to simmer until hot again. Finish by adding cream to the pot, and give it a final season with salt and pepper.

Basil Mint Pesto

Put all the ingredients into a food processor and pulse until well combined and the pesto is creamy but still has a little texture. Yields 4 to 6 servings.

To Serve

Serve each bowl with a spoonful of basil mint pesto on top, a drizzle of extra-virgin olive oil and some freshly ground black pepper. Garnish with a leafy stem of basil.

RECOMMENDED PAIRINGS

Sullivan St Bakery — Pane alle Olive

Edmunds St. John (White Blend) "Heart of Gold" 2007

executive chef
Carmen Quagliata

Papa al Pomodoro con Spiedini di Gamberini

Yields four servings / Requires advance preparation / This summer soup is best served at room temperature

Ingredients

1 large red vine-ripened tomato

5 large yellow Brandywine tomatoes

1 pint vine-ripened Sweet 100 tomatoes

3 cloves garlic, divided

8 tablespoons extra virgin olive oil, divided

5 basil leaves, chopped

2 teaspoon salt plus one pinch, divided

4 half-inch slices of country Italian bread, crusts removed, diced into half-inch squares

16 small (21-25) Ruby Red shrimp

1 shallot, chopped

1 pinch chile flakes

¼ cup white wine

1 cup water

Zest of half a lemon

½ teaspoon lemon juice

4 firm rosemary sprigs, at least 6 inches

Black pepper, as needed

Celery heart leaves, as needed

Procedure

Cook the red tomato in boiling water for 15 seconds. Remove and place in ice water to cool. Peel the tomato and cut in half horizontally. Squeeze over a strainer, removing the seeds and reserving the juice. Chop the tomato into half-inch dice. Set aside. Repeat the process with the yellow tomatoes keeping the red and yellow tomato juices together but diced flesh separate. Set aside.

Preheat oven to 180°F. Score the Sweet 100 tomatoes by making one small cut through both ends. Dip in boiling water for five to ten seconds, cool in ice water, peel. Set aside.

In a 10-inch sauté pan over medium flame, heat one of the garlic cloves and one tablespoon of the extra virgin oil together until the garlic starts to blister and turn a light golden brown color. Remove the garlic and add to the Sweet 100 tomatoes. To the hot oil, add the basil, chopped red tomatoes and one-half teaspoon of salt. Bring the chopped tomato to a boil and simmer hard for 30 seconds. Remove the red tomato to a container and toss with the diced bread. Cover and set aside until needed for serving.

Toss the Sweet 100 tomatoes and blistered garlic clove with 1 tablespoon of extra virgin olive oil and ½ teaspoon of salt. Place in the 180°F oven and slowly dry out for 3 hours. After 1½ hours, very carefully move the tomatoes from the outside to the center to ensure even drying. Remove the tomatoes from the oven and set aside in the same pan they dried in. Peel the shrimp and devein saving the shells.

Recipe continues on page 206

RECOMMENDED PAIRINGS

Sullivan St Bakery — Pane Pugliese

Podere Le Berne Rosso di Montalcino

**THE WAVERLY
INN & GARDEN**

executive chef
John DeLucie

Cauliflower Soup
with seared cauliflower crouton

Yields six to eight servings

Ingredients

1 sweet onion, diced

1 sachet d'epices: thyme, 2 cloves of garlic smashed,
1 teaspoon peppercorns wrapped in cheesecloth and tied

1 tablespoon butter

2 heads organic cauliflower, roughly chopped

4 quarts cold filtered water

Salt and pepper, to taste

Garnish

1 head cauliflower

Butter, as needed

1½ teaspoons caviar

Procedure Sweat the onion and sachet d'epices slowly in butter until soft, and then sweat the cauliflower. Add the water and bring to a boil. Simmer for 25 minutes until the cauliflower is very soft. Purée in batches with a high speed blender. Adjust seasoning with salt and pepper as necessary.

With a very sharp knife, slice the cauliflower down the center keeping the stalks intact. Make another cut that yields a thin slice of the whole flower. Sauté with a little butter until brown.

To Serve Pour the soup into a bowl. Float the cauliflower crouton in the center. Set the caviar on top and serve.

RECOMMENDED PAIRINGS

Sullivan St Bakery — Pane alle Olive

Saxon Brown Semillon "Casa Santinamaria" 2006 (California)

THE FOUR SEASONS
RESTAURANT

executive chef Christian Albin
chef de cuisine Fred Mero
chef de cuisine Peco Zantilaveevan

Short Ribs of Beef
with bone marrow and vegetable toss

Yields one serving

Ingredients

1 cleaned short ribs of beef with bone, (about 1 pound)

2 quarts double beef stock or consommé

1 beef bone marrow

2 golden beets

2 red beets

4 baby carrots

6 morel mushrooms

6 fiddlehead ferns

2 white and green asparagus

1 baby spring leek

12 English peas

1 star anise

1 cinnamon stick

1 fresh bay leaf

2 whole cloves

Salt and pepper, to taste

Garnish

Fresh thyme, as needed

Star anise, as needed

Procedure

Slowly braise the short rib in beef stock for about two hours or until very tender, remove the rib from the stock. Poach the bone with the marrow in stock for eight minutes and remove.

Peel and cut all the vegetables into bite-size pieces. Cook all of the vegetables in the stock starting with the hardest and successively adding softer ones so that everything is finished simultaneously. Begin with the beets, then the carrots, then the mushrooms, ferns, asparagus and leeks, and finally the peas at the very end. Remove all the vegetables from the stock.

Simmer the stock with the spices and season with salt pepper to taste for 30 minutes. Then strain the stock slowly with cheesecloth over a fine strainer.

To Serve

Arrange the short rib with the bone marrow in a square bowl and place the cooked vegetables around the short rib. Pour over the hot double beef broth into the bowl. Garnish with fresh thyme and star anise for final plate presentation.

RECOMMENDED PAIRINGS

Sullivan St Bakery — Stirato

Yannick Amirault Bourgeuil "Les Quartiers" 2006

Woo Lae Oak

executive chef
Harold Soo Hyung Kim

Den Jang Chige / Korean Miso Stew

Yields four servings

Ingredients

3 cups water

4 ounces lean pork, cubed

2 tablespoons Korean red soybean paste (den jang)

¾ tablespoon Korean red chili paste (go chu jang)

½ cup zucchini, cut into half-inch cubes

¼ cup white onion, roughly diced

1 Korean green chili, diced

1 green onion, chopped

1 teaspoon minced garlic

1 teaspoon shrimp powder (se woo caru)

1 teaspoon ground Korean chili pepper (go chu caru)

2 ounces firm tofu, cubed

2 ounces button mushroom, quartered

Procedure

In a Korean style stone bowl, bring the water to a boil, add pork, reduce heat to simmer and cook approximately five to seven minutes until the meat is tender, skimming the excess fat as needed.

Push the soybean paste and red chili pasted through a fine strainer into the simmering pork.

Add remaining ingredients and return to a boil for five minutes, reduce to simmer and cook an additional ten minutes. Serve directly in stone bowl.

RECOMMENDED PAIRINGS

Sullivan St Bakery — Stirato

Karthauserhof Eitelsbacher Karthauserhofberg Riesling Auslese 2006

chef / owner
Alex Volfman

Split Pea Soup

Yields four to six servings

194

SOUP

Ingredients

1 pound split peas

1½ quarts water

1 medium-large potato, diced

1 medium carrot, diced

1 stalk celery, diced

Salt and pepper, to taste

Procedure   Boil the peas in the 1½ quarts of water for 45 minutes. Meanwhile, in another pot, boil the vegetables for 15 minutes, or until tender. Remove the vegetables, reserving the liquid. Add the vegetables to the peas when the latter is finished cooking. Add some of the reserved water the vegetables cooked in until the desired consistency is achieved. Season to taste with salt and pepper.

RECOMMENDED PAIRINGS

Sullivan St Bakery — Rye Bread*

Pelaquie Tavel Rosé 2007 (France)

Vichyssoise

Yields four quarts

Ingredients

1½ pounds leeks (after trimming), white part only

1½ pounds leek (after trimming), tender green part

1 medium size onion, diced, divided

8 ounces butter, divided

Salt, to taste

2 pounds potato, small dice, divided

8 cups chicken stock, divided

24 ounces heavy cream, divided

1 cup chives, snipped

Procedure In four ounces of butter, sweat the white parts of the leeks and half of the onion, being careful not to brown. Season with a good pinch of salt. Add half of the potatoes and four cups of the hot chicken stock. Simmer until the leeks and potatoes are very tender, about 25 minutes. Process the soup in a blender. Strain through a sieve. Chill in an ice bath.

Repeat the procedure with the green parts of the leeks.

To Serve When ready to serve, incorporate half of the cream in each soup. Adjust seasoning. Pour half of each soup in chilled bowls and garnish with snipped chives.

RECOMMENDED PAIRINGS

Sullivan St Bakery — Rye Bread*

Albert Mann Pinot Gris "Cuvee Albert" 2006

Callaloo

Yields four servings

Ingredients

2 tablespoons peanut oil

1 medium Spanish onion, chopped

2 garlic cloves, minced

2 bird's-eye chilies, seeds and ribs removed, finely chopped

1½ teaspoons ground cumin

1½ teaspoons coriander seeds

2 cups chicken stock

1 cup coconut milk

1 cup bottled clam juice

1 cup heavy cream

2 ten-ounce packages frozen chopped spinach

Juice of three limes

Garnish

16 pieces baby bok choy or water spinach

Vegetable oil, as needed

1 dozen manila clams

½ cup water

Procedure

Heat the peanut oil in a large sauté pan over high heat. When it shimmers, add the onion, garlic, and chilies and sauté until the onion is translucent, about five minutes. Add the cumin, coriander, chicken stock, coconut milk, clam juice, and heavy cream, and bring to a simmer. Reduce heat and simmer gently for 30 minutes. Add spinach and bring to a boil. Reduce the heat and simmer, stirring occasionally, five minutes or until the spinach is cooked. Transfer the soup to a blender, in batches if necessary, and purée.

Transfer soup to a bowl and stir in the lime juice. Serve hot.

Garnish

Steam bok choy and/or water spinach with salted water, until tender. Remove from steamer and drain on paper towel. Heat sauté pan with a small amount of oil until it shimmers, add clams. Sauté the clams on high heat, for about a minute. Remove from heat and add half a cup of water. Return pan to the heat, steam clams until they open.

To Serve

Garnish each bowl with three clams and four pieces of bok choy.

RECOMMENDED PAIRINGS

Sullivan St Bakery — Ciabatta

Schoffit Riesling Harth "Cuvee Tradition" 2005 (Alsace, France)

chef / owner
Charlie Trotter

Globe Artichoke Soup
with pine nuts, white anchovy and pineapple mint

Yields two servings

Artichoke Soup

2 shallots minced

6 tablespoons olive oil

1 tablespoon coriander, ground

1 tablespoon cumin, ground

½ tablespoon chili flakes, ground

1 tablespoon grains of paradise, ground

8 large globe artichokes hearts

8 cups vegetable stock

Salt, to taste

Lemon juice, to taste

Garnish

¼ cup toasted pine nuts

6 white anchovies

A few sprigs of pineapple mint

Procedure Sweat the minced shallots in the olive oil, being careful not to brown. Add the spices and the artichoke hearts. Stir in the vegetable stock. Cook for about 25 minutes until the artichokes are soft. Next, pour contents into a vita prep and blend to desired thickness. Pass through a chinois and season with salt and lemon juice.

To Serve Pour the soup into a warm bowl and top with toasted pine nuts, white anchovies and pineapple mint.

RECOMMENDED PAIRINGS

Sullivan St Bakery — Integrale

Rebholz Weissburgunder "Im Sonnenschein" 2004 (Germany)

wd~50

chef / owner
Wylie Dufresne

Popcorn Soup with Popcorn Shrimp Rolls, Jicama and Tamarind

Yields four servings

Tamarind Water

1 ¾ ounces tamarind paste

3 ½ ounces water

Jicama

1 jicama

Popcorn Soup

35 ounces water

1 bag of popcorn, popped

2 ⅓ ounces freeze dried corn

1.8 ounces butter, melted

Salt, to taste

Popcorn Shrimp

250 shrimp shelled, cleaned, deveined, roughly chopped

¾ gram (tiny pinch) transglutaminase (RM)

2 grams (tiny pinch) lemon confit, diced

2 grams (tiny pinch) parsley, chopped

Salt, to taste

Cayenne pepper powder, to taste

Popcorn Powder

1 bag popcorn

Shiso Oil

Shiso leaves, cleaned, as needed

3 ½ ounces grapeseed oil

Garnish

Micro shiso greens, as needed

Tamarind Water Bring tamarind paste and water up to a boil and let simmer for 45 minutes. Remove from heat and strain through a coffee filter.

Jicama Cut jicama into rounds using a cutter or a ring. Cook in tamarind water for 30 to 45 minutes.

Popcorn Soup Combine the water, popcorn and freeze dried corn and blend well, slowly adding the melted butter. Strain twice through a fine mesh strainer. Add salt to taste.

Popcorn Shrimp Put ingredients in a bowl and mix together so that the transglutaminase is evenly dispersed. Using plastic wrap, roll the shrimp into rolls. Cook the rolls at 125°F for 25 minutes. Cool in an ice bath.

Popcorn Powder Pop popcorn and blend in a blender. Pass the powder through a tamis or very fine sieve to remove the large pieces.

Shiso Oil Blanch shiso in water for 30 seconds. Blend in a blender with grapeseed oil. Filter through a coffee filter.

To Serve Dot jicama on bottom of bowl. Pour in soup. Place shrimp rolls in middle of dish. Dust with popcorn powder. Garnish with shiso oil and micro shiso greens.

RECOMMENDED PAIRINGS

Sullivan St Bakery — Corn Bread*

Eric/Kent Chardonnay "Sonoma Coast" 2006

Recipe continued from page 4

Swiss Ale Cheese Soup / Gilt

Pretzel Dissolve 5 ounces of the water, yeast and glucose. Place flours and salt on a wooden work surface or cutting board and create a well in the center. Pour in the liquid and create a slurry by stirring in the flour a little at a time. Continue until the mix is workable, then scrape down your board, sprinkle lightly with flour, and kneed until smooth. Let rest for 30 minutes, covered, at room temperature.

Roll dough ½-inch thick, then proceed to cut into 1 by ½-inch rectangles. Then roll each rectangle into a 3-inch rope and tie into a pretzel knot. Place knot on a tray lined with parchment or Silpat and let proof for 20 minutes. Mix remaining 8 ounces of water with the baking soda. Carefully place each knot into baking soda/water solution for 5 minutes then return to tray. Sprinkle with pretzel salt and bake at 375°F until golden.

Recipe continued from page 12

Beef Consommé / Allen & Delancey

Garnish Cut all the vegetables into desired shapes. Poach until tender in the beef consommé. Reserve. Poach the bone marrow in the beef consommé until just cooked, then pack into a small teflon mold and freeze until needed.

To Serve (per person) Warm the vegetables in six ounces of the beef consommé. In a non-stick pan, heat the olive oil, flour the bone marrow lightly and then sear at a high heat until golden brown. Drain and reserve. Heat the cabbage ball in a pan of boiling water for four to five minutes. Neatly arrange the vegetables, cabbage ball, and bone marrow in a bowl, pour in the consommé and finish with herbs and sea salt.

Recipe continued from page 56

Clam Chowder and Croissants / Dovetail

Black Pepper Croissants Sprinkle the three tablespoons flour over the butter and blend together on the work surface. On a length of foil, fashion a six-inch square of the butter; fold over the foil to enclose. Place in the refrigerator to chill for two to three hours.

While the butter is chilling, prepare the dough. Blend two cups of flour with salt and sugar. Dissolve the yeast in the ¼-cup warm water. Add the yeast, warmed milk and half-and-half to the flour mixture. Stir with a wooden spoon to thoroughly blend, approximately two minutes. Stir in remaining flour, ¼ cup at a time, to make a soft but not sticky dough (it will stiffen when chilled.) Knead by hand for five minutes to form a solid mass. Place the dough in a bowl, cover with plastic wrap and chill for one hour.

Determine that both the butter and dough are about the same temperature, 65°F is ideal. The block of butter should bend but not break. This may mean taking the butter out of the refrigerator an hour or so early to reach a workable temperature. Likewise for the dough. Place dough on a floured work surface and press it into a 10-inch square. Unwrap the block of butter and lay diagonally on the dough. Bring each point of dough into the center, overlapping the edges by at least 1-inch. Press the dough into a neat package. With a heavy rolling pin, roll the dough into a rectangle, approximately 8 by 18-inch. Fold the length of dough into thirds, like a letter. Turn so that the open ends are at twelve and six o'clock. Roll again into a rectangle. This time, fold both ends into the middle and then close, like a book. The dough will now be in four layers. Wrap the package of dough in a cloth that has been soaked in cold water and wrung dry. Place the wrapped dough in the refrigerator to relax and chill for one or two hours.

Remove the dough from the refrigerator and place on the floured work surface. Unwrap, roll out, and fold in thirds, like a letter. This is the final turn before it is rolled out and cut into croissants. Dampen cloth again and wrap loosely around the dough. Place the package in a plastic bag so moisture will be retained. Leave in the refrigerator four to six hours or overnight.

Sprinkle work surface with flour. Roll the dough until it is a 10 by 38-inch rectangle, ¼-inch thick. This is a crucial dimension, since it determines the size and texture of the croissants. Trim irregularities to make the strip uniform in width. Cut the strip lengthwise to make two 5-inch pieces. Mark strip into triangles, 5-inch wide on the bottom. Using a yardstick as a guide, cut through the dough with a pizza cutter or knife. Separate the triangles, place them on a baking sheet, and chill for 15 to 20 minutes. Roll the dough into the traditional croissant shape, by rolling the triangle from the bottom to the point. At this point that the croissants are formed but not risen, you can freeze them individually.

To make the egg wash, mix together the egg and water.

Place the croissants on a baking sheet and allow to rise for one to two hours, in which they will double in volume. Lightly brush the dough and sprinkle with black pepper. It should be a generous seasoning of black pepper.

Preheat oven to 425°F. Bake croissants for 22 to 25 minutes. Allow to cool on a rack before serving.

To Serve Heat the soup and ladle it into the bowls. Garnish with smoked potatoes and chorizo. Serve two croissants per person on the side. Yields 24 to 30 croissants.

recipe continued from page 70

Chilled Spring Pea Soup / Daniel

The Cream Bring the cream, rosemary and garlic to a boil in a small pot. Reduce heat and simmer for five minutes, just until the cream thickens a little. Strain the cream, discarding the rosemary and garlic, season with salt and pepper and chill.

While the cream is cooling, brown and lightly crisp the bacon in a pan over medium heat, then drain well between several layers of paper towels. When the bacon is cool, chop into small bits.

To Serve Ladle the soup into cold bowls and drizzle a bit of rosemary cream over each portion, top with a sprinkling of bacon.

recipe continued from page 90

Black Tea and Mint Broth / The Institute of Culinary Education

Caramelized Tomato and Feta Flan Butter the inside of four two-ounce ramekins and dust with flour. In a small frying pan, heat the one teaspoon of butter. Add the minced garlic and shallots. Cook until translucent. Add the tomato paste and turn the heat up to medium. Caramelize the tomato paste for about one minute. Remove and cool. In a blender, add the eggs, cream, tomato paste and feta cheese. Blend for about 15 seconds. Season with nutmeg and salt and pepper. Blend 10 more seconds.

Pre-heat oven to 275°F. Heat two cups hot water for a water bath. After the bubbles settle, pour the custard into the prepared ramekins. Place in a small, shallow baking dish. Add the hot water to cover ⅔ of the ramekins and place a small piece of buttered parchment paper on top to protect the custard. Cook approximately 20 to 25 minutes until custard sets. Remove from the water bath. Keep warm to serve.

Petite White Asparagus Trim and blanch the asparagus and then refresh in the braising liquid from the lamb shanks.

Honshemeji Mushrooms Blanch the mushrooms in the braising tea broth.

Fried Phyllo In a small saucepot, heat the grapeseed oil to 265°F. Sprinkle in the phyllo chiffonade and cook ten seconds until lightly brown. Remove and place onto a dry towel to drain and sprinkle with sea salt. Keep dry until ready to serve.

To Serve Place lamb shanks with the remaining braising liquid in a small pan covered with foil into a pre-heated 350°F oven. Bring the clear 3 cups of black tea broth to a boil and adjust the seasoning. Add the lamb beggars' purses and simmer for 20 seconds. In a heated soup bowl, place the hot lamb shank, bone side up in the back of the bowl. Place the warm tomato and feta flan in front of the lamb shank. Place the cooked beggar's purse to the right of the flan and place the blanched honshemeji mushrooms to the left of the lamb shank and the blanched asparagus in between the mushrooms and the lamb shank. Slowly pour the black tea broth in the bowl, to almost cover the lamb shank. Place a small bundle of fried phyllo dough on top of the flan. Garnish with the nasturtium buds and mint sprigs.

recipe continued from page 94

Pot Pie of Florida Frog's Legs Velouté / Daniel

Glazed Mushroom And Onion Melt the butter in a medium sauté pan over medium to low heat. Add the pearl onions, three tablespoons of water, a pinch of salt and pepper and cook until tender, stirring, for about eight minutes. Add the button mushrooms and continue to cook for another four minutes. Add the bordelaise sauce or demi-glace and cook, stirring, to glaze the onions and mushrooms. Check for additional seasoning and keep warm.

Fried Frog's Legs Lollipops With the reserved frog's legs, separate the legs and thighs at the joint. Using a small knife, scrape the meat of the frog's legs and thighs down towards the knuckles to form a lollipop shape. Combine the flour, espellette pepper, salt and pepper. Coat the meat of the frog's legs in the flour mixture, then the eggs, and then the bread crumbs. Pour the vegetable oil into a small pot (it should reach about ⅓ of the way up the side) and heat to 350° F. When you are ready to serve the soup, fry the frog's legs in batches, remove with a slotted spoon and sprinkle lightly with salt.

Parsley Cream Bring a large pot of salted water to a boil and place a bowl of ice water on the side. Boil the parsley leaves for approximately 20 seconds, strain, chill in the ice water and pat dry. In a small saucepan over high heat, bring the cream to a simmer. Transfer to a blender with the cooked parsley. Purée on high speed until well combined and bright green. Strain through a fine meshed sieve, season with salt and pepper to taste, chill rapidly.

To Serve Pre-heat oven to 430°F and place a rack in the center. Place the soup bowls on a sheet tray and place in the oven, making sure there is about four inches of space above the top of the bowls for the puff pastry to rise. Bake for 12 minutes; the puff pastry will rise and turn a golden brown color. Serve with a spoonful of the glazed mushrooms and onions, three fried frog leg lollipops, and two strips of crisped bacon per portion. When presenting the soup, poke through the center of the pastry crust with a long spoon and drizzle in a bit of the parsley cream.

Recipe continued from page 186

Papa al Pomodoro con Spiedini di Gamberini / Union Square Café

Over medium flame, heat two tablespoon of the extra virgin oil in a medium saucepot until the oil is wavy but not smoking. Add the shallot and one garlic clove, sauté for 30 to 45 seconds or until the shallots and garlic just start to brown. Add the shrimp shells and sauté for another minute stirring constantly. Add the pinch of chile flakes and white wine. Reduce until almost dry. Immediately add the yellow tomatoes, tomato juice, water and one teaspoon of the salt. Simmer gently for 30 minutes. Strain the tomatoes by running them through a fine sieve or food mill. Adjust the seasoning, if needed, cover and set aside at room temperature until needed for serving.

One hour before serving, chop one of the garlic cloves and toss with the shrimp, lemon zest, lemon juice and one tablespoon of olive oil. Strip the leaves off of the bottom three inches of the rosemary sprigs. Rinse the rosemary in cold water and gently scrape the bottom portion of the sprig with a pairing knife to clean off a little of the resin. However, do not scrape all the way down to the yellow center of the sprig. Create a sharp edge at the bottom, by cutting off ⅛ of an inch of the sprig with a sharp knife at an angle. Arrange two of the shrimp in a Yin and Yang fashion on a cutting board. Slide the skewer through the center of the shrimps securing them to the skewer. Repeat with two more shrimps on the same rosemary skewer and then repeat the process with the three remaining skewers and set aside.

Check the tomato and bread mixture for seasoning. Gently fold in the oven-dried Sweet 100 tomatoes. Ladle three ounces of the yellow tomato soup in each bowl. Gently mound one cup of the red tomato and bread soup on the yellow tomato soup. Line the grill grates (off center of the hot coals) with a strip of aluminum foil (approximately 4 by 10 inches) to protect the rosemary leaves on the end of the shrimp skewers. Season the shrimp with the remaining pinch of salt and four twists of a pepper mill. Place the shrimp on the grill with the top end with rosemary over the foil. Grill the shrimp skewers over hot coals for one minute on the first side. Turn them over and grill for another 30 seconds. Remove and place a skewer on top of each mound of the Papa al Pomodoro. Drizzle the bowls of soup with the rest of the extra virgin olive. Garnish with the celery heart leaves and serve.

Five additional tabletop books from Battman Studios

Contents

Readers' Choice Homes 2

Two-Story Traditional Homes 17

Two-Story Contemporary Homes...97

Signature Series and History House Estates 113

Victorians and Farmhouses..129

Sun Country Homes...161

1½-Story Homes 193

One-Story Homes Under 2,000 Square Feet 209

One-Story Homes Over 2,000 Square Feet 257

Multi-Level and Hillside Homes 305

Vacation and Second Homes 321

Ordering Information..334

The Deck Blueprint Package 338

The Landscape Blueprint Package...340

The Blueprint Order Form 349

Home Construction and Improvement Books 350

Note: Many of the homes featured in this book have a matching or corresponding Landscape or Deck Plan available from Home Planners. Some have both. These plans have an **L** or a **D** following their design number and square-footage notations. For information on how to order plans for landscapes and decks, see pages 338-347.

Copyright © 1994 Home Planners, A Division of Hanley-Wood, Inc.

Published by Creative Homeowner Press®
A Division of Federal Marketing Corp.
24 Park Way
Upper Saddle River, NJ 07458

Current Printing (last digit)
10   9   8   7   6   5   4

Printed in the United States of America.

Library of Congress Number: 93-74013

ISBN: 1-880029-35-9

On The Cover: A lovely Cape Cod for family living (Design N2520). Plan is shown in reverse of original floor plan. Another version is shown on page 4. Photo by Steve Becker, Creative Images.

Design N2774

First Floor: 1,366 square feet
Second Floor: 969 square feet
Total: 2,335 square feet

L **D**

CUSTOMIZABLE

Custom Alterations? See page 349 for customizing this plan to your specifications.

● This design has something for the whole family. There is the quiet corner living room, an efficient U-shaped kitchen with pass-through to the beamed-ceiling breakfast room, sliding glass doors to the rear terrace, and a service entrance with laundry and pantry. The basement can be finished at a later time for expanded space. Upstairs are four bedrooms including a master suite with private bath.

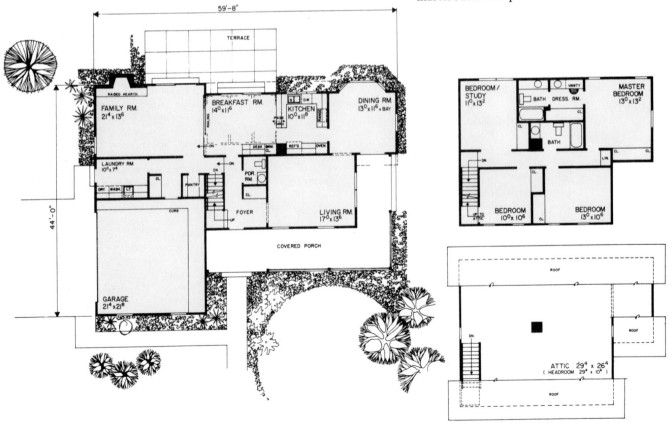

Design N2683 First Floor: 2,126 square feet; Second Floor: 1,882 square feet; Total: 4,008 square feet

L **D**

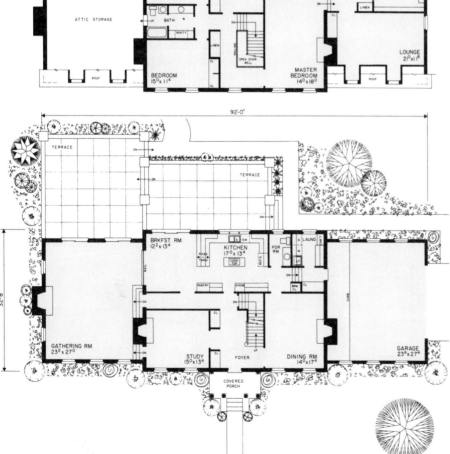

● This historical Georgian home has its roots in the 18th-Century. Dignified symmetry is a hallmark of both front and rear elevations. The full two-story center section is delightfully complimented by the 1½-story wings. Interior livability has been planned to serve today's active family. The elegant gathering room, three steps down from the rest of the house, has ample space for entertaining on a grand scale. It fills an entire wing and is dead-ended so that traffic does not pass through it. Guests and family alike will enjoy the two rooms flanking the foyer, the study and formal dining room. Each of these rooms will have a fireplace as its highlight. The breakfast room, kitchen, powder room and laundry are arranged for maximum efficiency. This area will always have that desired light and airy atmosphere with the sliding glass door and the triple window over the kitchen sink. The second floor houses the family bedrooms. Take special note of the spacious master bedroom suite. It has a deluxe bath, fireplace and sunken lounge with dressing room and walk-in closet. Surely an area to be appreciated.

Design N2520 First Floor: 1,419 square feet
Second Floor: 1,040 square feet; Total: 2,459 square feet

● From Tidewater Virginia comes this historic adaptation, a positive reminder of the charm of Early American architecture. Note how the center entrance opens to a fine floor plan.

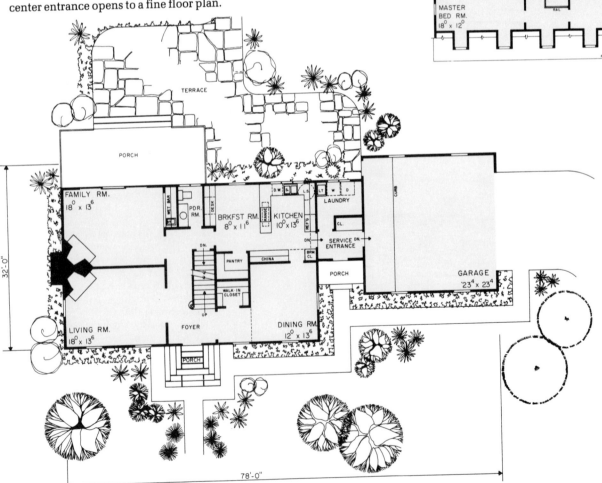

CUSTOMIZABLE

Custom Alterations? See page 349 for customizing this plan to your specifications.

Design N2563

First Floor: 1,500 square feet
Second Floor: 690 square feet
Total: 2,190 square feet

L **D**

● You'll have all kinds of fun deciding just how your family will function in this dramatically expanded half-house. There is lots of attic storage, too. Observe three car garage.

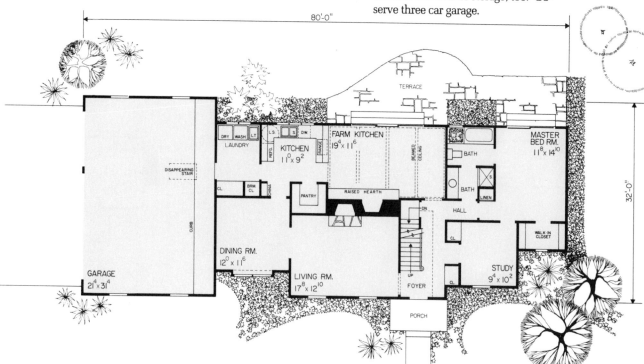

Photo by Laszlo Regos

Design N2921

First Floor: 3,215 square feet
Second Floor: 711 square feet
Total: 3,926 square feet

L **D**

CUSTOMIZABLE

Custom Alterations? See page 349
for customizing this plan to your
specifications.

● This popular traditionally styled house
features bay windows, shutters, a fanlight and
a cupola on the roof. Interior planning was
designed for empty-nesters whose children are
grown and moved out on their own. Open planning is geared for entertaining and relaxing
rather than child-rearing.

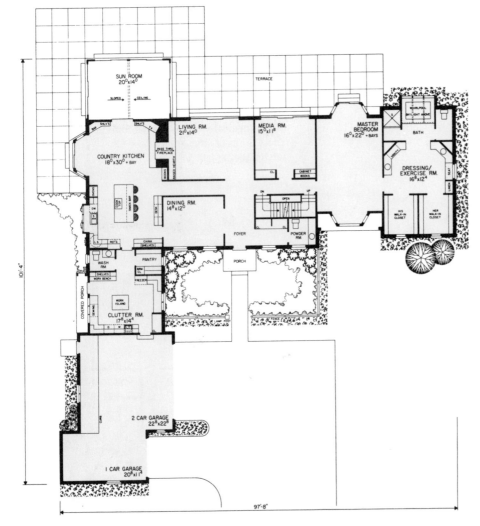

6

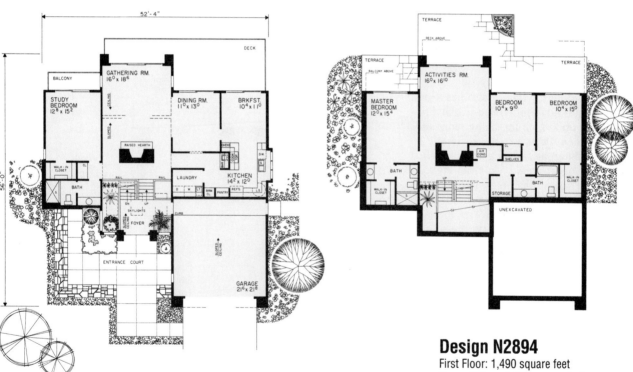

Design N2894

First Floor: 1,490 square feet
Second Floor: 1,357 square feet
Total: 2,847 square feet

L

● The foyer of this contemporary bi-level leads to upper and lower levels. In the large gathering room is a fireplace and sloped ceiling. To the left is the study/bedroom with full bath and walk-in closet. The lower level has two bedrooms and a bath to one side; a master bedroom suite to the other. In between is the activities room with raised-hearth fireplace.

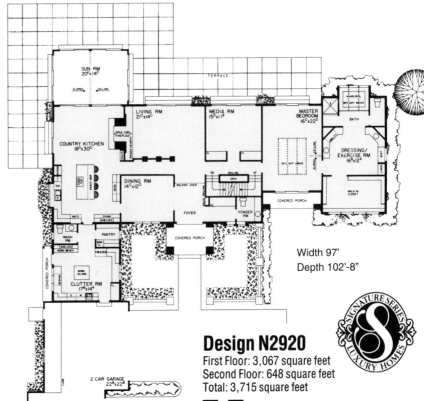

This contemporary design also has a great deal to offer. Study the living areas. A fireplace opens up to both the living room and country kitchen. Privacy is the key word when describing the sleeping areas. the first floor master bedroom is away from the traffic of the house and features a dressing/exercise room, whirlpool tub and shower and a spacious walk-in closet. Two more bedrooms and a full bath are on the second floor. The three car garage is arranged so that the owners have use of a double-garage with an attached single on reserve for guests. The cheerful sun room adds 296 sq. ft. to the total.

Width 97'
Depth 102'-8"

Design N2920

First Floor: 3,067 square feet
Second Floor: 648 square feet
Total: 3,715 square feet

L **D**

CUSTOMIZABLE

Custom Alterations? See page 349 for customizing this plan to your specifications.

● Something new? Something new, indeed!! Here is the introduction of two rooms which will make a wonderful contribution to family living. The clutter room is strategically placed between the kitchen and garage. It is the nerve center of the work area. It houses the laundry, provides space for sewing, has a large sorting table, and even plenty of space for the family's tool bench. A handy potting area is next to the laundry tray. Adjacent to

the clutter room, and a significant part of the planning of this whole zone, are the pantry and freezer with their nearby counter space. These facilities surely will expedite the unloading of groceries from the car and their convenient storing. Wardrobe and broom closets, plus washroom complete the outstanding utility of this area. The location of the clutter room with all its fine cabinet and counter space means that the often numerous family projects

can be on-going. This room is ideally isolated from the family's daily living patterns. The media room may be thought of as the family's entertainment center. While this is the room for the large or small TV, the home movies, the stereo and VCR equipment, it will serve as the library or study. It would be ideal as the family's home office with its computer equipment. Your family will decide just how it will utilize this outstanding area.

Design N2915
Square Footage: 2,758

L **D**

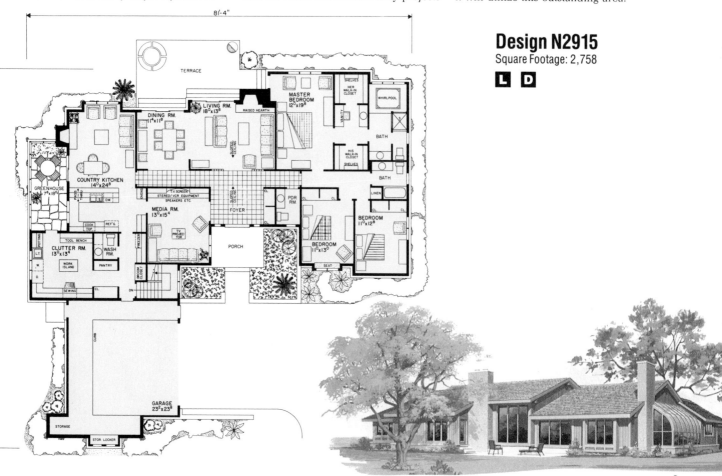

Design N3355
Square Footage: 1,387

L **D**

● Though it's only just under 1,400 total
square feet, this plan offers three bedrooms (or
two with study) and a sizable gathering room
with fireplace and sloped ceiling. The galley
kitchen provides a pass-through snack bar and
has a planning desk and attached breakfast
room. Besides two smaller bedrooms with a full
bath, there's an extravagant master suite with
large dressing area, double vanity and raised
whirlpool tub.

CUSTOMIZABLE

Custom Alterations? See page 349
for customizing this plan to your
specifications.

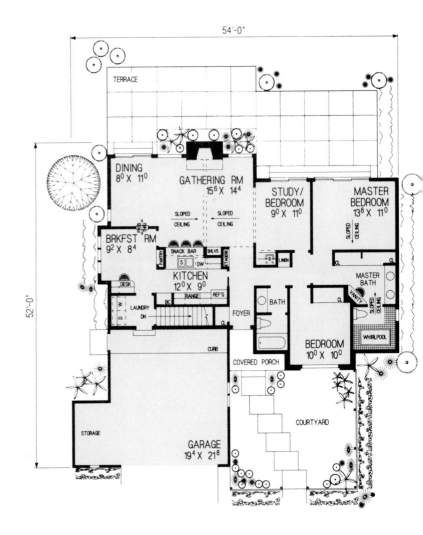

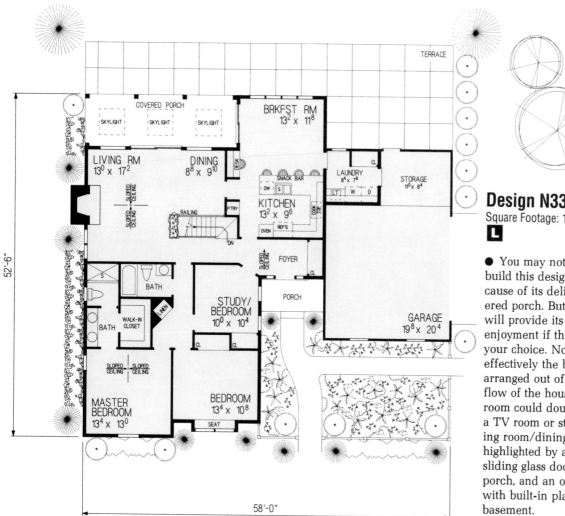

TERRACE

COVERED PORCH

SKYLIGHT | SKYLIGHT | SKYLIGHT

BRKFST RM
13² x 11⁸

LIVING RM
13⁰ x 17²

DINING
8⁸ x 9¹⁰

DESK

SNACK BAR

DW | S

RAILING

KITCHEN
13² x 9⁶

COOK TOP

OVEN | REF'G

DN

P'TRY

LAUNDRY
8⁴ x 7⁸

LT | W | D

CL

STORAGE
11⁰ x 8⁴

SLOPED CEILING

FOYER

CL

SLOPED CEILING

PORCH

CL

52'-6"

BATH

S

BATH

WALK-IN CLOSET

LINEN

STUDY/ BEDROOM
10⁰ x 10⁴

CL | CL

GARAGE
19⁸ x 20⁴

SLOPED CEILING | SLOPED CEILING

MASTER BEDROOM
13⁴ x 13⁰

BEDROOM
13⁴ x 10⁸

SEAT

58'-0"

Design N3340
Square Footage: 1,611

L

● You may not decide to build this design simply because of its delightful covered porch. But it certainly will provide its share of enjoyment if this plan is your choice. Notice also how effectively the bedrooms are arranged out of the traffic flow of the house. One bedroom could double nicely as a TV room or study. The living room/dining area is highlighted by a fireplace, sliding glass doors to the porch, and an open staircase with built-in planter to the basement.

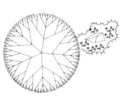

Design N3314

Square Footage: 1,951

L

● Formal living areas in this plan are joined by a three-bedroom sleeping wing. One bedroom, with foyer access, could function as a study. Two verandas and a screened porch enlarge the plan and enhance indoor/outdoor livability. Notice the abundant storage space.

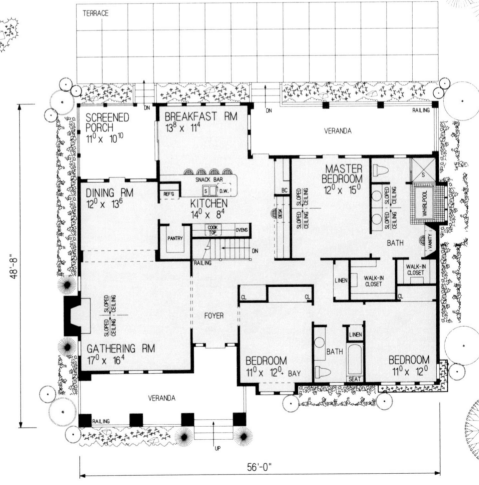

TERRACE

SCREENED PORCH
11⁰ x 10¹⁰

BREAKFAST RM
13⁸ x 11⁴

VERANDA

RAILING

DN

DN

DINING RM
12⁰ x 13⁶

SNACK BAR

REF'G

S

D.W.

KITCHEN
14⁰ x 8⁴

MASTER BEDROOM
12⁰ x 15⁰

SLOPED CEILING

SLOPED CEILING

BC

DESK

S

WHIRLPOOL

PANTRY

COOK TOP

OVENS

DN

BATH

VANITY

RAILING

WALK-IN CLOSET

LINEN

WALK-IN CLOSET

SLOPED CEILING

SLOPED CEILING

CL

CL

CL

GATHERING RM
17⁰ x 16⁴

FOYER

BEDROOM
11⁰ x 12⁰ + BAY

BATH

LINEN

SEAT

BEDROOM
11⁰ x 12⁰

VERANDA

RAILING

UP

48'-8"

56'-0"

Design N3315

First Floor: 2,918 square feet
Second Floor: 330 square feet
Total: 3,248 square feet

Besides the covered front veranda, look for another full-width veranda to the rear of this charming home. The master bedroom, breakfast room, and gathering room all have French doors to this outdoor space. A handy wet bar/tavern enhances entertainment options. The upper lounge could be a welcome haven.

Design N2947
Square Footage: 1,830

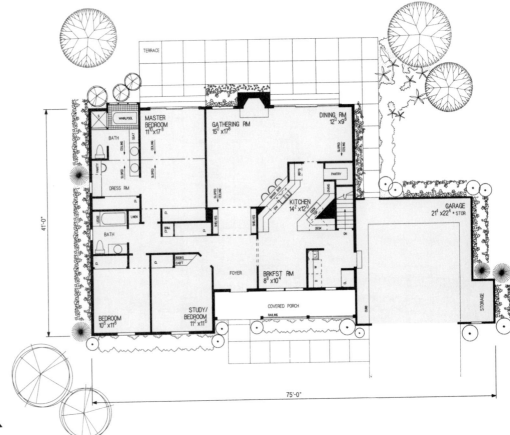

● This charming one-
story Traditional home
greets visitors with a
covered porch. A galley-
style kitchen shares a
snack bar with the spa-
cious gathering room
where a fireplace is the
focal point. An ample
master suite includes a
luxury bath with whirl-
pool tub and separate
dressing room. Two addi-
tional bedrooms, one that
could double as a study,
are located at the front of
the home.

CUSTOMIZABLE
Custom Alterations? See page 349
for customizing this plan to your
specifications.

CUSTOMIZABLE

Custom Alterations? See page 349 for customizing this plan to your specifications.

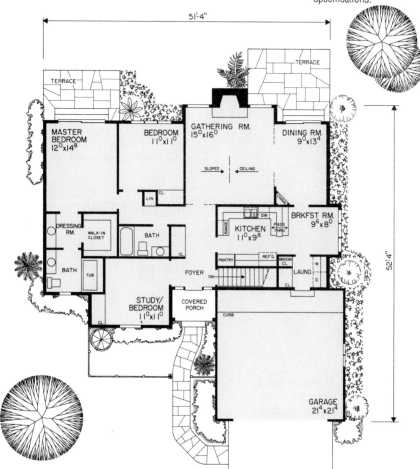

Design N2878

Square Footage: 1,521

L **D**

● There is a great deal of livability in this one-story design. The efficient floor plan makes optimum use of limited floor space. Ideally located, the gathering room is warmed by a fireplace. Its sloped-ceiling gives it a spacious appeal. Adjacent is the dining room which opens up to the rear terrace via sliding glass doors for dining alfresco. Ready to serve the breakfast room and dining room, there is the interior kitchen. The laundry, basement stairs and garage door are nearby. Two with an optional third bedroom are tucked away from the more active areas of the house. The master bedroom has sliding glass doors to the terrace for outdoor enjoyment. Study this cozy, clapboard cottage and imagine it as your next home.

CUSTOMIZABLE

Custom Alterations? See page 349 for customizing this plan to your specifications.

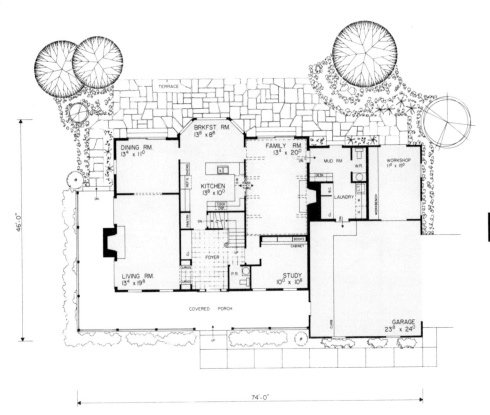

Design N2946

First Floor: 1,581 square feet
Second Floor: 1,344 square feet
Total: 2,925 square feet

L D

● Here's a traditional design that's made for down-home hospitality, the pleasures of casual conversation, and the good grace of pleasant company. The star attractions are the large covered porch and terrace, perfectly relaxing gathering points for family and

friends. Inside, though, the design is truly a hard worker; separate living room and family room, each with its own fireplace; formal dining room; large kitchen and breakfast area with bay windows; separate study; workshop with plenty of room to ma-

neuver; mud room; and four bedrooms up, including a master suite. Not to be overlooked are the curio niches, the powder room, the built-in bookshelves, the kitchen pass-through, the pantry, the planning desk, the workbench, and the stairs to the basement.

Design N2889

First Floor: 2,349 square feet
Second Floor: 1,918 square feet
Total: 4,267 square feet

L **D**

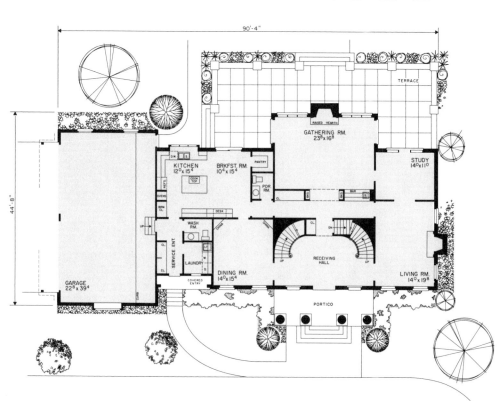

● This is truly classical Georgian design at its best. Some of the exterior highlights of this two-story include the pediment gable with cornice work and dentils, the beautifully proportioned columns, the front door detailing and the window treatment. These are just some of the features which make this design so unique and appealing. Behind the facade of this design is an equally elegant interior. Imagine greeting your guests in the large receiving hall. It is graced by two curving staircases and opens to the formal living and dining rooms. Beyond the living room is the study. It has access to the rear terrace. Those large, informal occasions for family get-togethers or entertaining will be enjoyed in the spacious gathering room. It has a centered fireplace flanked by windows on each side, access to the terrace and a wet bar. The work center is efficient: the kitchen with island cook top, breakfast room, washroom, laundry and service entrance. The second floor also is outstanding. Three family bedrooms and two full baths are joined by the feature filled master suite. If you like this basic floor plan but prefer a French exterior, see Design N2543.

Design N2984

First Floor: 3,116 square feet
Second Floor: 1,997 square feet
Total: 5,113 square feet

L

● An echo of Whitehall, built in
1765 in Anne Arundel County,
Maryland, resounds in this home.
Its classic symmetry and columned
facade herald a grand interior.
There's no lack of space whether
entertaining formally or just enjoying a family get-together, and all
are kept cozy with fireplaces in
the gathering room, study, and
family room. An island kitchen
with attached breakfast room
handily serves the nearby dining
room. Four second floor bedrooms
include a large master suite with
another fireplace, a whirlpool, and
His and Hers closets in the bath.
Three more full baths are found
on this floor.

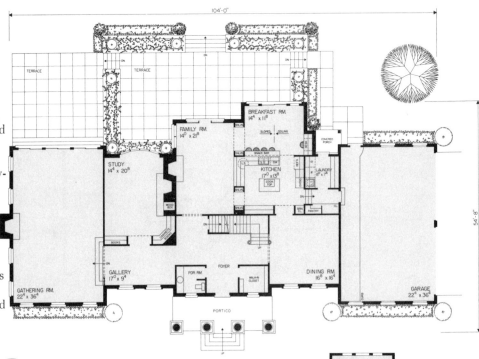

18

Design N3303

First Floor: 2,563 square feet; Second Floor: 1,496 square feet
Total: 4,059 square feet

L

● With its stately columns and one-story wings, this design is a fine representation of 18th Century adaptations. Formal living and dining areas flank the entry foyer at the front of the home. Look for a fireplace in the living room, china cabinet built-ins in the dining room. More casual living dominates the back section in a family room and kitchen/breakfast room combination that features access to the rear terrace and plenty of space for cooking and informal dining. The left wing garage is connected to the main structure by a service entrance adjacent to the laundry. The right wing contains the private master suite. Four second floor bedrooms share two full baths and each has its own walk-in closet.

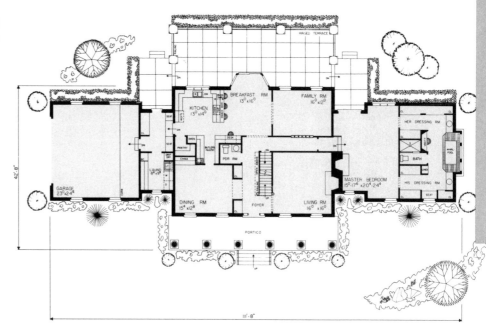

Design N2899 First Floor: 1,685 square feet
Second Floor: 1,437 square feet; Total: 3,122 square feet

L

● This impressive Georgian home with massive twin chimneys and slender Roman doric columns is authentic in its 18th-Century detailing. Inside, the home offers comfort and elegance with living room, study, large formal dining room, breakfast room and even a butler's pantry. Upstairs is thoughtfully zoned, too, with three family bedrooms and a master suite.

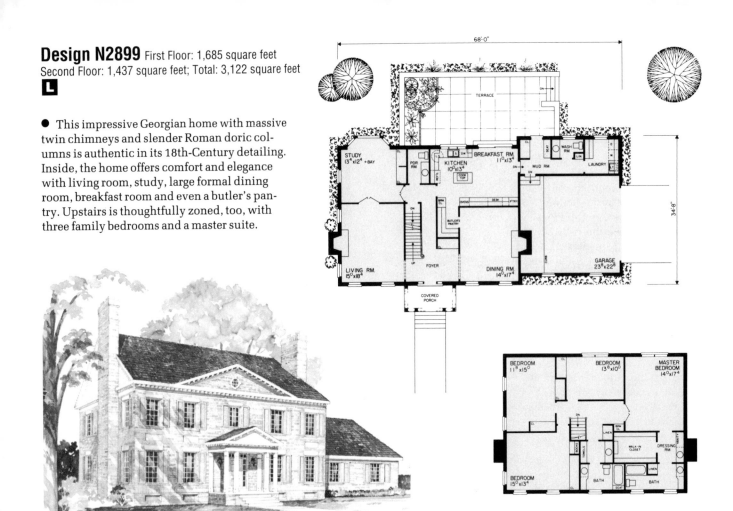

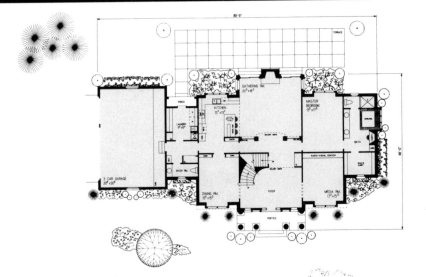

Design N3320 First Floor: 2,337 square feet
Second Floor: 1,232 square feet; Total: 3,569 square feet

L

● What a grand impression this home makes! A spacious two-story foyer with circular staircase greets visitors and leads to the dining room, media room and two-story gathering room with fireplace. The well-equipped kitchen includes a snack bar for informal meals. A luxurious master suite downstairs and four bedrooms upstairs complete this impressive plan.

ATTIC 29² x 26⁴
(HEADROOM 29² x 10⁴)

BEDROOM 11⁰ x 10⁸

MASTER BEDROOM 13⁴ x 13⁴

BATH   DRESS RM

VANITY

BATH

BEDROOM 10⁸ x 9²

BEDROOM 12⁰ x 10⁶

LINEN

DN

CL

CL

CL

UPPER PORTICO

Design N3339

First Floor: 1,460 square feet
Second Floor: 1,014 square feet
Total: 2,474 square feet

L

● This Colonial four-bedroom features the livable kind of plan you're looking for. A formal living room extends from the front foyer and leads to the formal dining area and nearby kitchen. A sunken family room has a raised-hearth fireplace. Three family bedrooms share a bath and are joined by the master bedroom with its own full bath.

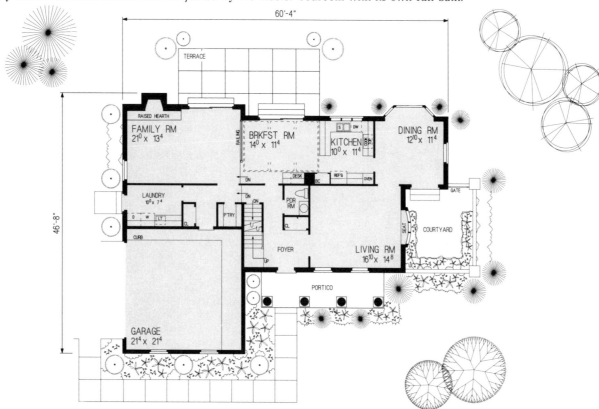

60'-4"

46'-8"

TERRACE

RAISED HEARTH

FAMILY RM 21⁰ x 13⁴

BRKFST RM 14⁰ x 11⁴

KITCHEN 10⁰ x 11⁴

DINING RM 12¹⁰ x 11⁴

LAUNDRY 10⁰ x 7⁴

PDR RM

FOYER

LIVING RM 16¹⁰ x 14⁸

GARAGE 21⁴ x 21⁴

PORTICO

COURTYARD

GATE

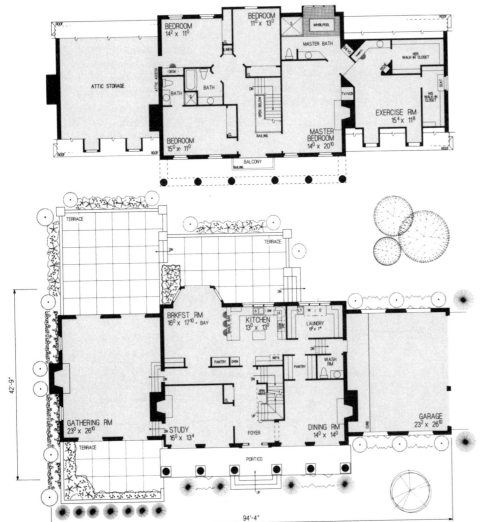

Design N3337

First Floor: 2,167 square feet
Second Floor: 1,992 square feet
Total: 4,159 square feet

L

● The elegant facade of this design with its columned portico, fanlights, and dormers houses an amenity-filled interior. The gathering room, study and dining room, each with fireplace, provide plenty of room for relaxing and entertaining. A large work area contains a kitchen with breakfast room and snack bar, laundry room and pantry. The four-bedroom upstairs includes a master suite with a sumptuous bath and an exercise room.

Design N2987

First Floor: 2,822 square feet
Second Floor: 1,335 square feet
Total: 4,157 square feet

● Andrew Jackson's dream of white-pillared splendor resulted in the building of The Hermitage. The essence of that grand dream is recaptured in this modern variation. One wing of the first floor contains a luxurious master suite which accommodates everyone's needs gracefully. The opposite wing features a country kitchen, laundry, washroom and two-car garage. The family room, dining room and living room are centrally located. On the second floor are three bedrooms (one a guest room) and one and a half baths.

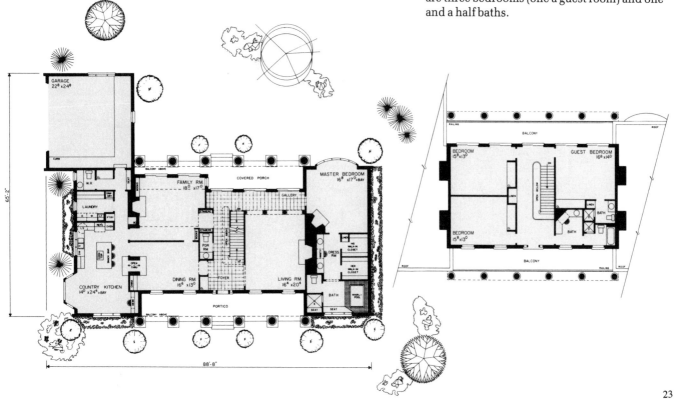

23

Design N2133 First Floor: 3,024 square feet; Second Floor: 826 square feet; Total: 3,850 square feet

D

● A country-estate home which will command all the attention it truly deserves. The projecting pediment gable supported by the finely proportioned columns lends an aura of elegance. The window treatment, the front door detailing, the massive, capped chimney, the cupola, the brick veneer exterior and the varying roof planes complete the characterization of an impressive home. Inside, there are 3,024 square feet on the first floor. In addition, there is a two bedroom second floor should its development be necessary. However, whether called upon to function as one, or 1-1/2 story home it will provide a lifetime of gracious living. Don't overlook the compartment baths, the big library, the coat room, the beamed ceiling family room, the two fireplaces, the breakfast room and the efficient kitchen. Note pass-thru to breakfast room.

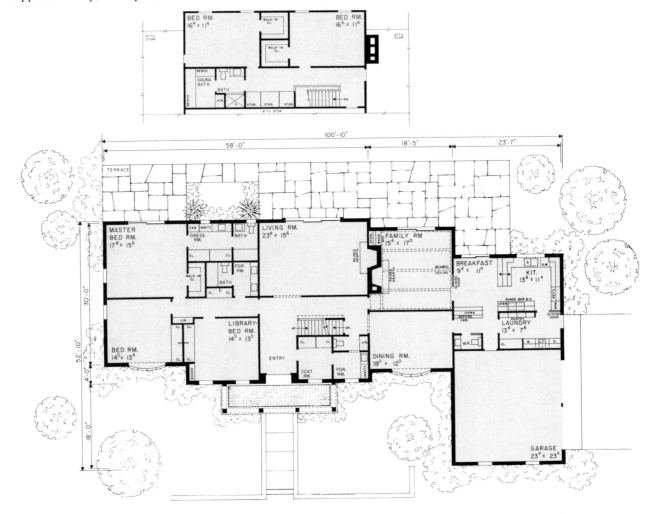

Design N2977 First Floor: 4,104 square feet; Second Floor: 979 square feet; Total: 5,083 square feet

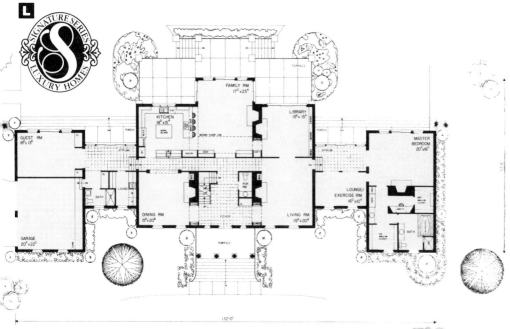

● Both front and rear facades of this elegant brick manor depict classic Georgian symmetry. A columned, Greek entry opens to an impressive two-story foyer. Fireplaces, built-in shelves, and cabinets highlight each of the four main gathering areas: living room, dining room, family room, and library.

Design N3349

First Floor: 2,807 square feet
Second Floor: 1,363 square feet
Total: 4,170 square feet

L **D**

● Grand traditional design comes to the forefront in this elegant two-story. From the dramatic front entry with curving double stairs to the less formal gathering room with fireplace and terrace access, this plan accommodates family lifestyles. Notice the split-bedroom plan with the master suite on the first floor and family bedrooms upstairs. A four-car garage handles the

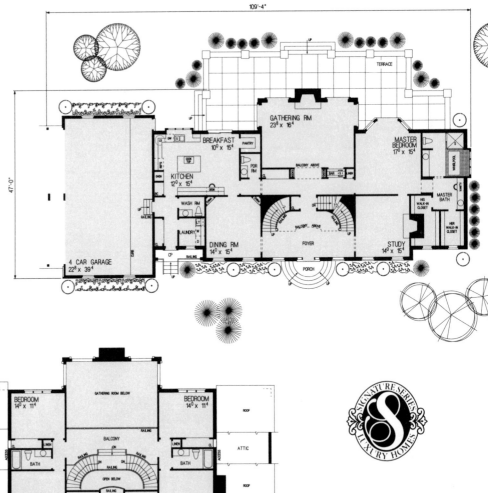

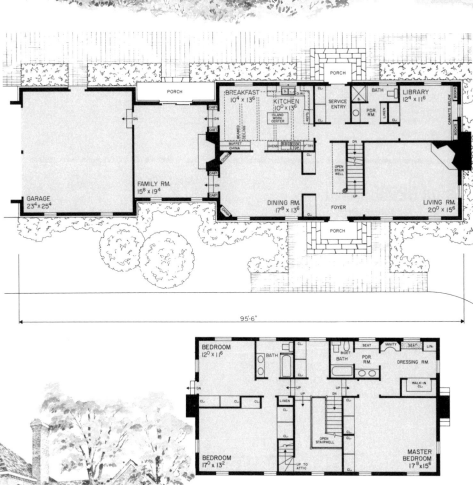

Design N2192

First Floor: 1,884 square feet
Second Floor: 1,521 square feet
Total: 3,405 square feet

L **D**

● This is surely a fine adaptation from the 18th-Century when formality and elegance were by-words. The authentic detailing of this design centers around the fine proportions, the dentils, the window symmetry, the front door and entranceway, the massive chimneys and the masonry work. The rear elevation retains all the grandeur exemplary of exquisite architecture. The appeal of this outstanding home does not end with its exterior elevations. Consider the formal living room with its corner fireplace. Also, the library with its wall of bookshelves and cabinets. Further, the dining room highlights corner china cabinets. Continue to study this elegant plan.

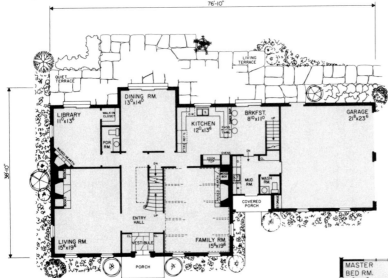

Design N1858

First Floor: 1,794 square feet
Second Floor: 1,474 square feet
Studio: 424 square feet
Total: 3,692 square feet

D

● From the delightful spacious front entry hall, to the studio or maid's room over the garage, this home is unique: four fireplaces, three full baths, two extra washrooms, a family room plus a quiet library. Note the separate set of stairs to the studio or maid's room. The kitchen is well-planned and strategically located between dining room and breakfast room.

Design N2633

First Floor: 1,338 square feet
Second Floor: 1,200 square feet
Third Floor: 506 square feet
Total: 3,044 square feet

● This pleasing Georgian features a front porch with a roof supported by 12″ diameter wooden columns. Sliding glass doors link the terrace and family room, providing an indoor/ outdoor area for entertaining. The floor plan has been designed to serve the family efficiently. The stairway in the foyer leads to four second-floor bedrooms. The third floor is windowed and can be used as a studio and study.

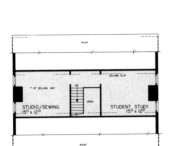

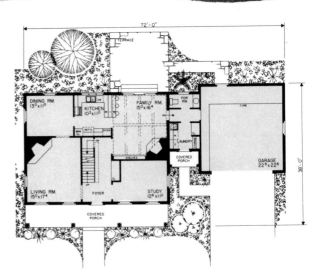

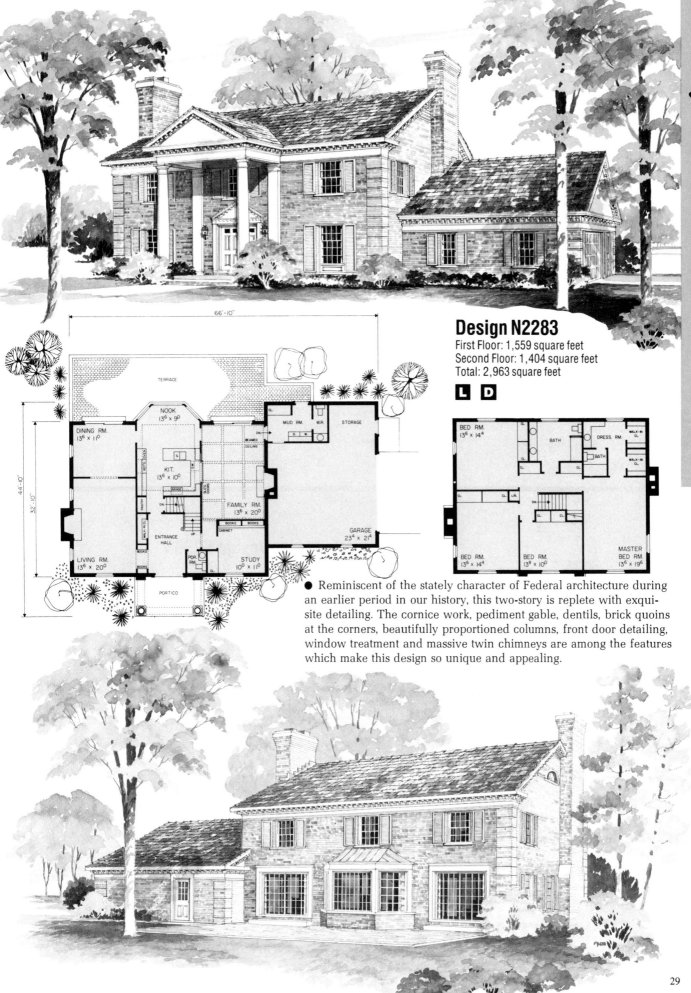

66'-10"

TERRACE

NOOK
13⁶ x 9⁰

DINING RM.
13⁶ x 11⁰

KIT.
13⁶ x 10⁰

MUD RM.   W.R.   STORAGE

BEAMED CEILING

FAMILY RM.
13⁶ x 20⁰

GARAGE
23⁴ x 21⁴

ENTRANCE HALL

LIVING RM.
13⁶ x 20⁰

BOOKS   CABINET   BOOKS

PDR. RM.

STUDY
10⁰ x 11⁰

PORTICO

32'-10"

44'-10"

Design N2283
First Floor: 1,559 square feet
Second Floor: 1,404 square feet
Total: 2,963 square feet

L D

BED RM.
13⁶ x 14⁴

BATH

DRESS. RM.

WALK-IN CL.

BATH

WALK-IN CL.

BED RM.
13⁶ x 14⁴

BED RM.
13⁸ x 10⁰

MASTER BED RM.
13⁶ x 19⁶

● Reminiscent of the stately character of Federal architecture during an earlier period in our history, this two-story is replete with exqui-site detailing. The cornice work, pediment gable, dentils, brick quoins at the corners, beautifully proportioned columns, front door detailing, window treatment and massive twin chimneys are among the features which make this design so unique and appealing.

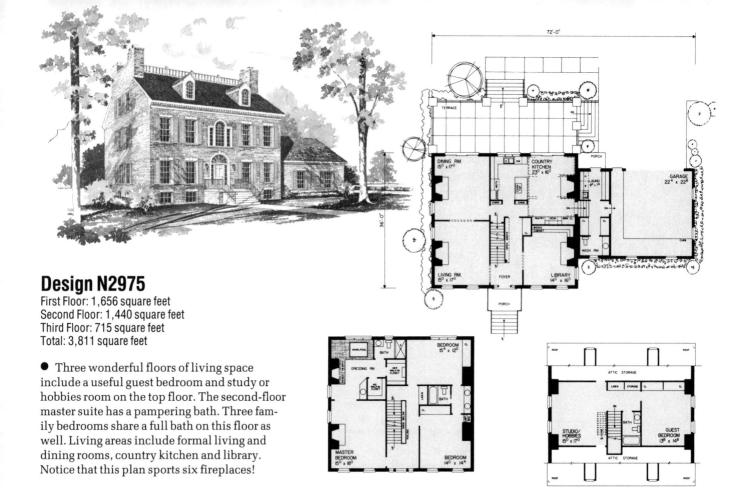

Design N2975

First Floor: 1,656 square feet
Second Floor: 1,440 square feet
Third Floor: 715 square feet
Total: 3,811 square feet

● Three wonderful floors of living space include a useful guest bedroom and study or hobbies room on the top floor. The second-floor master suite has a pampering bath. Three family bedrooms share a full bath on this floor as well. Living areas include formal living and dining rooms, country kitchen and library. Notice that this plan sports six fireplaces!

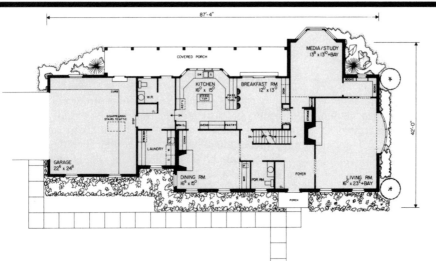

Design N2963

First Floor: 2,046 square feet
Second Floor: 1,644 square feet
Total: 3,690 square feet

● The rambling proportions of this house reflect Colonial precedents. Both the dining and living rooms boast large fireplaces. Family meals are likely to be served in the cozy breakfast room attached to the kitchen. The study is tucked away behind the living room. Upstairs, four bedrooms provide a comfortable retreat for each family member.

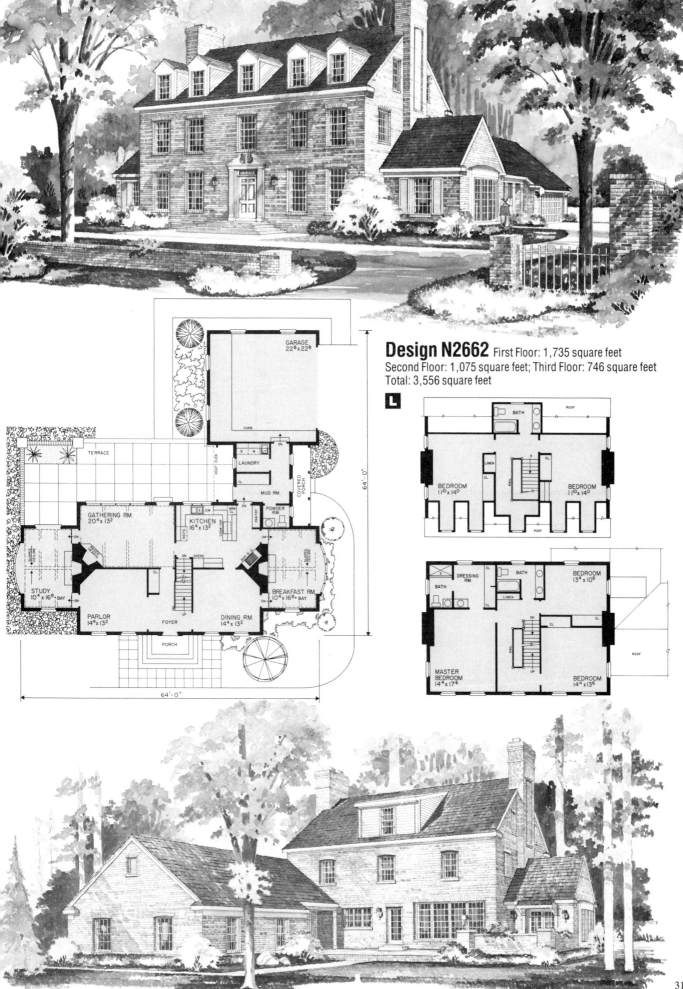

GARAGE
22⁸ x 22⁸

CURB

TERRACE

LAUNDRY

MUD RM.

POWDER RM.

COVERED PORCH

GATHERING RM.
20⁴ x 13²

KITCHEN
16⁴ x 13²

COOK TOP

PANTRY

OVENS

BREAKFAST RM.
10⁴ x 16⁸+ BAY

STUDY
10⁴ x 16⁸+ BAY

SLOPED CEILING

SLOPED CEILING

PARLOR
14⁴ x 13²

FOYER

DINING RM.
14⁴ x 13²

PORCH

64'-0"

64'-0"

Design N2662 First Floor: 1,735 square feet

Second Floor: 1,075 square feet; Third Floor: 746 square feet
Total: 3,556 square feet

L

BATH

ROOF

LINEN

CL.

RAIL

BEDROOM
11¹⁰ x 14⁰

BEDROOM
11¹⁰ x 14⁰

ROOF

BATH

DRESSING RM.

BATH

CL.

BATH

LINEN

BEDROOM
13⁴ x 10⁶

RAIL

CL.

MASTER BEDROOM
14⁴ x 17⁶

BEDROOM
14⁴ x 13⁶

ROOF

31

Design N2176

First Floor: 1,485 square feet
Second Floor: 1,175 square feet
Total: 2,660 square feet

L **D**

● A big, end living room featuring a fireplace and sliding glass doors is the focal point of this Georgian design. Adjacent is the formal dining room strategically located but a couple of steps from the efficient kitchen. Functioning closely with the kitchen is the family room.

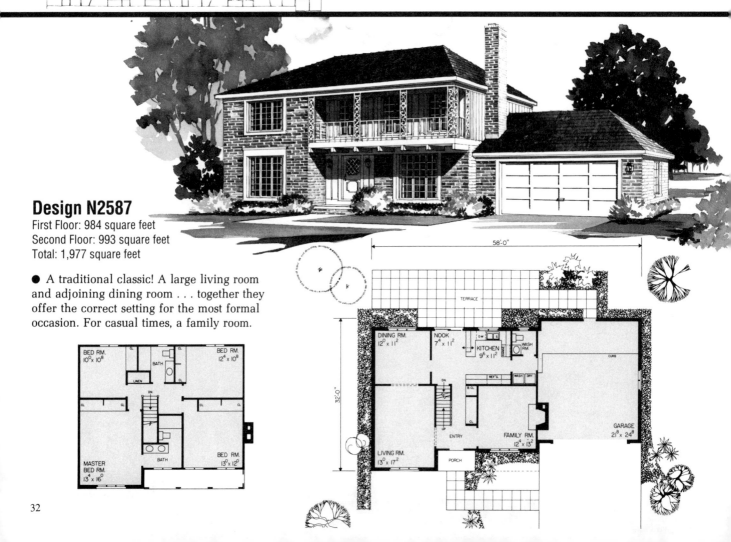

Design N2587

First Floor: 984 square feet
Second Floor: 993 square feet
Total: 1,977 square feet

● A traditional classic! A large living room and adjoining dining room . . . together they offer the correct setting for the most formal occasion. For casual times, a family room.

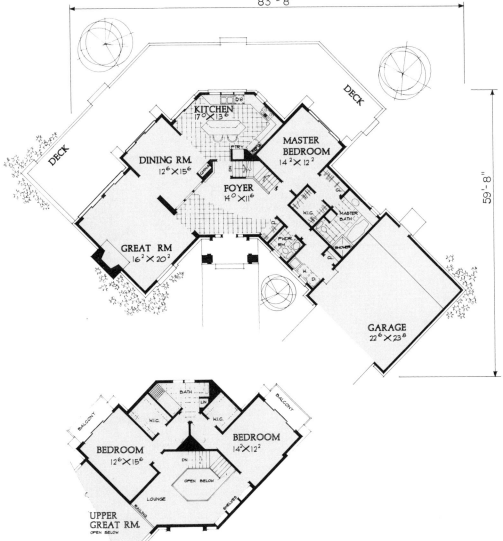

83' - 8"

59' - 8"

DECK

DECK

KITCHEN
17⁰ X 13⁶

DINING RM.
12⁶ X 15⁶

MASTER
BEDROOM
14² X 12²

FOYER
14⁰ X 11⁶

GREAT RM
16² X 20²

W.I.C.

MASTER
BATH

PWDR.
RM.

SHOWER

GARAGE
22⁶ X 23⁸

BATH

LIN

BALCONY

W.I.C.

W.I.C.

BALCONY

BEDROOM
12⁶ X 15⁶

BEDROOM
14² X 12²

DN

OPEN BELOW

LOUNGE

SHELVES

UPPER
GREAT RM.
OPEN BELOW

Design N3310
First Floor: 1,668 square feet
Second Floor: 905 square feet
Total: 2,573 square feet

● If you're looking for a different angle on a new home, try this enchanting transitional house. The open foyer creates a rich atmosphere. To the left you'll find a great room with raised-brick hearth and sliding glass doors that lead out onto a wraparound deck. The kitchen enhances the first floor with a snack bar and deck access. The master bedroom, with balcony and bath with whirlpool, is located on the first floor for privacy. Upstairs, two family bedrooms, both with balconies and walk-in closets, share a full bath. Don't overlook the lounge and elliptical window that give the second floor added charisma.

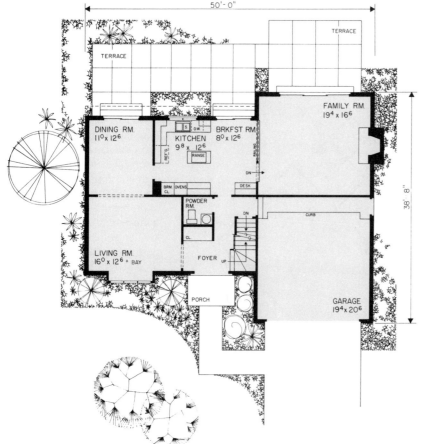

Design N2798

First Floor: 1,149 square feet
Second Floor: 850 square feet
Total: 1,999 square feet

● An island range in the kitchen is a great feature of the work center in this two-story French designed home. The breakfast room has an open railing to the sunken family room so it can enjoy the view of the family room's fireplace.

Sliding glass doors in each of the major rear rooms, dining, breakfast and family rooms, lead to the terrace for outdoor enjoyment. The front, formal living room is highlighted by a bay window. A powder room is conven-

iently located on the first floor near all of the major areas. All of the sleeping facilities are housed on the second floor. Each of the four bedrooms will serve its occupants ideally. A relatively narrow lot can house this design.

Design N2543 First Floor: 2,345 square feet
Second Floor: 1,687 square feet; Total: 4,032 square feet

L **D**

● Though quite different on the outside, the homes on these two pages have floor plans that are nearly identical. This best selling French adaptation is highlighted by effective window treatment, delicate cornice detailing, appealing brick quoins and excellent proportion. Inside are a gathering room, formal living and dining rooms, study, gourmet kitchen and four upstairs bedrooms.

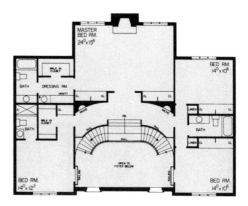

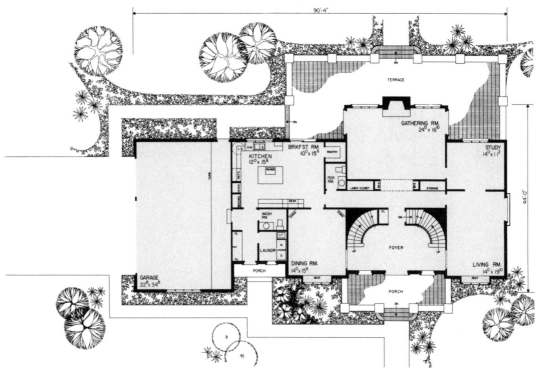

Design N1228

First Floor: 2,583 square feet
Second Floor: 697 square feet
Total: 3,280 square feet

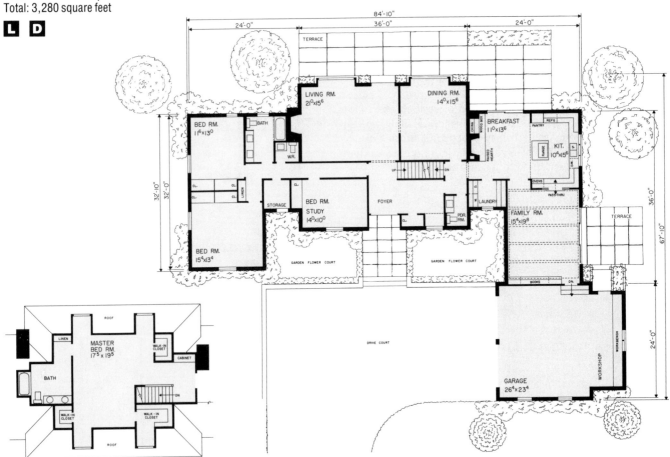

● This beautiful house has a wealth of detail taken from the rich traditions of French Regency design. The roof itself is a study in pleasant dormers and the hips and valleys of a big flowing area. A close examination of the plan shows the careful arrangement of space for privacy as well as good circulation of traffic. The spacious formal entrance hall sets the stage for good zoning. The informal living area is highlighted by the updated version of the old country kitchen. Observe the fireplace, built-in wood box, and china cabinet. While there is a half-story devoted to the master bedroom suite, this home functons more as a one-story country estate design than as a 1½ story.

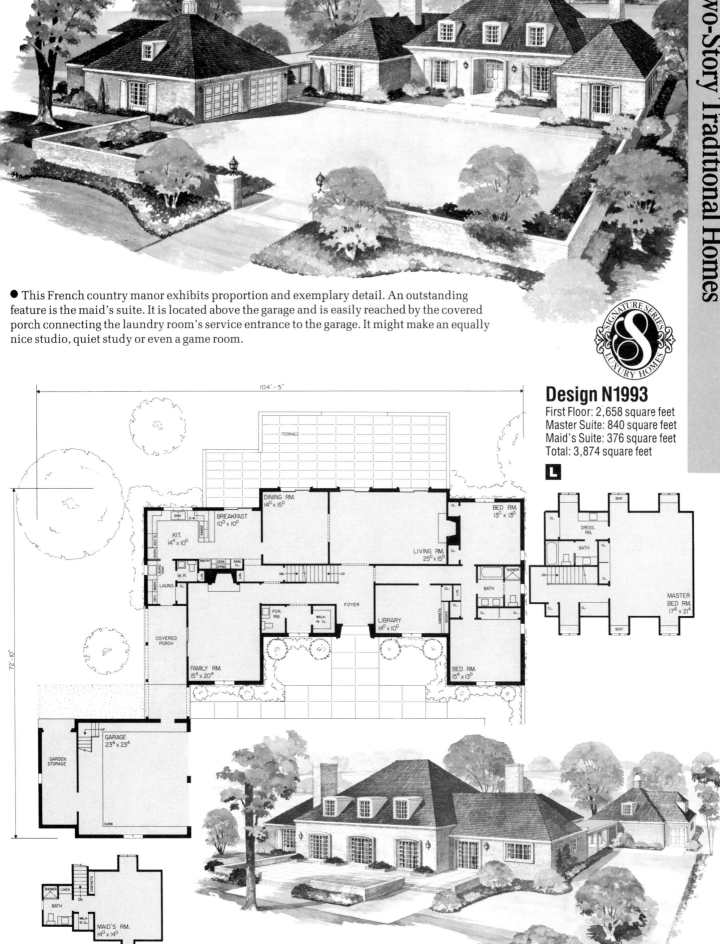

● This French country manor exhibits proportion and exemplary detail. An outstanding feature is the maid's suite. It is located above the garage and is easily reached by the covered porch connecting the laundry room's service entrance to the garage. It might make an equally nice studio, quiet study or even a game room.

Design N1993

First Floor: 2,658 square feet
Master Suite: 840 square feet
Maid's Suite: 376 square feet
Total: 3,874 square feet

L

Design N2610

First Floor: 1,505 square feet
Second Floor: 1,344 square feet
Total: 2,849 square feet

L **D**

BED RM.
13⁴ x 14⁴

BATH

DRESSING RM.

WALK-IN CLOSET

WALK-IN CLOSET

BATH

BED RM.
13⁶ x 14⁴

BED RM.
13⁶ x 10⁰

MASTER BED RM.
13⁶ x 19⁶

● This full two-story traditional will be worthy of note wherever built. It strongly recalls images of a New England of yesteryear. And well it might; for the window treatment is delightful. The front entrance detail is inviting. The narrow horizontal siding and the corner boards are appealing as are the two massive chimneys. The center entrance hall is large with a handy powder room nearby. The study has built-in bookshelves and offers a full measure of privacy. The interior kitchen has a pass-through to the family room and enjoys all that natural light from the bay window of the nook. A beamed ceiling, fireplace and sliding glass doors are features of the family room. The mud room highlights a closet, laundry equipment and an extra wash room. Study the upstairs with those four bedrooms, two baths and plenty of closets. An excellent arrangement for all.

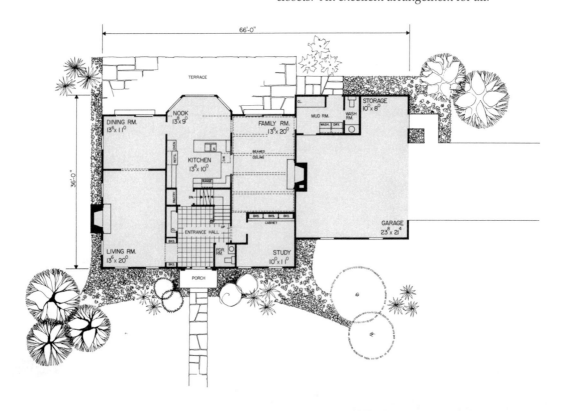

Design N2640

First Floor: 1,386 square feet
Second Floor: 1,232 square feet
Total: 2,618 square feet

L **D**

● Here is a gracious exterior which adopts many features common to New England-style Federal homes. The symmetry and proportions are outstanding. Inside, a fine, functioning plan. Note stairs to attic for additional storage and livability.

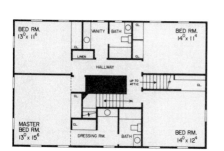

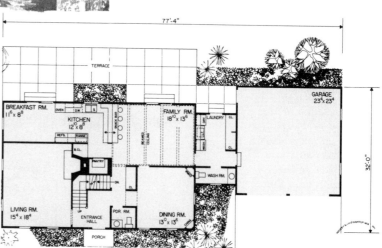

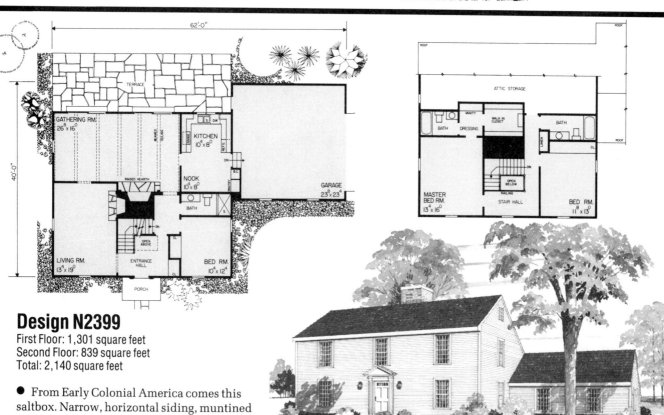

Design N2399

First Floor: 1,301 square feet
Second Floor: 839 square feet
Total: 2,140 square feet

● From Early Colonial America comes this saltbox. Narrow, horizontal siding, muntined windows, a massive central chimney, carriage lamps and a classic front entrance set the exterior character. Inside, three bedrooms, three baths and two living areas make the plan most livable.

Design N3503

First Floor: 1,748 square feet
Second Floor: 1,748 square feet
Third Floor: 1,100 square feet
Total: 4,596 square feet

L **D**

● A brick exterior serves as a nice introduction to a charming home. Enter the eleven-foot-high foyer and take a seat in the warm living room and its focal-point fireplace. Built-in shelves grace the hallway as well as the living and dining rooms. The handy kitchen with island and snack bar opens up into a conversation room with bay and fireplace. The service entrance leads to both laundry and garage. This house features four bedrooms: the master with fireplace, walk-in closet and whirlpool; two family bedrooms that share a full bath with double-bowl vanity; and a guest bedroom that shares the third floor with the library. This design would work well on a narrow lot.

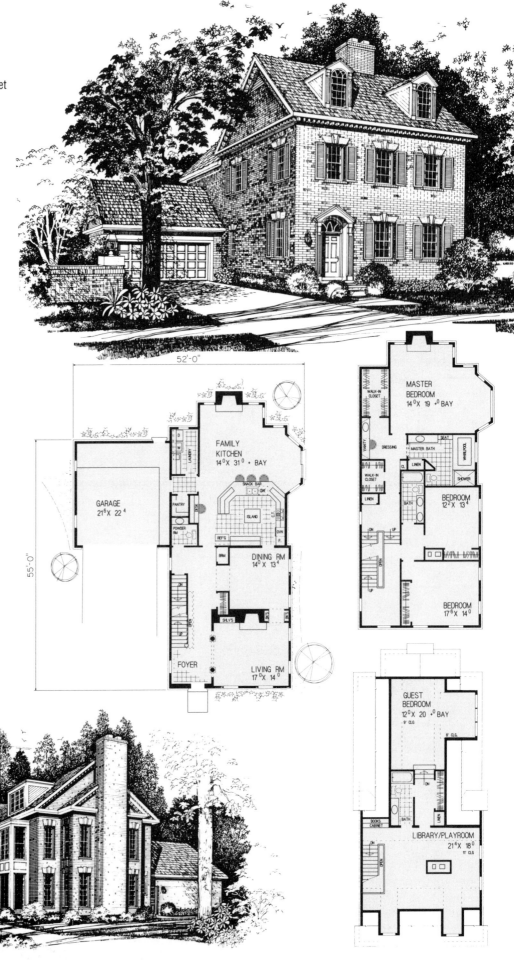

Design N2659
First Floor: 1,023 square feet
Second Floor: 1,008 square feet; Third Floor: 476 square feet
Total: 2,507 square feet

L **D**

● The facade of this three-storied, pitch-roofed house has a symmetrical placement of windows and a restrained but elegant central entrance. The central hall, or foyer, expands midway through the house to a family kitchen. Off the foyer are two rooms, a living room with fireplace and a study. The windowed third floor attic can be used as a study and studio. Three bedrooms are housed on the second floor.

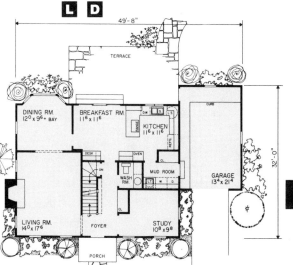

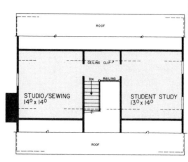

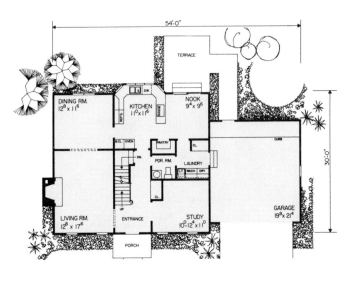

Design N2731 First Floor: 1,039 square feet
Second Floor: 973 square feet; Total: 2,012 square feet

L D

● The multi-paned windows with shutters of this two-story highlight the exterior delightfully. Inside the livability is ideal. Formal and informal areas are sure to serve your family with ease. Note efficient U-shaped kitchen with handy first-floor laundry. Sleeping facilities on second floor.

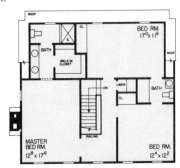

● The appeal of this Colonial home will be virtually everlasting. It will improve with age and service the growing family well. Imagine your family living here. There are four bedrooms, 2½ baths, plus plenty of first floor living space.

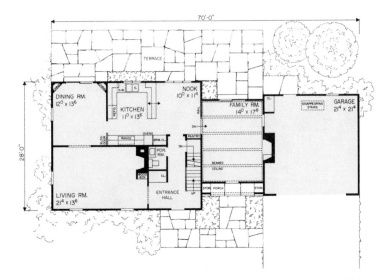

Design N2211 First Floor: 1,214 square feet
Second Floor: 1,146 square feet; Total: 2,360 square feet

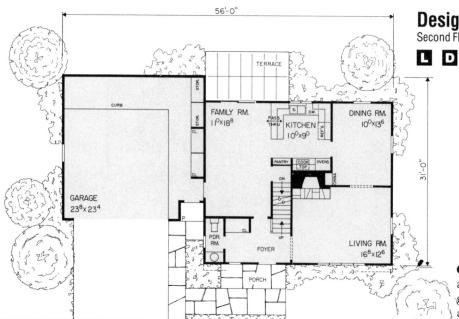

Design N1719 First Floor: 864 square feet
Second Floor: 896 square feet; Total: 1,760 square feet

L **D**

● What an appealing low-cost Colonial adaptation. Most of the livability features generally found in the largest of homes are present to cater to family needs.

Design N2733 First Floor: 1,177 square feet; Second Floor: 1,003 square feet; Total: 2,180 square feet

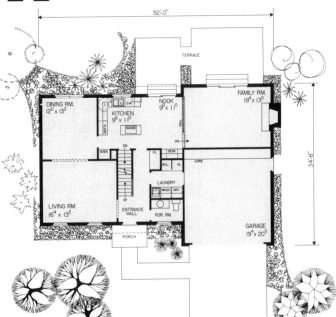

● This is definitely a four bedroom Colonial with charm galore. The kitchen features an island range and other built-ins. All will enjoy the sunken family room with fireplace, which has sliding glass doors leading to the terrace. Also a basement for recreational activities with laundry remaining on first floor for extra convenience.

Design N2538
First Floor: 1,503 square feet
Second Floor: 1,095 square feet
Total: 2,598 square feet

L **D**

● This Salt Box is charming, indeed. The livability it has to offer to the large and growing family is great. The entry is spacious and is open to the second floor balcony. For living areas, there is the study in addition to the living and family rooms.

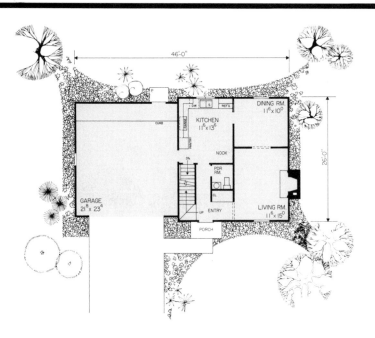

Design N2622
First Floor: 624 square feet
Second Floor: 624 square feet
Total: 1,248 square feet

L **D**

CUSTOMIZABLE

Custom Alterations? See page 349 for customizing this plan to your specifications.

Design N3485

First Floor: 1,586 square feet
Second Floor: 1,057 square feet
Total: 2,643 square feet

L

● A covered porch introduces the foyer of this delightful two-story plan. From here, formal areas open up with the living room on the right and the dining room on the left. Note the pot-shelf that extends around the dining room. A den backs up the formal areas of the house and shares a two-way fireplace with the family room. In the kitchen, an island cooktop facilitates food preparation. A double oven is built-in nearby. Upstairs, three bedrooms include a master suite with its own bath. The secondary bedrooms each partake in a hall bath with dual lavatories.

FAMILY ROOM BELOW
SLOPED CEILING

RAILING

READING ALCOVE

BEDRM
10⁶ x 11⁶

PLANT SHELF

DINING ROOM BELOW

LINEN

BATH

FOYER BELOW

PLANT

MASTER BATH

SHWR

TUB

BEDRM
15⁶ x 10²

MASTER BEDRM
14⁶ x 14⁰

WALK-IN CLOSET

LINEN

PLANT SHELF ABOVE

COVERED DECK

RAILING

SLOPED CEILING

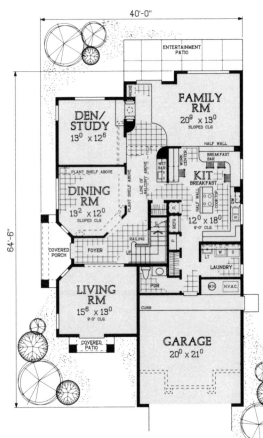

40'-0"

ENTERTAINMENT PATIO

DEN/ STUDY
13⁰ x 12⁶

FAMILY RM
20⁹ x 13⁰
SLOPED CLG

HALF WALL

PLANT SHELF ABOVE

WET BAR

WORK CENTER

BREAKFAST BAR

DINING RM
13² x 12⁰
SLOPED CLG

KIT
12⁰ x 18⁰
9'-0" CLG

BREAKFAST

64'-6"

COVERED PORCH

FOYER

RAILING

LAUNDRY

LIVING RM
15⁶ x 13⁰
9'-0" CLG

PDR

H.V.A.C.

COVERED PATIO

CURB

GARAGE
20⁰ x 21⁰

CUSTOMIZABLE
Custom Alterations? See page 349 for customizing this plan to your specifications.

46

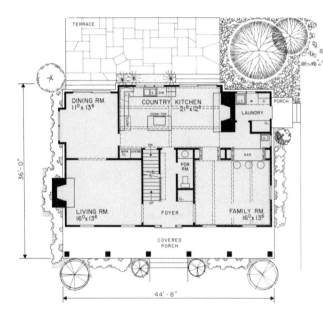

The exterior of this full two-story is highlighted by the covered porch and balcony. Many enjoyable hours will be spent at these outdoor areas. The interior is highlighted by a spacious country kitchen. Be sure to notice its island cook-top, fireplace and the beamed ceiling. A built-in bar is in the family room.

Design N2664 First Floor: 1,308 square feet
Second Floor: 1,262 square feet; Total: 2,570 square feet

D

Design N2668 First Floor: 1,206 square feet
Second Floor: 1,254 square feet; Total: 2,460 square feet

L

● This elegant exterior houses a very livable plan. Every bit of space has been put to good use. The front country kitchen is a good place to begin. It is efficiently planned with its island cook top, built-ins and pass-thru to the dining room. The large great room will be the center of all family activities. Quiet times can be enjoyed in the front library. Study the second floor sleeping areas.

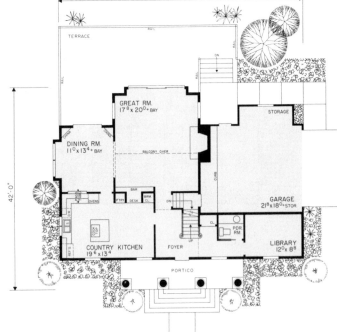

Design N2979

First Floor: 1,440 square feet
Second Floor: 1,394 square feet
Total: 2,834 square feet

● The memory of Noah Webster's house, built in 1823, in New Hampshire is recalled by this Greek Revival adaptation. In addition to the formal living and dining rooms, there is a huge country kitchen and handy mud room. There is also a study. Upstairs there are four bedrooms and three full baths. Don't miss the four fireplaces or the outdoor balcony of the master bedroom. A basement provides additional space for recreation and the pursuit of hobbies.

Design N2667

First Floor: 1,827 square feet
Second Floor: 697 square feet
Total: 2,524 square feet

L

● Two one-story wings flank the two-story center section of this design which echoes the architectural forms of 18th-Century Tidewater Virginia. The left wing is a huge living room; the right the master bedroom suite, service areas and garage. The kitchen, dining room and family room are centrally located with the three bedrooms above.

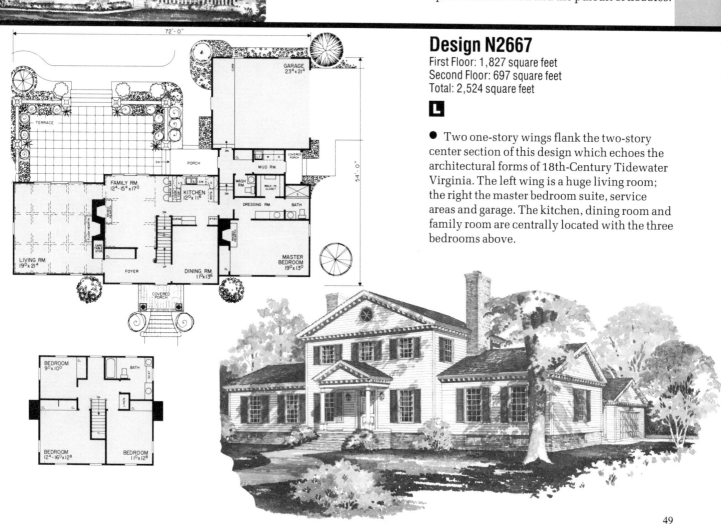

A Mount Vernon Reminiscence

● This magnificent manor's streetview illustrates a centralized mansion connected by curving galleries to matching wings. What a grand presentation this home will make! The origin of this house dates back to 1787 and George Washington's stately Mount Vernon. The underlying aesthetics for this de-sign come from the rational balancing of porticoes, fenestration and chimneys. The rear elevation of this home also deserves mention. Six two-story columns, along with four sets of French doors, highlight this view. Study all of the intricate detailing that is featured all around these exteriors.

The flanking wings create a large formal courtyard where guests of today can park their cars. This home, designed from architecture of the past, is efficient and compact enough to fit many suburban lots. Its interior has been well planned and is ready to serve a family of any size.

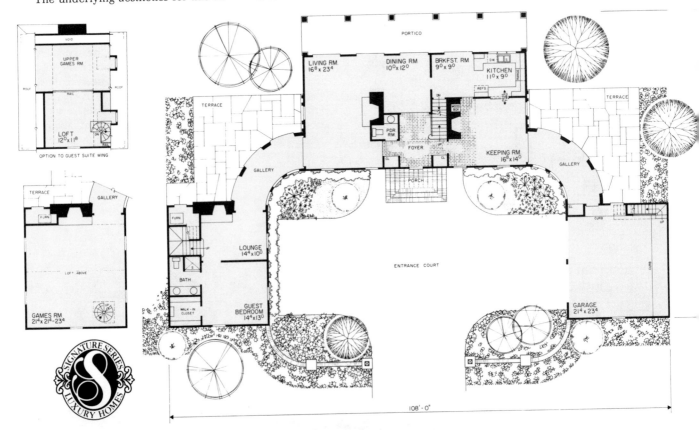

Design N2665 First Floor: 1,152 square feet; Second Floor: 1,152 square feet
Total: 2,304 square feet (Excludes Guest Suite and Galleries)

● The main, two-story section of this home houses the living areas. First - there is the large, tiled foyer with two closets and powder room. Then there is the living room which is the entire width of the house. This room has a fireplace and leads into the formal dining room. Three sets of double French doors lead to the rear portico from this formal area. The kitchen and breakfast room will function together. There is a pass-thru from the kitchen to the keeping room. All of the sleeping facilities, four bedrooms, are on the second floor. The gallery on the right leads to the garage; the one on the left, to a lounge and guest suite with studio above. The square footages quoted above do not include the guest suite or gallery areas. The first floor of the guest suite contains 688 sq. ft.; the second floor studio, 306 sq. ft. The optional plan shows a game room with a loft above having 162 sq. ft.

Design N3457

First Floor: 1,252 square feet
Second Floor: 972 square feet
Total: 2,224 square feet

L

● For family living, this delightful three-bedroom plan scores big. Stretching across the back of the plan, casual living areas take precedence. The family room focuses on a fireplace and enjoys direct access to a covered porch. The breakfast room allows plenty of space for friendly meals—the island kitchen remains open to this room thus providing ease in serving meals and, of course, conversations with the cook. From the two-car garage, a utility area opens to the main-floor living areas. Upstairs, the master suite affords a quiet retreat with its private bath; here you'll find a whirlpool tub set in a sunny nook. A balcony further enhances this bedroom. The two secondary bedrooms share a full hall bath with a double-bowl vanity.

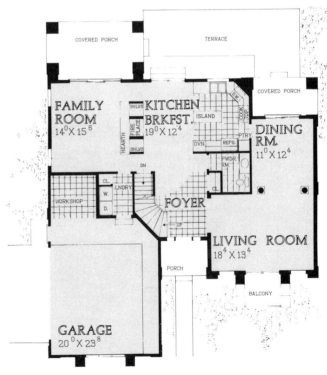

WIDTH 48'
DEPTH 58'

52

Design N3459

First Floor: 1,392 square feet
Second Floor: 1,178 square feet
Total: 2,570 square feet

L

● This innovative, compact plan affords over 2,500 square feet in living space! A central, angled staircase provides an interesting pivot with which to admire the floor plan. To begin with, the living room rises to two stories and even sports a front porch. The dining room, with its bumped-out nook, enjoys the use of a china alcove. The island kitchen finds easy access to the dining room and blends nicely into the airy breakfast room. A large pantry and a built-in desk also grace the kitchen and the breakfast room, respectively. In the family room, relaxed living comes through with the introduction of a fireplace and access to a covered patio and a terrace. The second floor will please all your family members with its four bedrooms, including a master suite with a private bath.

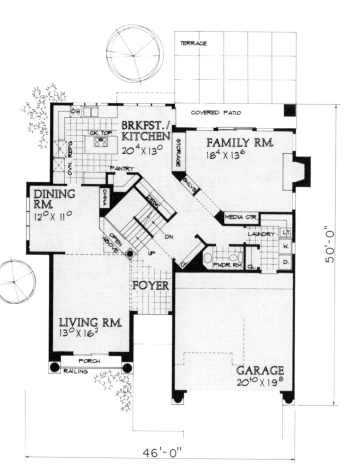

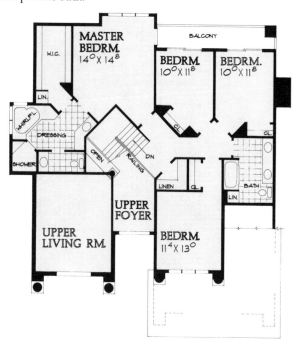

Design N3463

First Floor: 1,163 square feet
Second Floor: 1,077 square feet
Total: 2,240 square feet

L

● Fine family living takes off in this grand two-story plan. The tiled foyer leads to a stately living room with sliding glass doors to the back terrace. Columns separate it from the dining room. For casual living, the family room/breakfast room combination works well. On the second floor, the master bedroom draws attention with a fireplace, access to a deck and a spoiling bath. The study niche in the hallway shares the outside deck. Two family bedrooms are also on the second floor.

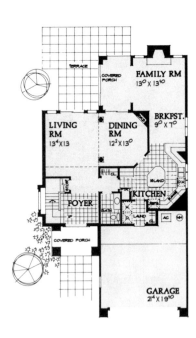

Width 36'
Depth 63'

Width 42'
Depth 72'-8"

Design N3464

First Floor: 1,776 square feet
Second Floor: 876 square feet
Total: 2,652 square feet

L **D**

● This dramatic home offers something a little different. A two-story foyer introduces an open formal area consisting of a volume living room and a dining room, separated by columns. The kitchen sits to the rear of the plan and shares space with the breakfast room. The family room has access to a terrace as well as a through fireplace and volume ceiling. Also on the first floor, the master bedroom offers a pampering bath. The sleeping accommodations are completed with three upstairs bedrooms.

Design N3455

First Floor: 1,408 square feet
Second Floor: 667 square feet
Total: 2,075 square feet

L **D**

● Whether you're just starting out or looking to retire, this 1½-story, sun-country design will make an excellent home. The focal point of the first floor, the two-story living room utilizes a central fireplace and columns for comfort and elegance. Open to the living room, the dining room complements this space with its influx of natural light. The kitchen services this room easily and also enjoys a cozy breakfast nook. An island work counter in the kitchen guarantees ease in food preparation. Note the service entry to the garage; a full washer/dryer set-up adds convenience to laundry chores. On the second floor you'll find a skylit balcony—a dramatic yet purposeful design feature—leading to two bedrooms.

48'-0"

54'-0"

SITTING RM. 7¹⁰ X 9⁰

MASTER BEDROOM 12⁰ X 15⁸

LIVING ROOM 14⁰ X 15⁴

DINING RM. 12⁰ X 10⁰

DRESSING ROOM

SHOWER

VANITY

WHIRLPOOL

DN

UP

FOYER

PWDR RM.

CL CL

BRKFST. 12⁴ X 9⁰

KITCHEN 12⁴ X 9⁰

WORK ISLAND

OVEN

D.W.

REFG.

DESK

PORCH

GARAGE 20⁴ X 22⁸

BEDROOM 7¹⁰ X 9⁰

BEDROOM 12⁸ X 10⁰

OPEN BELOW

RAILING

BALCONY

RAILING

LINEN

BATH

STORAGE

UPPER FOYER

STORAGE

Design N2680

First Floor: 1,707 square feet

Second Floor: 1,439 square feet

Total: 3,146 square feet

L **D**

● This Early American, Dutch Colonial offers many fine features. The foyer allows easy access to all rooms on the first floor. Note the large country kitchen with beamed ceiling and fireplace. A large, formal dining room and powder room are only a few steps away. The study and the living room also have fireplaces. Two bedrooms, a full bath and the master bedroom suite are on the second floor. A fourth bedroom and bath are accessible through the master bedroom or by stairs in the service entrance.

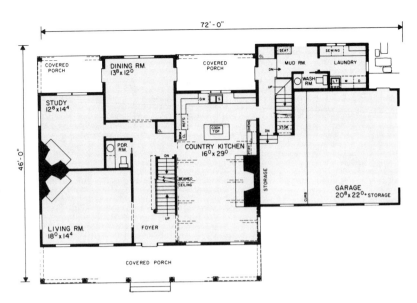

CUSTOMIZABLE

Custom Alterations? See page 349 for customizing this plan to your specifications.

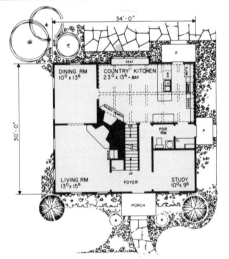

Design N2661

First Floor: 1,020 square feet

Second Floor: 777 square feet

Total: 1,797 square feet

L **D**

● Any other starter house or retirement home couldn't have more charm than this design. Its compact frame houses a very livable plan. An outstanding feature of the first floor is the large country kitchen. Its fine attractions include a beamed ceiling, raised-hearth fireplace, built-in window seat and a door leading to the outdoors. A living room in the front of the plan has another fireplace which shares the single chimney. The rear dormered second floor houses the sleeping and bath facilities.

56

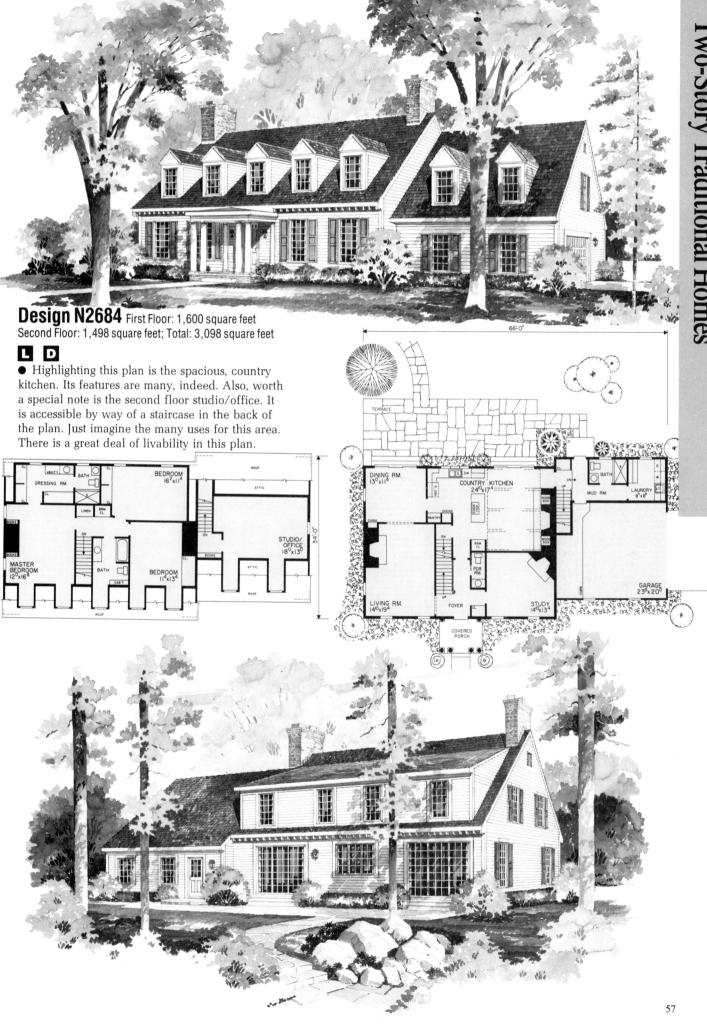

Design N2684 First Floor: 1,600 square feet
Second Floor: 1,498 square feet; Total: 3,098 square feet

L **D**

● Highlighting this plan is the spacious, country kitchen. Its features are many, indeed. Also, worth a special note is the second floor studio/office. It is accessible by way of a staircase in the back of the plan. Just imagine the many uses for this area. There is a great deal of livability in this plan.

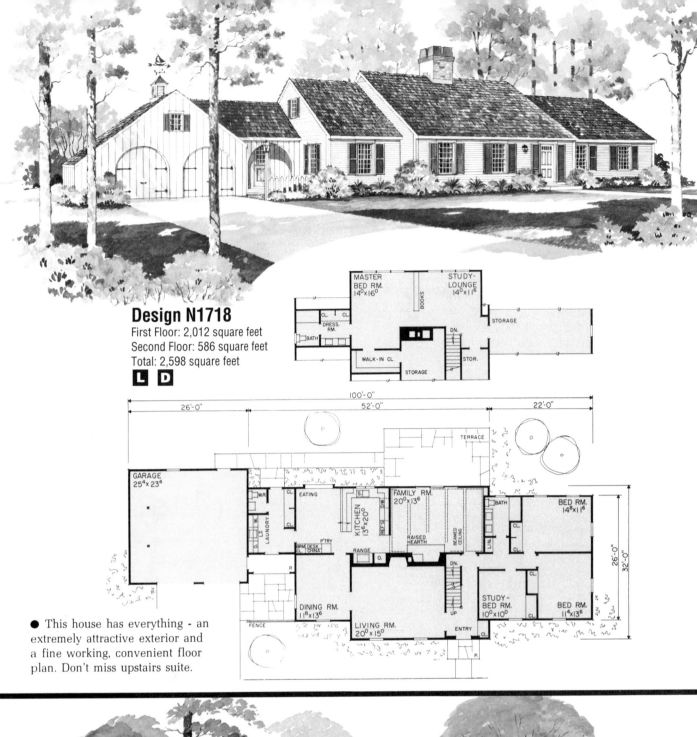

Design N1718

First Floor: 2,012 square feet
Second Floor: 586 square feet
Total: 2,598 square feet

L **D**

● This house has everything - an extremely attractive exterior and a fine working, convenient floor plan. Don't miss upstairs suite.

Second Floor Plan Labels

MASTER BED RM. 14⁰x16⁰
STUDY-LOUNGE 14⁰x11⁶
BOOKS
CL.
CL.
DRESS. RM.
BATH
STORAGE
DN.
WALK-IN CL.
STORAGE
STOR.

First Floor Plan Labels

100'-0"
26'-0"
52'-0"
22'-0"
26'-0"
32'-0"

GARAGE 25⁴x23⁴
TERRACE
W.R.
EATING
CL.
S.
DW.
FAMILY RM. 20⁰x13⁶
BATH
BED RM. 14⁸x11⁶
W.
LAUNDRY
CL.
KITCHEN 13⁴x20⁰
REF'G
RAISED HEARTH
BEAMED CEILING
LIN.
CL.
CL.
BRM. DESK CHINA CL.
P'TRY
RANGE
DN.
CL.
P.
O.
UP
STUDY-BED RM. 10⁰x10⁰
CL.
BED RM. 11⁴x13⁶
DINING RM. 11⁸x13⁶
CL.
FENCE
LIVING RM. 20⁰x15⁰
ENTRY
CL.
P.

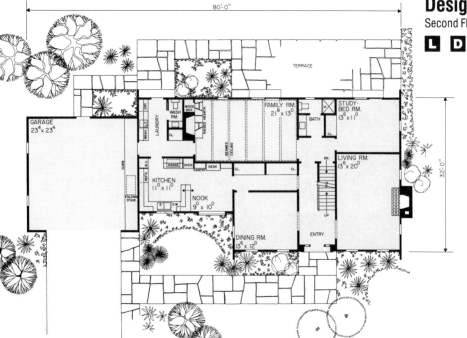

80'-0"

TERRACE

GARAGE
23⁴ x 23⁴

LAUNDRY

WASH RM.

FAMILY RM.
21⁸ x 13⁰

STUDY-
BED RM.
13⁶ x 11⁰

BATH

RANGE OVEN PANTRY DESK

KITCHEN
11' x 11'

NOOK
9⁰ x 10⁰

LIVING RM.
13⁶ x 20⁰

DINING RM.
13⁶ x 12⁰

ENTRY

32'-0"

Design N1987 First Floor: 1,632 square feet
Second Floor: 980 square feet; Total: 2,612 square feet

L   **D**

● The comforts of home will be endless and enduring when experienced
and enjoyed in this Colonial adaptation. What's your favorite feature?

BED RM.
13⁶ x 13⁰

BATH

BATH

DRESSING RM.

WALK-IN CLOSET

LINEN

BED RM.
13⁶ x 12⁰

WALK-IN CLOSET

MASTER BED RM.
13⁶ x 16⁰

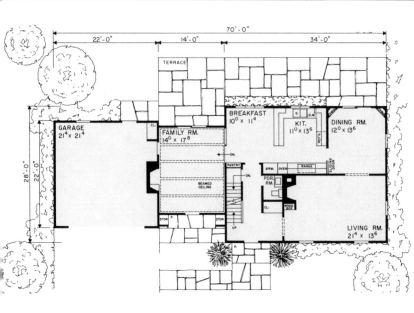

70'-0"

22'-0"   14'-0"   34'-0"

TERRACE

GARAGE
21⁴ x 21⁴

FAMILY RM.
14⁰ x 17⁸

BEAMED CEILING

BREAKFAST
10⁰ x 11⁴

KIT.
11' x 13⁶

DINING RM.
12⁰ x 13⁶

PANTRY

PDR. RM.

BRM. OVEN RANGE

LIVING RM.
21⁴ x 13⁶

28'-0"   22'-0"

Design N2131

First Floor: 1,214 square feet
Second Floor: 1,097 square feet
Total: 2,311 square feet

L   **D**

● The Gambrel-roof home is often the very embodiment of charm from the Early Colonial Period in American architechtural history. Fine proportion and excellent detailing were the hall-
marks of the era.

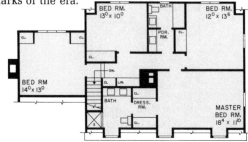

BED RM.
13⁰ x 10⁰

BATH

BED RM.
12⁰ x 13⁶

PDR. RM.

BED RM
14⁰ x 13⁰

DRESS. RM.

BATH

MASTER BED RM.
18⁴ x 11⁰

Design N1791 First Floor: 1,157 square feet
Second Floor: 875 square feet; Total: 2,032 square feet

L **D**

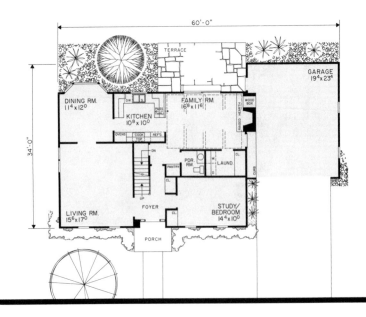

● Wherever you build this moderately sized house an aura of Cape Cod is sure to unfold. The symmetry is pleasing, indeed. The authentic center entrance seems to project a beckoning call.

Design N1870 First Floor: 1,136 square feet
Second Floor: 936 square feet; Total: 2,072 square feet

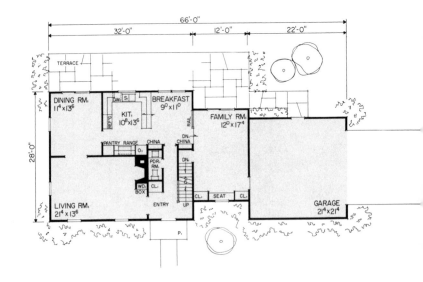

● Besides an enchanting exterior, this home has formal dining and living rooms, plus informal family and breakfast rooms. Built-ins are located in both of these informal rooms. U-shaped, the kitchen will efficiently service both of the dining areas. Study the sleeping facilities of the second floor.

Design N2396 First Floor: 1,616 square feet
Second Floor: 993 square feet; Total: 2,609 square feet

D

● Another picturesque facade right from the pages of our Colonial heritage. The authentic features are many. Don't miss the stairs to area over the garage.

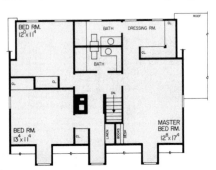

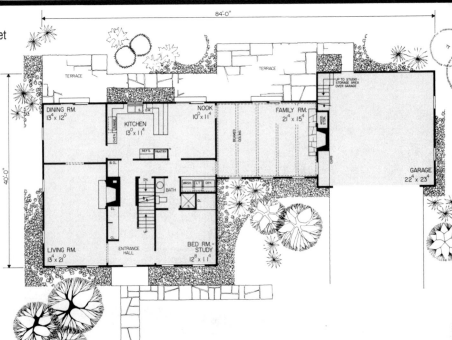

Design N3372

First Floor: 1,259 square feet
Second Floor: 942 square feet
Total: 2,201 square feet

L **D**

● Charm is the key word for this delightful plan's exterior, but don't miss the great floor plan inside. Formal living and dining rooms flank the entry foyer to the front; a family room and breakfast room with beamed ceilings are to the rear. The kitchen and service areas function well together and are near the garage and service entrance for convenience. Upstairs are the sleeping accommodations: two family bedrooms and a master suite of nice proportion.

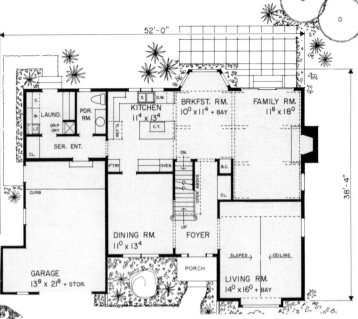

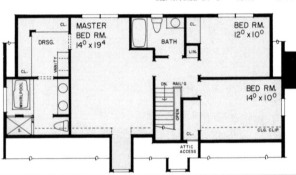

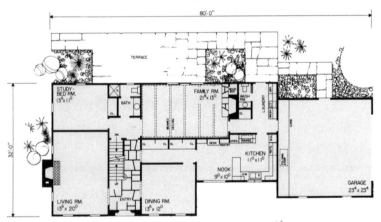

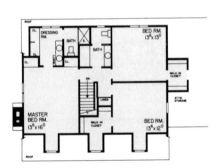

Design N2631

First Floor: 1,634 square feet
Second Floor: 1,011 square feet
Total: 2,645 square feet

L **D**

● Two fireplaces and a wealth of other amenities abound in this design. Notice how all the rooms are accessible from the main hall — keeping traffic in each room to a minimum. A large family room featuring a beamed ceiling, a fireplace with built-in wood box and double doors onto the terrace is nearby an exceptional U-shaped kitchen. Three upstairs bedrooms include a master suite with dressing room and private bath.

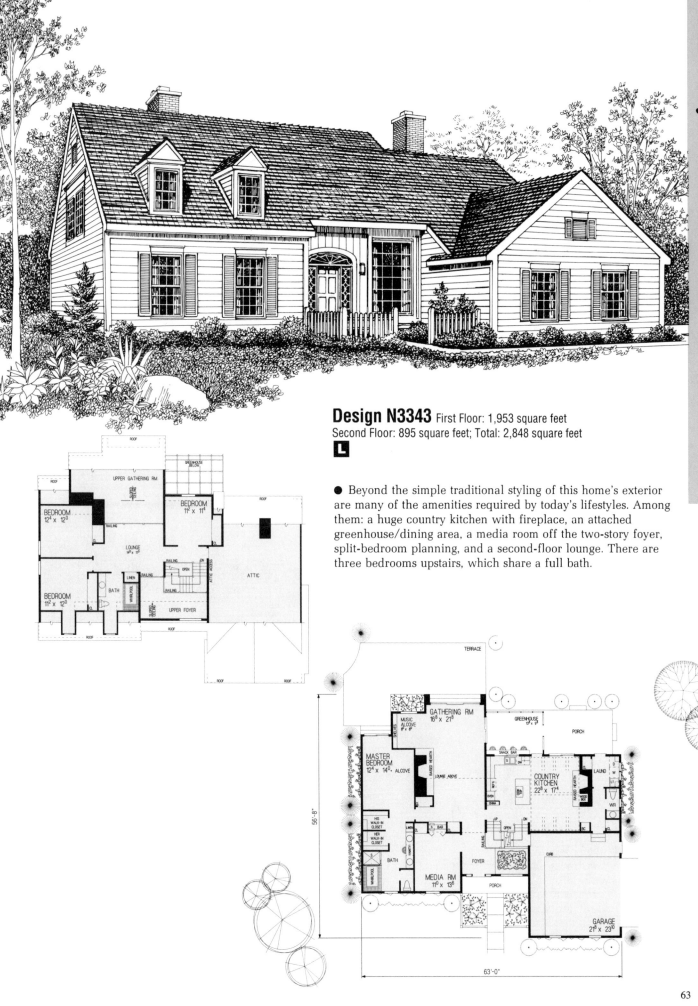

Design N3343 First Floor: 1,953 square feet
Second Floor: 895 square feet; Total: 2,848 square feet

L

● Beyond the simple traditional styling of this home's exterior are many of the amenities required by today's lifestyles. Among them: a huge country kitchen with fireplace, an attached greenhouse/dining area, a media room off the two-story foyer, split-bedroom planning, and a second-floor lounge. There are three bedrooms upstairs, which share a full bath.

Design N3367 First Floor: 3,634 square feet
Second Floor: 1,450 square feet; Total: 5,084 square feet

L

● This may be the perfect plan for you if your proposed building site is narrow but quite deep. First-floor living areas include a two-story gathering room, more casual keeping room (note fireplaces in both rooms), media room (another fireplace!), dining room with bay window, and kitchen with butler's pantry. The master bedroom on this level has a sloped ceiling and His and Hers walk-ins. Three family bedrooms are upstairs. One of these has its own private bath; the other two share a full bath.

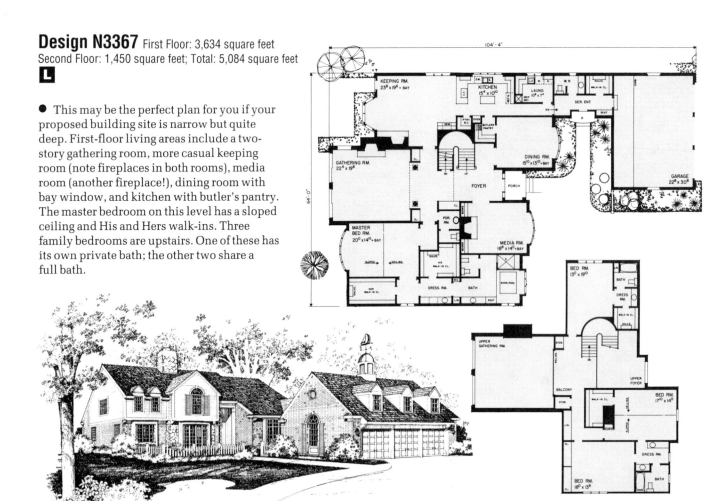

Design N3334 First Floor: 2,193 square feet
Second Floor: 831 square feet; Total: 3,024 square feet

L

● A traditional favorite, this home combines classic style with progressive floor planning. Four bedrooms are split — master suite and one bedroom on the first floor, two more bedrooms upstairs. The second-floor lounge overlooks a large, sunken gathering room near the formal dining area. A handy butler's pantry connects the dining room and kitchen.

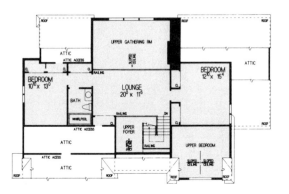

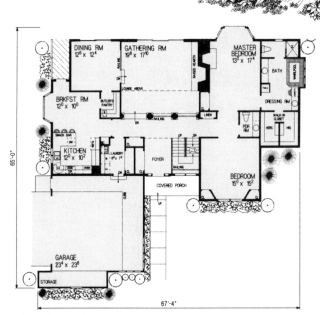

Design N3450

First Floor: 1,801 square feet
Second Floor: 1,086 square feet
Total: 2,887 square feet

L **D**

● A striking facade includes a covered front porch with four columns.
To the left of the foyer is a large
gathering room with a fireplace and bay
window. The adjoining dining room leads
to a covered side porch. The kitchen
includes a snack bar, pantry, desk, and eating area. The first-floor master suite provides a spacious bath with walk-in closet,
whirlpool and shower. Also on the first
floor: a study and a garage workshop. Two
bedrooms and a lavish guest suite share
the second floor.

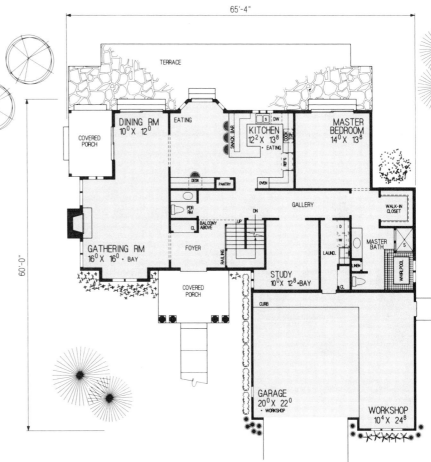

CUSTOMIZABLE

Custom Alterations? See page 349
for customizing this plan to your
specifications.

Design N2967 First Floor: 1,877 square feet
Second Floor: 467 square feet; Total: 2,344 square feet

L

● Special interior amenities abound in this unique 1½-story Tudor. Living areas include an open gathering room/dining room area with fireplace and pass-through to the breakfast room. Quiet time can be spent in a sloped-ceiling study. Look for plenty of workspace in the island kitchen and workshop/storage area. Sleeping areas are separated for utmost privacy: an elegant master suite on the first floor, two bedrooms and a full bath on the second.

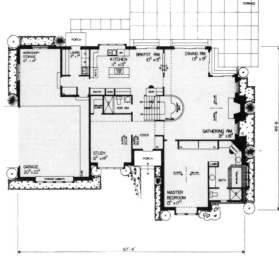

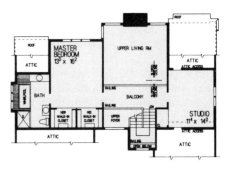

Design N3342 First Floor: 1,467 square feet
Second Floor: 715 square feet; Total: 2,182 square feet

L

● Just the right amount of living space is contained in this charming traditional house and it's arranged in a great floor plan. The split-bedroom configuration, with two bedrooms (or optional study) on the first floor and the master suite on the second floor with its own studio, assures complete privacy. The living room has a second-floor balcony overlook and a warming fireplace. The full-width terrace in back is counterbalanced nicely by the entry garden court.

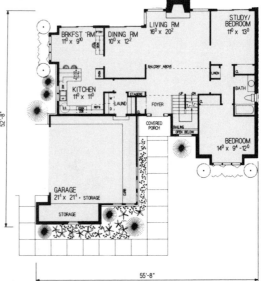

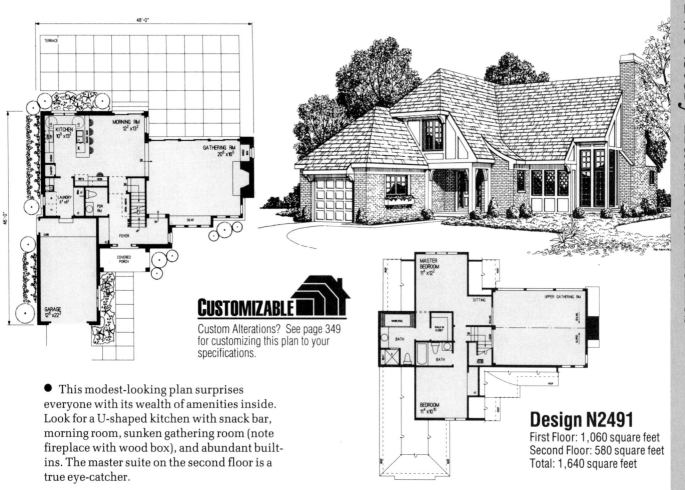

CUSTOMIZABLE

Custom Alterations? See page 349 for customizing this plan to your specifications.

● This modest-looking plan surprises everyone with its wealth of amenities inside. Look for a U-shaped kitchen with snack bar, morning room, sunken gathering room (note fireplace with wood box), and abundant built-ins. The master suite on the second floor is a true eye-catcher.

Design N2491

First Floor: 1,060 square feet
Second Floor: 580 square feet
Total: 1,640 square feet

Design N3331
First Floor: 1,115 square feet
Second Floor: 690 square feet; Total: 1,805 square feet

L

● Who could guess that this compact design contains three bedrooms and two full baths? The kitchen is close to indoor eating space in the dining room and outdoor eating space in an attached deck. A fireplace in the two-story gathering room welcomes company.

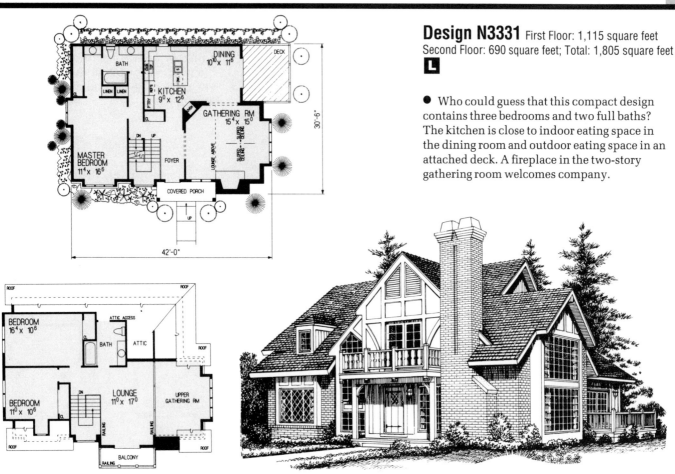

Design N3302

First Floor: 1,326 square feet
Second Floor: 542 square feet
Total: 1,868 square feet

L

● A cottage fit for a king! Appreciate the highlights: a two-story foyer, a rear living zone (gathering room, terrace, and dining room), pass-through snack bar in kitchen, a two-story master bedroom. Two upstairs bedrooms share a full bath.

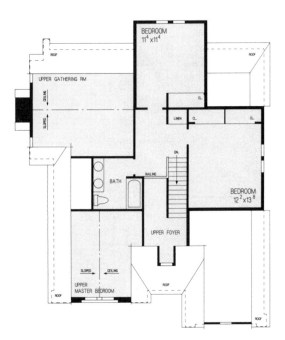

TERRACE

DINING RM
10⁴×14⁶

GATHERING RM
16¹⁰×17⁰

PASS THRU

KITCHEN
9²×15⁰

39'-7"

49'-4"

PANTRY

LAUNDRY

BAR

WALK-IN CLOSET

BATH

FOYER

UP

SECOND FLOOR ABOVE

MASTER BEDROOM
14²×14⁰

COVERED PORCH

GARAGE
12²×20⁰

BEDROOM
11⁴×11⁴

UPPER GATHERING RM

LINEN

BATH

RAILING

BEDROOM
12²×13⁸

UPPER FOYER

SLOPED CEILING

UPPER MASTER BEDROOM

CUSTOMIZABLE

Custom Alterations? See page 349 for customizing this plan to your specifications.

● This Tudor design has many fine features. The exterior is enhanced by front and side bay windows in the family and dining rooms. Along with an outstanding exterior, it also contains a modern and efficient floor plan within its modest proportions. Flanking the entrance foyer is a comfortable living room. The U-shaped kitchen is conveniently located between the dining and breakfast rooms.

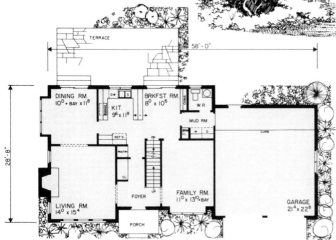

Design N2800 First Floor: 999 square feet
Second Floor: 997 square feet; Total: 1,996 square feet

L **D**

● The charm of old England has been captured in this outstanding two-story design. Interior livability will efficiently serve the various needs of all family members. The first floor offers both formal and informal areas along with the work centers. Features include: a wet bar in the dining room, the kitchen's snack bar, first-floor laundry and a rear covered porch.

CUSTOMIZABLE

Custom Alterations? See page 349 for customizing this plan to your specifications.

Design N2854 First Floor: 1,261 square feet
Second Floor: 950 square feet; Total: 2,211 square feet

L **D**

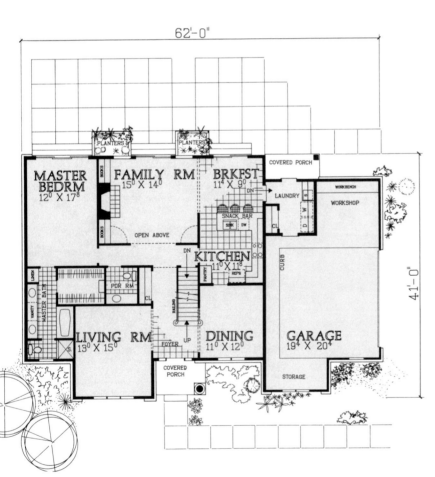

Design N3458

First Floor: 1,617 square feet
Second Floor: 725 square feet
Total: 2,342 square feet

L **D**

● Palladian windows adorn the facade of this excellent, fully functional plan. The foyer introduces the formal zones of the house with a volume living room to the left and a dining room to the right. The kitchen easily services this area and also enjoys a large breakfast room on the other side. A step away, the service entry presents a washer and dryer as well as passage to the two-car, side-load garage. A curb in the garage expands to storage space or becomes a perfect spot for a workbench. For sleeping, four bedrooms each exhibit uniqueness. The master suite—on the ground level—has terrace access, a generous, private bath and a walk-in closet. Upstairs, a balcony overlooking the two-story family room leads to the secondary bedrooms. A compartmented bath with dual lavs adds to convenience.

Design N3452

First Floor: 1,545 square feet
Second Floor: 805 square feet
Total: 2,350 square feet

L

● Clean lines and tasteful window treatment create a pleasing facade. The formal living room (with vaulted ceiling) and dining room are open to each other. To the right of the foyer is a parlor that may serve as a guest bedroom, with a full bath nearby. The island kitchen easily serves the octagonal breakfast room and the family room with a vaulted ceiling and a fireplace. A rear patio can be accessed from the family room or breakfast room. Two stairways lead to the second floor. Balconies overlook the living and family rooms. The master bedroom features a luxurious bath and a walk-in closet, while two family bedrooms share a full bath.

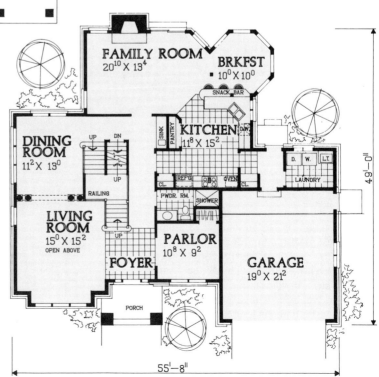

Design N2914
First Floor: 1,143 square feet
Second Floor: 845 square feet; Total: 1,988 square feet

L

● This striking Tudor adaptation offers plenty of comfort and livability on two floors. Two large bedrooms including a luxurious master suite are located on the second floor. The master suite includes its own whirlpool and twin walk-in closets. Downstairs are a media room, powder room for guests, a large rear gathering room, and dining room which adjoins the gathering room via a through-fireplace. Built-in storage space enhances the two-car garage.

Design N2959
First Floor: 1,003 square feet
Second Floor: 1,056 square feet
Total: 2,059 square feet

● Here the stateliness of Tudor styling is captured in a design suited for a narrow building site. This two-story has all the livability found in many much larger homes. The 29-foot living/dining area stretches across the entire rear of the house and opens to a large terrace. The efficient U-shaped kitchen is found near the mud room with adjacent wash room. Enhancing first-floor livability is the study with huge walk-in closet. Upstairs are three bedrooms, two baths and an outdoor balcony.

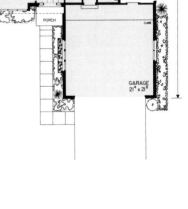

Design N2957

First Floor: 2,557 square feet
Second Floor: 1,939 square feet
Total: 4,496 square feet

L **D**

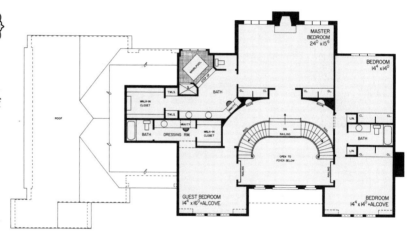

● The decorative half timbers and stone wall-cladding on this manor are stately examples of Tudor architecture. A grand double staircase is the highlight of the elegant, two-story foyer that opens to each of the main living areas. The living and gathering rooms are anchored by impressive central fireplaces. Handy built-ins, including a lazy susan and desk, and an island workstation with sink and cooktop, are convenient amenities in the kitchen. The adjacent breakfast room opens to the terrace for a sunny start to the day. Functioning with both the kitchen and the formal dining room is the butler's pantry. It has an abundance of cabinet and cupboard space and even a sink for a wet bar. Accessible from both the gathering and living rooms is the quiet study. If desired this could become a media center, sewing room or home office. The outstanding master suite features a cozy bedroom fireplace, picturesque whirlpool bath, and a convenient walk-in closet. Three additional second-floor bedrooms include a guest suite with dressing room and walk-in closet. Every part of this house speaks elegance, formality and the time-honored values for which Tudor is renowned.

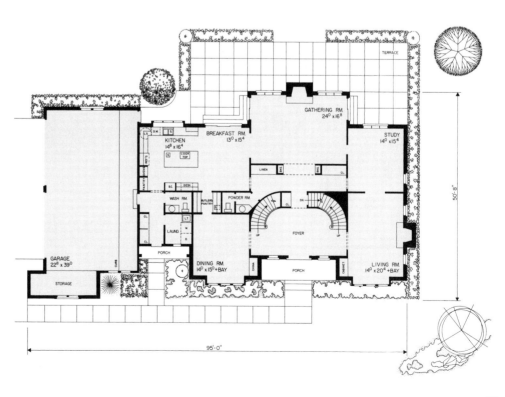

Design N3369

First Floor: 2,740 square feet
Second Floor: 2,257 square feet
Total: 4,997 square feet

L **D**

● Tudor styling at its best graces this home's facade and the floor plan is laid out in a complementary grand manner. There's living space for any activity: a quiet library, a great hall with fireplace for entertaining, cozy family room with adjacent breakfast room, and a laundry room large enough to double as a hobbies center. The second floor holds three family bedrooms each with its own bath and a private master suite with garden whirlpool.

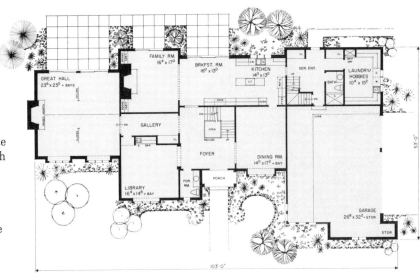

Design N2391

First Floor: 2,496 square feet
Second Floor: 958 square feet
Total: 3,454 square feet

● This impressive English adaptation allows complete one-story convenience with additional sleeping and study space on a second floor. Note the large living areas: family room with raised-hearth fireplace and beamed ceiling, L-shaped living/dining room area with bay window — all arranged around the kitchen and breakfast room. Three first-floor bedrooms have access to two full baths while an entry hall powder room serves guests nicely. The large three-car garage provides a service entrance to the laundry.

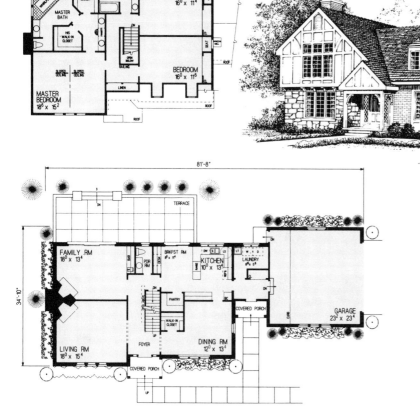

Design N3335

First Floor: 1,504 square feet
Second Floor: 1,348 square feet
Total: 2,852 square feet

L

● This is a first-rate Tudor with three bedrooms upstairs and casual and formal living downstairs. Corner fireplaces in the family room and living room will be favorite gathering spots. From the efficient U-shaped kitchen move to a convenient service area and two-car garage.

Design N3354

First Floor: 3,556 square feet
Second Floor: 684 square feet
Total: 4,240 square feet

L **D**

● This 1½-story Tudor design makes the most of living spaces on its first floor. There are formal living and dining rooms, a media room with built-ins, and a large country kitchen for informal gatherings. The master suite is enhanced with its own exercise room. Upstairs are two family bedrooms which will serve nicely as guest rooms if needed.

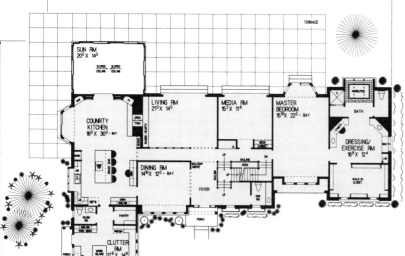

Design N3381

First Floor: 2,485 square feet
Second Floor: 1,864 square feet
Total: 4,349 square feet

L **D**

● A place for everything and everything in its place. If that's your motto, this is your house. A central foyer allows access to every part of the home. To the left sits the spacious gathering room with fireplace and music alcove. Straight ahead, the open living and dining rooms offer sweeping views of the back yard. The modern kitchen and conversation area are situated to the right of the home. Near the entrance, a library with bay window and built-in bookcase is found. Look for extra amenities throughout the home: curio cabinets in the foyer, stairwell, conversation area and hall; built-in desk; walk-in closet and a second fireplace. Upstairs, the master suite features an enormous walk-in closet and a pampering bath. Another bedroom has a private bath, while the remaining two bedrooms share a bath with dual lavs.

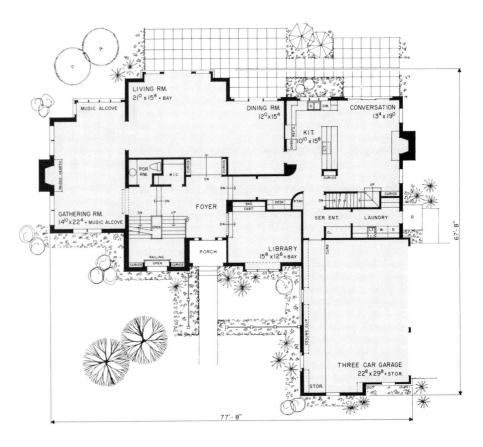

CUSTOMIZABLE

Custom Alterations? See page 349 for customizing this plan to your specifications.

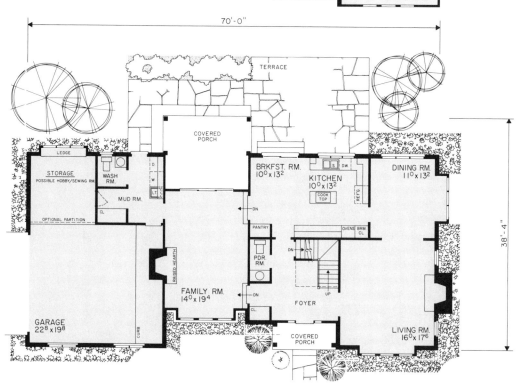

Design N2855

First Floor: 1,372 square feet
Second Floor: 1,245 square feet
Total: 2,617 square feet

L **D**

● This elegant Tudor house is perfect for the family who wants to move-up in living area, style and luxury. As you enter this home you will find a large living room with a fire-place on your right. Adja-cent, the formal dining room has easy access to both the living room and the kitchen. The kitchen/breakfast room has an open plan and access to the rear terrace. Sunken a few steps, the spacious family room is highlighted with a fireplace and access to the rear, covered porch. Note the optional planning of the garage storage area. Plan this area according to the needs of your family. Upstairs, your family will enjoy three bedrooms and a full bath, along with a spacious master bedroom suite. Truly a house that will bring many years of pleasure to your family.

Design N3558

First Floor: 2,328 square feet
Second Floor: 603 square feet
Total: 2,931 square feet

L **D**

● This home will keep even the most active family from feeling cramped. A broad foyer opens to a living room that measures 24 feet across and features sliding glass doors to a rear terrace and a covered porch. Adjacent to the kitchen is a conversation area with additional access to the covered porch, a snack bar, fireplace and a window bay. A butler's pantry leads to the formal dining room. Placed conveniently on the first floor, the master suite features a roomy bath with a huge walk-in closet and dual vanities. Two large bedrooms are found on the second floor.

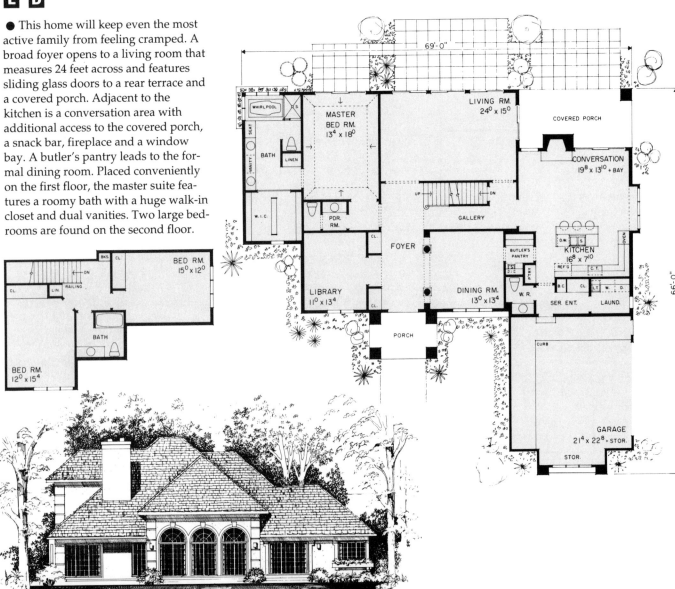

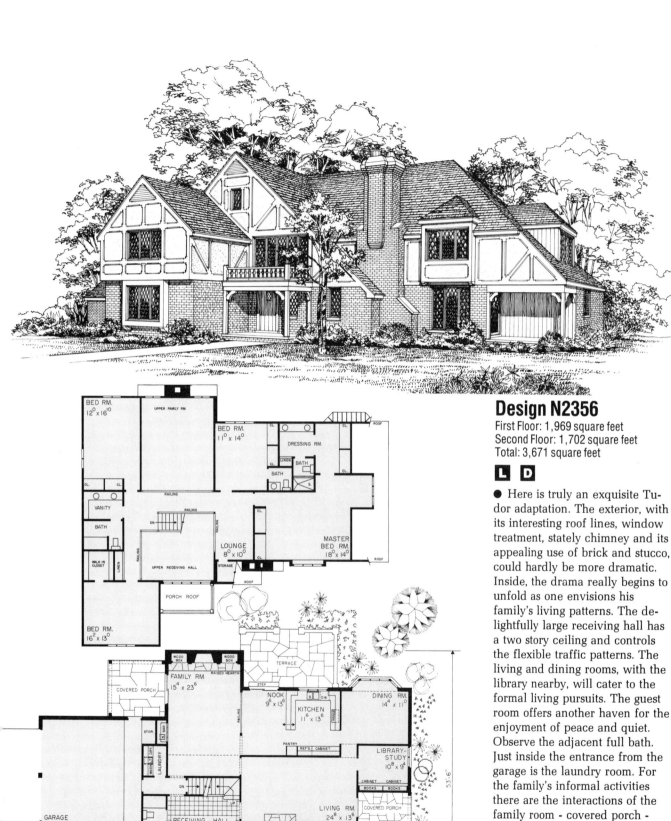

Design N2356

First Floor: 1,969 square feet
Second Floor: 1,702 square feet
Total: 3,671 square feet

L **D**

● Here is truly an exquisite Tudor adaptation. The exterior, with its interesting roof lines, window treatment, stately chimney and its appealing use of brick and stucco, could hardly be more dramatic. Inside, the drama really begins to unfold as one envisions his family's living patterns. The delightfully large receiving hall has a two story ceiling and controls the flexible traffic patterns. The living and dining rooms, with the library nearby, will cater to the formal living pursuits. The guest room offers another haven for the enjoyment of peace and quiet. Observe the adjacent full bath. Just inside the entrance from the garage is the laundry room. For the family's informal activities there are the interactions of the family room - covered porch - nook - kitchen zone. Notice the raised hearth fireplace, the wood boxes, the sliding glass doors, built-in bar and the kitchen pass-thru. Adding to the charm of the family room is its high ceiling. From the second floor hall one can look down and observe the activities below.

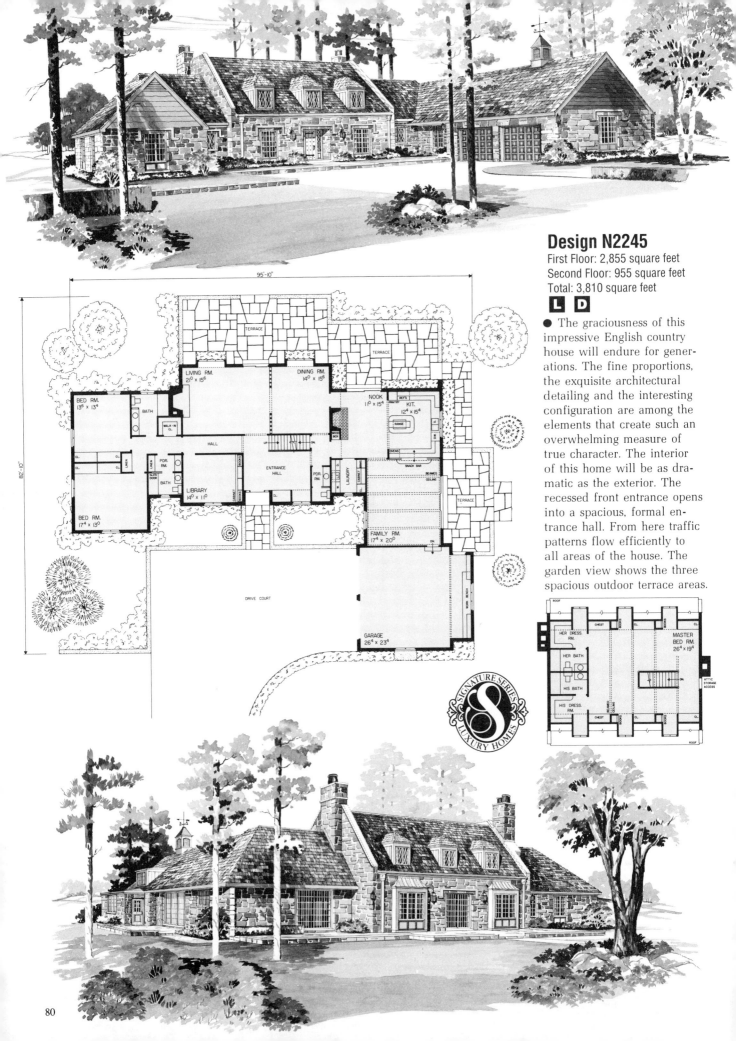

Design N2245

First Floor: 2,855 square feet
Second Floor: 955 square feet
Total: 3,810 square feet

L **D**

● The graciousness of this impressive English country house will endure for generations. The fine proportions, the exquisite architectural detailing and the interesting configuration are among the elements that create such an overwhelming measure of true character. The interior of this home will be as dramatic as the exterior. The recessed front entrance opens into a spacious, formal entrance hall. From here traffic patterns flow efficiently to all areas of the house. The garden view shows the three spacious outdoor terrace areas.

Design N1787

First Floor: 2,656 square feet
Second Floor: 744 square feet
Total: 3,400 square feet

● Can't you picture this dramatic home sitting on your property? The curving front drive is impressive as it passes the walks to the front door and the service entrance. The roof masses, the centered masonry chimney, the window symmetry and the 108 foot expanse across the front are among the features that make this a distinctive home. Of interest are the living and family rooms — both similar in size and each having its own fireplace.

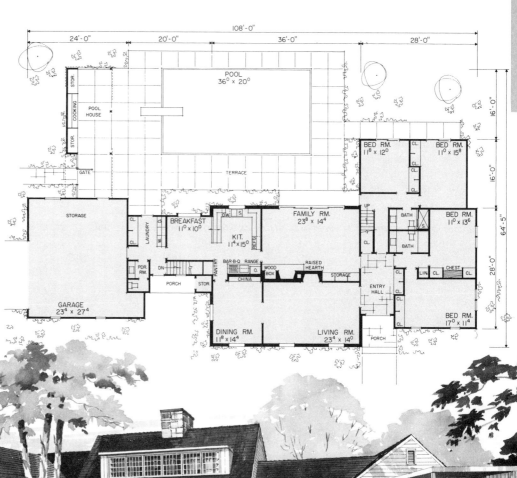

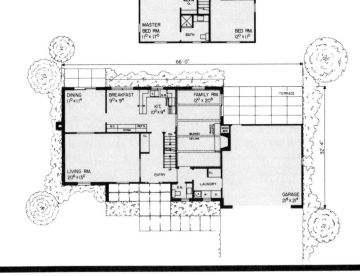

Design N1285

First Floor: 1,202 square feet
Second Floor: 896 square feet
Total: 2,098 square feet

L **D**

● Such a pretty traditional farmhouse design — and with so much to offer in the way of floor planning. From the front entry, turn left into a good-sized living room with attached dining room. A right turn leads to a well-placed powder room and laundry or farther back to the beamed-ceiling family room (note the fireplace with wood box here). The kitchen and adjacent breakfast room will make mealtimes a pleasure. Upstairs, four bedrooms share space with two baths.

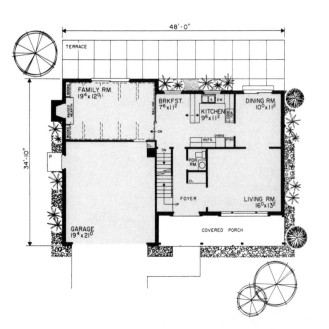

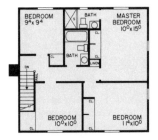

OPTIONAL 3-BEDROOM PLAN

Design N1956

First Floor: 990 square feet
Second Floor: 728 square feet
Total: 1,718 square feet

D

● The blueprints for this home include details for both the three-bedroom and the four-bedroom options. The first-floor livability does not change.

CUSTOMIZABLE

Custom Alterations? See page 349 for customizing this plan to your specifications.

Design N2540 First Floor: 1,306 square feet
Second Floor: 1,360 square feet; Total: 2,666 square feet

L **D**

● This efficient Colonial abounds in features. A spacious entry flanked by living areas. A kitchen flanked by eating areas. Upstairs, four bedrooms including a sitting room in the master suite.

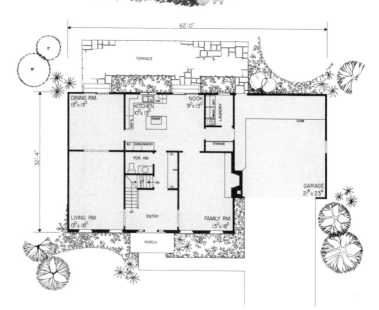

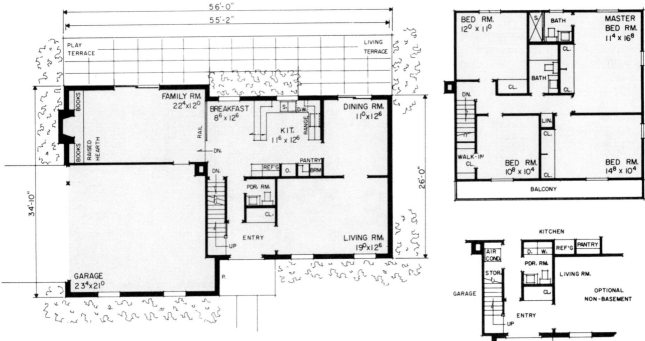

PLAY TERRACE

LIVING TERRACE

FAMILY RM.
22⁴ x 12⁰

BREAKFAST
8⁶ x 12⁶

KIT.
11⁶ x 12⁶

DINING RM.
11⁰ x 12⁶

RAISED HEARTH

BOOKS

DN.

DN.

PANTRY

REF'G

O.

BRM.

PDR. RM.

CL.

ENTRY

UP

LIVING RM.
19⁰ x 12⁶

GARAGE
23⁴ x 21⁰

56'-0"

55'-2"

34'-10"

26'-0"

BED RM.
12⁰ x 11⁰

MASTER
BED RM.
11⁴ x 16⁸

BATH

CL.

DN.

BATH

CL.

CL.

LIN.

CL.

WALK-IN
CL.

BED RM.
10⁸ x 10⁴

CL.

BED RM.
14⁸ x 10⁴

BALCONY

KITCHEN

D.

W.

REF'G

PANTRY

AIR
COND.

STOR.

PDR. RM.

LIVING RM.

GARAGE

CL.

OPTIONAL
NON-BASEMENT

ENTRY

UP

Design N1371 First Floor: 1,172 square feet; Second Floor: 896 square feet; Total: 2,068 square feet

L **D**

● If you like traditional charm and the tried and true living patterns of the conventional two-story idea, you'll not go wrong in selecting this design as your next home. In fact, when you order blueprints for N1371 you'll receive details for building all three optional elevations. So, you needn't decide which front exterior is your favorite right now. Any one of these will surely add a touch of class to your new neighborhood.

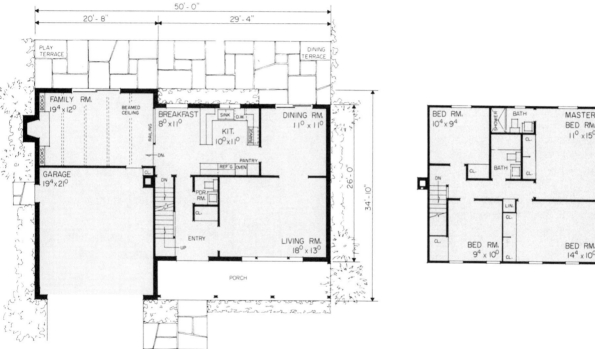

Design N1957 First Floor: 1,042 square feet; Second Floor: 780 square feet; Total: 1,822 square feet

L **D**

● When you order your blueprints for this design you will receive details for the construction of each of the three charming exteriors pictured above. Whichever the exterior you finally decide to build, the floor plan will be essentially the same except the location of the windows. This will be a fine home for the growing family. It will serve well for many years. There are four bedrooms and two full baths (one with a stall shower) upstairs.

Design N3444

First Floor: 1,453 square feet
Second Floor: 520 square feet
Total: 1,973 square feet

L **D**

● This compact plan offers full-scale livability on two floors. The first floor begins with an elegant living room—a bay window here allows for an infiltration of natural light. The dining room remains open to this room and will delight with its spaciousness. The kitchen is just beyond and extends room enough for a dinette set. Comfortable gatherings are the name of the game in the family room which enjoys shared space with the kitchen area. A warming fireplace gains attention here as do a pair of graceful windows that flank it. Also on the first floor, the master bedroom expands into a spacious and luxurious bathroom. A garden tub set below a window is sure to satisfy as is a large walk-in closet. For family and guests, two upstairs bedrooms are situated around a Hollywood bath.

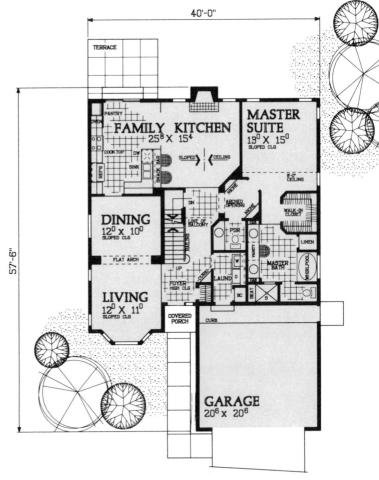

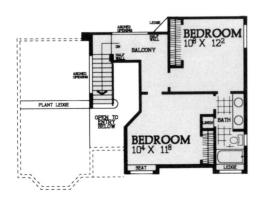

CUSTOMIZABLE

Custom Alterations? See page 349 for customizing this plan to your specifications.

Design N3484

First Floor: 1,139 square feet
Second Floor: 948 square feet
Total: 2,087 square feet

L **D**

● An angled entry offers a new perspective on the formal areas of this house: living room on the left; dining room on the right. Both rooms exchange views through a columned hallway; a potshelf and a niche add custom touches to this already attention-getting arrangement. At the back of the first floor, a family room with built-in bookshelves and an entertainment-center niche opens to the kitchen and nook where both cooking and dining become a delight. The second floor provides interest with its balcony open to the living and family rooms. Three bedrooms include a master suite with a sloped ceiling, separate closets and a private bath. The two-car garage has direct access to the house.

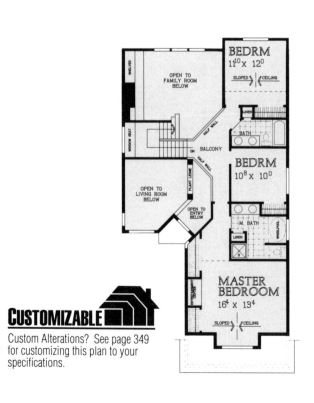

CUSTOMIZABLE
Custom Alterations? See page 349 for customizing this plan to your specifications.

Design N3479

First Floor: 914 square feet
Second Floor: 1,050 square feet
Total: 1,964 square feet

L **D**

● This four-bedroom family home has a distinctive interior design. The gathering room features two bay windows, a sloped ceiling, a fireplace and a built-in entertainment center. A low wall separates the gathering room from the formal dining area. A rear terrace can be accessed from sliding glass doors here. Informal meals may take place in the bay-windowed breakfast nook. The kitchen includes a snack bar, a built-in planning desk and a walk-in pantry. The sleeping area is located quietly on the second floor. The master bedroom is highlighted by a sloped ceiling and includes two closets and a deluxe master bath with dual vanities and a whirlpool tub.

CUSTOMIZABLE

Custom Alterations? See page 349 for customizing this plan to your specifications.

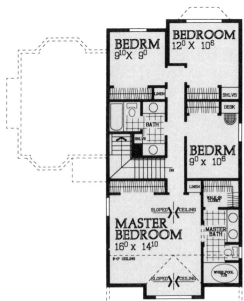

Design N3445

First Floor: 1,147 square feet
Second Floor: 1,116 square feet
Total: 2,263 square feet

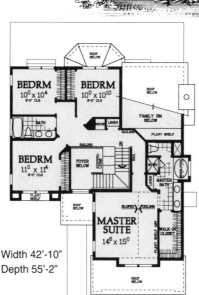

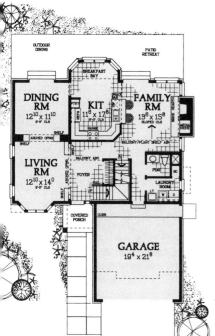

Width 42'-10"
Depth 55'-2"

● A two-story foyer opens to a formal living room with a front-facing bay window. Traffic flows easily to the adjacent dining room. The U-shaped kitchen opens to a sunny breakfast nook. It also enjoys the convenience of two Lazy Susans. Informal activities take place in the spacious family room with fireplace. A powder room and utility area are conveniently located on the first floor. On the second floor, the master bedroom features a sloped ceiling and a bath with tub and shower. Three family bedrooms share a full bath with dual vanities.

CUSTOMIZABLE
Custom Alterations? See page 349 for customizing this plan to your specifications.

CUSTOMIZABLE
Custom Alterations? See page 349 for customizing this plan to your specifications.

Width 42'-8"
Depth 62'

Design N3495

First Floor: 1,457 square feet
Second Floor: 1,288 square feet
Total: 2,745 square feet

● The very best in modern design comes into play with this extraordinary two-story home. Columns and half walls define the formal living and dining rooms—a curved niche adds appeal to the latter. The family room contains a sloped ceiling and angled corner fireplace. In the kitchen is an abundance of counter and storage space. Two full bathrooms grace the upstairs: one in the master suite and one that serves three secondary bedrooms.

Design N2599

First Floor: 2,075 square feet
Second Floor: 1,398 square feet
Total: 3,473 square feet

● This traditional two-story with its projecting one-story wings is delightfully proportional. The symmetrical window treatment is most appealing. Inside, there is a large foyer with curving, open staircase to the second floor. Besides a formal living room and dining room, there are a formal study and upstairs sitting room. The second floor also offers a three- or four-bedroom sleeping area. The master suite has a large dressing area with plenty of closet space.

Design N2927

First Floor: 1,425 square feet
Second Floor: 704 square feet
Total: 2,129 square feet

CUSTOMIZABLE

Custom Alterations? See page 349 for customizing this plan to your specifications.

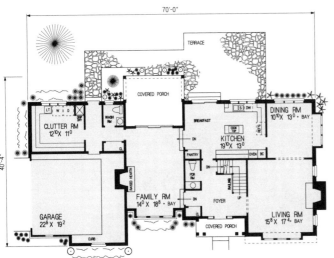

Design N3356

First Floor: 1,610 square feet
Second Floor: 1,200 square feet
Total: 2,810 square feet

L **D**

● Traditionally speaking, this home takes blue ribbons. Its family room has a raised-hearth fireplace and there's a covered porch reached through sliding glass doors for informal eating. The living room also has a fireplace and is near the boxed-windowed dining room. A clutter room off the garage could be turned into a hobby or sewing room. Three bedrooms on the second floor include a master suite with His and Hers walk-in closets and three family bedrooms.

Design N3370

First Floor: 2,055 square feet
Second Floor: 1,288 square feet
Total: 3,343 square feet

L **D**

● The combination of stone and brick allow an impressive facade on this traditional two-story. The symmetrically designed interior will provide efficient traffic patterns. Note the formal living and dining areas to the right and huge family room to the rear. The U-shaped kitchen has an attached breakfast room and built-ins. There are four bedrooms on the second floor. The master features a walk-in closet, double vanity and whirlpool tub.

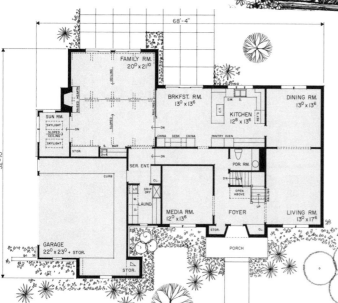

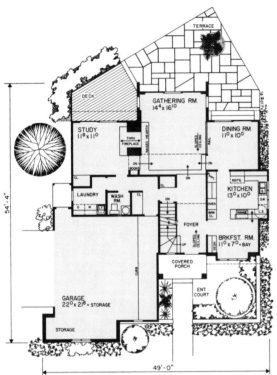

Design N2826 First Floor: 1,112 square feet
Second Floor: 881 square feet; Total: 1,993 square feet

D

ALTERNATE KITCHEN / DINING RM. /
BREAKFAST RM. FLOOR PLAN

● This is an outstanding example of the type of informal, traditional-style architecture that has captured the modern imagination. The interior plan houses all of the features that people want most - a spacious gathering room, formal and informal dining areas, efficient, U-shaped kitchen, master bedroom, two children's bedrooms, second floor lounge, entrance court and rear terrace and deck. Study all areas of this plan carefully.

CUSTOMIZABLE

Custom Alterations? See page 349 for customizing this plan to your specifications.

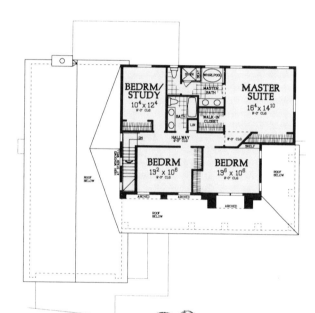

Design N3326

First Floor: 1,595 square feet
Second Floor: 1,112 square feet
Total: 2,707 square feet

● This four-bedroom family plan makes the grade with defining exterior details that create a Southwestern charmer. The floor plan opens with a foyer that introduces a grand living room. In the U-shaped kitchen, a central island facilitates cooking ease. A pass-through snack bar connects the kitchen and breakfast room. Nearby, the family room delights with its warming hearth and access to an entertainment patio. A large utility area sits near the garage. Upstairs, the master bedroom suite includes two closets and a private bath with a garden tub and dual lavatories.

CUSTOMIZABLE

Custom Alterations? See page 349 for customizing this plan to your specifications.

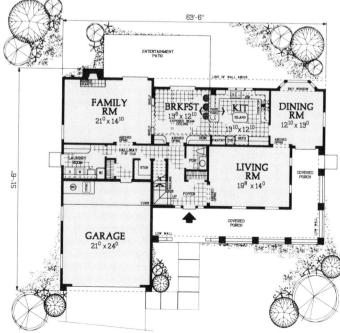

Design N3476

First Floor: 1,170 square feet
Second Floor: 838 square feet
Total: 2,008 square feet

● A vaulted ceiling in the living room and a centered fire-place in the family room set the stage for the formal and casual areas of this home. A hub kitchen boasts a round counter for serving both the family room and the breakfast area; a pantry in this area offers plenty of storage space. The utility room, separating the main-floor living areas from the garage, acquires both light and views from a side window. Three bedrooms—all with ample closet space, including a walk-in closet in the master suite—define the second-floor sleeping quarters. A full hall bath with a double-bowl vanity services two of the bedrooms—the master bedroom utilizes its own bath.

CUSTOMIZABLE

Custom Alterations? See page 349 for customizing this plan to your specifications.

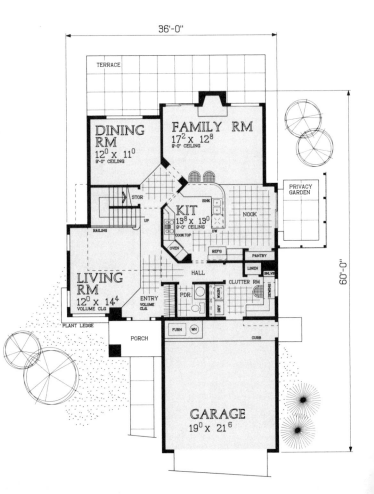

Design N3330

First Floor: 1,394 square feet
Second Floor: 320 square feet
Total: 1,714 square feet

● Outdoor living and open floor planning are highlights of this moderately sized plan. Amenities include a private hot tub on a wooden deck that is accessible via sliding glass doors in both bedrooms, and a two-story gathering room. An optional second-floor plan allows for a full 503 square feet of space with a balcony.

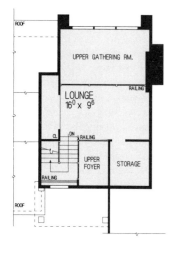

Design N3471

First Floor: 3,166 square feet
Second Floor: 950 square feet
Guest Living Area: 680
Total: 4,796 square feet

L

● Western farmhouse-style living is captured in this handsome design. The central entrance leads into a cozy parlor—half walls provide a view of the grand dining room. Entertaining's a cinch with the dining room's built-in china alcove, service counter and fireplace. The country kitchen, with a large island cooktop, overlooks the gathering room with its full wall of glass. The master bedroom will satisfy even the most discerning tastes. It boasts a raised hearth, porch access and a bath with a walk-in closet, separate vanities and a whirlpool. You may want to use one of the additional first-floor bedrooms as a study, the other as a guest room. To round out the first floor, you'll also find a clutter room with a pantry, freezer space and access to storage space. Two family bedrooms and attic storage make up the second floor. Note, too, the separate garage and guest house which make this such a winning design.

WIDTH 154'
DEPTH 94'-8"

FAMILY RM BELOW

RAILING

BALCONY

BATH

LINEN

RAILING

MECH AC

OPEN TO FIRE PIT

CL

CL

LEDGE

OPEN TO FOYER

BEDROOM 13 X 11 • BAY

BEDROOM 13 X 11 • BAY

Design N3404

First Floor: 3,358 square feet
Second Floor: 868 square feet
Total: 4,226 square feet

L **D**

● Farmhouse design does a double take in this unusual and elegant rendition. Notice that most of the living takes place on the first floor: formal living room and dining room, gigantic family room with enormous firepit and porch access, guest bedroom or den and master bedroom suite. Upstairs there are two smaller bedrooms and a dramatic balcony overlook to the family room below.

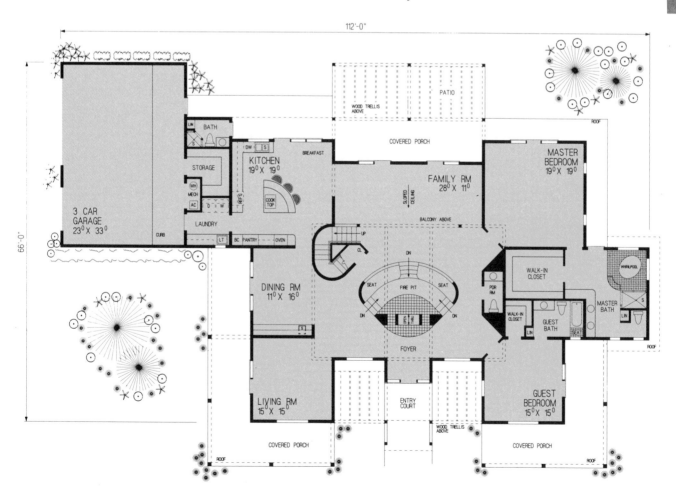

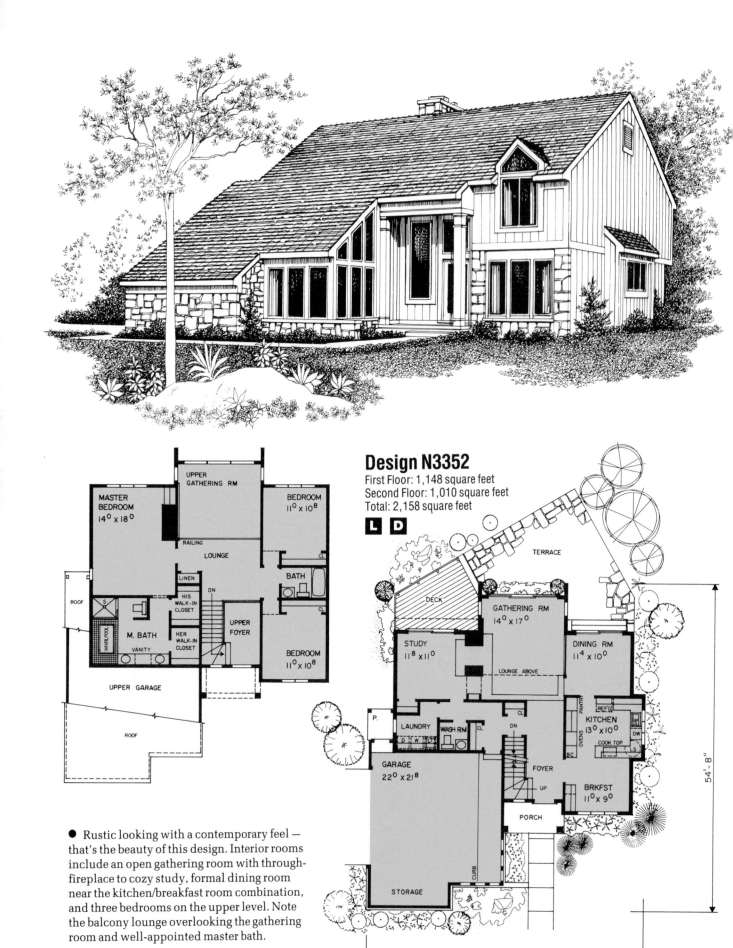

Design N3352

First Floor: 1,148 square feet
Second Floor: 1,010 square feet
Total: 2,158 square feet

L **D**

UPPER GATHERING RM

MASTER BEDROOM
14⁰ x 18⁰

BEDROOM
11⁰ x 10⁸

LOUNGE

RAILING

CL

BATH

ROOF

LINEN

DN

HIS WALK-IN CLOSET

M. BATH

WHIRLPOOL

HER WALK-IN CLOSET

UPPER FOYER

S

VANITY

CL

BEDROOM
11⁰ x 10⁸

UPPER GARAGE

ROOF

TERRACE

DECK

GATHERING RM
14⁰ x 17⁰

STUDY
11⁸ x 11⁰

DINING RM
11⁴ x 10⁰

LOUNGE ABOVE

PANTRY

REF'G

KITCHEN
13⁰ x 10⁰

P.

CL

LAUNDRY

WASH RM

CL

DN

OVENS

DW

COOK TOP

LS

D W

BC

GARAGE
22⁰ x 21⁸

FOYER

UP

BRKFST
11⁰ x 9⁰

PORCH

STORAGE

CURB

54' - 8"

47' - 0"

● Rustic looking with a contemporary feel — that's the beauty of this design. Interior rooms include an open gathering room with through-fireplace to cozy study, formal dining room near the kitchen/breakfast room combination, and three bedrooms on the upper level. Note the balcony lounge overlooking the gathering room and well-appointed master bath.

Design N3563

First Floor: 1,023 square feet
Second Floor: 866 square feet
Total: 1,889 square feet

L **D**

● Practical to build, this wonderful transitional plan combines the best of contemporary and traditional styling. Its stucco exterior is enhanced by arched windows and a recessed arched entry plus a lovely balcony off the second-floor master bedroom. A walled entry court extends the living room to the outside. The double front doors open to a foyer with a hall closet and a powder room. The service entrance is just to the right and accesses the two-car garage. The large living room adjoins directly to the dining room. The family room is set off behind the garage and features a sloped ceiling and a fireplace. Sleeping quarters consist of two secondary bedrooms with a shared bath and a generous master suite with a well-appointed bath.

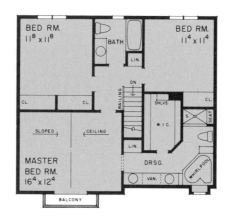

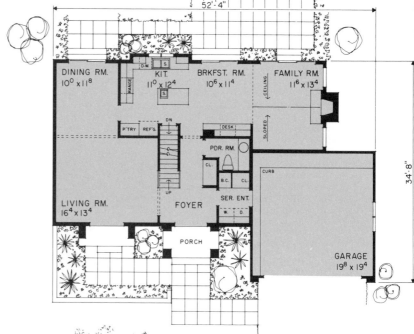

Design N2905

First Floor: 1,342 square feet
Second Floor: 619 square feet
Total: 1,961 square feet

L **D**

● All of the livability in this plan is in the back! Each first-floor room, except the kitchen, has access to the rear terrace via sliding glass doors — a great way to capture an excellent view. This plan is also ideal for a narrow lot because its width is less than 50 feet. Two bedrooms and a lounge, overlooking the gathering room, are on the second floor.

Design N2562

First Floor: 2,459 square feet
Second Floor: 1,107 square feet
Lower Level: 851 square feet
Total: 4,417 square feet

D

● Here is an exciting contemporary design for the large, active family. It can function as either a four- or five-bedroom home. As a four-bedroom home the parents will enjoy a wonderful suite with study and exceptional bath facilities. Note stall shower, plus sunken tub. The upstairs features the children's bedrooms and a spacious balcony lounge which looks down to the floor below. The sunken gathering room has a sloped, beamed ceiling, dramatic raised-hearth fireplace and direct access to the rear terrace.

Design N3409

First Floor: 1,481 square feet
Second Floor: 1,287 square feet
Total: 2,768 square feet

L

● Glass block walls and a foyer with barrel vaulted ceiling create an interesting exterior. Covered porches to the front and rear provide for excellent indoor/outdoor living relationships. Inside, a large planter and through-fireplace enhance the living room and family room. The dining room has a stepped ceiling. A desk, eating area and snack bar are special features in the kitchen. The master suite features a large walk-in closet, bath with double bowl vanity and separate tub and shower, and a private deck. Three additional bedrooms share a full bath.

Design N3338

First Floor: 1,314 square feet

Second Floor: 970 square feet

Total: 2,284 square feet

L

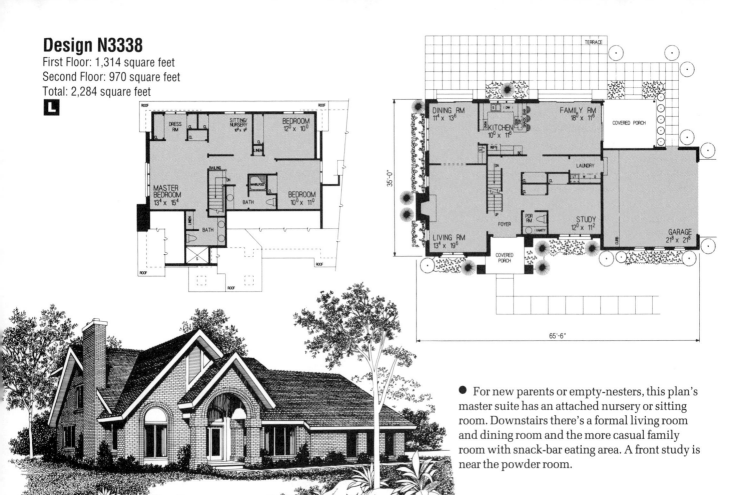

● For new parents or empty-nesters, this plan's master suite has an attached nursery or sitting room. Downstairs there's a formal living room and dining room and the more casual family room with snack-bar eating area. A front study is near the powder room.

Design N3347

First Floor: 1,915 square feet

Second Floor: 759 square feet; Total: 2,674 square feet

L

● Open living is the key to the abundant livability of this design. The gigantic gathering room/dining room area shares a through-fireplace with a unique sunken conversation area. An L-shaped kitchen has a pass-through snack bar to the breakfast room. On the second floor, two bedrooms are separated by a lounge with a balcony overlook.

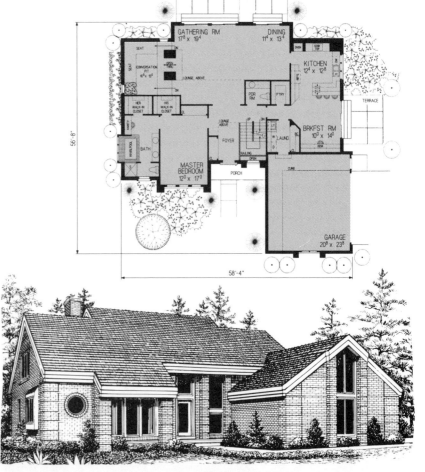

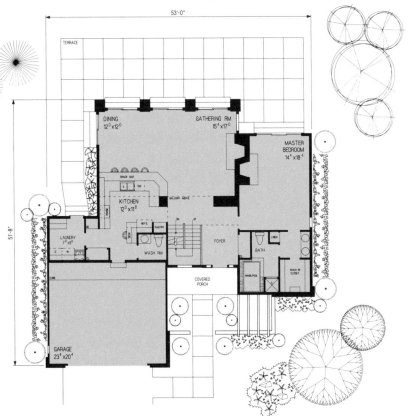

53'-0"

TERRACE

DINING
12⁰x12⁰

GATHERING RM
15⁴x17⁰

MASTER
BEDROOM
14⁴x18⁴

SNACK BAR

BALCONY ABOVE

KITCHEN
12⁰x11⁸

51'-8"

PANTRY

REF'G

WASH RM

LAUNDRY
7⁵x8⁵

FOYER

LINEN

BATH

WALK-IN
CLOSET

WHIRLPOOL

COVERED
PORCH

GARAGE
23⁴x20⁴

Design N2490
First Floor: 1,414 square feet
Second Floor: 620 square feet
Total: 2,034 square feet

● Split-bedroom planning makes the most of this contemporary plan. The master suite pampers with a lavish bath and a fireplace. The living areas are open and have easy access to the rear terrace.

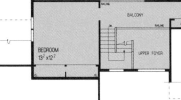

CUSTOMIZABLE
Custom Alterations? See page 349 for customizing this plan to your specifications.

UPPER DINING

UPPER GATHERING RM.

BALCONY

BEDROOM
11⁰x11⁸

BALCONY

RAILING

RAILING

BATH

LINEN

BEDROOM
13²x12²

UPPER FOYER

ROOF

ROOF

ROOF

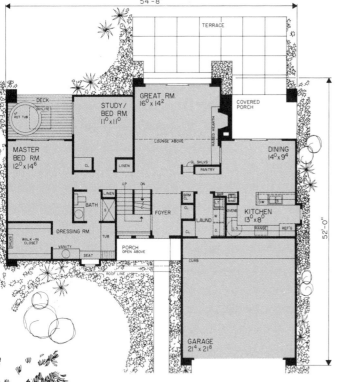

TERRACE

GREAT RM.
16⁰ x 14²

COVERED PORCH

STUDY / BED RM.
11⁰ x 11⁰

DECK
SKYLITE

HOT TUB

LOUNGE ABOVE

RAISED HEARTH

MASTER BED RM.
12⁰ x 14⁶

CL

LINEN

G. SHLVS

PANTRY

DINING
14⁰ x 9⁴

BATH

LINEN

UP DN

FOYER

RM CL

BAR

DW

KITCHEN
13⁵ x 8⁰

DRESSING RM.

TUB

CL

LAUND
W OVEN
D L.S.
RANGE REF'G

WALK-IN CLOSET

VANITY

SEAT

PORCH
OPEN ABOVE

CURB

ROOF LINE

GARAGE
21⁴ x 21⁸

54'-8"

52'-0"

UPPER GREAT RM.

RAILING

CL

LOUNGE / HOBBIES
16⁰ x 9²

SKYLITE

CL

DN

RAILING

UPPER FOYER

STOR / BATH

RAILING

Design N2822

First Floor: 1,363 square feet
Second Floor: 351 square feet
Total: 1,714 square feet

L

● Here is a truly unique house whose interior was designed with the current decade's economies, lifestyles and demographics in mind. While functioning as a one-story home, the second floor provides an extra measure of livability when required. In addition, this two-story section adds to the dramatic appeal of both the exterior and the interior. Within only 1,363 square feet, this contemporary delivers refreshing and outstanding living patterns for those who are buying their first home, those who have raised their family and are looking for a smaller home and those in search of a retirement home.

BALCONY

LOUNGE / GUEST RM. / GRANDCHILDREN'S RM.
16⁰ x 19²

CL

CL

DN

RAILING

UPPER FOYER

BATH

RAILING

ALTERNATE SECOND FLOOR

Design N3562

First Floor: 1,182 square feet
Second Floor: 927 square feet
Total: 2,109 square feet

L **D**

● Interesting detailing marks the exterior of this home as a beauty. Its interior makes it a livable option for any family. Entry occurs through double doors to the left side of the plan. A powder room with curved wall is handy to the entry. Living areas of the home are open and well-planned. The formal living room shares a through fireplace with the large family room. The dining room is adjoining and has a pass-through counter to the L-shaped kitchen. Special details on this floor include a wealth of sliding glass doors to the rear terrace and built-ins throughout. Upstairs are three bedrooms with two full baths.

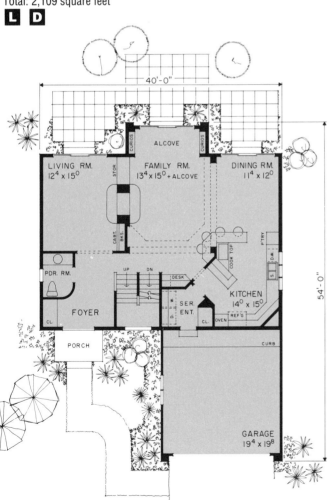

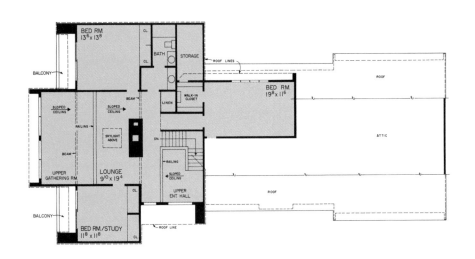

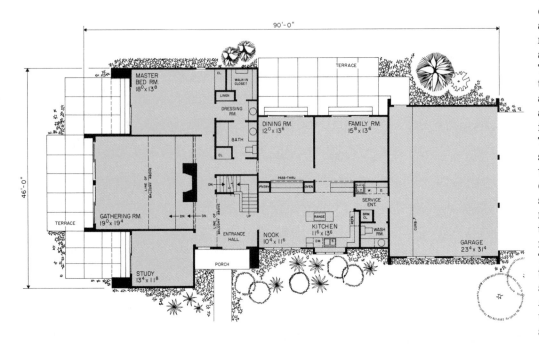

Design N2781

First Floor: 2,132 square feet
Second Floor: 1,156 square feet
Total: 3,288 square feet

L **D**

● This beautifully designed two-story has an eye-catching exterior. The floor plan is a perfect complement. The front kitchen features an island range, adjacent breakfast nook and pass-through to a formal dining room. The master bedroom suite has a spacious walk-in closet and dressing room. The side terrace can be reached from the master suite, the gathering room and the study. The second floor has three bedrooms and storage space galore. Also notice the lounge with sloped ceiling and skylight.

Design N3439
First Floor: 1,424 square feet
Second Floor: 995 square feet
Total: 2,419 square feet
L

● Featuring a facade of wood and window glass, this home presents a striking first impression. Its floor plan is equally as splendid. Formal living and dining areas flank the entry foyer—both are sunken two steps down. Also sunken from the foyer is the family room with attached break-fast nook. A fireplace in this area sits adjacent to a built-in audiovisual center. A nearby study with adjacent full bath doubles as a guest room. Upstairs are three bedrooms including a master suite with whirlpool spa and walk-in closet. Plant shelves adorn the entire floor plan.

CUSTOMIZABLE

Custom Alterations? See page 349 for customizing this plan to your specifications.

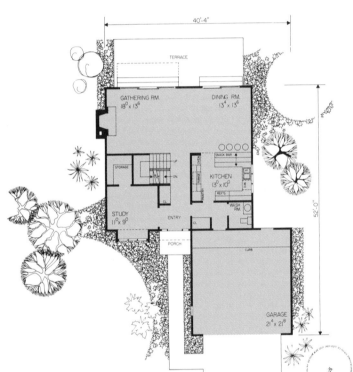

Design N2711 First Floor: 975 square feet
Second Floor: 1,024 square feet; Total: 1,999 square feet

L D

● Special features! A complete master suite with a private balcony plus two more bedrooms and a bath upstairs. The first floor has a study with a storage closet. A convenient snack bar between kitchen and dining room. The kitchen offers many built-in appliances. Plus a gathering room and dining room that measures 31 feet wide. Note the curb area in the garage and fireplace in gathering room.

CUSTOMIZABLE

Custom Alterations? See page 349 for customizing this plan to your specifications.

Design N2925 First Floor: 1,128 square feet; Second Floor: 844 square feet; Total: 1,972 square feet

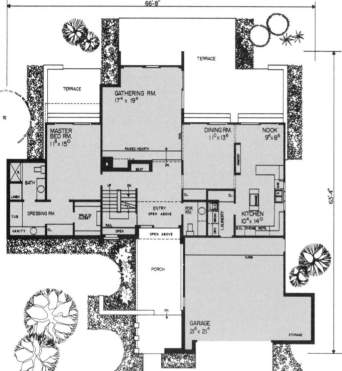

Design N2729 First Floor: 1,590 square feet
Second Floor: 756 square feet; Total: 2,346 square feet

L

● Entering this home will be a pleasure through the sheltered walk-way to the double front doors. And the pleasure and beauty does not stop there. The entry hall and sunken gathering room are open to the upstairs for added dimension. There is fine indoor-outdoor living relationships in this design. Note the private terrace, a living terrace plus the balcony.

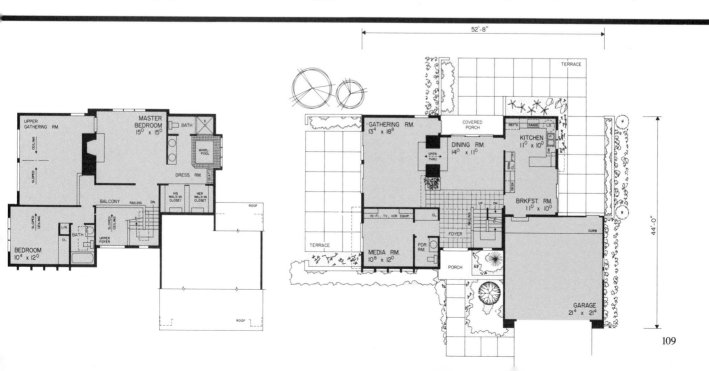

Design N3446

First Floor: 1,532 square feet
Second Floor: 1,200 square feet
Total: 2,732 square feet

L **D**

● A unique facade harbors a spacious, two-story foyer with an angled stairway. To the left is the formal living room with fireplace, and the formal dining room. To the right is a quiet den. The kitchen and breakfast room take advantage of a sunny bay. The family room features a second fireplace and a vaulted ceiling with three skylights. Another fireplace is found in the master bedroom. Secondary bedrooms share a full bath.

Width 60'-4"
Depth 48'-8"

Width 40'-7"
Depth 57'-8"

Design N3456

First Floor: 1,130 square feet
Second Floor: 1,189 square feet
Total: 2,319 square feet

L

● This volume home opens to a wealth of living potential with a media room to the right and formal living and dining rooms to the left. A covered porch, accessed from both the dining and breakfast rooms, adds outdoor dining potential. The kitchen contains a built-in desk and a snack bar pass-through to the breakfast area. Upstairs, four bedrooms include a master suite with balcony and three family bedrooms.

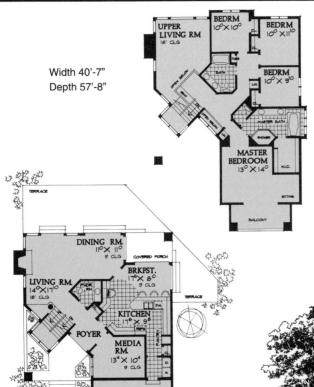

Design N4334

First Floor: 1,838 square feet
Second Floor: 640 square feet
Total: 2,478 square feet

L

● Grand sloping rooflines and a design created for southern orientation are the unique features of this contemporary home. Outdoor living is enhanced by a solar greenhouse off the breakfast room, a sun space off the master bedroom, a greenhouse window in the dining room, a casual breakfast deck, and full-width deck to the rear. The split-bedroom plan allows for the master suite to be situated on the first floor and two family bedrooms and a full bath to find space on the second floor.

LIFESTYLE HOME PLANS

Design N4287

First Floor: 930 square feet
Second Floor: 1,362 square feet
Total: 2,292 square feet

L **D**

LIFESTYLE HOME PLANS

● This contemporary uses windows as a major part of its elegant design. Other special amenities include a convenient U-shaped kitchen, a screened porch and attached deck, and fireplace in the living room. All four bedrooms on the second floor have sloped ceilings.

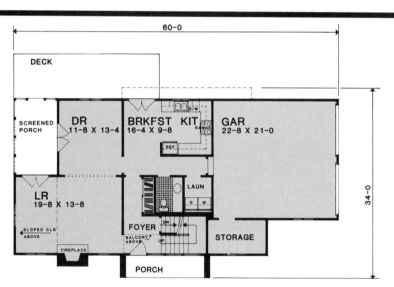

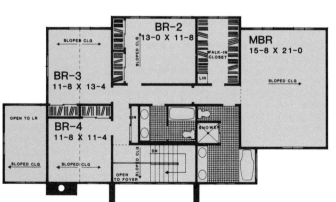

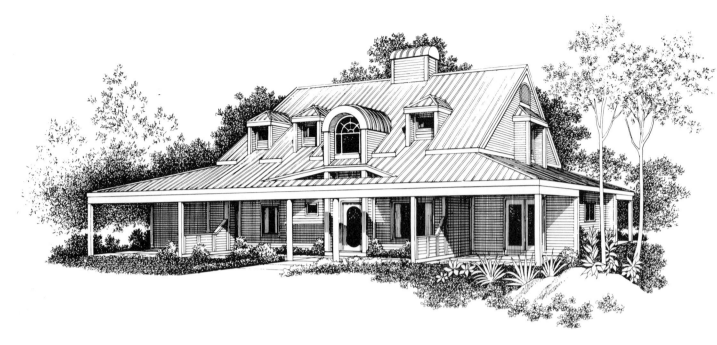

Design N3438

First Floor: 1,489 square feet
Second Floor: 741 square feet
Total: 2,230 square feet

L

● A unique farmhouse plan which provides a grand floor plan, this home is comfortable in country or suburban settings. Formal entertaining areas share first-floor space with family gathering rooms and work and service areas. The master suite is also on this floor for convenience and privacy. Upstairs is a guest bedroom, private bath and loft area that makes a perfect studio. Special features make this a great place to come home to.

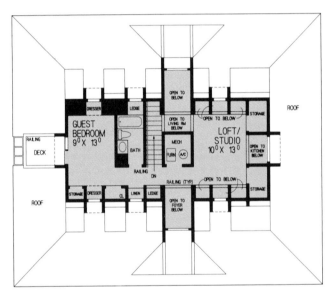

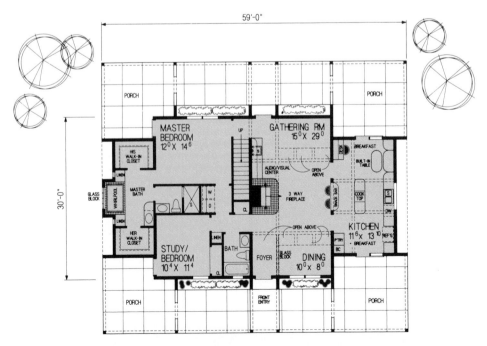

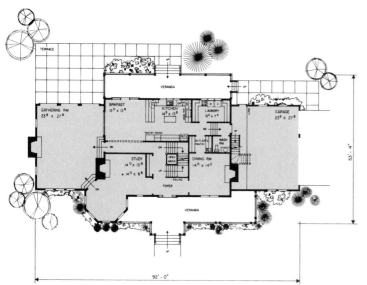

Design N3395

First Floor: 2,248 square feet
Second Floor: 2,020 square feet
Third Floor: 1,117 square feet
Total: 5,385 square feet

L **D**

● This home is a lovely example of classic
Queen Anne architecture. Its floor plan offers:
a gathering room with fireplace, a study with an
octagonal window area, a formal dining room
and a kitchen with attached breakfast room.
Bedrooms on the second floor include three
family bedrooms and a grand master suite. On
the third floor are a guest room with private
bath and sitting room and a game room with
attached library.

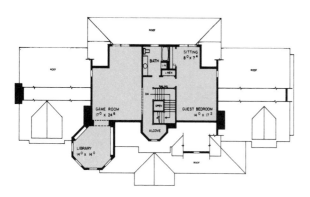

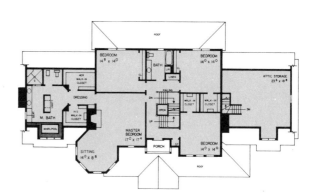

113

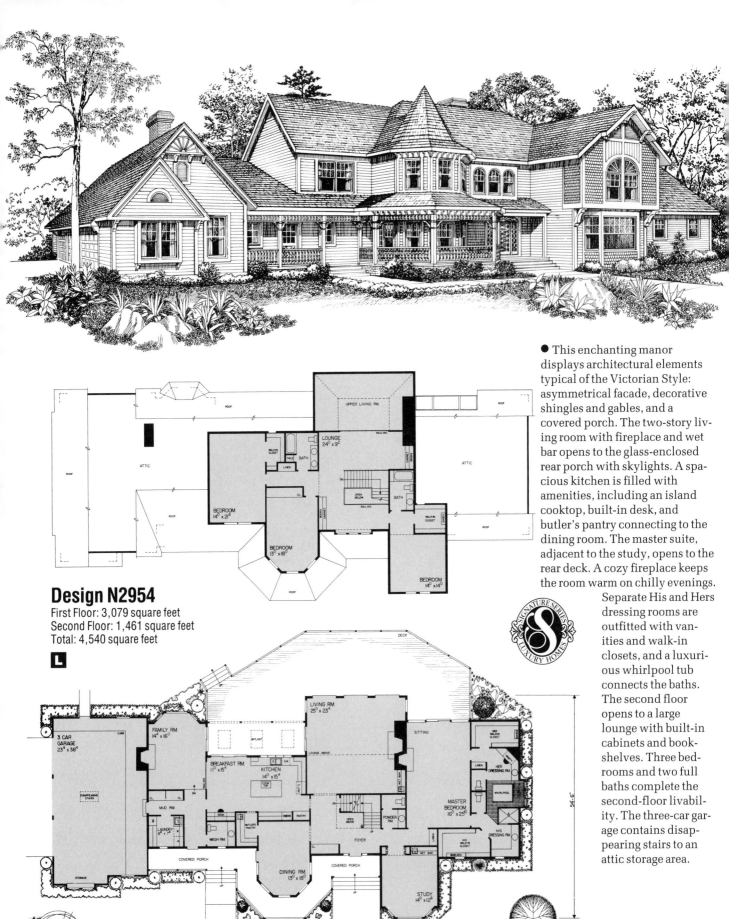

Design N2954

First Floor: 3,079 square feet
Second Floor: 1,461 square feet
Total: 4,540 square feet

L

● This enchanting manor displays architectural elements typical of the Victorian Style: asymmetrical facade, decorative shingles and gables, and a covered porch. The two-story living room with fireplace and wet bar opens to the glass-enclosed rear porch with skylights. A spacious kitchen is filled with amenities, including an island cooktop, built-in desk, and butler's pantry connecting to the dining room. The master suite, adjacent to the study, opens to the rear deck. A cozy fireplace keeps the room warm on chilly evenings.

Separate His and Hers dressing rooms are outfitted with vanities and walk-in closets, and a luxurious whirlpool tub connects the baths. The second floor opens to a large lounge with built-in cabinets and bookshelves. Three bedrooms and two full baths complete the second-floor livability. The three-car garage contains disappearing stairs to an attic storage area.

● A magnificent, finely wrought covered porch wraps around this impressive Victorian estate home. The gracious two-story foyer provides a direct view past the stylish bannister and into the great room with large central fireplace. To the left of the foyer is a bookshelf-lined library and to the right is a dramatic, octagonal-shaped dining room. The island cooktop completes a convenient work triangle in the kitchen, and a pass-through connects this room with the Victorian-style morning room. A butler's pantry, walk-in closet, and broom closet offer plenty of storage space. A luxurious master suite is located on the first floor and opens to the rear covered porch. A through-fireplace warms the bedroom, sitting room, and dressing room, which includes His and Hers walk-in closets. The step-up whirlpool tub is an elegant focal point to the master bath. Four uniquely designed bedrooms, three full baths, and a restful lounge with fireplace are located on the second floor. Who says you can't combine the absolute best of today's amenities with the quaint styling and comfortable warmth of the Victorian past!

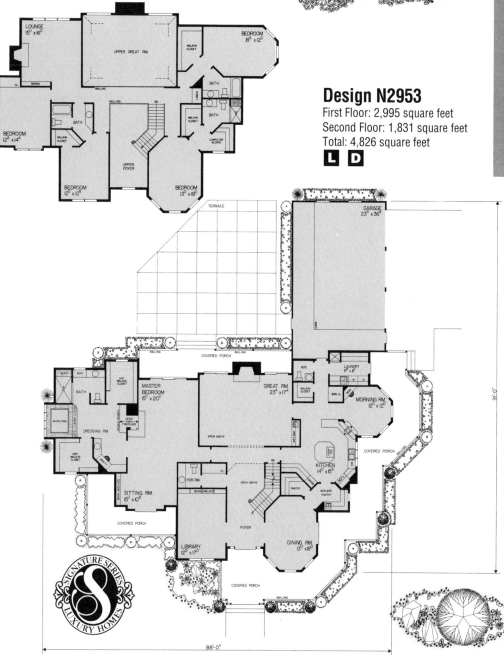

Design N2953

First Floor: 2,995 square feet
Second Floor: 1,831 square feet
Total: 4,826 square feet

L **D**

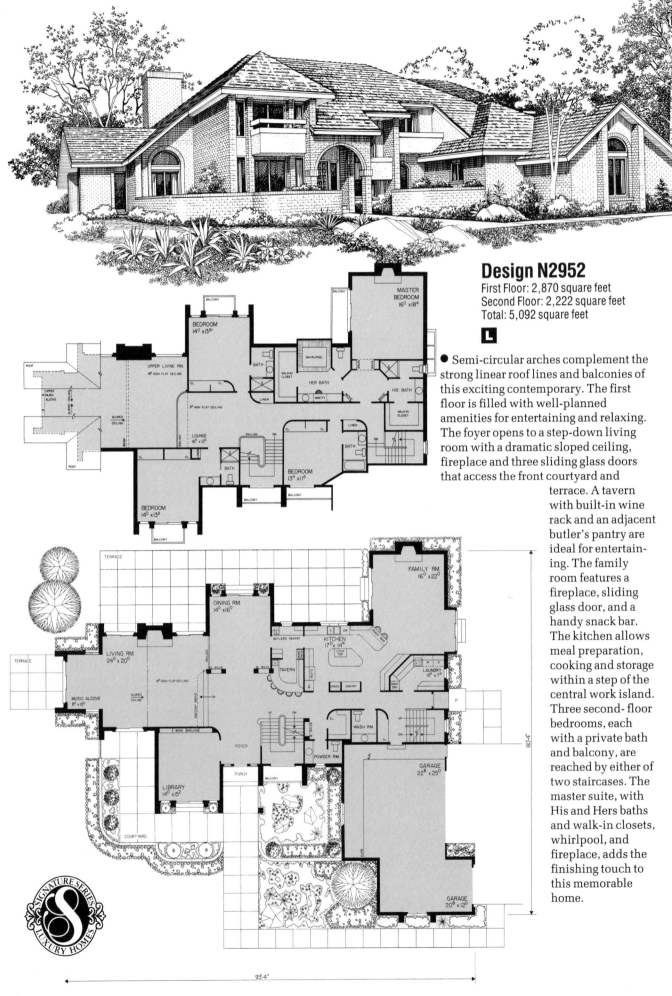

Design N2952

First Floor: 2,870 square feet
Second Floor: 2,222 square feet
Total: 5,092 square feet

L

● Semi-circular arches complement the strong linear roof lines and balconies of this exciting contemporary. The first floor is filled with well-planned amenities for entertaining and relaxing. The foyer opens to a step-down living room with a dramatic sloped ceiling, fireplace and three sliding glass doors that access the front courtyard and terrace. A tavern with built-in wine rack and an adjacent butler's pantry are ideal for entertaining. The family room features a fireplace, sliding glass door, and a handy snack bar. The kitchen allows meal preparation, cooking and storage within a step of the central work island. Three second-floor bedrooms, each with a private bath and balcony, are reached by either of two staircases. The master suite, with His and Hers baths and walk-in closets, whirlpool, and fireplace, adds the finishing touch to this memorable home.

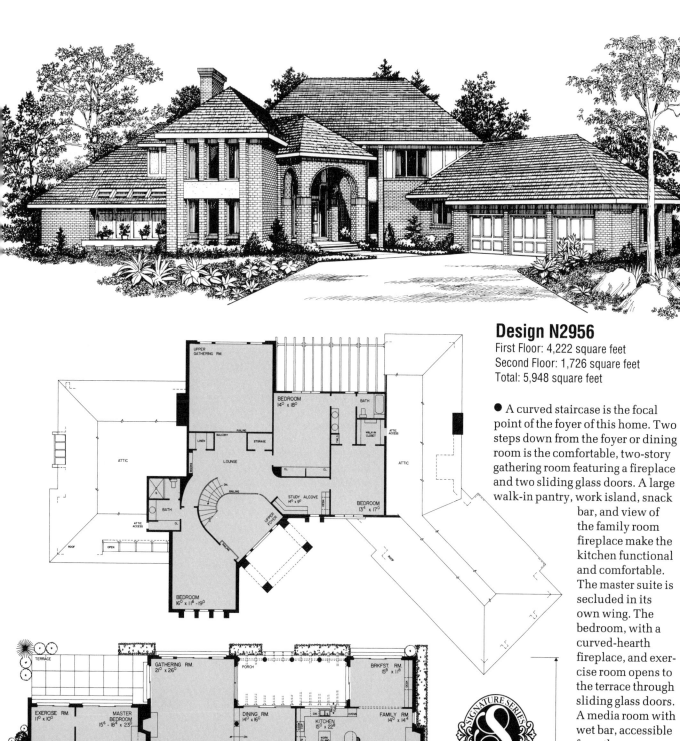

Design N2956

First Floor: 4,222 square feet
Second Floor: 1,726 square feet
Total: 5,948 square feet

● A curved staircase is the focal point of the foyer of this home. Two steps down from the foyer or dining room is the comfortable, two-story gathering room featuring a fireplace and two sliding glass doors. A large walk-in pantry, work island, snack bar, and view of the family room fireplace make the kitchen functional and comfortable. The master suite is secluded in its own wing. The bedroom, with a curved-hearth fireplace, and exercise room opens to the terrace through sliding glass doors. A media room with wet bar, accessible from the master bedroom and foyer, is the perfect place to relax. The second-floor stairs open to a lounge which overlooks the gathering room. Three additional bedrooms and a quiet study alcove on the second floor round out this gracious home.

Design N2940 First Floor: 4,786 square feet; Second Floor: 1,842 square feet; Total: 6,628 square feet
L D

● Graceful window arches soften the massive chimneys and steeply gabled roof of this grand Norman manor. A two-story gathering room is two steps down from the adjacent lounge with impressive wet bar and semi-circular music alcove. The highly efficient galley-style kitchen overlooks the family room fireplace and spectacular windowed breakfast room. The master suite is a private retreat with fireplace and wood box tucked into the corner of its sitting room. Separate His and Hers baths and dressing rooms guarantee plenty of space and privacy. A large, built-in whirlpool tub adds the final touch. Upstairs, a second-floor balcony overlooks the gathering room below. There are also four additional bedrooms, each with private bath.

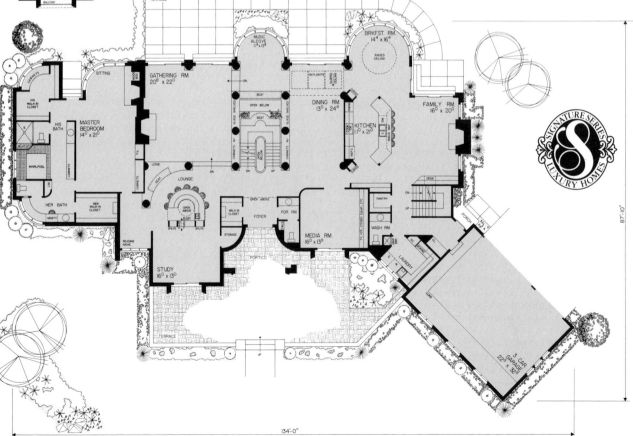

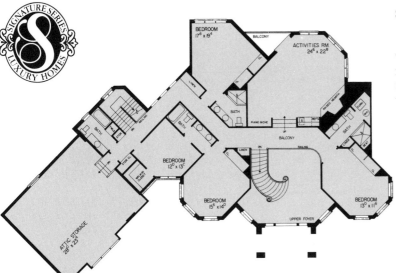

Design N2968 First Floor: 3,736 square feet
Second Floor: 2,264 square feet; Total: 6,000 square feet

L

● The distinctive covered entry to this stunning manor, flanked by twin turrets, leads to a gracious foyer with impressive fan lights. The plan opens from the foyer to a formal dining room, master study and step-down gathering room. The spacious kitchen has numerous amenities including an island workstation and built-in desk. The adjacent morning room and gathering room with wet bar and raised-hearth fireplace are bathed in light and open to the terrace for outdoor entertaining. The luxurious master suite has a wealth of amenities as well. The second floor features four bedrooms and an oversized activities room with fireplace and balcony. Unfinished attic space can be completed to your specifications.

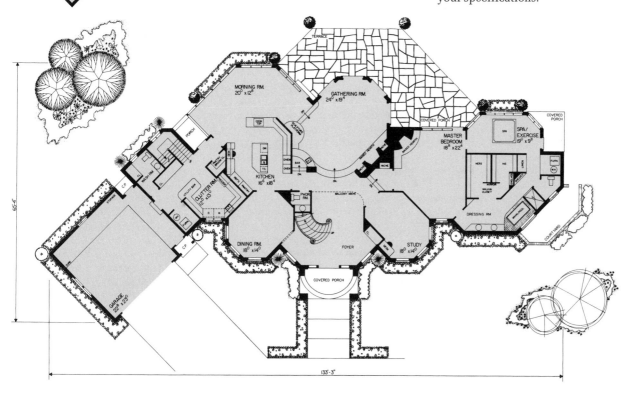

119

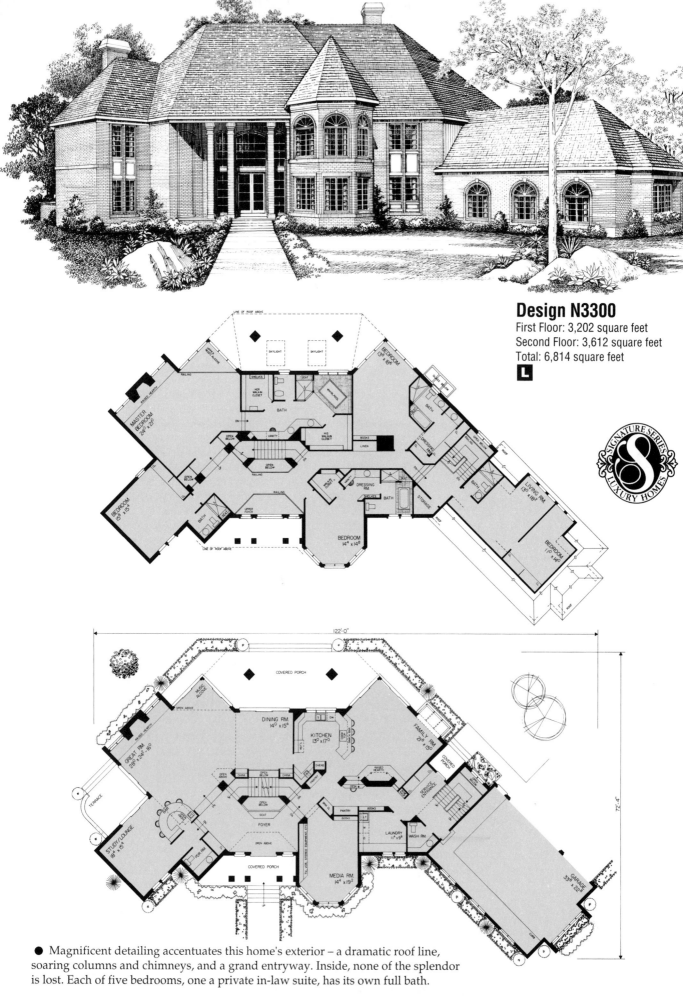

Design N3300
First Floor: 3,202 square feet
Second Floor: 3,612 square feet
Total: 6,814 square feet

● Magnificent detailing accentuates this home's exterior – a dramatic roof line, soaring columns and chimneys, and a grand entryway. Inside, none of the splendor is lost. Each of five bedrooms, one a private in-law suite, has its own full bath.

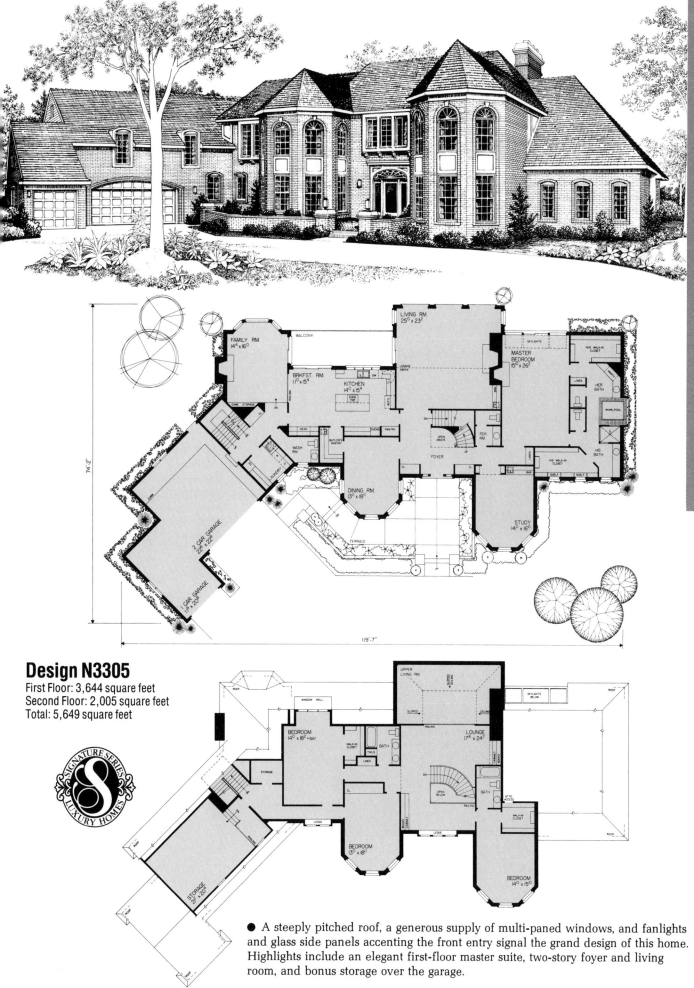

Design N3305

First Floor: 3,644 square feet
Second Floor: 2,005 square feet
Total: 5,649 square feet

● A steeply pitched roof, a generous supply of multi-paned windows, and fanlights and glass side panels accenting the front entry signal the grand design of this home. Highlights include an elegant first-floor master suite, two-story foyer and living room, and bonus storage over the garage.

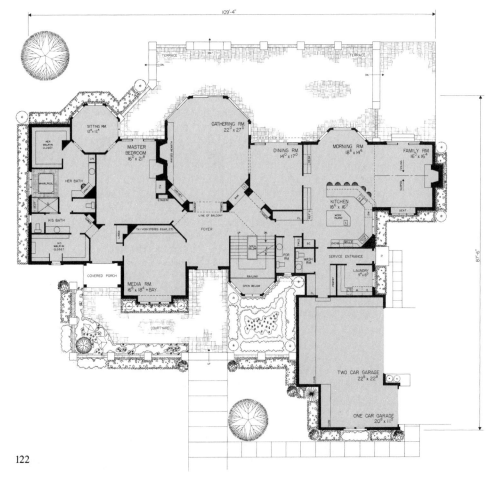

Design N2951

First Floor: 4,195 square feet
Second Floor: 2,094 square feet
Total: 6,289 square feet

● A single prominent turret with two-story divided windows draws attention to this stately Tudor home. The open foyer allows an uninterrupted view into the impressive, two-story great room with wet bar, where a fireplace with raised hearth runs the entire length of one wall. The expansive kitchen, conveniently located near the service entrance, has a U-shaped work area and a snack bar that opens to the morning room. The adjacent sloped-ceiling family room has an additional fireplace and a comfortable window seat. A Victorian-inspired, octagon-shaped sitting room is tucked into the corner of the unique master bedroom. His and Hers baths and walk-in closets complete the impressive first-floor suite. Two bedrooms, a study, and a guest suite with private sitting room are located on the second floor. A magnificent second-floor bridge overlooks foyer and gathering room and provides extraordinary views to guests on the way to their bedroom.

Design N2955 First Floor: 3,840 square feet
Second Floor: 3,435 square feet; Total: 7,275 square feet

● A circular staircase housed in the turret makes an impressive opening statement in the two-story foyer of this Tudor. Two steps down lead to the elegant living room with music alcove or the sumptuous library with wet bar. The kitchen is a chef's delight with work island, full cooking counter and butler's pantry leading to a formal dining room. The second floor features four bedrooms, two with fireplaces, and each with private bath and abundant closet space. The master has an additional fireplace. Adjacent to the master bedroom is a nursery that would make an ideal exercise room.

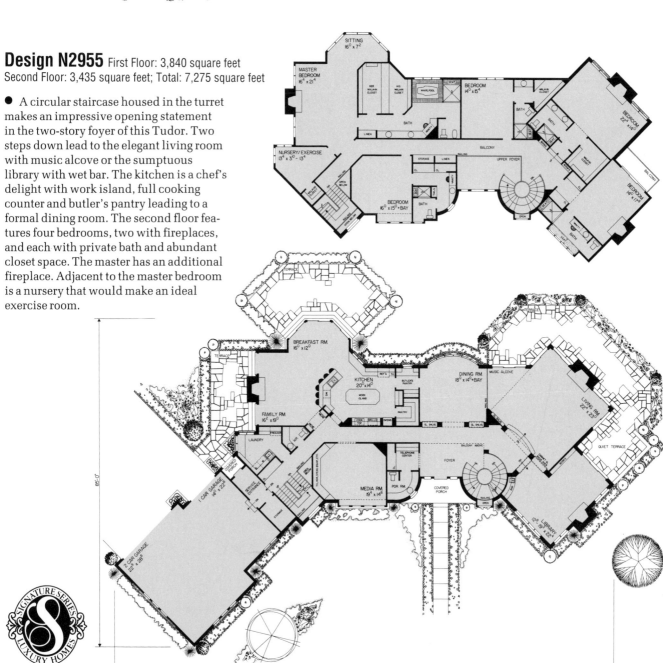

Design N3301

First Floor: 3,425 square feet
Second Floor: 2,501 square feet
Total: 5,926 square feet

● Masterful use of space with a profusion of windows and terrace access are all employed in this Tudor treasure. A two-story foyer points the way directly to the living room which features a raised-hearth fireplace, huge bay window, and curved bar. The angular kitchen has a center island and is strategically placed with relationship to the formal dining room, the family room and its gracious fireplace, and a captivating breakfast room. A media room to the left of the foyer provides built-in space for an entertainment system. The sloped-ceiling master bedroom contains a third fireplace and another gigantic bay window. Its adjoining bath is divided into His and Hers dressing areas and closets, and centers around a relaxing whirlpool spa. Guests are easily accommodated in a full suite with its own living room and bath on the second floor. Three other bedrooms and a lounge on this floor share a balcony overlook to the living room below.

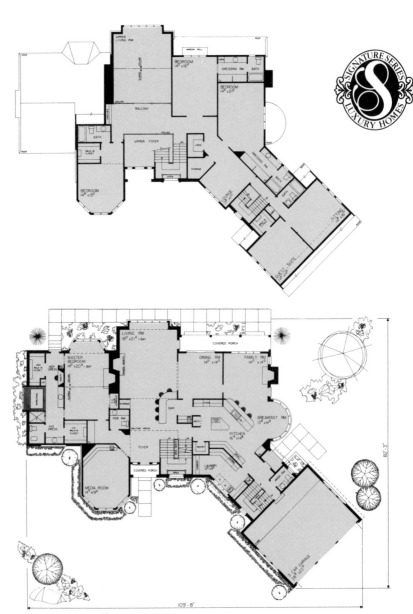

Design N2993

First Floor: 2,440 square feet
Second Floor: 2,250 square feet
Total: 4,690 square feet

L **D**

● This dramatically columned home delivers beautiful proportions and great livability on two levels. The main area of the house, the first floor, holds a gathering room, library, family room, dining room and gourmet kitchen. The master bedroom features a whirlpool tub and through fireplace. Two family bedrooms on the second floor share a full bath. A fourth bedroom is the perfect guest bedroom with its own private bath.

Design N2990

First Floor: 2,615 square feet
Second Floor: 1,726 square feet
Guest Bedroom: 437 square feet
Total: 4,778 square feet

L

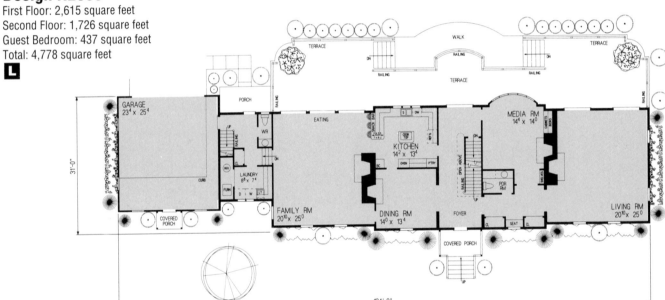

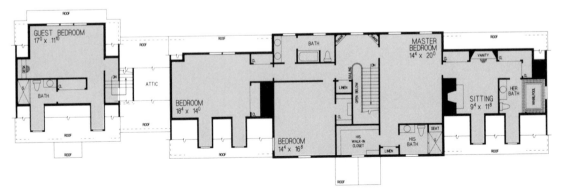

● Designed to resemble the St. George Tucker house in Williamsburg, this stately home offers a floor plan for today's family. First-floor rooms include a family room with informal dining space at one end of the plan and a formal living room at the other end. In between are the media room, guest powder room, dining room and kitchen. Three second-floor bedrooms include a luxurious master suite with sitting room. There is also a guest room with private bath over the garage.

Design N2992

First Floor: 1,541 square feet
Second Floor: 1,541 square feet
Third Floor: 1,016 square feet
Total: 4,098 square feet

L **D**

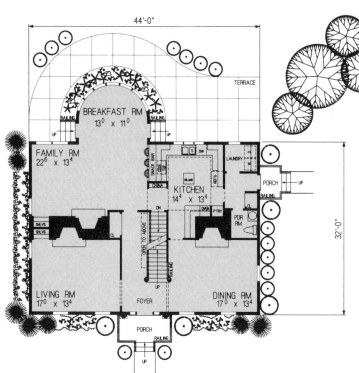

44'-0"

TERRACE

BREAKFAST RM
13⁰ x 11⁰

FAMILY RM
22⁶ x 13⁴

LAUNDRY

PORCH

SNACK BAR

KITCHEN
14⁴ x 13⁴

ISLAND

CHINA

OVEN

PTRY

PDR RM

32'-0"

SHLVS

SHLVS

OPEN TO ABOVE

DN

LIVING RM
17⁰ x 13⁴

FOYER

DINING RM
17⁰ x 13⁴

UP

PORCH

RAILING

UP

ROOF

ROOF

ROOF

WALK-IN CLOSET

LINEN

SEAT

BATH

TWLS

DN

GUEST BEDROOM
12⁴ x 19⁰

RAILING

DESK

STUDIO
17⁰ x 19⁰

ROOF

ROOF

ROOF

MASTER BEDROOM
21⁴ x 13⁴

BATH

BEDROOM
13⁰ x 13⁴

WALK-IN CLOSET

LINEN

DN

LINEN

WALK-IN CLOSET

VANITY

RAILING OPEN TO BELOW

UP

WHIRL POOL

MASTER BATH

SEAT

SEAT

BEDROOM
17⁰ x 13⁴

● The Dalton house, built between 1750 and 1760 in Newburyport, Massachusetts, inspired our plan shown here. Its lovely proportion and graceful exterior give way to a floor plan designed for the times. Left of the entry foyer is the formal living room; to the right formal dining. Both rooms have warming hearths. A family room to the rear of the plan connects with a unique glass-enclosed breakfast room. Nearby is the kitchen with pass-through snack bar. The second floor holds three bedrooms — the master suite and two family bedrooms. On the third floor is a guest bedroom with private bath and studio.

Design N2989

First Floor: 1,972 square feet
Second Floor: 1,533 square feet
Total: 3,505 square feet

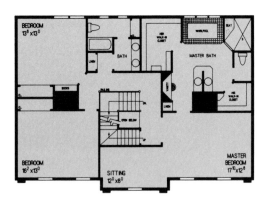

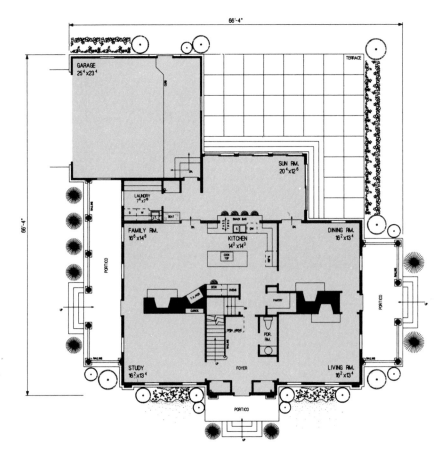

● This dramatic residence, patterned after one built in 1759 by Major John Vassall in Cambridge, offers a floor plan that is intriguing in its wealth of amenities. On the first floor are the formal living and dining rooms, each with fireplace. A front study connects to the family room with built-ins and another fireplace. Opening to the rear terrace is a most-welcome sun room with pass- through snack bar to the kitchen. Upstairs are three bedrooms. The master has a sitting room, double vanity, whirlpool tub, His and Hers closets, and built-in vanity. Two family bedrooms share a full bath.

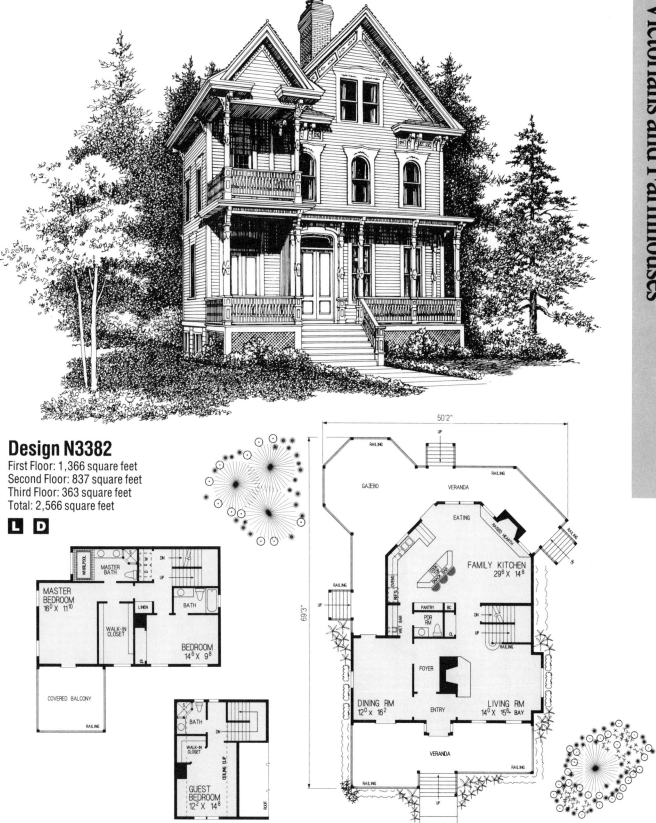

Design N3382

First Floor: 1,366 square feet
Second Floor: 837 square feet
Third Floor: 363 square feet
Total: 2,566 square feet

L **D**

● A simple but charming Queen Anne Victorian, this enchanting three-story home boasts delicately turned rails and decorated columns on its covered front porch. Inside is a floor plan that includes a living room with fireplace and dining room that connects to the kitchen via a wet bar. The adjoining family room contains another fireplace. The second floor holds two bedrooms, one a master suite with grand bath. A tucked-away guest suite on the third floor has a private bath.

Design N3391

First Floor: 1,230 square feet
Second Floor: 962 square feet
Total: 2,192 square feet

L **D**

● Detailing is one of the characteristic features of Queen Anne Victorians and this home has no lack of it. Interior rooms add special living patterns. Features include a powder room for guests in the front hallway, a through-fireplace between the ample gathering room and cozy study, an efficient U-shaped kitchen with pantry, and a full-width terrace to the rear. On the second floor are three bedrooms — one a master suite with walk-in closet and amenity-filled bath. An open balcony overlooks the gathering room.

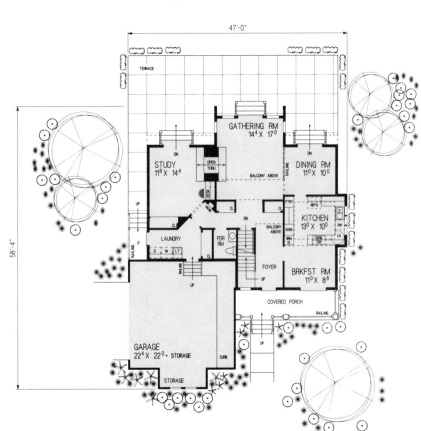

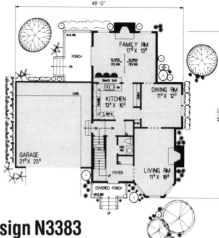

Design N3383

First Floor: 995 square feet
Second Floor: 1,064 square feet
Third Floor: 425 square feet
Total: 2,484 square feet

L **D**

● This delightful Victorian cottage features exterior details that perfectly complement the convenient plan inside. Note the central placement of the kitchen, near to the dining room and the family room. Two fireplaces keep things warm and cozy. Three second-floor bedrooms include a master suite with bay window and two family bedrooms, one with an alcove and walk-in closet. Use the third-floor studio as a study, office or playroom for the children.

Design N3384

First Floor: 1,399 square feet
Second Floor: 1,123 square feet
Total: 2,522 square feet

L **D**

● Classic Victorian styling comes to the forefront in this Queen Anne. The interior boasts comfortable living quarters for the entire family. On opposite sides of the foyer are the formal dining and living rooms. To the rear is a country-style island kitchen with attached family room. A small library shares a covered porch with this informal gathering area and also has its own fireplace. Three bedrooms on the second floor include a master suite with grand bath. The two family bathrooms share a full bath.

● This two-story farmhouse will be a delight for those who work at home. The second floor has a secluded master bedroom and a studio. A U-shaped kitchen with snack bar and breakfast area with bay window are only the first of the eating areas, which extend to a formal dining room and a covered rear porch for dining al fresco. The two-story living room features a cozy fireplace. A versatile room to the back could serve as a media room or a third bedroom.

Design N3390

First Floor: 1,508 square feet
Second Floor: 760 square feet
Total: 2,268 square feet

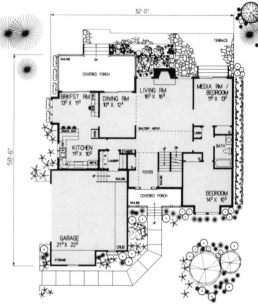

Design N3385

First Floor: 1,096 square feet
Second Floor: 900 square feet
Total: 1,996 square feet

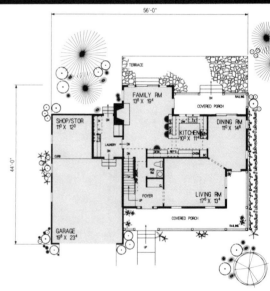

● Covered porches front and rear are complemented by a grand plan for family living. A formal living room and attached dining room provide space for entertaining guests. The large family room with fireplace is a gathering room for everyday use. Four bedrooms occupy the second floor. The master suite features two lavatories, a window seat and three closets. One of the family bedrooms has its own private balcony and could be used as a study.

Design N2974 First Floor: 911 square feet
Second Floor: 861 square feet; Total: 1,772 square feet

L

● Victorian houses are well known for their orientation on narrow building sites. And when this occurs nothing is lost to captivating exterior styling. This house is but 38 feet wide. Its narrow width belies the tremendous amount of livability found inside. And, of course, the ubiquitous porch/veranda contributes mightily to style as well as livability. The efficient, U-shape kitchen is flanked by the informal breakfast room and formal dining room. The rear living area is spacious and functions in an exciting manner with the outdoor areas. Bonus recreational, hobby and storage space is offered by the basement and the attic.

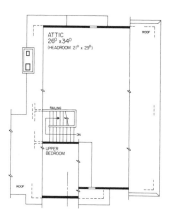

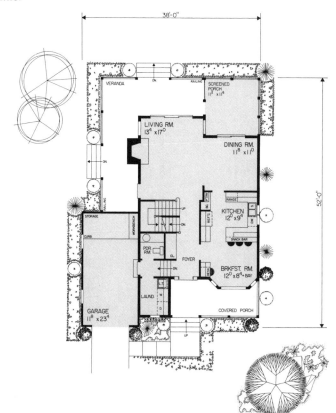

Design N2971 First Floor: 1,766 square feet
Second Floor: 1,519 square feet; Total: 3,285 square feet

L

● The stately proportions and the exquisite detailing of Victorian styling are exciting, indeed. Like so many Victorian houses, interesting roof lines set the character with this design. Observe the delightful mixture of gable roof, hip roof, and the dramatic turret. Horizontal siding, wood shingling, wide fascia, rake and corner boards make a strong statement. Of course, the delicate detailing of the windows, railings, cornices and front entry is most appealing to the eye. Inside, a great four-bedroom family living plan.

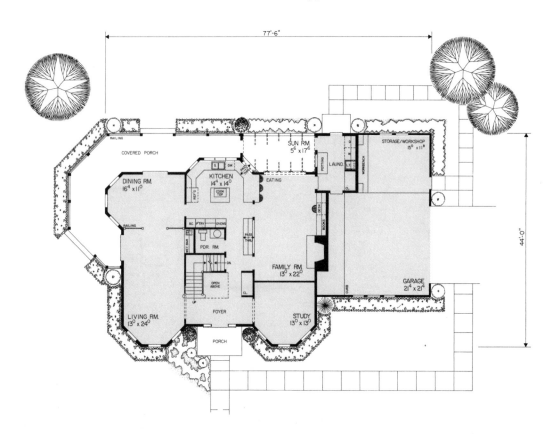

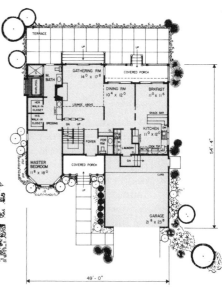

● A grand facade makes this Victorian stand out. Inside, guests and family are well accommodated: gathering room with terrace access, fireplace and attached formal dining room; split-bedroom sleeping arrangements. The master suite contains His and Hers walk-in closets, a separate shower and whirlpool tub and a delightful bay-windowed area. Upstairs there are three more bedrooms (one could serve as a study, one as a media room), a full bath and an open lounge area overlooking the gathering room.

Design N3393

First Floor: 1,449 square feet
Second Floor: 902 square feet
Total: 2,351 square feet

L **D**

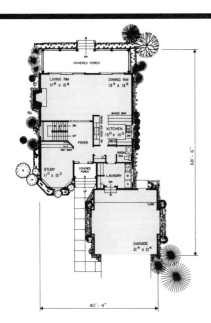

Design N3389

First Floor: 1,161 square feet
Second Floor: 1,090 square feet
Third Floor: 488 square feet
Total: 2,739 square feet

L **D**

● A Victorian turret accents the facade of this compact three-story. Downstairs rooms include a grand-sized living room/dining room combination. The U-shaped kitchen has a snack-bar pass-through to the dining room. Just to the left of the entry foyer is a private study. On the second floor are three bedrooms and two full baths. The master bedroom has a whirlpool spa and large walk-in closet. The third floor is a perfect location for a guest bedroom with private bath.

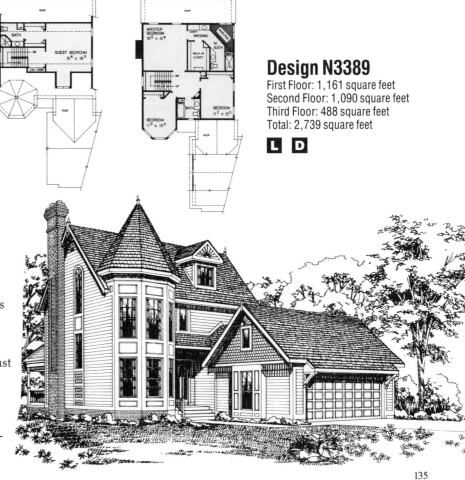

Design N2973

First Floor: 1,269 square feet
Second Floor: 1,227 square feet
Total: 2,496 square feet

● A most popular feature of the Victorian house has always been its covered porches. In addition to being an appealing exterior design feature, covered porches have their practical side, too. They provide wonderful indoor-outdoor living relationships. Notice sheltered outdoor living facilities for the various formal and informal living and dining areas of the plan. This home has a myriad of features to cater to the living requirements of the growing, active family.

CUSTOMIZABLE

Custom Alterations? See page 349 for customizing this plan to your specifications.

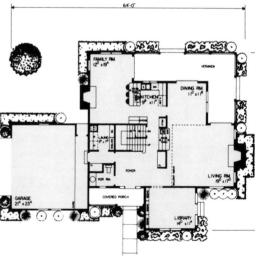

Design N2972

First Floor: 1,432 square feet
Second Floor: 1,108 square feet
Total: 2,540 square feet

● The spacious foyer of this Victorian is prelude to a practical and efficient interior. The formal living and dining area is located to one side of the plan. The more informal area of the plan includes the fine U-shaped kitchen which opens to the big family room. Just inside the entrance from the garage is the laundry; a closet and the powder room are a few steps away. The library will enjoy its full measure of privacy. Upstairs is the three-bedroom sleeping zone with a fireplace.

CUSTOMIZABLE

Custom Alterations? See page 349 for customizing this plan to your specifications.

Design N3309

First Floor: 1,375 square feet
Second Floor: 1,016 square feet
Total: 2,391 square feet

L

● Covered porches, front and back, are a fine preview to the livable nature of this Victorian. Living areas are defined in a family room with fireplace, formal living and dining rooms, and a kitchen with breakfast room. An ample laundry room, garage with storage area, and powder room round out the first floor. Three second floor bedrooms are joined by a study and two full baths.

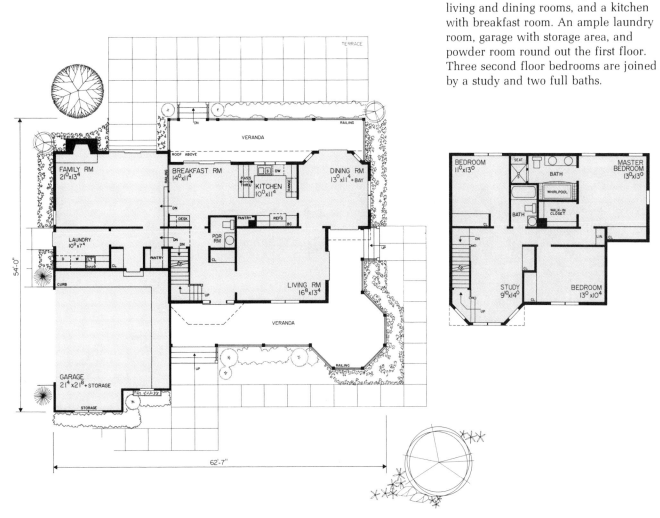

Design N3388

First Floor: 1,517 square feet
Second Floor: 1,267 square feet
Third Floor: 480 square feet
Total: 3,264 square feet

L D

● This delightful home offers the best in thoughtful floor planning. The home opens to a well-executed entry foyer. To the left is the casual family room with fireplace. To the right is the formal living room which connects to the formal dining area. The kitchen/breakfast room combination features an island cook top and large pantry. Second-floor bedrooms include a master suite and two family bedrooms served by a full bath. A guest room dominates the third floor.

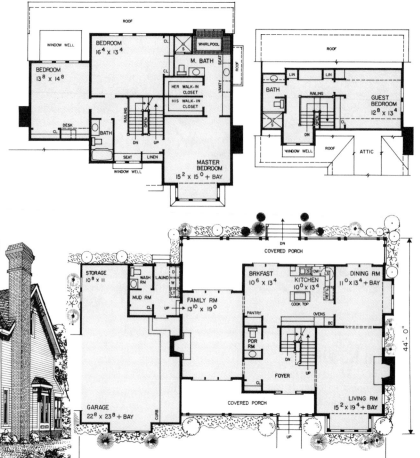

Design N3394

First Floor: 1,531 square feet
Second Floor: 1,307 square feet
Third Floor: 664 square feet
Total: 3,502 square feet

L D

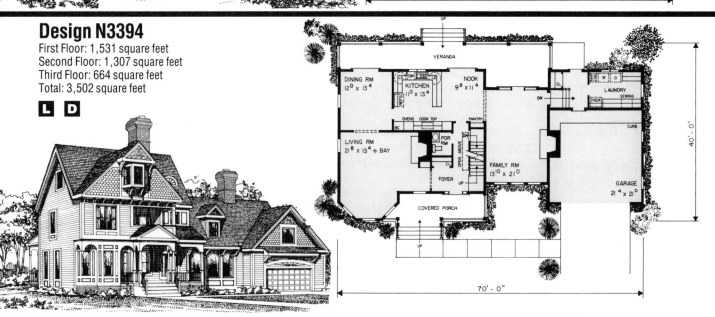

● The Folk Victorian is an important and delightful interpretation. And this version offers the finest in modern floor plans. The formal living areas are set off by a family room which connects the main house to the service areas. The second floor holds three bedrooms and two full baths. A sitting area in the master suite separates it from family bedrooms. On the third floor is a guest bedroom with gracious bath and large walk-in closet.

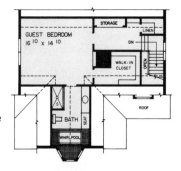

Design N3386

First Floor: 1,683 square feet
Second Floor: 1,388 square feet
Third Floor: 808 square feet
Total: 3,879 square feet

L D

● This beautiful Folk Victorian has all the properties of others in its class. Living areas include a formal Victorian parlor, a private study and large gathering room. The formal dining room has its more casual counterpart in a bay-windowed breakfast room. Both are near the well-appointed kitchen. Five bedrooms serve family and guest needs handily. Three bedrooms on the second floor include a luxurious master suite. For outdoor entertaining, there is a covered rear porch leading to a terrace.

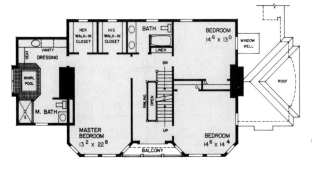

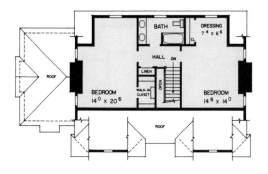

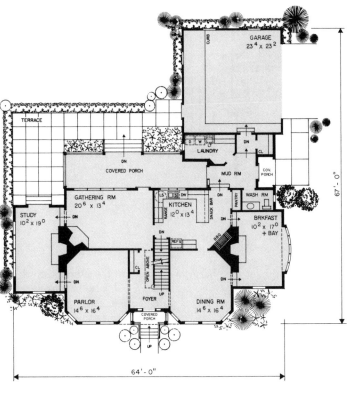

139

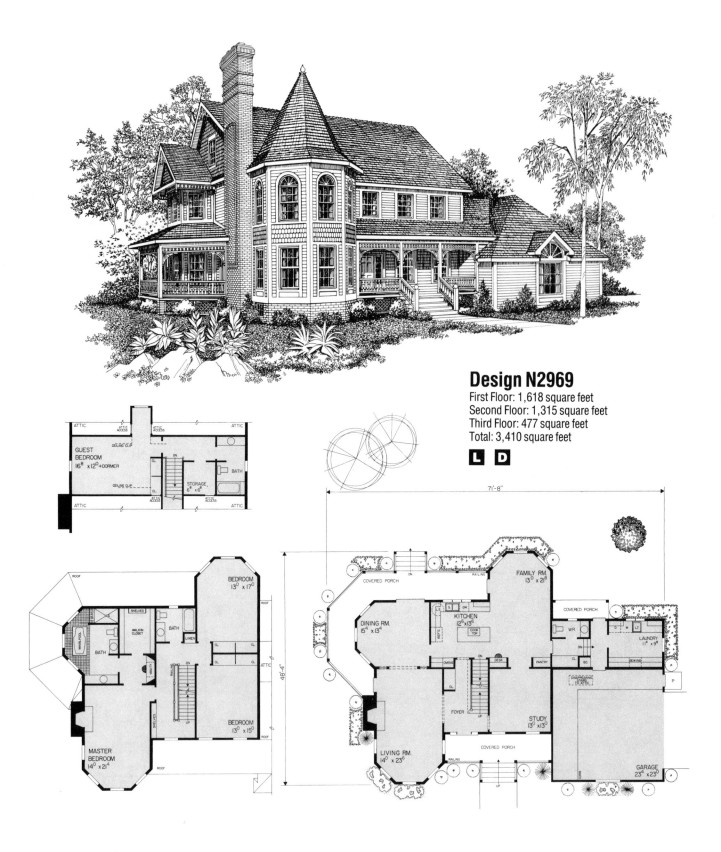

Design N2969

First Floor: 1,618 square feet
Second Floor: 1,315 square feet
Third Floor: 477 square feet
Total: 3,410 square feet

● What could beat the charm of a turreted Victorian with covered porches to the front, side and rear? This delicately detailed exterior houses an outstanding family oriented floor plan. Projecting bays make their contribution to the exterior styling. In addition, they provide an extra measure of livability to the living, dining and family rooms, plus two of the bedrooms. The efficient kitchen, with its island cooking station, functions well with the dining and family rooms. A study provides a quiet first floor haven for the family's less active pursuits. Upstairs there are three big bedrooms and a fine master bath.

The third floor provides a guest suite and huge bulk storage area (make it a cedar closet if you wish). This house has a basement for the development of further recreational and storage facilities. Don't miss the two fireplaces, large laundry and attached two-car garage. A great investment.

Design N2970 First Floor: 1,538 square feet
Second Floor: 1,526 square feet; Third Floor: 658 square feet
Total: 3,722 square feet

L

● A porch, is a porch, is a porch. But, when it wraps around to a side, or even two sides, of the house, we have called it a veranda. This charming Victorian features a covered outdoor living area on all four sides! It even ends at a screened porch which features a sun deck above. This interesting plan offers three floors of livability. And what livability it is! Plenty of formal and informal living facilities to go along with the potential of five bedrooms. The master suite is just that. It is adjacent to an interesting sitting room. It has a sun deck and excellent bath/personal care facilities. The third floor will make a wonderful haven for the family's student members.

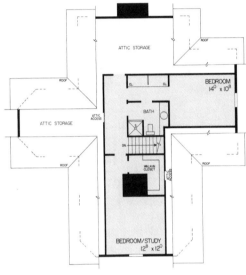

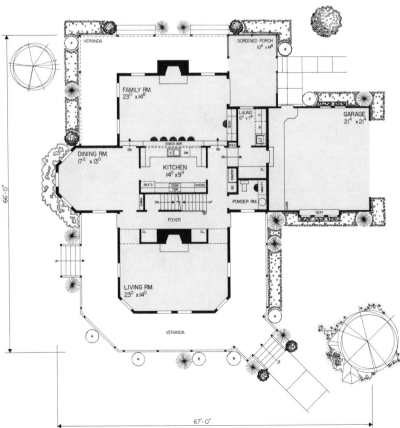

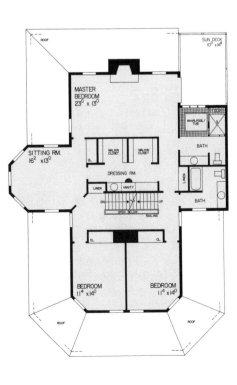

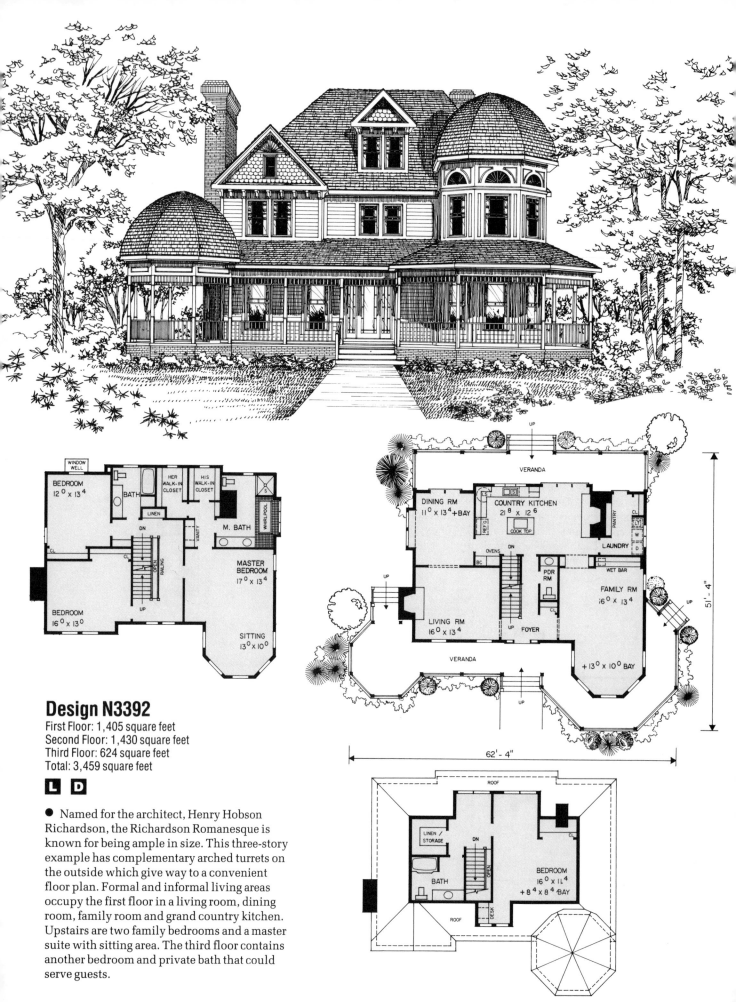

Design N3392

First Floor: 1,405 square feet
Second Floor: 1,430 square feet
Third Floor: 624 square feet
Total: 3,459 square feet

L **D**

● Named for the architect, Henry Hobson Richardson, the Richardson Romanesque is known for being ample in size. This three-story example has complementary arched turrets on the outside which give way to a convenient floor plan. Formal and informal living areas occupy the first floor in a living room, dining room, family room and grand country kitchen. Upstairs are two family bedrooms and a master suite with sitting area. The third floor contains another bedroom and private bath that could serve guests.

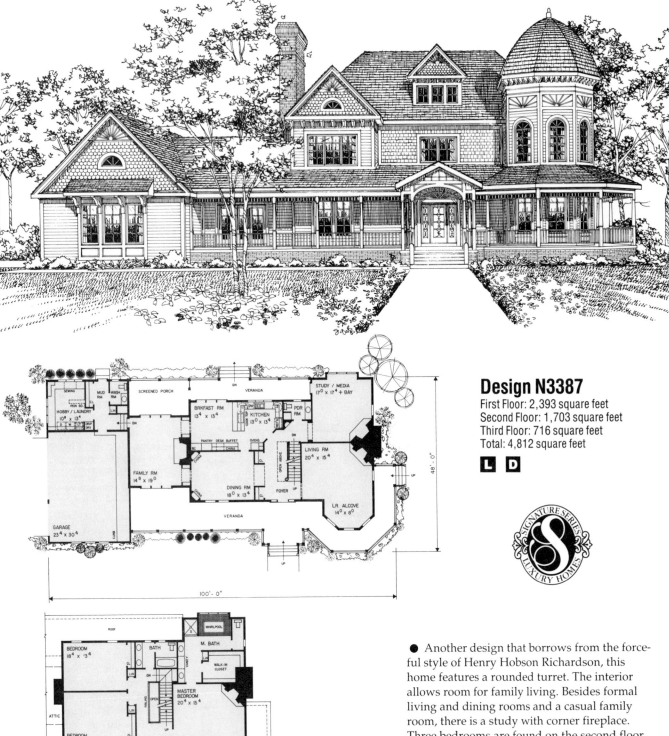

Design N3387

First Floor: 2,393 square feet
Second Floor: 1,703 square feet
Third Floor: 716 square feet
Total: 4,812 square feet

L **D**

● Another design that borrows from the forceful style of Henry Hobson Richardson, this home features a rounded turret. The interior allows room for family living. Besides formal living and dining rooms and a casual family room, there is a study with corner fireplace. Three bedrooms are found on the second floor along with two full baths. The third floor contains another bedroom with full bath and small alcove. Wide verandas both front and rear and a screened porch allow good indoor/outdoor living relationships.

143

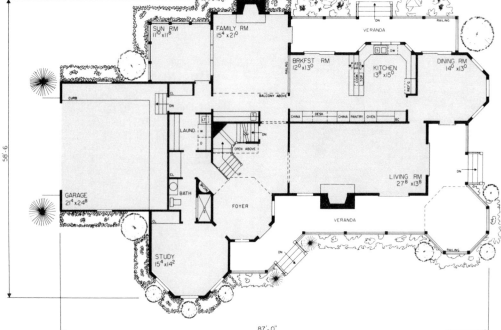

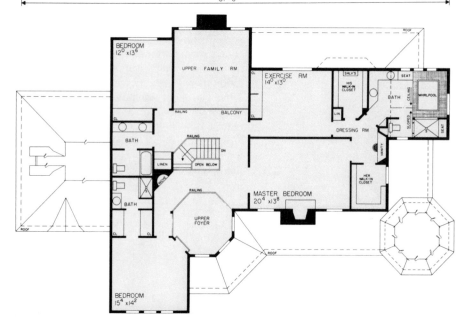

Design N3304

First Floor: 2,102 square feet
Second Floor: 1,971 square feet
Total: 4,073 square feet

L

● Victorian style is displayed in most exquisite proportions in this three-bedroom, four-bath home. From verandas, both front and rear, to the stately turrets and impressive chimney stack, this is a beauty. Inside is a great lay-out with many thoughtful amenities. Besides the large living room, formal dining room, and two-story family room, there is a cozy study for private time. A gourmet kitchen with built-ins has a pass-through counter to the breakfast room. The master suite on the second floor includes many special features: whirlpool spa, His and Hers walk-in closets, exercise room, and fireplace. There are two more bedrooms, each with a full bath, on the second floor.

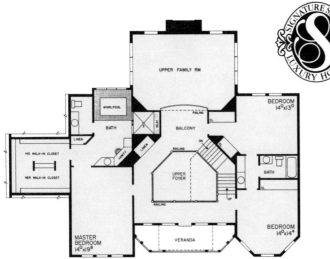

Design N3308

First Floor: 2,515 square feet
Second Floor: 1,708 square feet
Third Floor: 1,001 square feet
Total: 5,224 square feet

L

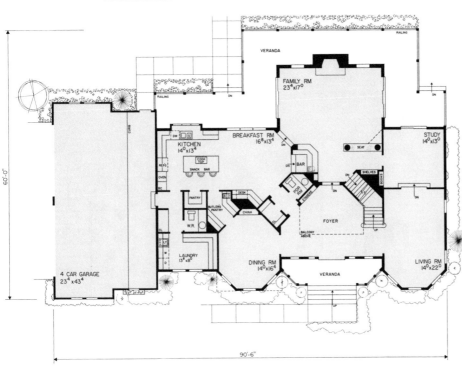

● Uniquely shaped rooms and a cache of amenities highlight this three-story beauty. Downstairs rooms accommodate both formal and informal entertaining and also provide a liberal share of work space in the kitchen and laundry. The second floor has two bedrooms and a full bath plus a master suite with His and Hers closets and whirlpool bath. An exercise room on the third floor has its own sauna and bath, while a guest room on this floor is complemented by a charming alcove and another full bath.

145

Width 53'-8"
Depth 57'

Design N3462

First Floor: 1,395 square feet
Second Floor: 813 square feet
Total: 2,208 square feet

L

● Get off to a great start with this handsome family farmhouse. Distinct formal and informal living zones provide space for any occasion. The central kitchen serves the large family room. The master bedroom is on the first floor and comes complete with double closets and master bath with double-bowl vanity, whirlpool tub and separate shower. Upstairs, three family bedrooms extend fabulous livability.

Design N3443

First Floor: 1,211 square feet
Second Floor: 614 square feet
Total: 1,825 square feet

L **D**

● The master suite in this house is on a level all its own. The 21-foot bedroom includes a sitting area and a bath with walk-in closet, dual vanities, separate tub and shower and a compartmented toilet. A second bedroom or optional den, with a full bath nearby, is located on the first floor. The formal living and dining rooms have sloped ceilings separated by a plant shelf, and bay windows. The family room features a snack bar to the kitchen and patio access. The garage contains a hobby shop.

CUSTOMIZABLE
Custom Alterations? See page 349 for customizing this plan to your specifications.

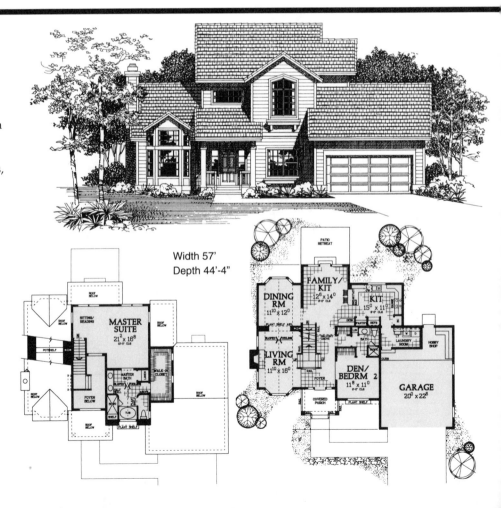

Width 57'
Depth 44'-4"

Design N3461

First Floor: 1,391 square feet
Second Floor: 611 square feet
Total: 2,002 square feet

L

● A Palladian window set in a dormer provides a nice introduction to this 1½-story country home. The two-story foyer draws on natural light and a pair of columns to set a comfortable, yet elegant mood. The living room, to the left, presents a grand space for entertaining. From full-course dinners to family suppers, the dining room will serve its purpose well. The kitchen delights with an island work station and openness to the keeping room. Here, a raised-hearth fireplace provides added comfort. Sleeping accommodations are comprised of four bedrooms, one a first-floor master suite. With a luxurious private bath, including dual lavatories, this room will surely be a favorite retreat. Upstairs, three secondary bedrooms meet the needs of the growing family.

147

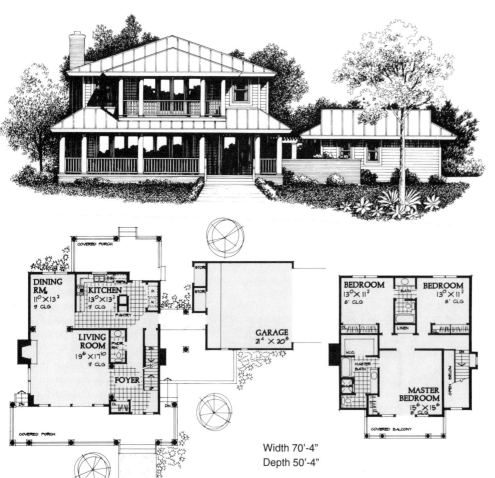

Design N3469

First Floor: 1,066 square feet
Second Floor: 1,006 square feet
Total: 2,072 square feet

L

● Our neo-classic farmhouse offers plenty of room for delightful diversions; a sheet-metal roof adds old-fashioned charm. Inside, a large living area with a fireplace connects to a formal dining room. The fully functional kitchen, the powder room and the utility room round out the first floor. The second floor provides well-arranged sleeping quarters—a large master bedroom and two family bedrooms. A mud yard separates the garage from the main house.

Width 70'-4"
Depth 50'-4"

Width 65'
Depth 51'-8"

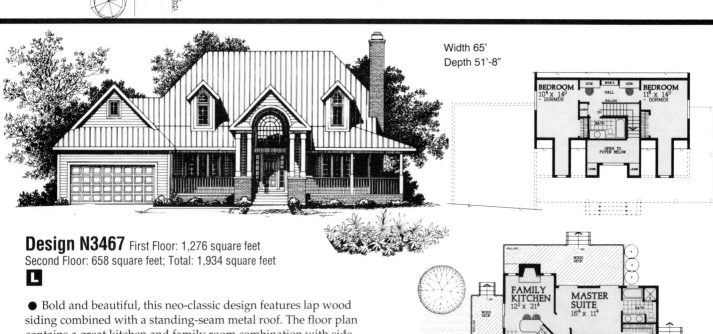

Design N3467
First Floor: 1,276 square feet
Second Floor: 658 square feet; Total: 1,934 square feet

L

● Bold and beautiful, this neo-classic design features lap wood siding combined with a standing-seam metal roof. The floor plan contains a great kitchen and family room combination with side deck for outdoor dining. For more formal occasions, the dining and living rooms serve well. A covered wraparound porch is accessible from both rooms. At the rear of the first floor, the master bedroom contains a private bath and walk-in closet. Two family bedrooms with dormers are located on the second floor.

CUSTOMIZABLE
Custom Alterations? See page 349 for customizing this plan to your specifications.

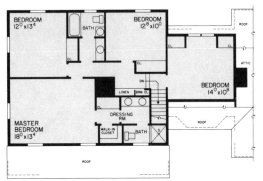

CUSTOMIZABLE

Custom Alterations? See page 349 for customizing this plan to your specifications.

Design N2908

First Floor: 1,427 square feet
Second Floor: 1,153 square feet
Total: 2,580 square feet

L **D**

● This Early American farmhouse offers plenty of modern comfort with its covered front porch with pillars and rails, double chimneys, building attachment, and four upstairs bedrooms. The first floor attachment includes a family room with bay window. It leads from the main house to a two-car garage. The family room certainly is the central focus of this fine design, with its own fireplace and rear entrance to a laundry and sewing room behind the garage. Disappearing stairs in the building attachment lead to attic space over the garage. The upstairs also is accessible from stairs just off the front foyer. Included is a master bedroom suite. Downstairs one finds a modern kitchen with breakfast room, dining room, and front living room.

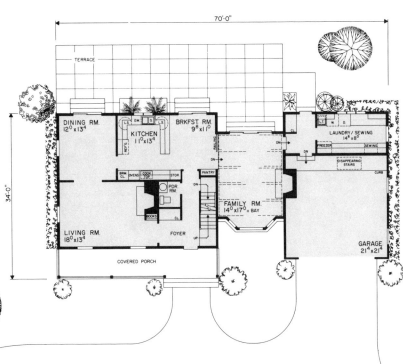

149

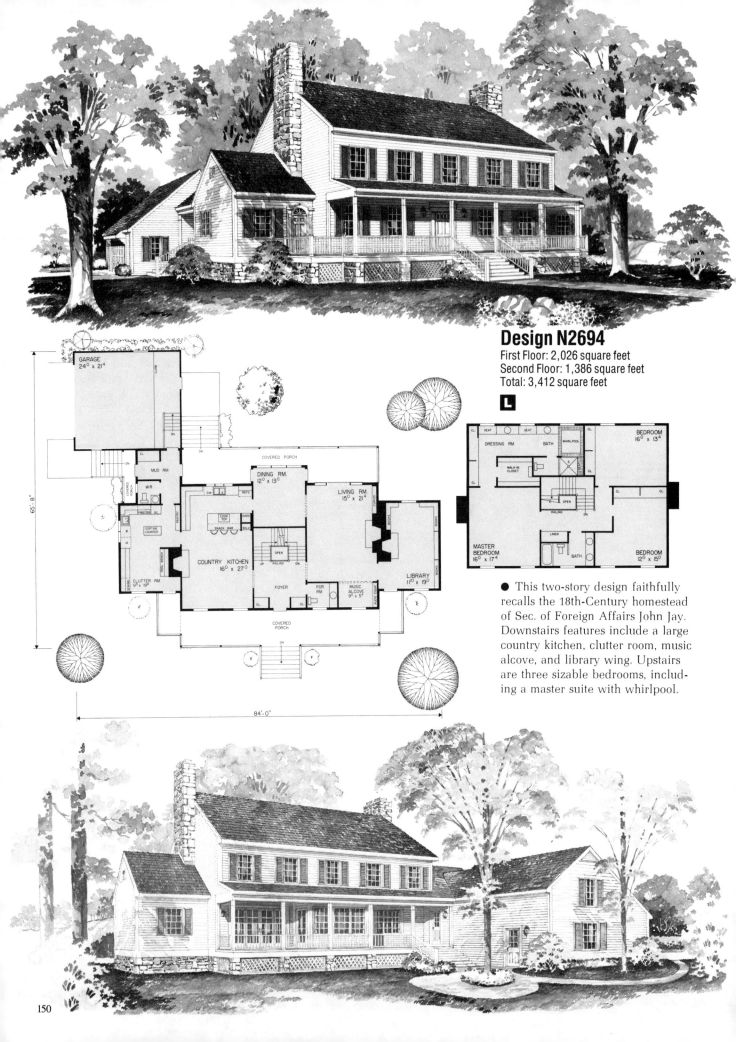

Design N2694

First Floor: 2,026 square feet
Second Floor: 1,386 square feet
Total: 3,412 square feet

L

● This two-story design faithfully recalls the 18th-Century homestead of Sec. of Foreign Affairs John Jay. Downstairs features include a large country kitchen, clutter room, music alcove, and library wing. Upstairs are three sizable bedrooms, including a master suite with whirlpool.

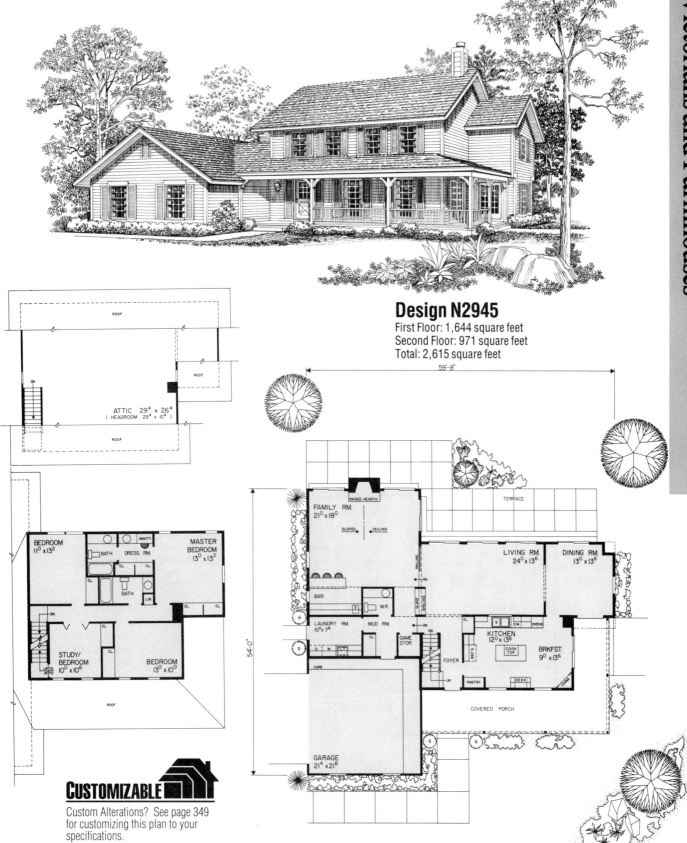

Design N2945

First Floor: 1,644 square feet
Second Floor: 971 square feet
Total: 2,615 square feet

CUSTOMIZABLE

Custom Alterations? See page 349
for customizing this plan to your
specifications.

● Here is a new floor plan designed to go with the almost identical exterior of one of Home Planners' most popular houses. A masterfully affordable design, this plan manages to include all the basics - and then adds a little more. Note the wraparound covered porch, large family room with raised-hearth fireplace and wet bar, spacious kitchen with island cook top, formal dining room, rear terrace, and extra storage on the first floor. Upstairs, the plan's as flexible as they come: three or four bedrooms (the fourth could easily be a study or playroom) and lots of unfinished attic just waiting for you to transform it into living space. This could make a fine studio, sewing room, home office, or just a place for the safe, dry storage of the family's paraphernalia, Christmas decorations, etc.

Design N2907

First Floor: 1,546 square feet
Second Floor: 1,144 square feet
Total: 2,690 square feet

L

● This traditional L-shaped farmhouse is charming indeed with dormer windows and covered porch supported by slender columns. A spacious country kitchen with a bay provides a convenient place for food preparation with its central work island and size. There's a formal dining room also adjacent to the kitchen. A rear family room features its own fireplace, as does a large living room in the front. All four bedrooms are isolated upstairs. Included is a large master bedroom suite with its own bath, dressing room and abundant closet space.

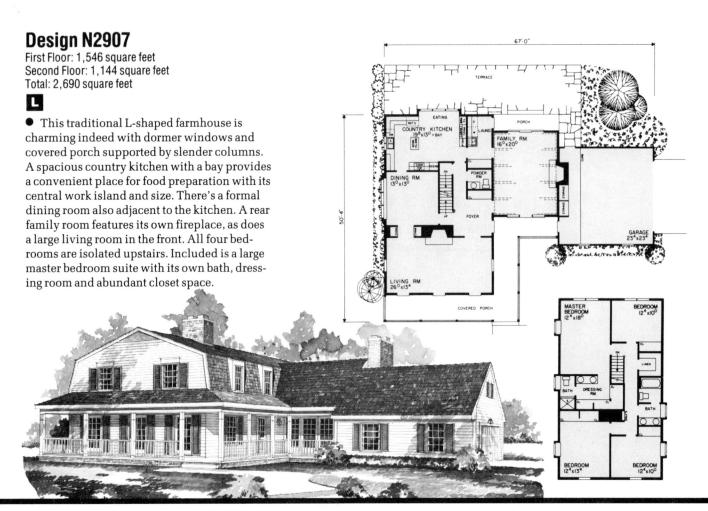

Design N3325

First Floor: 1,595 square feet
Second Floor: 1,112 square feet
Total: 2,707 square feet

L D

● This four-bedroom farmhouse plan is one of the most popular styles in America today. The floor plan begins with a foyer that introduces a grand living room. The U-shaped kitchen has a central island and a pass-through snack bar that connects it to the breakfast room. Nearby, the family room delights with its warming hearth and access to an entertainment patio. A large utility area sits near the garage. Upstairs, the master bedroom suite includes two closets and a private bath with a garden tub and dual lavatories.

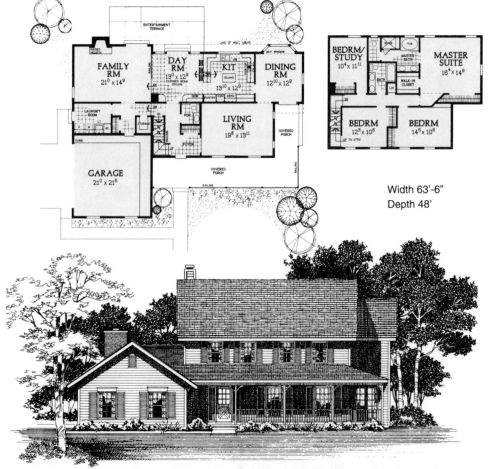

Width 63'-6"
Depth 48'

Design N2981

First Floor: 2,104 square feet
Second Floor: 2,015 square feet; Total: 4,119 square feet

L

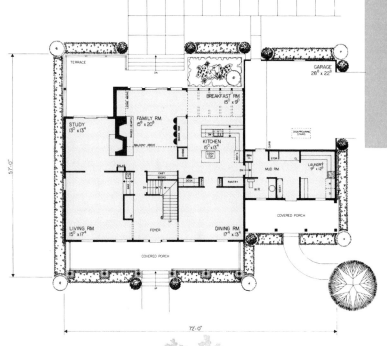

● This formal two-story recalls a Louisiana plantation house, Land's End, built in 1857. The Ionic columns of the front porch and the pediment gable echo the Greek Revival style. Highlighting the interior is the bright and cheerful spaciousness of the informal family room area. It features a wall of glass stretching to the second story sloping ceiling. Enhancing the drama of this area is the adjacent glass area of the breakfast room. Note the "His/Her" areas of the master bedroom.

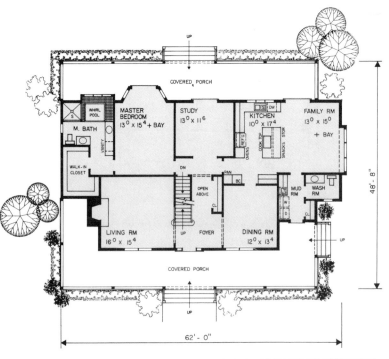

Design N3396

First Floor: 1,829 square feet
Second Floor: 947 square feet
Total: 2,776 square feet

L **D**

● Rustic charm abounds in this pleasant farmhouse rendition. Covered porches to the front and rear enclose living potential for the whole family. Flanking the entrance foyer are the living and dining rooms. To the rear is the L-shaped kitchen with island cook top and snack bar. A small family room/breakfast nook is attached. A private study is tucked away on this floor next to the master suite. On the second floor are three bedrooms and a full bath. Two of the bedrooms have charming dormer windows.

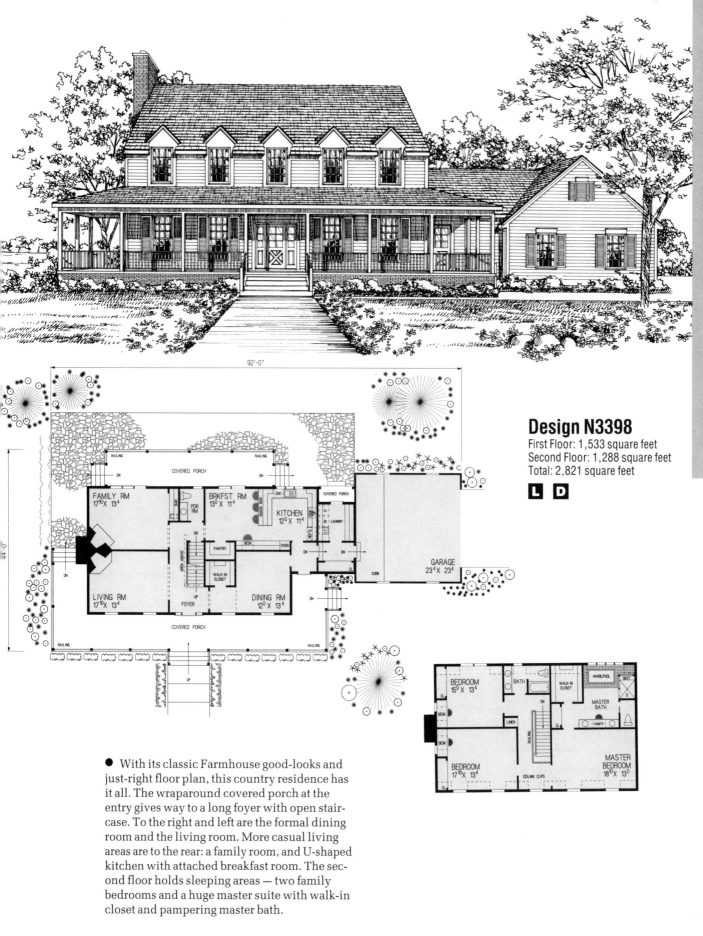

Design N3398
First Floor: 1,533 square feet
Second Floor: 1,288 square feet
Total: 2,821 square feet

L **D**

● With its classic Farmhouse good-looks and
just-right floor plan, this country residence has
it all. The wraparound covered porch at the
entry gives way to a long foyer with open staircase. To the right and left are the formal dining
room and the living room. More casual living
areas are to the rear: a family room, and U-shaped
kitchen with attached breakfast room. The second floor holds sleeping areas — two family
bedrooms and a huge master suite with walk-in
closet and pampering master bath.

Design N3397

First Floor: 1,855 square feet
Second Floor: 1,241 square feet
Total: 3,096 square feet

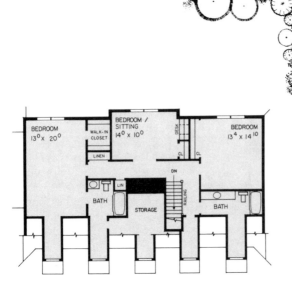

● Five second-story dormers and a wide covered front porch add to the charm of this farmhouse design. Inside, the entry foyer opens to the left to a formal living room with fireplace and attached dining room. To the right is a private study. The back of the plan is dominated by a huge country kitchen featuring an island cook top. On this floor is the master suite with a large walk-in closet. The second floor holds three bedrooms (or two and a sitting room) with two full baths.

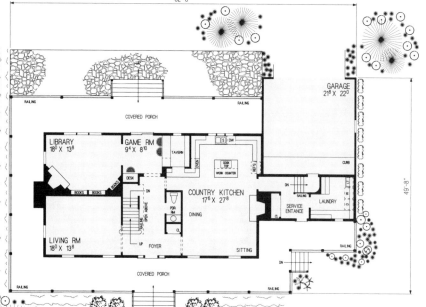

Design N3399

First Floor: 1,716 square feet
Second Floor: 2,102 square feet
Total: 3,818 square feet

L **D**

● This is the ultimate in farmhouse living — six dormer windows and a porch that stretches essentially around the entire house. Inside, the plan is open and inviting. Besides the large country kitchen with fireplace, there is a small game room with attached tavern, a library with built-in bookshelves and a fireplace, and a formal living room. The second floor has four bedrooms and three full baths. The service entrance features a laundry area conveniently just off the garage.

Design N2776

First Floor: 1,134 square feet
Second Floor: 874 square feet
Total: 2,008 square feet

CUSTOMIZABLE

Custom Alterations? See page 349 for customizing this plan to your specifications.

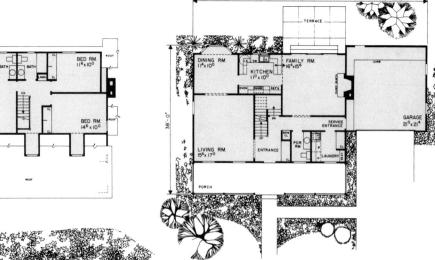

● This board-and-batten farmhouse design has all of the country charm of New England. Immediately off the front entrance is the delightful corner living room. The dining room with bay window is easily served by the U-shaped kitchen. Informal family living enjoyment resides in the family room which features a raised-hearth fireplace and sliding glass doors to the rear terrace. The second floor houses all of the sleeping facilities.

Design N2865

First Floor: 1,703 square feet
Second Floor: 1,044 square feet
Total: 2,747 square feet

● Here's a cozy traditional farmhouse with a big wraparound covered porch. Up front, flanking the entry foyer, are a living room with fireplace and formal dining room. To the rear are a study, that could be used as a guest room, and the family room with another fireplace. The kitchen/breakfast room combination is conveniently located near the service entrance off the garage. Note bedrooms with dormer windows upstairs.

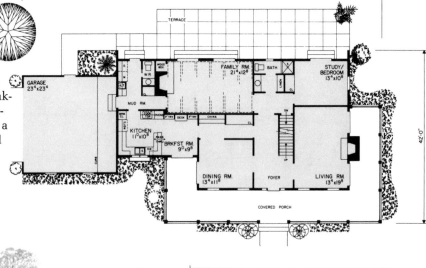

158

Design N2988

First Floor: 1,458 square feet
Second Floor: 1,075 square feet
Total: 2,533 square feet

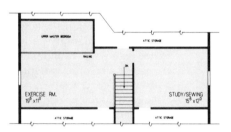

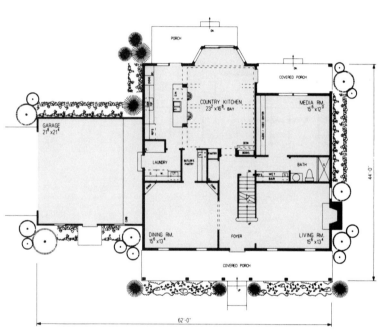

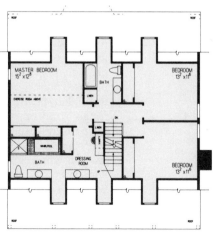

● The Joseph Guyon farmhouse, built in 1740, served as inspiration for this beautiful modern version. Three floors of living space encompass a country kitchen, living room, media room and dining room on the first floor; three bedrooms and two baths on the second floor; and an exercise room and study or sewing room on the third floor. Don't miss the covered porches front and rear, full guest bath near the media room and built-in wet bar.

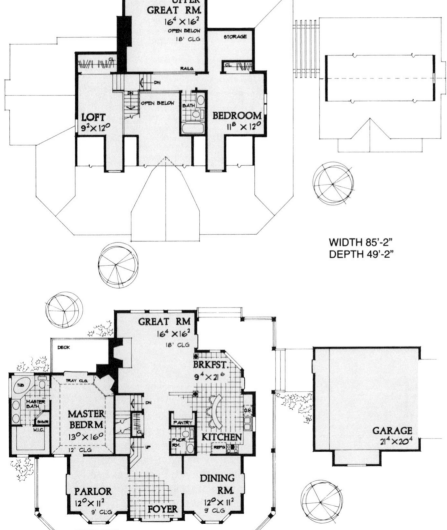

UPPER GREAT RM.
16⁴ × 16²
OPEN BELOW
18' CLG

STORAGE

RAILG.

GL.

LOFT
9² × 12⁰

OPEN BELOW

DN

BATH

BEDROOM
11⁶ × 12⁰

WIDTH 85'-2"
DEPTH 49'-2"

DECK

TRAY CLG.

TUB

MASTER BATH

SHWR

W.I.C.

MASTER BEDRM
13⁰ × 16⁰
12' CLG

GREAT RM
16⁴ × 16²
18' CLG

BRKFST.
9⁴ × 21⁶

DN

PANTRY

PWDR. RM.

UP

KITCHEN

REFG.

PARLOR
12⁰ × 11²
9' CLG

FOYER

DINING RM.
12⁰ × 11²
9' CLG

COVERED PORCH

GARAGE
21⁴ × 20⁴

Design N3468

First Floor: 1,618 square feet
Second Floor: 510 square feet
Total: 2,128 square feet

L

● There's nothing lacking
in this contemporary farmhouse. A wraparound porch
ensures a favorite spot for
enjoying good weather. A
large great room sports a
fireplace and lots of natural
light. Grab a snack at the
kitchen island/snack bar or
in the bright breakfast room.
The vaulted foyer grandly
introduces the dining room
and parlor—the master bedroom is just off this room.
Inside it: tray ceiling, fireplace, luxury bath and walk-
in closet. Stairs lead up to a
quaint loft/bedroom—per-
fect for study or snoozing—a
full bath and an additional
bedroom. Designated storage
space also makes this one a
winner.

Design N3405
Square Footage: 3,144

CUSTOMIZABLE

Custom Alterations? See page 349 for customizing this plan to your specifications.

● In classic Santa Fe style, this home strikes a beautiful combination of historic exterior detailing and open floor planning on the inside. A covered porch running the width of the facade leads to an entry foyer that connects to a huge gathering room with fireplace and formal dining room. The family kitchen allows special space for casual gatherings. The right wing of the home contains two family bedrooms and full bath. The left wing is devoted to the master suite and guest room or study. Built-ins abound throughout the house.

Width 139'-10"
Depth 63'-8"

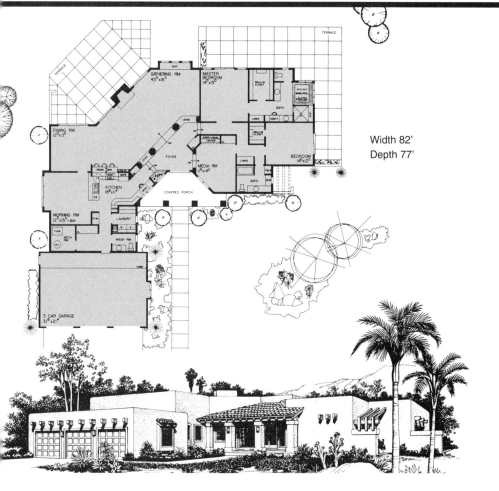

Design N2949
Square Footage: 2922

Width 82'
Depth 77'

● Spanish and Western influences take center stage in a long, low stucco design. You'll enjoy the Texas-sized gathering room that opens to a formal dining area and has a snack bar through to the kitchen. More casual dining is accommodated in the nook. A luxurious master suite is graced by plenty of closet space and a soothing whirlpool spa. Besides another bedroom and full bath, there is a media room that could easily double as a third bedroom or guest room.

Design N3565

First Floor: 1,248 square feet
Second Floor: 1,012 square feet
Total: 2,260 square feet

L **D**

● Every detail of this plan speaks of modern design. The exterior is simple yet elegant, while interior floor planning is thorough yet efficient. The formal living and dining rooms are to the left of the home, separated by columns. The living room features a wall of windows and a fireplace. The kitchen with island cooktop is adjacent to the large family room with terrace access. A study with additional terrace access completes the first floor. The master bedroom features a balcony and a spectacular bath with whirlpool tub, shower with seat, separate vanities and a walk-in closet. Two family bedrooms share access to a full bath. Also notice the three-car garage.

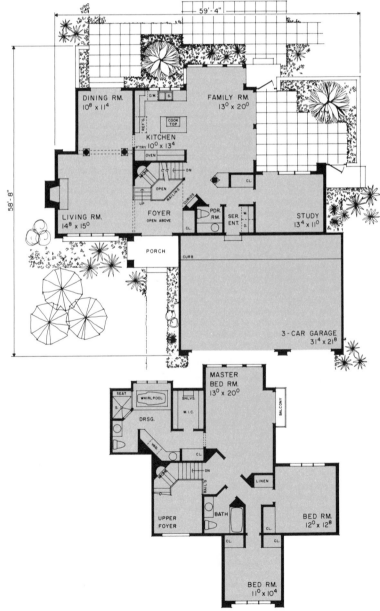

Design N3569
Square Footage: 1,981

L **D**

● A graceful entry opens this impressive one-story design; the foyer introduces an open gathering room/dining room combination. A front-facing study could easily convert into a bedroom for guests—a full bath is directly accessible from the rear of the room. In the kitchen, such features as an island cooktop and a built-in desk add to livability. A corner bedroom takes advantage of front and side views. The master bedroom accesses the rear terrace and also sports a bath with dual lavatories and a whirlpool. Other special features of the house include multi-pane windows, a warming fireplace, a cozy covered dining porch and a two-car garage. Note the handy storage closet in the laundry area.

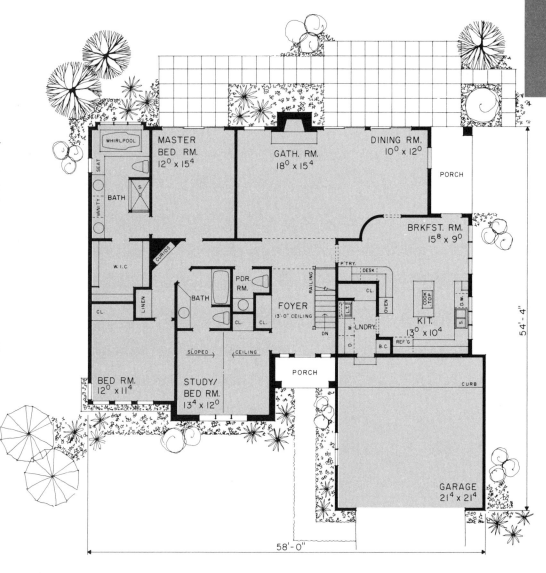

Design N3421
Square Footage: 2,145

 L

● Split-bedroom planning makes the most of a one-story design. In this case the master suite is on the opposite side of the house from two family bedrooms. Gourmets can rejoice at the abundant work space in the U-shaped kitchen and will appreciate the natural light afforded by the large bay window in the breakfast room. A formal living room has a sunken conversation area with a cozy fireplace as its focus. The rear covered porch can be reached through sliding glass doors in the family room.

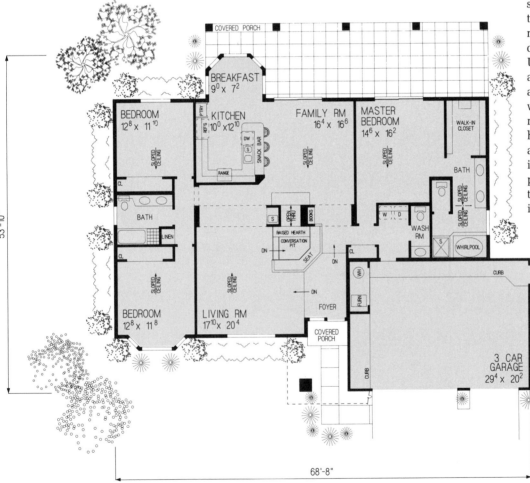

COVERED PORCH

BREAKFAST
9⁰ x 7²

BEDROOM
12⁸ x 11¹⁰

KITCHEN
10⁰ x 12¹⁰

FAMILY RM
16⁴ x 16⁶

MASTER BEDROOM
14⁶ x 16²

WALK-IN CLOSET

SLOPED CEILING

SLOPED CEILING

SLOPED CEILING

BATH

BATH

LINEN

CL

SLOPED CEILING

SLOPED CEILING

W D

WASH RM

WHIRLPOOL

SNACK BAR

DW

RANGE

REFG

PTRY

OPEN THRU

BOOKS

RAISED HEARTH

CONVERSATION PIT

SEAT

DN

DN

CL

DN

53'-10"

BEDROOM
12⁸ x 11⁸

LIVING RM
17¹⁰ x 20⁴

FOYER

WH

FURN

COVERED PORCH

CURB

CURB

3 CAR GARAGE
29⁴ x 20²

68'-8"

CUSTOMIZABLE
Custom Alterations? See page 349
for customizing this plan to your
specifications.

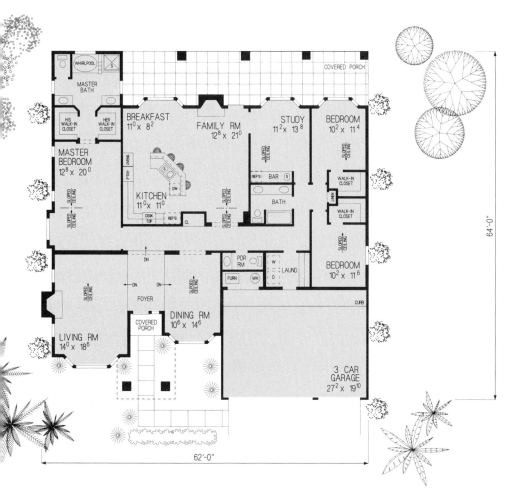

Design N3413

Square Footage: 2,517

L

● Though distinctly Southwest in design, this home
has some features that are
universally appealing. Note,
for instance, the central gallery, perpendicular to the
raised entry hall, and running almost the entire width
of the house. An L-shaped,
angled kitchen serves the
breakfast room and family
room in equal fashion.
Sleeping areas are found in
four bedrooms including an
optional study and exquisite
master suite.

CUSTOMIZABLE

Custom Alterations? See page 349
for customizing this plan to your
specifications.

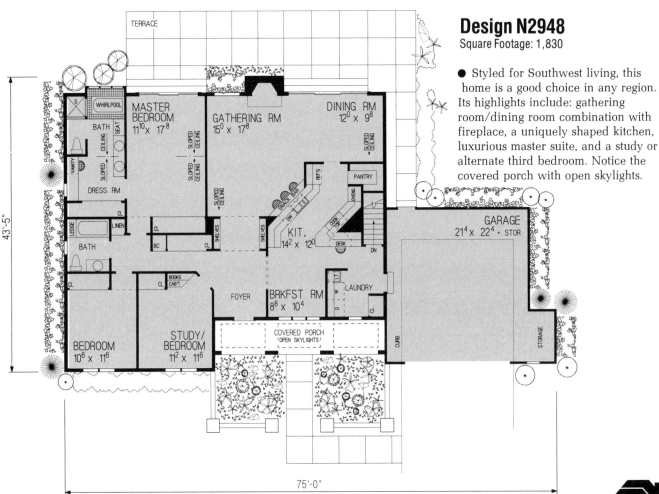

Design N2948

Square Footage: 1,830

● Styled for Southwest living, this home is a good choice in any region. Its highlights include: gathering room/dining room combination with fireplace, a uniquely shaped kitchen, luxurious master suite, and a study or alternate third bedroom. Notice the covered porch with open skylights.

CUSTOMIZABLE

Custom Alterations? See page 349 for customizing this plan to your specifications.

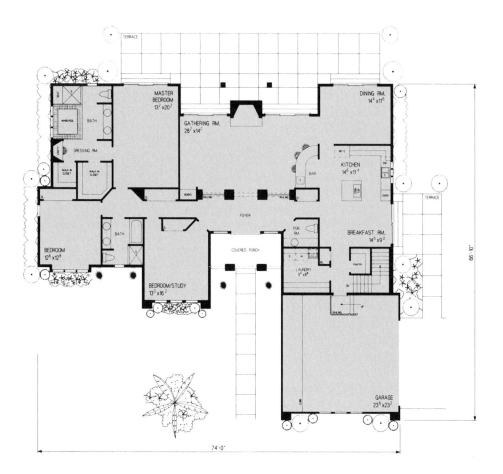

Design N2950
Square Footage 2,559

● A natural desert dweller, this stucco, tile-roofed beauty is equally comfortable in any clime. Inside, there's a well-planned design. Common living areas — gathering room, formal dining room, and breakfast room — are offset by a quiet study that could be used as a bedroom or guest room. A master suite features two walk-in closets, a double vanity, and whirlpool spa. The two-car garage has a service entrance; close by is an adequate laundry area and a pantry. Notice the warming hearth in the gathering room and the snack bar area for casual dining.

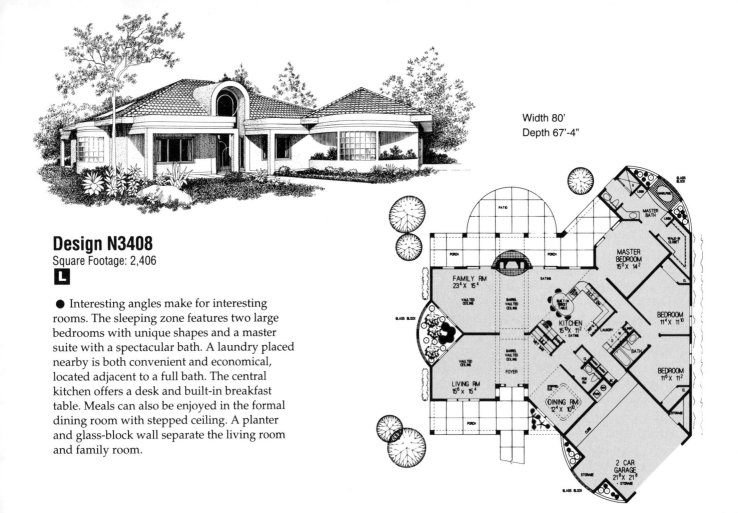

Width 80'
Depth 67'-4"

Design N3408

Square Footage: 2,406

L

● Interesting angles make for interesting rooms. The sleeping zone features two large bedrooms with unique shapes and a master suite with a spectacular bath. A laundry placed nearby is both convenient and economical, located adjacent to a full bath. The central kitchen offers a desk and built-in breakfast table. Meals can also be enjoyed in the formal dining room with stepped ceiling. A planter and glass-block wall separate the living room and family room.

Design N3419

Square Footage: 1,965

L

● This attractive, multi-gabled exterior houses a compact, livable interior. The entry foyer effectively routes traffic to all areas: left to the family room and kitchen, straight back to the dining room and living room, and right to the four-bedroom sleeping area. The spacious family room provides an informal gathering space while the living and dining rooms are perfect for formal occasions. The highlight of the sleeping area is the master bedroom with its whirlpool, walk-in closet and view of the back yard.

CUSTOMIZABLE

Custom Alterations? See page 349 for customizing this plan to your specifications.

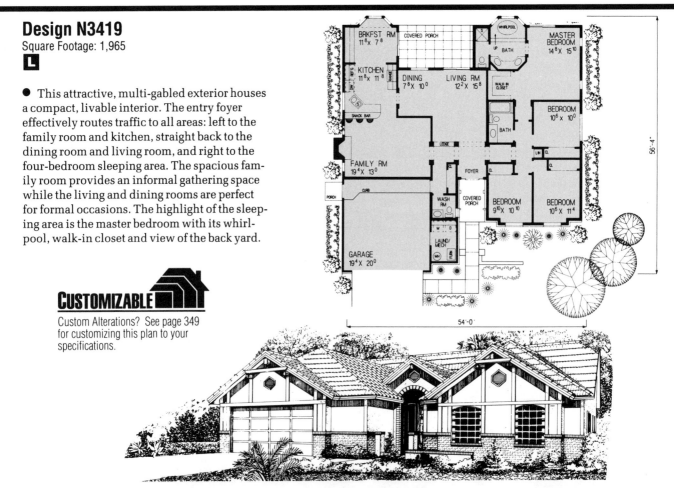

168

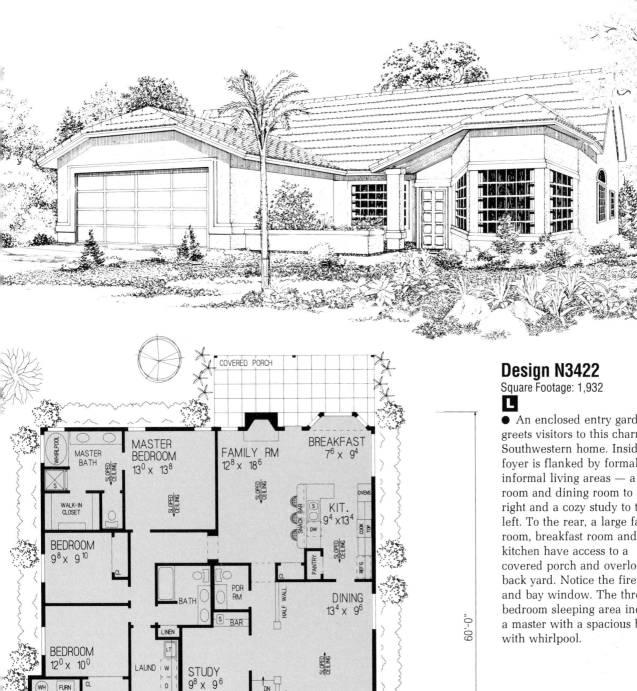

Design N3422

Square Footage: 1,932

L

● An enclosed entry garden greets visitors to this charming Southwestern home. Inside, the foyer is flanked by formal and informal living areas — a living room and dining room to the right and a cozy study to the left. To the rear, a large family room, breakfast room and open kitchen have access to a covered porch and overlook the back yard. Notice the fireplace and bay window. The three-bedroom sleeping area includes a master with a spacious bath with whirlpool.

CUSTOMIZABLE

Custom Alterations? See page 349 for customizing this plan to your specifications.

CUSTOMIZABLE

Custom Alterations? See page 349 for customizing this plan to your specifications.

Design N3427 First Floor: 1,574 square feet
Second Floor: 1,177 square feet; Total: 2,751 square feet

L

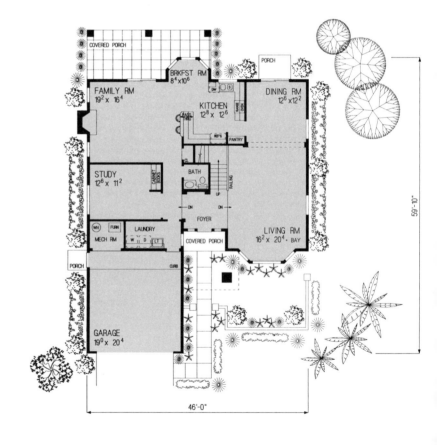

● Varying rooflines and unusual window treatments will make this home a standout anywhere. The transom-lit foyer opens onto a cozy study and a spacious living room with dramatic bay window. To the rear, the kitchen easily serves the dining room and the bay-windowed breakfast room. The family room features a large fireplace. Upstairs are four bedrooms including a master with whirlpool bath.

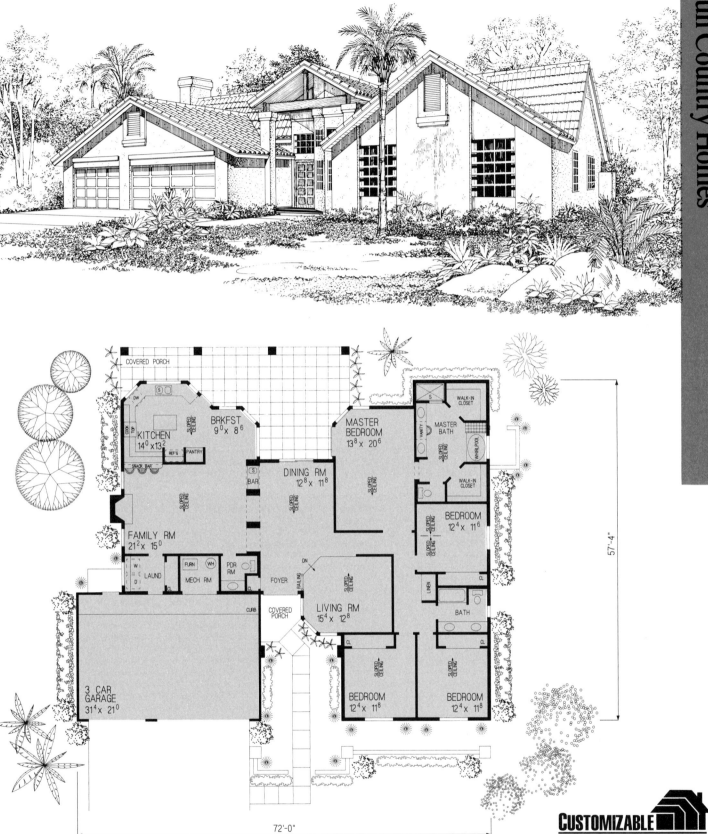

COVERED PORCH

KITCHEN
14⁰ x 13²

BRKFST
9⁰ x 8⁶

MASTER
BEDROOM
13⁸ x 20⁶

WALK-IN
CLOSET

MASTER
BATH

WHIRLPOOL

DINING RM
12⁸ x 11⁸

WALK-IN
CLOSET

FAMILY RM
21² x 15⁰

BEDROOM
12⁴ x 11⁶

LAUND

FURN

WH

PDR
RM

MECH RM

FOYER

DN

RAILING

LIVING RM
15⁴ x 12⁸

LINEN

BATH

CURB

COVERED
PORCH

3 CAR
GARAGE
31⁴ x 21⁰

BEDROOM
12⁴ x 11⁸

BEDROOM
12⁴ x 11⁸

57'-4"

72'-0"

CUSTOMIZABLE

Custom Alterations? See page 349
for customizing this plan to your
specifications.

Design N3423 Square Footage: 2,577

● This spacious Southwestern home
will be a pleasure to come home to.
Immediately off the foyer are the dining room and step-down living room
with bay window. The highlight of the

four-bedroom sleeping area is the
master suite with porch access and a
whirlpool for soaking away the day's
worries. The informal living area features an enormous family room with

fireplace and bay-windowed kitchen
and breakfast room. Notice the snack
bar pass-through to the family room.

Design N3440

Square Footage: 2,300

● Pack 'em in! There's plenty of
room for everyone in this three-, or
optional four-bedroom home. The
expansive gathering room welcomes
family and guests with a through-
fireplace to the dining room, an
audio/visual center, and a door to
the outside. The kitchen includes a
wide pantry, a snack bar, and a separate eating area. Included in the
master suite: two walk-in closets,
shower, whirlpool tub and seat, dual
vanities, and linen storage.

CUSTOMIZABLE

Custom Alterations? See page 349
for customizing this plan to your
specifications.

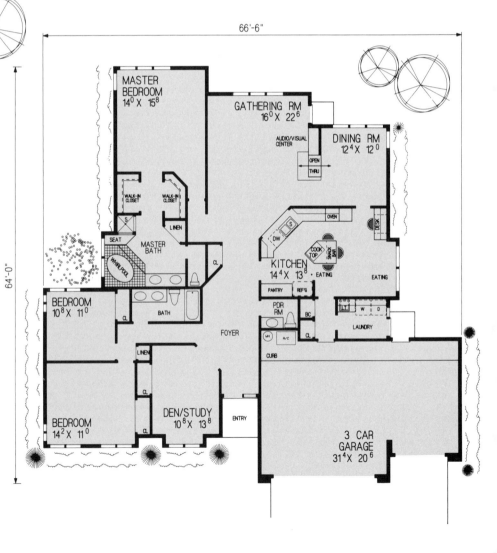

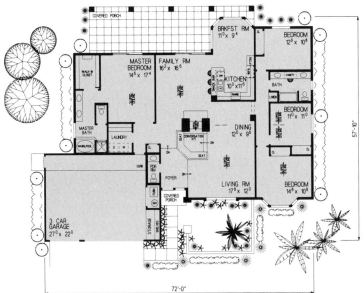

Design N3430

Square Footage: 2,394

L

● This dramatic design benefits from open planning. The centerpiece of the living area is a sunken conversation pit which shares a through-fireplace with the family room. The living room and dining room share space beneath a sloped ceiling. The open kitchen features a snack bar and breakfast room and conveniently serves all living areas. Split zoning in the sleeping area places the private master suite to the left of the plan and three more bedrooms, including one with a bay window, to the right.

CUSTOMIZABLE

Custom Alterations? See page 349 for customizing this plan to your specifications.

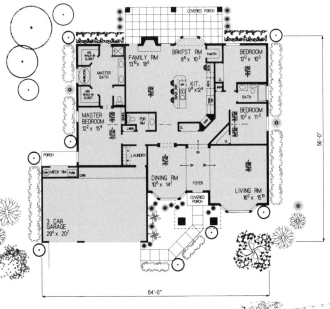

Design N3412

Square Footage: 2,150

L

● Although typically Southwestern in design, this home will bring style to any neighborhood. Huge bay windows flood the front living and dining rooms with plenty of natural light. An amenity-filled kitchen with attached family room will be the main gathering area, where the family works and relaxes together. Notice the fireplace, the island snack bar and walk-in pantry. A split sleeping zone separates the master suite with luxurious bath from the two family bedrooms. Also notice the covered porch off the family room.

CUSTOMIZABLE

Custom Alterations? See page 349 for customizing this plan to your specifications.

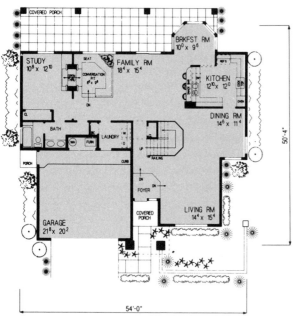

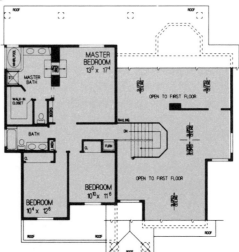

CUSTOMIZABLE

Custom Alterations? See page 349 for customizing this plan to your specifications.

Design N3424

First Floor: 1,625 square feet
Second Floor: 982 square feet
Total: 2,607 square feet

● You'll find plenty about this Spanish design that will convince you that this is the home for your family. Enjoy indoor/outdoor living in the gigantic family room with covered patio access and a sunken conversation area sharing a through-fireplace with the study. An L-shaped kitchen has an attached, glass-surrounded breakfast room and is conveniently located next to the formal dining room/living room combination. Besides the opulent master suite on the second floor, there are two family bedrooms and a full bath.

Design N3449

First Floor: 1,336 square feet
Second Floor: 1,186 square feet
Total: 2,522 square feet

L

● A covered porch leads inside to a wide, tiled foyer. A curving staircase makes an elegant statement in the open space between the living room and dining room. A through fireplace warms the nook and family room. Also look for a wet bar and glass shelves here. The master bedroom includes a sitting area, two closets and its own deck. Two family bedrooms share a full bath with dual vanities.

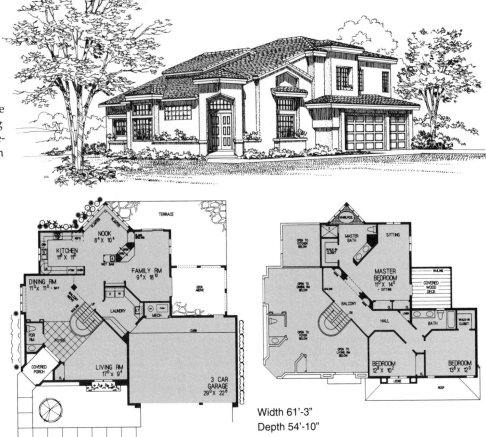

CUSTOMIZABLE

Custom Alterations? See page 349 for customizing this plan to your specifications.

Width 61'-3"
Depth 54'-10"

Design N3323

First Floor: 1,923 square feet
Second Floor: 838 square feet
Total: 2,751 square feet

L

● Take a step down from the foyer to a gathering room with fireplace and reading alcove, to a media room or to a dining room with sliding glass doors to the terrace. The kitchen has an island range and eating space. Also on the first floor is a large master suite including a sitting area with terrace access, a walk-in closet and whirlpool. An elegant spiral staircase leads to two family bedrooms which share a full bath and a guest bedroom with private bath.

CUSTOMIZABLE

Custom Alterations? See page 349 for customizing this plan to your specifications.

Width 53'
Depth 70'-4"

Design N3414

First Floor: 2,024 square feet
Second Floor: 1,144 square feet
Total: 3,168 square feet

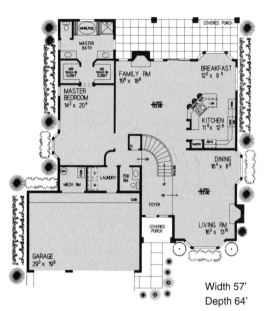

Width 57'
Depth 64'

● Though seemingly compact from the exterior, this home allows for "wide-open-spaces" living. The two-story entry connects directly to a formal living/dining area, a fitting complement to the more casual family room and cozy breakfast room. Split-bedroom planning puts the master suite on the first floor for utmost privacy. Up the curved staircase are three family bedrooms, a guest room with deck, and two full baths.

CUSTOMIZABLE

Custom Alterations? See page 349 for customizing this plan to your specifications.

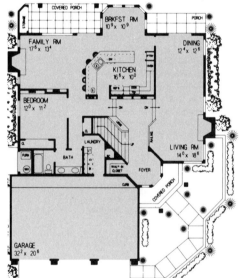

Width 52'
Depth 64'-4"

Design N3425

First Floor: 1,776 square feet
Second Floor: 1,035 square feet
Total: 2,811 square feet

● Here's a two-story Spanish design with an appealing, angled exterior. Inside is an interesting floor plan containing rooms with a variety of shapes. Formal areas are to the right of the entry tower: a living room with fireplace and

CUSTOMIZABLE

Custom Alterations? See page 349 for customizing this plan to your specifications.

large dining room. The kitchen has loads of counter space and is complemented by a bumped-out breakfast room. Note the second fireplace in the family room, and the first-floor bedroom. Three second-floor bedrooms include a master suite with balcony.

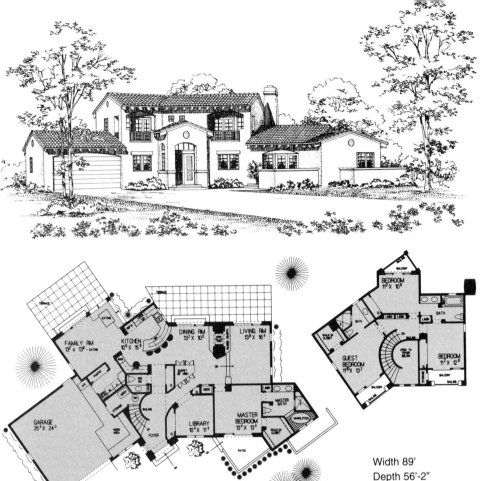

Design N3435

First Floor: 1,946 square feet
Second Floor: 986 square feet
Total: 2,932 square feet

L

● Here's a grand Spanish Mission home designed for family living. Enter at the angled foyer which contains a curved staircase to the second floor. Family bedrooms are here along with a spacious guest suite. The master bedroom is found on the first floor and has a private patio and whirlpool overlooking an enclosed garden area. Besides a living room and dining room connected by a through-fireplace, there is a family room with casual eating space. There is also a library with large closet. You'll appreciate the abundant built-ins and interesting shapes throughout the house.

Width 89'
Depth 56'-2"

CUSTOMIZABLE

Custom Alterations? See page 349 for customizing this plan to your specifications.

Design N3437

First Floor: 1,522 square feet
Second Floor: 800 square feet
Total: 2,322 square feet

L

● This two-story Spanish Mission-style home has character inside and out. The first-floor master suite features a fireplace and gracious bath with walk-in closet, whirlpool, shower, dual vanities and linen storage. A second fireplace serves both the gathering room and media room or library. The kitchen, with island cook top, includes a snack bar and an adjoining breakfast nook. Three bedrooms and two full baths occupy the second floor.

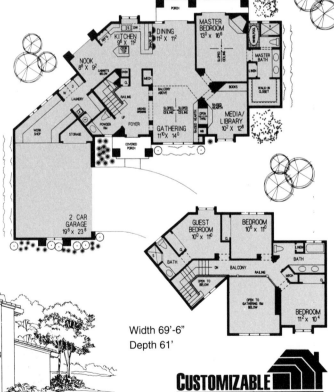

Width 69'-6"
Depth 61'

CUSTOMIZABLE

Custom Alterations? See page 349 for customizing this plan to your specifications.

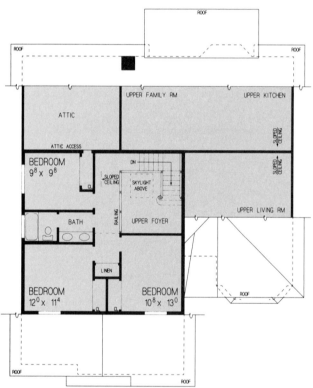

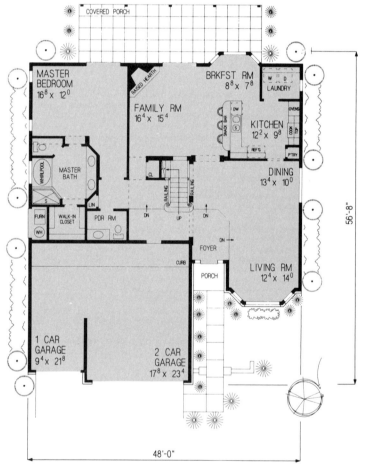

Design N3420 First Floor: 1,617 square feet
Second Floor: 658 square feet; Total: 2,275 square feet

L

● Here is a moderate-sized house with a wealth of amenities typical of much larger homes. Interesting window treatments include two bay windows, one in the living room and one in the breakfast room. In the kitchen there's a snack bar pass-through to the family room which boasts a corner raised-hearth fireplace. Also on this level, the master suite features a large bath with whirlpool and access to the rear covered porch. Upstairs are three more bedrooms and a shared bath. Notice the attic storage space.

CUSTOMIZABLE

Custom Alterations? See page 349 for customizing this plan to your specifications.

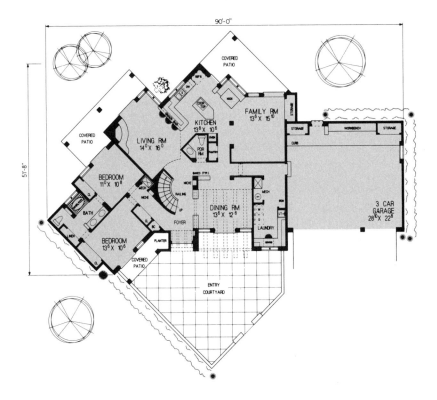

Design N3432

First Floor: 1,966 square feet
Second Floor: 831 square feet
Total: 2,797 square feet

L

● Unique in nature, this two-story Santa Fe-style home is as practical as it is lovely. The facade is elegantly enhanced by a large entry court, overlooked by windows in the dining room and a covered patio from one of two family bedrooms. The entry foyer leads to living areas at the back of the plan: a living room with corner fireplace and a family room connected to the kitchen via a built-in eating nook. Upstairs, the master suite features a grand bath and large walk-in closet. The guest bedroom has a private bath. Every room in this home has its own outdoor area.

CUSTOMIZABLE

Custom Alterations? See page 349 for customizing this plan to your specifications.

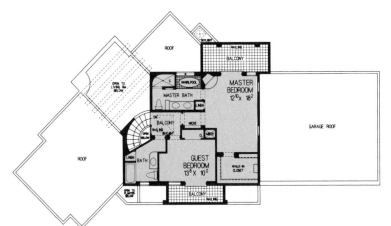

Design N3441

First Floor: 2,022 square feet
Second Floor: 845 square feet
Total: 2,867 square feet

L

Width 63'-8"
Depth 56'-2"

● Special details make the difference between a house and a home. A snack bar, audio/visual center and a fireplace make the family room livable. A desk, island cooktop, bay and sky-lights enhance the kitchen area. The dining room features two columns and a plant ledge. The first-floor master suite includes His and Hers walk-in closets, a spacious bath and a bay window. On the second floor, one bedroom features a walk-in closet and private bath, while two additional bedrooms share a full bath.

CUSTOMIZABLE

Custom Alterations? See page 349 for customizing this plan to your specifications.

Design N3447

First Floor: 1,861 square feet
Second Floor: 1,039 square feet
Total: 2,900 square feet

L **D**

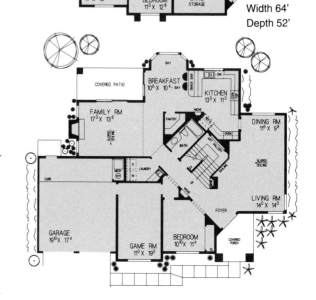

Width 64'
Depth 52'

● Family activities of all types have a distinct place in this home. The first floor contains a game room, along with a living room/dining room combination with sloped ceiling. The family room is also on this floor and has a cozy fireplace. The spacious, angled kitchen includes a snack bar, walk-in pantry, and adjacent breakfast area with a bay. An elegant staircase is accented by a niche and art gallery. The master bed-room features a private deck, two closets and a lavish bath. Two addi-tional bedrooms share a full bath.

CUSTOMIZABLE

Custom Alterations? See page 349 for customizing this plan to your specifications.

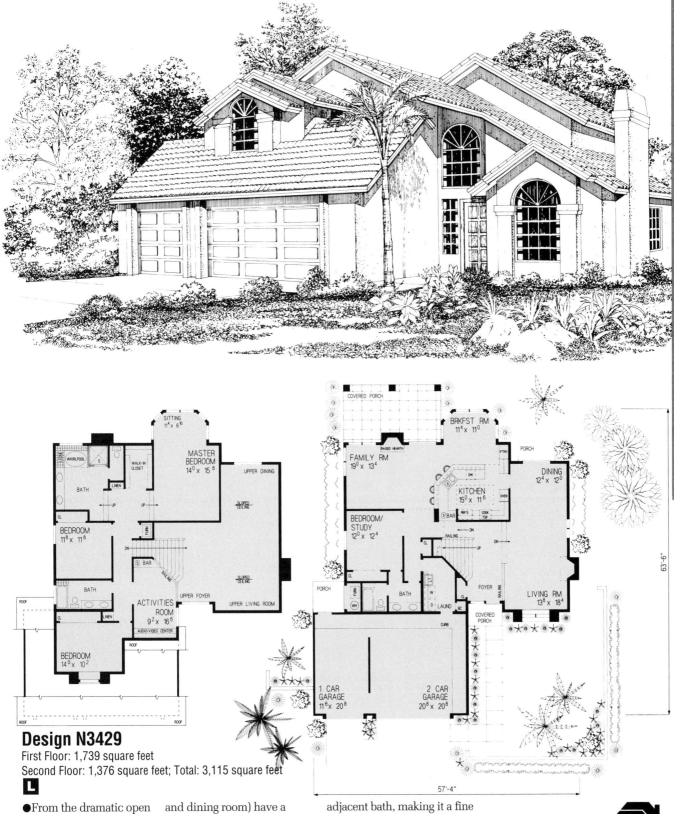

SITTING
11⁴ x 6¹⁰

WHIRLPOOL
S

WALK-IN
CLOSET

MASTER
BEDROOM
14⁰ x 15⁸

UPPER DINING

LINEN

BATH

SLOPED
CEILING

UP   UP

BEDROOM
11⁸ x 11⁸

FURN

DN

S   BAR

RAILING

BATH

SLOPED
CEILING

LINEN

CL

ACTIVITIES
ROOM
9² x 16⁶

UPPER FOYER

UPPER LIVING ROOM

AUDIO/VIDEO CENTER

ROOF

BEDROOM
14⁰ x 10²

ROOF

ROOF

ROOF

ROOF

COVERED PORCH

BRKFST RM
11⁴ x 11⁰

RAISED HEARTH

FAMILY RM
19⁰ x 13⁴

P'TRY

PORCH

DW

DINING
12⁴ x 12⁰

KITCHEN
15⁰ x 11⁶

OVEN

S   BAR

REF'S

COOK
TOP

BEDROOM/
STUDY
12⁰ x 12⁴

DN

RAILING

UP

DN

CL

PORCH

CL

FURN

WH

BATH

W

D

LAUND

BC

FOYER

RAILING

LIVING RM
13⁸ x 18⁴

COVERED
PORCH

CURB

1 CAR
GARAGE
11⁶ x 20⁸

2 CAR
GARAGE
20⁸ x 20⁸

63'-6"

57'-4"

Design N3429

First Floor: 1,739 square feet
Second Floor: 1,376 square feet; Total: 3,115 square feet

L

●From the dramatic open entry to the covered back porch, this home delivers a full measure of livability in Spanish design. Formal living areas (living room and dining room) have a counter-point in the family room and glassed-in breakfast room. The kitchen is a hub for both areas. Notice that the first-floor study has an adjacent bath, making it a fine guest room when needed. On the second floor, the activities room serves two family bedrooms and a grand master suite.

CUSTOMIZABLE

Custom Alterations? See page 349 for customizing this plan to your specifications.

Design N2850

Main Level: 1,530 square feet
Upper Level: 984 square feet
Lower Level: 951 square feet
Total: 3,465 square feet

L **D**

● Entering through the entry court of this Spanish design is very impressive. Down six steps from the foyer is the lower level, housing a bedroom and full bath, study and teenage activities room. Six steps up from the foyer is the upper-level bedroom area. The main level has the majority of the living areas: formal living and dining rooms, informal family room, kitchen with accompanying breakfast room and mud room consisting of laundry and wash room. This home even has a three-car garage.

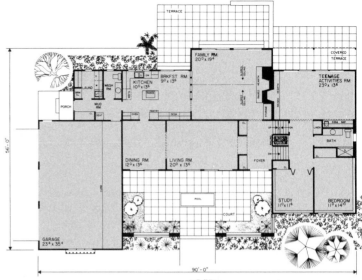

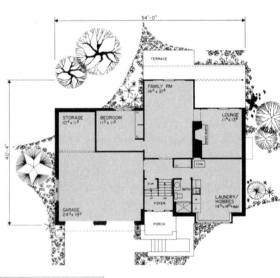

Design N2843

Upper Level: 1,861 square feet
Lower Level: 1,181 square feet
Total: 3,042 square feet

L

● Bi-level living will be enjoyed to its fullest in this Spanish- styled design. There is a lot of room for the various family activities. Informal living will take place on the lower level in the family room and lounge. The formal living and dining rooms, sharing a through-fireplace, are located on the upper level.

Design N2846

Main Level: 2,341 square feet; Lower Level: 1,380 square feet;
Total: 3,721 square feet

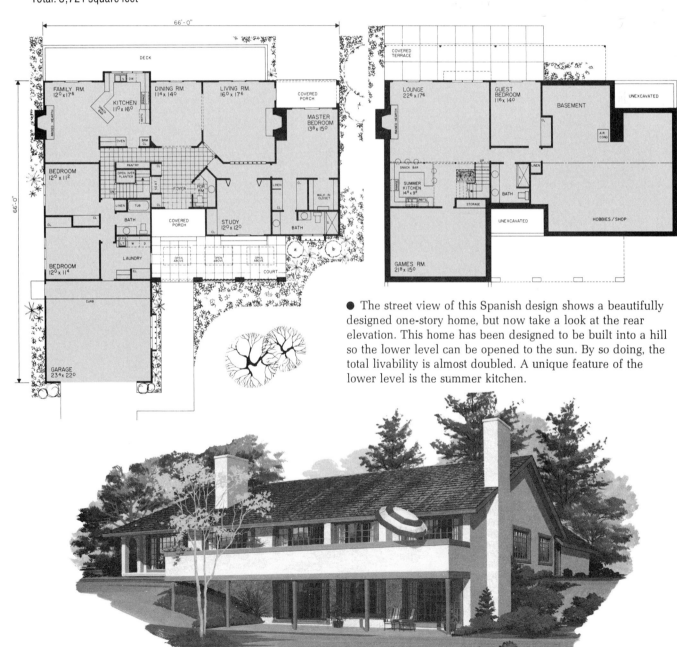

● The street view of this Spanish design shows a beautifully designed one-story home, but now take a look at the rear elevation. This home has been designed to be built into a hill so the lower level can be opened to the sun. By so doing, the total livability is almost doubled. A unique feature of the lower level is the summer kitchen.

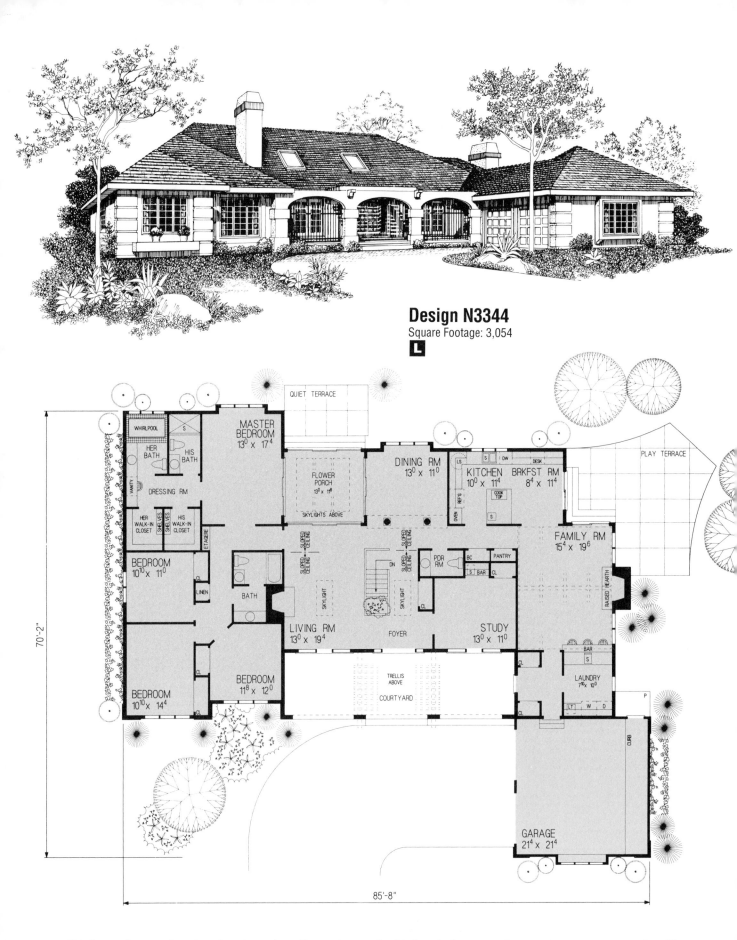

Design N3344

Square Footage: 3,054

L

● This home features interior planning for today's active family. Living areas include a living room with fireplace, a cozy study and family room with wet bar. Convenient to the kitchen is the formal dining room with attractive bay window overlooking the back yard. The four-bedroom sleeping area contains a sumptuous master suite. Also notice the cheerful flower porch with access from the master suite, living room and dining room.

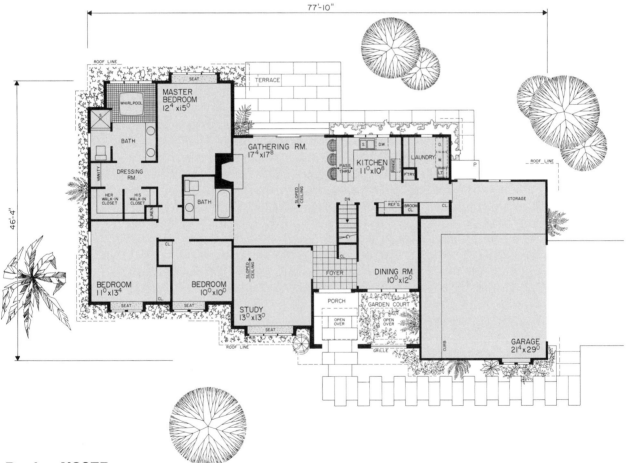

Design N2875

Square Footage: 1,913

L **D**

● This elegant Spanish design incorporates excellent indoor-outdoor living relationships for modern families who enjoy the sun and comforts of a well-planned new home. Note the overhead openings for rain and sun to fall upon a front garden, while a twin arched entry leads to the front porch and foyer. Inside the floor plan features a modern kitchen with pass-thru to a large gathering room with fireplace. Other features include a dining room, laundry room, a study off the foyer, plus three bedrooms including master bedroom with its own whirlpool.

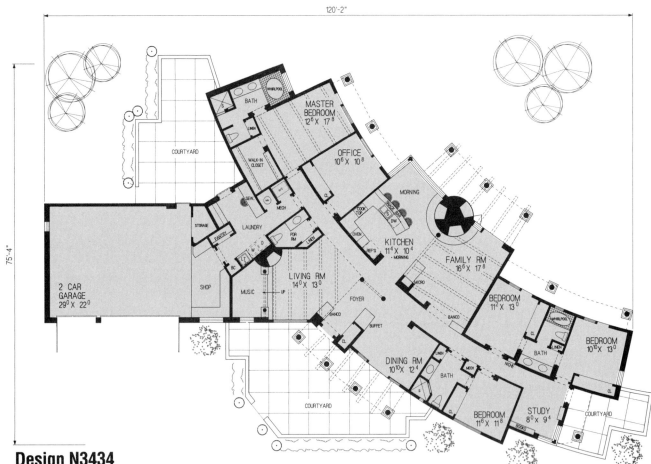

Floor plan labels:
BATH · WHIRLPOOL · MASTER BEDROOM 12⁶ X 17⁸ · COURTYARD · LINEN · WALK-IN CLOSET · OFFICE 10⁶ X 10⁸ · SEW. · MECH · CL · MORNING · SNACK BAR · DW · BOOK TOP · STORAGE · PANTRY · LAUNDRY · PDR RM · LINEN · OVEN · KITCHEN 11⁴ X 10⁴ · MORNING · REF'S · FAMILY RM 16⁶ X 17⁸ · SHOP · MUSIC · LIVING RM 14⁰ X 13⁰ · UP · FOYER · MICRO · BANCO · BEDROOM 11² X 13⁰ · 2 CAR GARAGE 29⁰ X 22⁰ · BANCO · BUFFET · CL · BANCO · CL · LINEN · WHIRLPOOL · BEDROOM 10¹⁰ X 13⁰ · DINING RM 10¹⁰ X 12⁴ · LINEN · MECH · BATH · LINEN · NICHE · BATH · CL · COURTYARD · CL · COURTYARD · BEDROOM 11⁶ X 11⁸ · STUDY 8⁰ X 9⁴ · BOOKS · CL

120'-2"

75'-4"

Design N3434
Square Footage: 3,428

L

● An in-line floor plan follows the tradition of the original Santa Fe-style homes. The slight curve to the overall configuration lends an interesting touch. From the front courtyard, the plan opens to a formal living room and dining room complemented by a family room and kitchen with morning room. The master bedroom is found to one side of the plan while family bedrooms share space at the opposite end. There's also a huge office and a study area for private times. With 3½ baths, a workshop garage, full laundry/sewing area, and three courtyards, this plan adds up to great livability.

CUSTOMIZABLE
Custom Alterations? See page 349 for customizing this plan to your specifications.

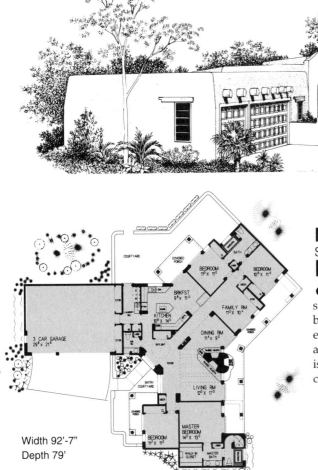

Design N3433

Square Footage: 2,350

L

● Santa Fe styling creates interesting angles in this one-story home. The master suite features a deluxe bath and a bedroom close at hand, perfect for a nursery, home office or exercise room. Fireplaces in the living room, dining room and covered porch create various shapes. Make note of the island range in the kitchen, extra storage in the garage, and covered porches on two sides.

Width 92'-7"
Depth 79'

CUSTOMIZABLE

Custom Alterations? See page 349 for customizing this plan to your specifications.

Design N3431

Square Footage: 1,907

● Graceful curves welcome you into the courtyard of this Santa Fe home. Inside, a gallery directs traffic to the work zone on the left or the sleeping zone on the right. Straight ahead lies a sunken gathering room with beamed ceiling and raised-hearth fireplace. A large pantry offers extra storage space for kitchen items. The covered rear porch is accessible from the dining room, gathering room and secluded master bedroom. Two family bedrooms share a compartmented bath. The study could serve as a guest room, media room or home office.

Width 61'-6"
Depth 67'-4"

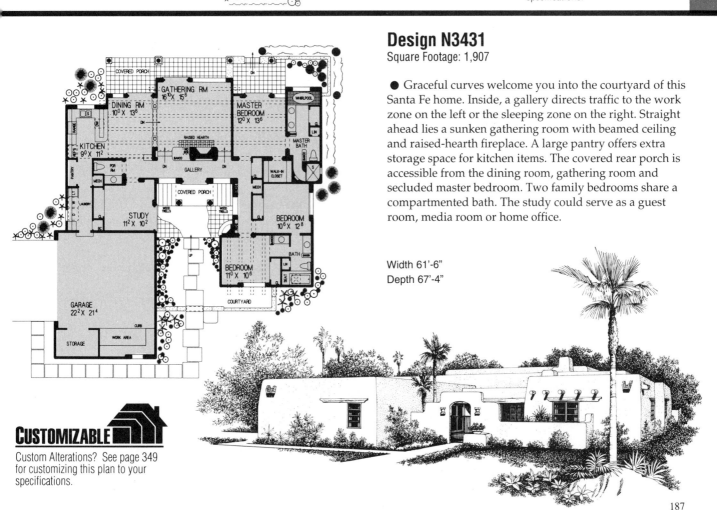

CUSTOMIZABLE

Custom Alterations? See page 349 for customizing this plan to your specifications.

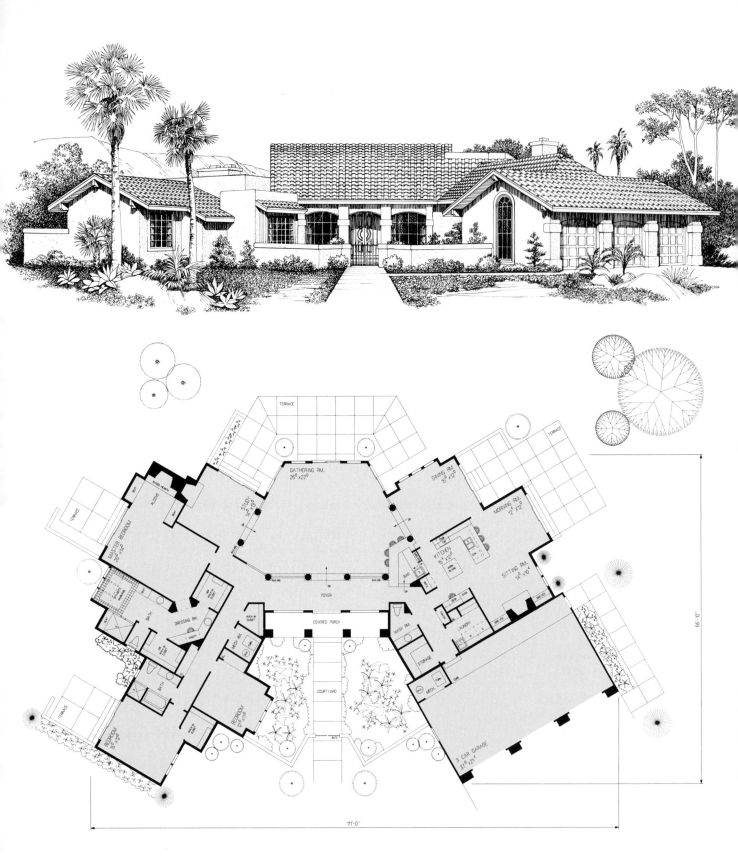

Design N2922
Square Footage: 3,505

● Loaded with custom features, this plan seems to have everything imaginable. There's an enormous sunken gathering room and cozy study. The country-style kitchen contains an efficient work area, as well as space for relaxing in the morning and sitting rooms. Two nice-sized bedrooms and a luxurious master suite round out the plan.

Design N3480

Square Footage: 1,845

L **D**

● The inviting facade of this sun-country home introduces a most livable floor plan. Beyond the grand entry, a comfortable gathering room, with a central fireplace, shares sweeping, open spaces with the dining room. An efficiently patterned kitchen makes use of a large, walk-in pantry and a breakfast room. Nearby, a full laundry room rounds out the modern livability of this utilitarian area. Away from the hustle and bustle of the day, three bedrooms provide ample sleeping accommodations for the whole family. Two secondary bedrooms each enjoy full proportions and the convenience of a nearby full bath. In the master bedroom, look for double closets and a pampering bath with double lavs, a vanity and a whirlpool bath.

CUSTOMIZABLE
Custom Alterations? See page 349 for customizing this plan to your specifications.

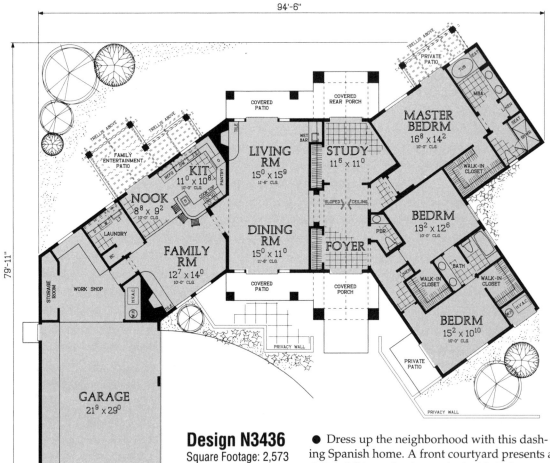

94'-6"

79'-11"

COVERED PATIO

COVERED REAR PORCH

PRIVATE PATIO

TRELLIS ABOVE

TUB

MBA

MASTER BEDRM
16⁸ x 14²
10'-0" CLG.

WALK-IN CLOSET

LINEN

SEAT

SHWR

LIVING RM
15⁰ x 15⁹
11'-6" CLG.

STUDY
11⁶ x 11⁰

WET BAR

FAMILY ENTERTAINMENT PATIO

TRELLIS ABOVE

KIT
11⁰ x 10⁸
10'-0" CLG.

REFG

DW

PANTRY

COOK TOP

SLOPED CEILING

PDR

BEDRM
13² x 12⁶
10'-0" CLG.

NOOK
8⁸ x 9²
10'-0" CLG.

LAUNDRY

DINING RM
15⁰ x 11⁰
11'-6" CLG.

FOYER

LINEN

BATH

FAMILY RM
12⁷ x 14⁰
10'-0" CLG.

WALK-IN CLOSET

WALK-IN CLOSET

STORAGE ROOM

WORK SHOP

HVAC

COVERED PATIO

COVERED PORCH

HVAC

BEDRM
15² x 10¹⁰
10'-0" CLG.

TILE

PRIVACY WALL

PRIVATE PATIO

GARAGE
21⁸ x 29⁰

CURB

PRIVACY WALL

Design N3436
Square Footage: 2,573

L

CUSTOMIZABLE

Custom Alterations? See page 349 for customizing this plan to your specifications.

● Dress up the neighborhood with this dashing Spanish home. A front courtyard presents a delightful introduction to the inside living spaces. These excel with a central living room/dining room combination. A wet bar here makes entertaining easy. In the kitchen, a huge pantry and interesting angles are sure to please the house gourmet. A breakfast nook with a corner fireplace further enhances this area. Notice the laundry room nearby as well as the expansive work shop just off the three-car garage. The master bedroom makes room for a private bath with a whirlpool tub and dual lavatories; a walk-in closet adds to the modern amenities here. Two additional bedrooms make use of a Hollywood bath. Each bedroom is highlighted by a spacious walk-in closet.

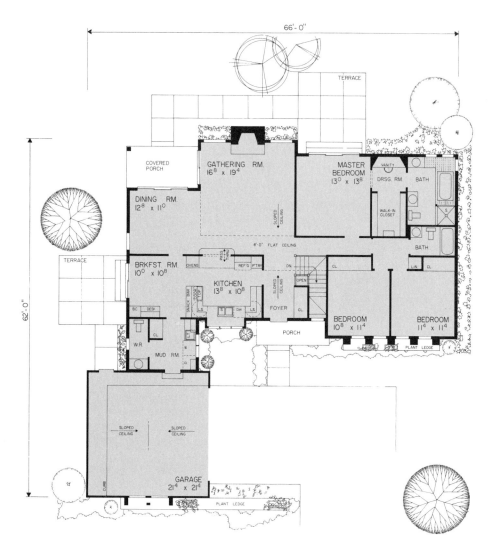

Design N2912
Square Footage: 1,864

● This modern design with
smart Spanish styling incorporates careful zoning by room
functions with lifestyle comfort.
All three bedrooms, including a
master bedroom suite, are isolated at one end of the one-story
home for privacy and out of traffic patterns. Entry to a breakfast
room and kitchen is possible
through a mud room off the garage. That's good news for people carrying groceries from car to
kitchen or people with muddy
shoes during inclement weather.
The modern kitchen includes a
snack bar and cook top with
multiple access to breakfast
room, side foyer, and pass-thru to
hallway. There's also a nearby
formal dining room. A large rear
gathering room features sloped
ceiling and its own fireplace.
Note the two-car garage and
built-in plant ledge in front.
Gabled end window treatment
plus varied roof lines further
enhance the striking appearance
of this efficient design.

Design N3403

First Floor: 2,240 square feet
Second Floor: 660 square feet
Total: 2,900 square feet

L D

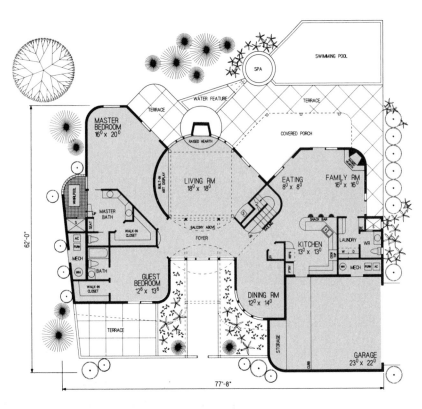

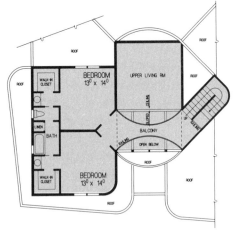

● There is no end to the distinctive features in this Southwestern contemporary. Formal living areas are concentrated in the center of the plan, perfect for entertaining. To the right of the plan, the kitchen and family room function well together as a working and living area. Also note the separate laundry room. The optional guest bedroom or den and the master bedroom are located to the left of the plan. Upstairs, the remaining two bedrooms are reached by a balcony overlooking the living room and share a bath with twin vanities.

Design N3316

First Floor: 1,111 square feet
Second Floor: 886 square feet
Total: 1,997 square feet

L

● Don't be fooled by a small-looking exterior. This plan offers three bedrooms and plenty of living space. Notice that the screened porch leads to a rear terrace with access to the breakfast room. A living room/dining room combination adds spaciousness to the first floor.

Design N2682

First Floor (Basic Plan): 976 square feet
First Floor (Expanded Plan): 1,230 square feet
Second Floor (Both Plans): 744 square feet
Total (Basic Plan): 1,720; Total (Expanded Plan): 1,974

L **D**

CUSTOMIZABLE

Custom Alterations? See page 349 for customizing this plan to your specifications.

● Here is an expandable Colonial with a full measure of Cape Cod Charm. For those who wish to build the basic house, there is an abundance of low-budget livability. Twin fireplaces serve the formal living room and the informal country kitchen. Note the spaciousness of both areas. A dining room and powder room are also on the first floor of this basic plan. Upstairs three bedrooms and two full baths.

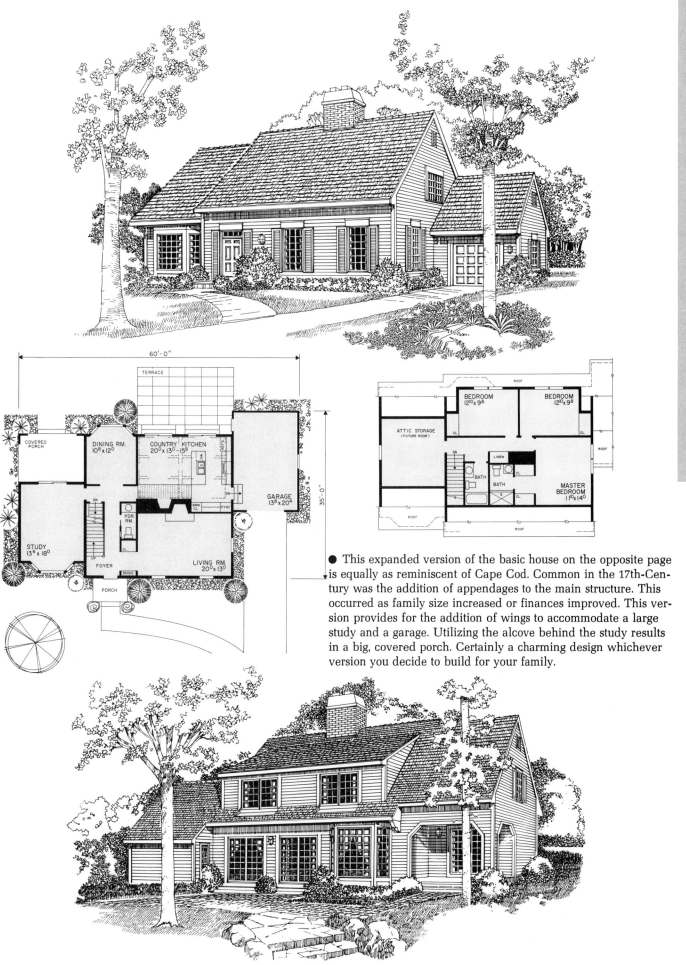

● This expanded version of the basic house on the opposite page is equally as reminiscent of Cape Cod. Common in the 17th-Century was the addition of appendages to the main structure. This occurred as family size increased or finances improved. This version provides for the addition of wings to accommodate a large study and a garage. Utilizing the alcove behind the study results in a big, covered porch. Certainly a charming design whichever version you decide to build for your family.

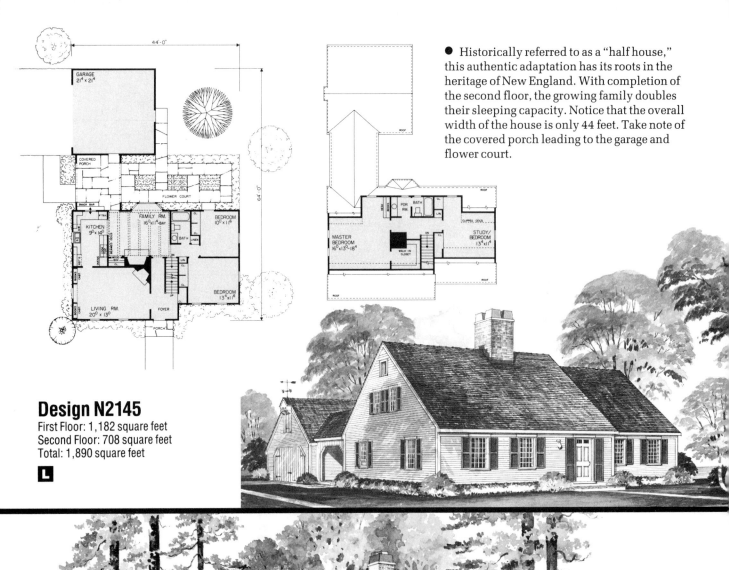

● Historically referred to as a "half house," this authentic adaptation has its roots in the heritage of New England. With completion of the second floor, the growing family doubles their sleeping capacity. Notice that the overall width of the house is only 44 feet. Take note of the covered porch leading to the garage and flower court.

Design N2145
First Floor: 1,182 square feet
Second Floor: 708 square feet
Total: 1,890 square feet

L

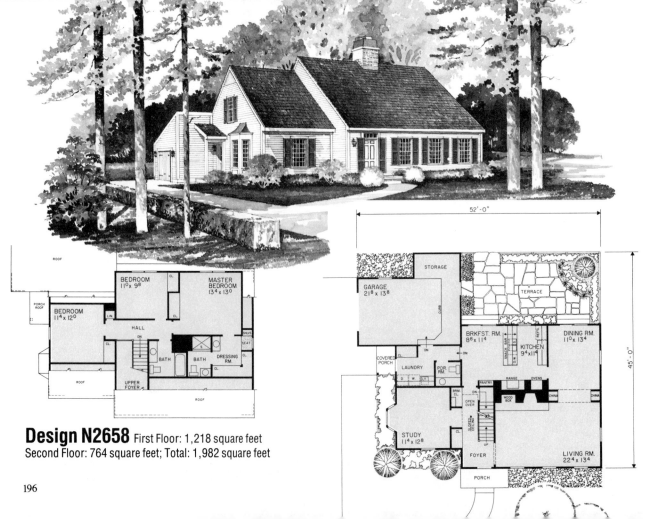

Design N2658 First Floor: 1,218 square feet
Second Floor: 764 square feet; Total: 1,982 square feet

● Captivating as a New England village! From the weather vane atop the garage to the roofed side entry and paned windows, this home is perfectly detailed. Inside, there is a lot of living space. An exceptionally large family room which is more than 29' by 13' including a dining area. The adjoining kitchen has a laundry just steps away. Two formal rooms are in the front.

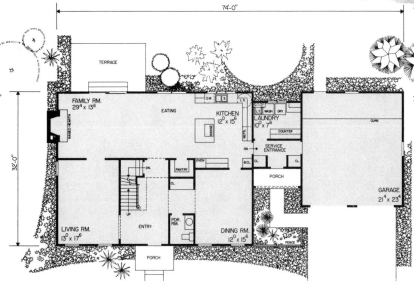

Design N2596
First Floor: 1,489 square feet
Second Floor: 982 square feet
Total: 2,471 square feet

L **D**

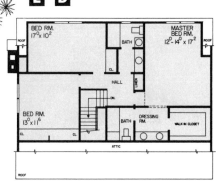

Design N2146
First Floor: 1,182 square feet
Second Floor: 708 square feet
Total: 1,890 square feet

L **D**

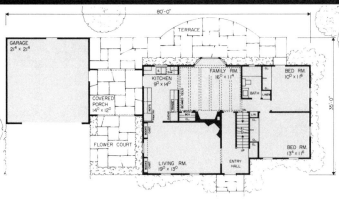

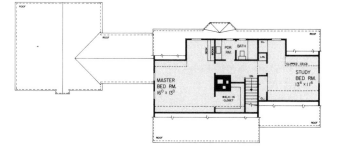

● Historically referred to as a "half house," this authentic adaptation has its roots in the heritage of New England. With completion of the second floor, the growing family doubles its sleeping capacity. Notice that both the family and living rooms have a fireplace. Don't overlook the many built-in units featured throughout the plan.

Design N2569 First Floor: 1,102 square feet
Second Floor: 764 square feet; Total: 1,866 square feet

L **D**

● What an enchanting updated version of the popular
Cape Cod cottage. There are facilities for both formal
and informal living pursuits. Note the spacious family
area, the formal dining/living room, the first floor laundry and the efficient kitchen. The second floor houses
the three bedrooms and two economically located baths.

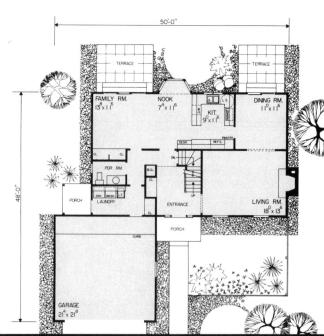

Design N2395 First Floor: 1,481 square feet
Second Floor: 861 square feet; Total: 2,342 square feet

L

● New England revisited. The appeal of
this type of home is ageless. As for its
livability, it will serve its occupants
admirably for generations to come. With two
bedrooms downstairs, you may want to finish
off the second floor at a later date.

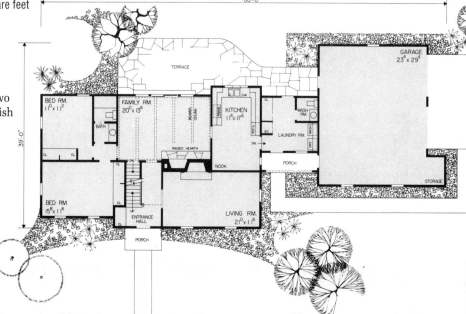

198

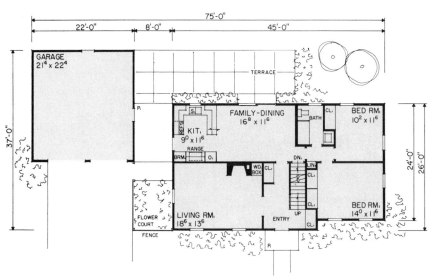

Design N3126

First Floor: 1,141 square feet
Second Floor: 630 square feet
Total: 1,771 square feet

L **D**

● This New England adaptation has a lot to offer. There is the U-shaped kitchen, family-dining room, four bedrooms, two full baths, fireplace, covered porch and two-car garage. A delightful addition to any neighborhood.

199

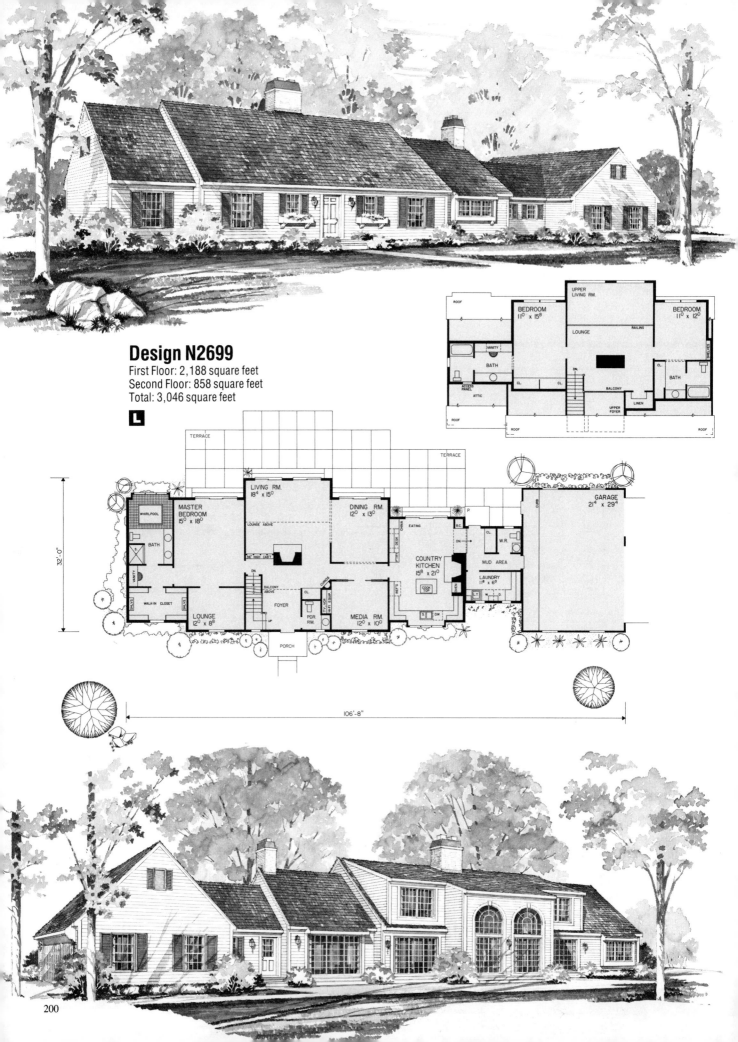

Design N2699

First Floor: 2,188 square feet
Second Floor: 858 square feet
Total: 3,046 square feet

L

The exterior detailing of this design recalls 18th-Century New England architecture. Enter by way of the centered front door and you are greeted into the foyer. Directly to the right is the study or optional bedroom or to the left is the living room. This large formal room features sliding glass doors to the sun-drenched solarium. The beauty of the solarium will be appreciated from the master bedroom and the dining room along with the living room.

Design N2615
First Floor: 2,563 square feet
Second Floor: 552 square feet
Total: 3,115 square feet

L   D

Design N2500

First Floor: 1,851 square feet
Second Floor: 762 square feet
Total: 2,613 square feet

L D

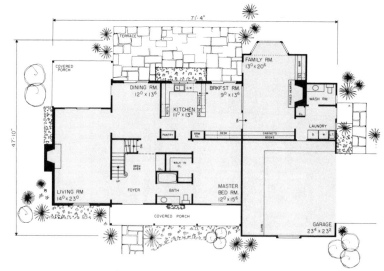

● Large families will enjoy the wonderful floor plan offered by this charming home. Don't miss the covered rear porch and the many features of the family room.

Design N2510

First Floor: 1,191 square feet
Second Floor: 533 square feet
Total: 1,724 square feet

L D

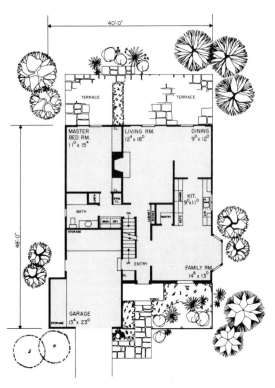

● The pleasant in-line kitchen is flanked by a separate dining room and a family room. The master bedroom is on the first floor with two more bedrooms upstairs.

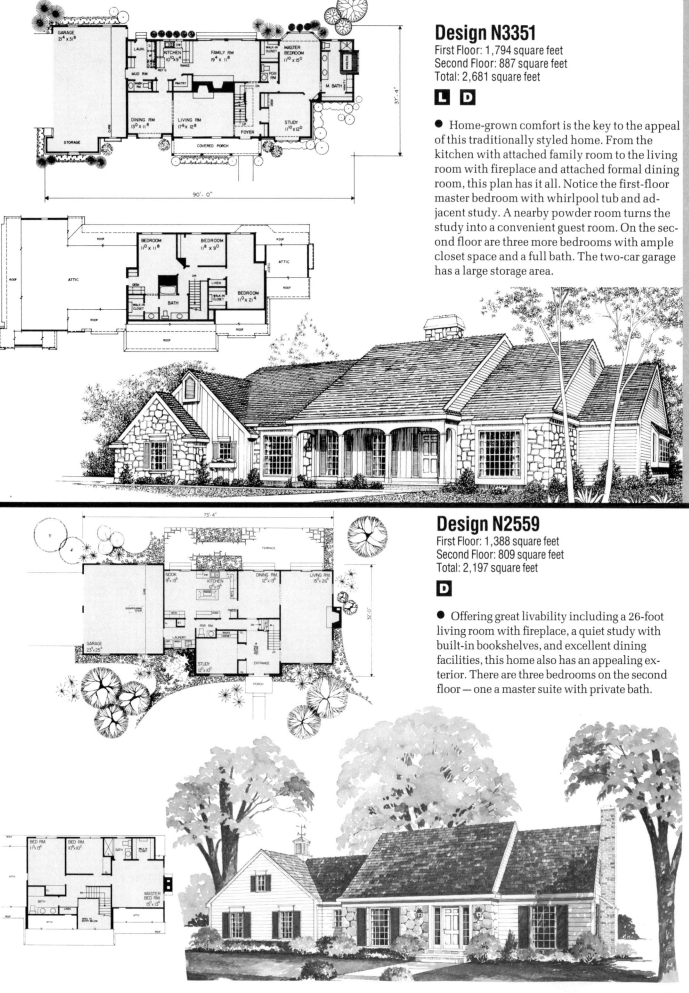

Design N3351

First Floor: 1,794 square feet
Second Floor: 887 square feet
Total: 2,681 square feet

L **D**

● Home-grown comfort is the key to the appeal of this traditionally styled home. From the kitchen with attached family room to the living room with fireplace and attached formal dining room, this plan has it all. Notice the first-floor master bedroom with whirlpool tub and adjacent study. A nearby powder room turns the study into a convenient guest room. On the second floor are three more bedrooms with ample closet space and a full bath. The two-car garage has a large storage area.

Design N2559

First Floor: 1,388 square feet
Second Floor: 809 square feet
Total: 2,197 square feet

D

● Offering great livability including a 26-foot living room with fireplace, a quiet study with built-in bookshelves, and excellent dining facilities, this home also has an appealing exterior. There are three bedrooms on the second floor — one a master suite with private bath.

Design N3353

First Floor: 2,191 square feet
Second Floor: 874 square feet
Total: 3,065 square feet

● This captivating 1½-story Southern Colonial provides the best in livability. On the first floor are the living room, dining room and private media room. A country kitchen with fireplace offers casual living space. The master suite is also located on this floor and has a lavish master bath with whirlpool spa. Upstairs are two family bedrooms, each with its own bath, and a central lounge overlooking the living room.

Design N2718

First Floor: 1,941 square feet
Second Floor: 791 square feet
Total: 2,732 square feet

D

● New living patterns are established in the 1½-story home. The front entry hall features an impressive open staircase to the upstairs and basement. Adjacent is the master bedroom which has a compartmented bath with both tub and stall shower. The spacious dressing room steps down into a unique, sunken conversation pit. This cozy area has a planter, built-in seat and a view of the through-fireplace opening to the gathering room. Here, the ceiling slopes to the top of the second-floor lounge which looks down into the gathering room.

63'-0"

Design N2883 First Floor: 1,919 square feet
Second Floor: 895 square feet; Total: 2,814 square feet

● A country-style home is part of America's fascination with the rural past. This home's emphasis of the traditional home is in its gambrel roof, dormers and fanlight windows. Having a traditional exterior from the street view, this home has win-

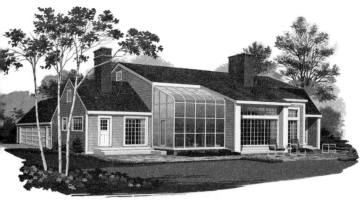

dow walls and a greenhouse, which opens the house to the outdoors in a thoroughly contemporary manner. The interior meets the requirements of today's active family. Like the country houses of the past, it has a gathering room for family get-togethers or entertaining. The adjacent two-story greenhouse doubles as the dining room. There is a pass-through snack bar to the country kitchen here. This country kitchen just might be the heart of the house with its two areas — work zone and sitting room. There are four bedrooms on the two floors — the master bedroom suite on the first floor; three more on the second floor. A lounge, overlooking the gathering room and front foyer, is also on the second floor.

Design N2892 First Floor: 1,623 square feet
Second Floor: 160 square feet; Total: 1,783 square feet

● What a striking contemporary! It houses an efficient floor plan with many outstanding features. The foyer has a sloped ceiling and an open staircase to the basement. To the right of the foyer is the work center. Note the snack bar, laundry and covered dining porch, along with the step-saving kitchen. Both the gathering and dining rooms overlook the backyard. Each of three bedrooms has access to an outdoor area. The second-floor loft could be used as a sewing room, den or lounge.

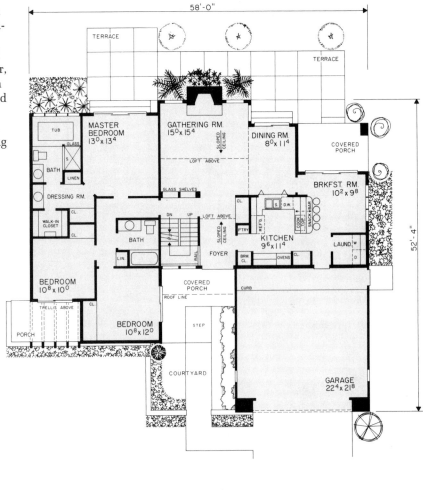

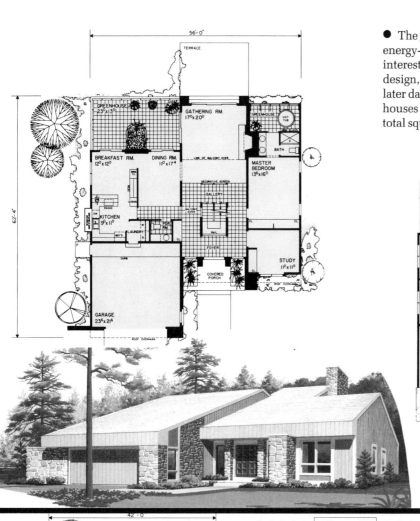

• The greenhouses in this design enhance its energy-efficiency and allow for spacious and interesting living patterns. Being a 1½-story design, the second floor could be developed at a later date when the space is needed. The greenhouses add an additional 418 square feet to the total square footage.

Design N2884

First Floor: 1,855 square feet
Second Floor: 837 square feet
Total: 2,692 square feet

Ⓛ

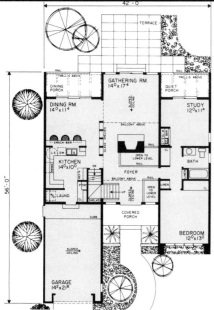

Design N2887

First Floor: 1,338 square feet
Second Floor: 661 square feet
Total: 1,999 square feet

• This attractive contemporary 1½-story will be the envy of many. The kitchen offers a snack bar for those quick meals but also serves a nearby dining room. The gathering room has a fireplace and access to the rear terrace. There is also a study with wet bar and a private porch. Upstairs, the large master suite occupies the entire floor. It has an oversized tub, walk-in closet and open lounge with fireplace. Additional space in the lower level can be developed later.

Design N3313

First Floor: 1,482 square feet
Second Floor: 885 square feet
Total: 2,367 square feet

L

● Cozy living abounds in a first-floor living room and family room, dining room, and kitchen with breakfast room. Two fireplaces keep things warm. Three bedrooms upstairs have more than adequate closet space.

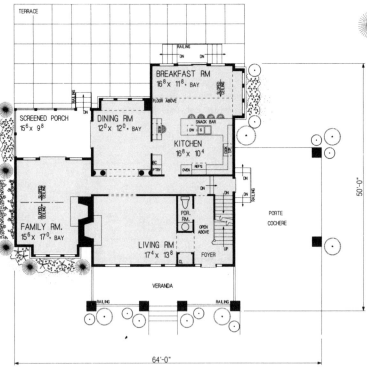

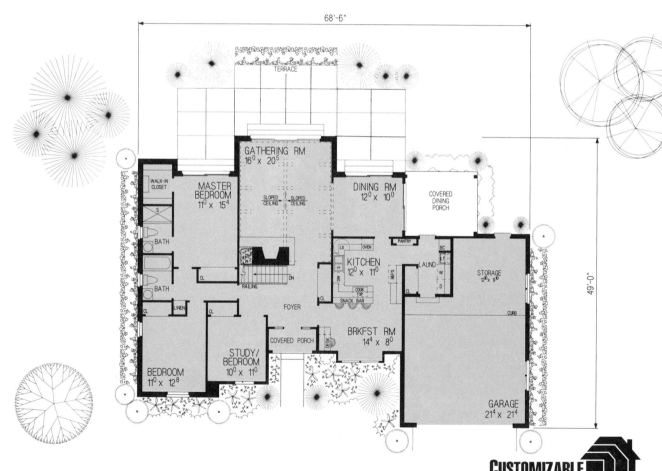

68'-6"

TERRACE

GATHERING RM
16⁰ x 20⁵

DINING RM
12⁰ x 10⁰

COVERED
DINING
PORCH

WALK-IN
CLOSET

MASTER
BEDROOM
11⁰ x 15⁴

SLOPED
CEILING

SLOPED
CEILING

BATH

PANTRY

KITCHEN
12⁰ x 11⁰

LS   OVEN

COOK
TOP

LAUND

BC

STORAGE
12⁰ x 9¹⁰

BATH

LINEN

FOYER

SNACK BAR

REFG

CL

49'-0"

CURB

BEDROOM
11⁰ x 12⁸

STUDY/
BEDROOM
10⁰ x 11⁰

COVERED PORCH

DESK

BRKFST RM
14⁴ x 8⁰

RAILING

DN

GARAGE
21⁴ x 21⁴

CUSTOMIZABLE

Custom Alterations? See page 349 for customizing this plan to your specifications.

Design N3345 Square Footage: 1,738
L

● This quaint shingled cottage offers an unexpected amount of living space in just over 1,700 square feet. The large gathering room with fireplace, dining room with covered porch, and kitchen with breakfast room handle formal parties as easily as they do the casual family get-together. Three bedrooms, one that could also serve as a study, are found in a separate wing of the house. Give special attention to the storage space in this home and the extra touches that set it apart from many homes of equal size.

Design N3454

Square Footage: 1,699

L **D**

● An efficient, spacious interior comes through in this compact floor plan. Through a pair of columns, an open living and dining room area creates a warm space for all sorts of living pursuits. Sliding glass doors guarantee a bright, cheerful interior while providing easy access to outdoor living. The L-shaped kitchen has an island work surface, a practical planning desk and an informal eating space. The breakfast area has access to an outdoor living area—perfect for enjoying a morning cup of coffee. Sleeping arrangements are emphasized by the master suite with its tray ceiling and sliding glass doors to the yard.

Width 52'-8"
Depth 49'

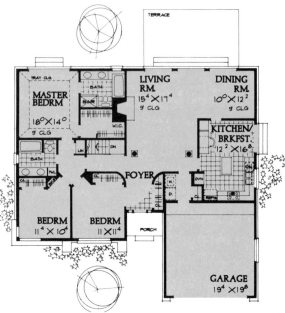

Design N3376

Square Footage: 1,999

L **D**

Width 60'
Depth 55'

● Small families or empty nesters will appreciate the layout of this traditional ranch. The foyer opens to the gathering room with fireplace and sloped ceiling. The dining room is open to the gathering room for entertaining ease and contains sliding doors to a rear terrace. The breakfast room also provides access to a covered porch for dining outdoors. The media room to the left of the home offers a bay window and a wet bar, or it can double as a third bedroom.

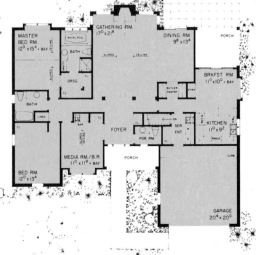

CUSTOMIZABLE

Custom Alterations? See page 349 for customizing this plan to your specifications.

Design N3451

Square Footage: 1,560

L

● This split-bedroom plan includes two bedrooms in only 1,560 square feet. The master bedroom is to the rear of the home and includes a private bath. A family bedroom or study is to the left of the home with a full bath. The washer and dryer are placed within easy reach of both bedrooms. A spacious gathering room with a fireplace provides space for relaxing or entertaining guests. A formal dining room adjacent to the kitchen offers access to a terrace for evening meals outside.

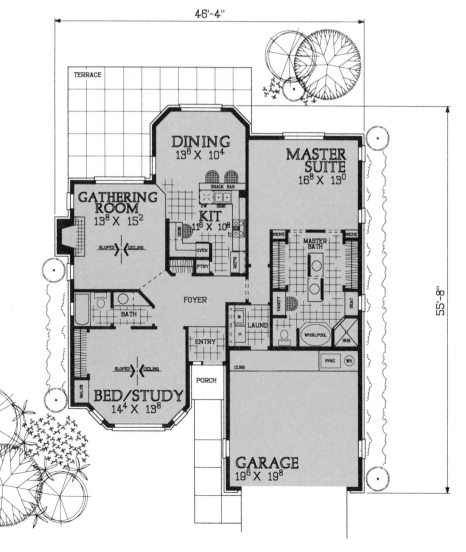

Design N2929
Square Footage: 1,608

● This efficient floor plan caters to the needs of the small family. The angled kitchen is located in a space convenient to the garage, dining room, dining terrace and front door. The spacious living area has a dramatic fireplace and rear terrace access. A favorite spot will be the media room with built-in cabinets for the TV, VCR and stereo. Storage space abounds in the master bedroom and its adjacent bath has twin lavatories, a tub and stall shower. There's an extra bedroom for guests or for use as a nursery.

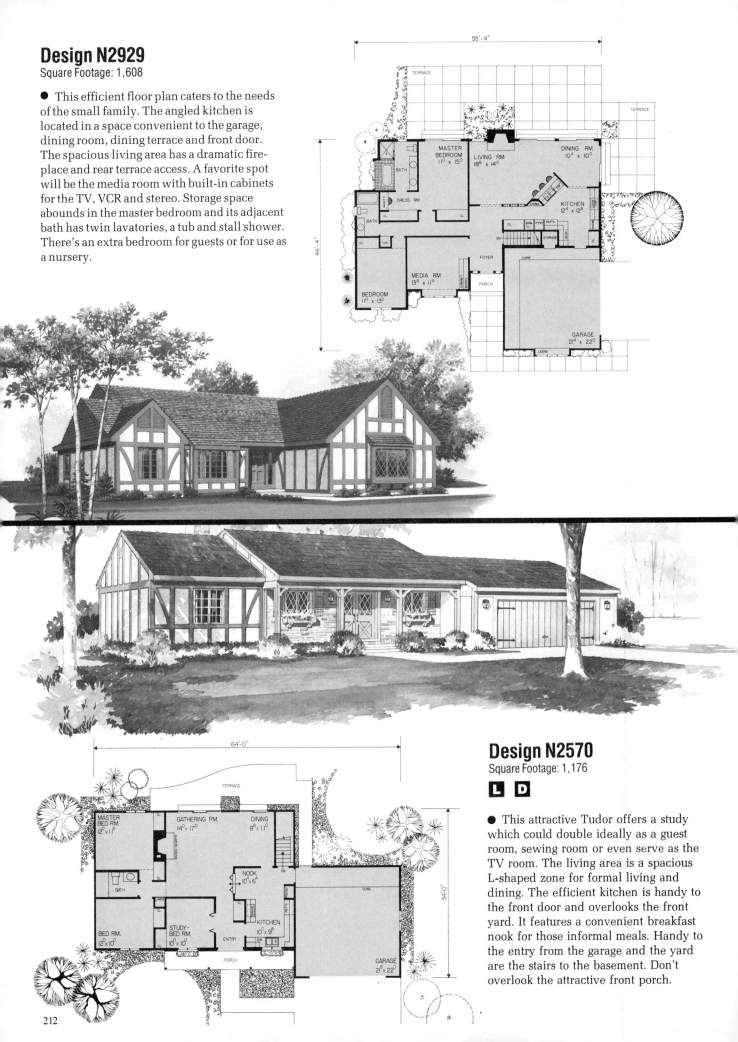

Design N2570
Square Footage: 1,176

L **D**

● This attractive Tudor offers a study which could double ideally as a guest room, sewing room or even serve as the TV room. The living area is a spacious L-shaped zone for formal living and dining. The efficient kitchen is handy to the front door and overlooks the front yard. It features a convenient breakfast nook for those informal meals. Handy to the entry from the garage and the yard are the stairs to the basement. Don't overlook the attractive front porch.

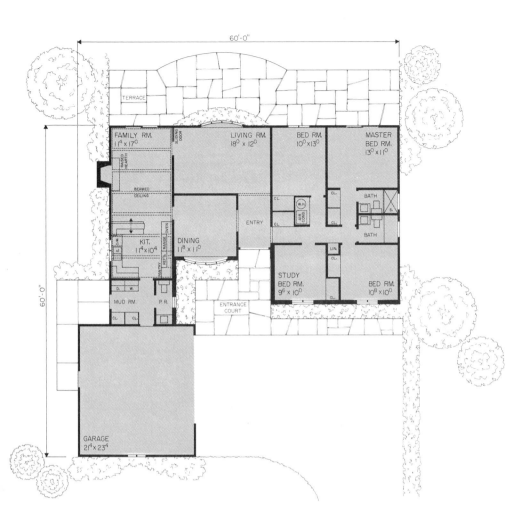

Design N2170
Square Footage: 1,646

● An L-shaped home with an enchanting Olde English styling. The wavy-edged siding, the simulated beams, the diamond lite windows, the unusual brick pattern and the interesting roof lines all are elements which set the character of authenticity. The center entry routes traffic directly to the formal living and sleeping zones of the house. Between the kitchen-family room area and the attached two-car garage is the mud room. Here is the washer and dryer with the extra powder room nearby. The family room is highlighted by the beamed ceilings, the raised hearth fireplace and sliding glass doors to the rear terrace. The work center with its abundance of cupboard space will be fun in which to function. Four bedrooms, two full baths and good closet space are features of the sleeping area.

Design N2604

Square Footage: 1,956

L

● This Tudor one-story home is set off by some very special features: an enormous country kitchen with warming hearth, a large keeping room with another hearth, three bedrooms and 2½ baths. Note the covered porch at the front and terrace area to the back.

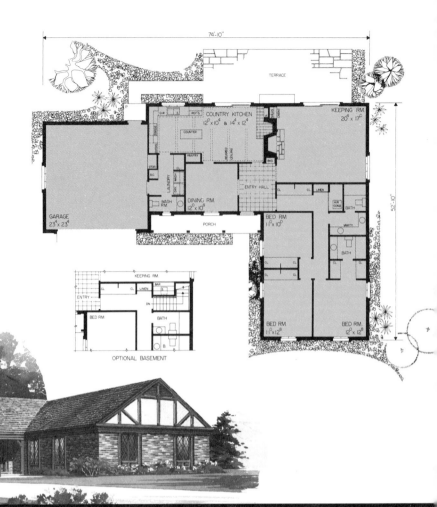

Design N2728

Square Footage: 1,825

L **D**

● This lovely L-shaped English adaptation presents a wonderful face with impressive exterior features. Its floor plan adds livability for modern families. Note the fireplace — a focal point in the living/dining room area. The kitchen is strategically placed to serve the dining room and family room. In addition to the two full baths in the sleeping zone, there is a handy washroom at the entrance from the garage. Note the fine master bath.

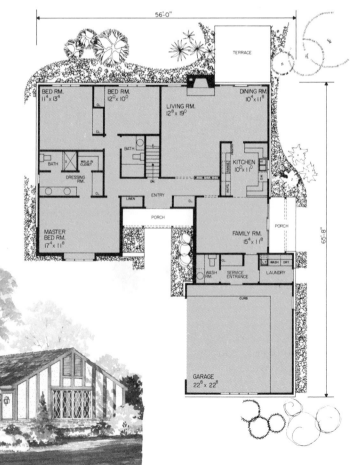

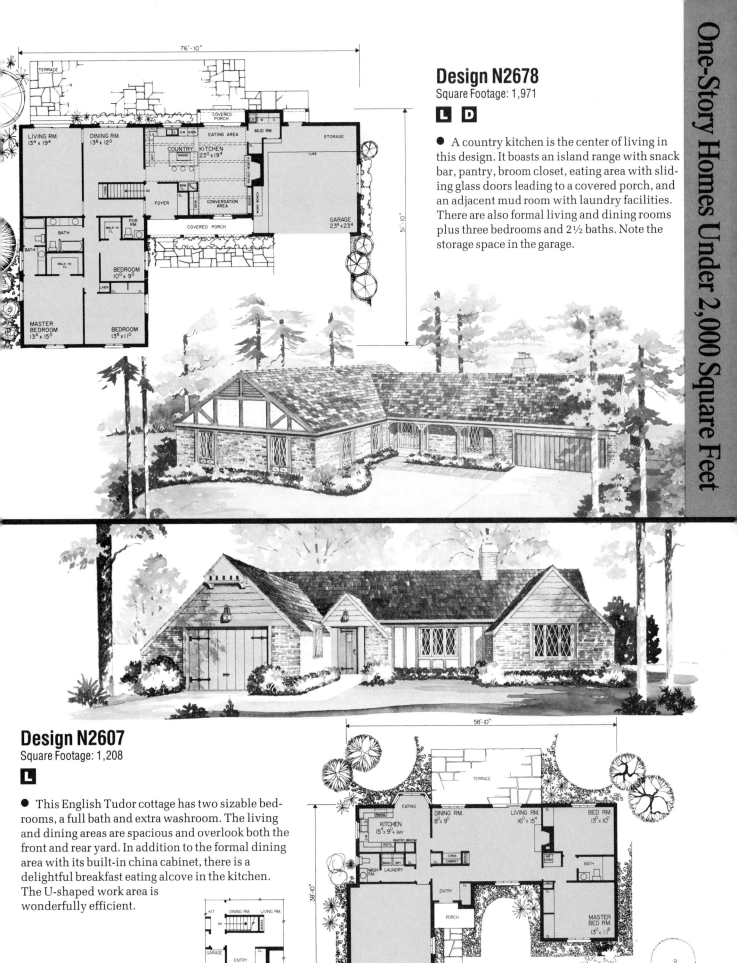

Design N2678
Square Footage: 1,971

L **D**

● A country kitchen is the center of living in this design. It boasts an island range with snack bar, pantry, broom closet, eating area with sliding glass doors leading to a covered porch, and an adjacent mud room with laundry facilities. There are also formal living and dining rooms plus three bedrooms and 2½ baths. Note the storage space in the garage.

Design N2607
Square Footage: 1,208

L

● This English Tudor cottage has two sizable bedrooms, a full bath and extra washroom. The living and dining areas are spacious and overlook both the front and rear yard. In addition to the formal dining area with its built-in china cabinet, there is a delightful breakfast eating alcove in the kitchen. The U-shaped work area is wonderfully efficient.

215

Design N2206
Square Footage: 1,769

L

● The charm of Tudor adaptations has become increasingly popular in recent years. And little wonder. Its freshness of character adds a unique touch to any neighborhood. This interesting one-story home will be a standout wherever you choose to have it built. The covered front porch leads to the formal front entry–the foyer. From this point traffic flows freely to the living and sleeping areas. The outstanding plan features a separate dining room, a beamed ceiling living room, an efficient kitchen and an informal family room.

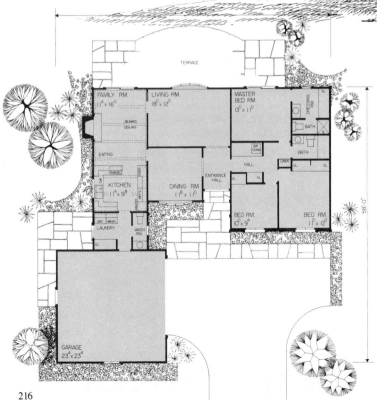

Design N2606
Square Footage: 1,499

L

CUSTOMIZABLE
Custom Alterations? See page 349 for customizing this plan to your specifications.

● This modest sized house with its 1,499 square feet could hardly offer more in the way of exterior charm and interior livability. Measuring only 60 feet in width means it will not require a huge, expensive piece of property. The orientation of the garage and the front drive court are features which promote an economical use of property. In addition to the formal, separate living and dining rooms, there is the informal kitchen/family room area. Note the beamed ceiling, the fireplace, the sliding glass doors and the eating area of the family room.

216

Design N2737
Square Footage: 1,796

L

● You will be able to build this distinctive, modified U-shaped one-story home on a relatively narrow site. But, then, if you so wished, with the help of your architect and builder you may want to locate the garage to the side of the house. Inside, the living potential is just great. The interior U-shaped kitchen handily services the dining and family rooms and nook. A rear covered porch functions ideally with the family room while the formal living room has its own terrace. Three bedrooms and two baths highlight the sleeping zone (or make it two bedrooms and a study). Notice the strategic location of the washroom, laundry, two storage closets and the basement stairs.

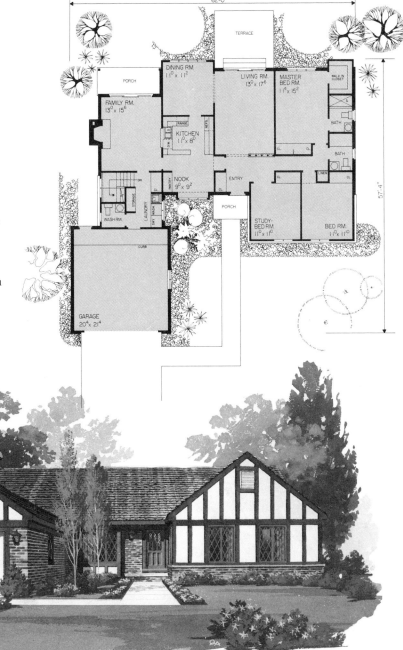

Design N2802
Square Footage: 1,729

L D

● The three exteriors shown at the left house the same, efficiently planned one-story floor plan shown below. Be sure to notice the design variations in the window placement and roof pitch. The Tudor design to the left is delightful. Half-timbered stucco and brick comprise the facade of this English Tudor variation of the plan. Note authentic bay window in the front bedroom.

Design N2803
Square Footage: 1,679

L D

● Housed in varying facades, this floor plan is very efficient. The front foyer leads to each of the living areas. The sleeping area of two, or optional three, bedrooms is ready to serve the family. Then there is the gathering room. This room is highlighted by its size, 16 x 20 feet. A contemporary mix of fieldstone and vertical wood siding characterizes this exterior. The absence of columns or posts gives a modern look to the covered porch.

Design N2804
Square Footage: 1,674

L D

● Stuccoed arches, multi-paned windows and a gracefully sloped roof accent the exterior of this Spanish-inspired design. Like the other two designs, the interior kitchen will efficiently serve the dining room, covered dining porch and breakfast room with great ease. Blueprints for all three designs include details for an optional non-basement plan.

CUSTOMIZABLE

Custom Alterations? See page 349 for customizing this plan to your specifications.

OPTIONAL NON - BASEMENT

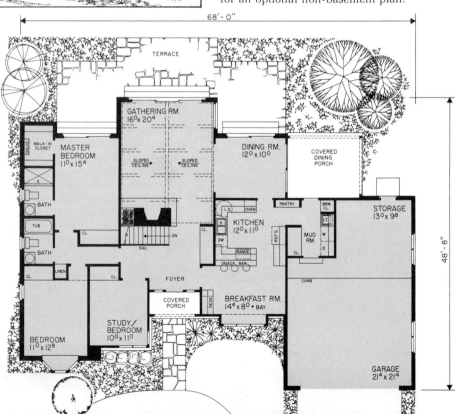

Design N2805
Square Footage: 1,547

● Three completely different exterior facades share one compact, practical and economical floor plan. The major design variations are roof pitch, window placement and garage openings. Each design will hold its own when comparing the three exteriors. The design on the left is a romantic stone-and-shingle cottage design. This design, along with the other two designs presented here, is outstanding.

Design N2806
Square Footage: 1,584

● This Tudor version of the plan is also very appealing. The living/dining room expands across the rear of the plan and has direct access to the covered porch. Notice the built-in planter adjacent to the open staircase leading to the basement.

Design N2807
Square Footage: 1,576

● The contemporary version may be your choice. In addition to living/dining areas, there is a breakfast room that overlooks the covered porch. A desk, snack bar and mud room house laundry facilities and are near the U-shaped kitchen. The master bedroom has a private bath.

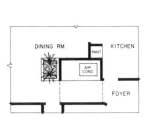

OPTIONAL NON-BASEMENT

Design N2941

Square Footage: 1,842

D

● Here is a basic floor plan which goes with each of the differently styled exteriors. The Early American version above is charming, indeed. Horizontal siding, stone, window boxes, a dovecote, a picket fence and a garden court enhance its appeal. Note the covered entrance.

Design N2942

Square Footage: 1,834

D

● The Tudor exterior above will be the favorite of many. Stucco, simulated timber work and diamond-lite windows set its unique character. Each of the delightful exteriors features eye-catching roof lines. Inside, there is an outstanding plan to cater to the living patterns of the small family, empty nesters, or retirees.

Design N2943

Square Footage: 1,834

D

● The Contemporary optional exterior above features vertical siding and a wide overhanging roof with exposed rafter ends. The foyer is spacious with sloped ceiling and a dramatic open staircase to the basement recreation area. Other ceilings in the house are also sloped. The breakfast, dining and media rooms are highlights, along with the laundry, the efficient kitchen, the snack bar and the master bath.

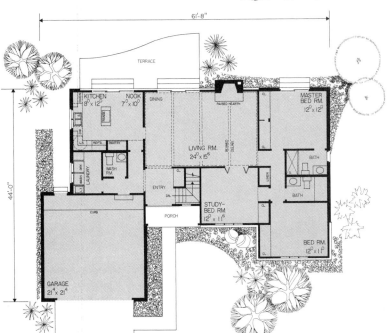

Design N2565
Square Footage: 1,540

L **D**

● This modest sized floor plan has much to offer in the way of livability. It may function as either a two or three bedroom home. The living room is huge and features a fine, raised hearth fireplace. The open stairway to the basement is handy and will lead to what may be developed as the recreation area. In addition to the two full baths, there is an extra wash room. Adjacent is the laundry room and the service entrance from the garage. The blueprints you order for this design will show details for each of the three delightful elevations above. Which is your favorite? The Tudor, the Colonial or the Contemporary?

221

Design N1305
Square Footage: 1,382

D

● Order blueprints for any one of the three exteriors shown on these two pages and you will receive details for building the outstanding floor plan at right. In less than 1,400 square feet there are three bedrooms, two full baths, a separate dining room, a formal living room, a fine kitchen overlooking the rear yard, and an informal family room. In addition, there is the attached two-car garage. Note the location of the stairs when this plan is built with a basement. Each of the exteriors is predominantly brick — the front of Design N1305 features both stone and vertical boards and battens with brick on the other three sides. Design N1382 and Design N1383 both have double front doors.

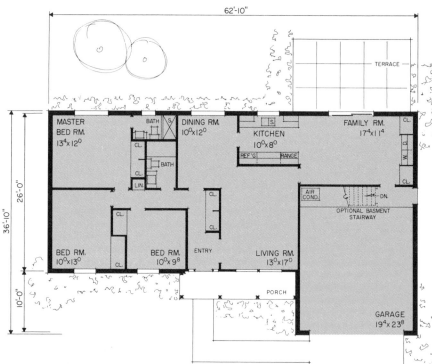

Design N1382
Square Footage: 1,382

D

Design N1383
Square Footage: 1,382

D

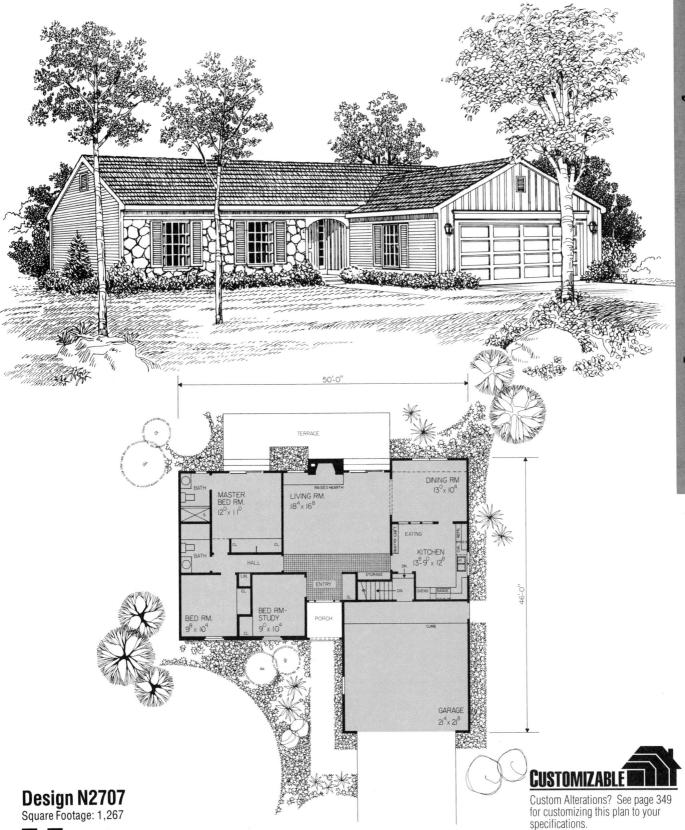

TERRACE

BATH

MASTER BED RM. 12'0" x 11'0"

LIVING RM. 18'4" x 16'8"

RAISED HEARTH

DINING RM. 13'0" x 10'4"

EATING

PANTRY CAB'T

KITCHEN 13'-9" x 12'8"

CL

CL

BATH

HALL

LIN.

CL

STORAGE

ENTRY

DN.

OVENS

RANGE

BED RM. 9'8" x 10'4"

BED RM-STUDY 9'0" x 10'4"

CL

PORCH

CURB

GARAGE 21'4" x 21'8"

50'-0"

46'-0"

CUSTOMIZABLE

Custom Alterations? See page 349 for customizing this plan to your specifications.

Design N2707
Square Footage: 1,267

L **D**

● Here is a charming Early American adaptation that will serve as a picturesque and practical retirement home. Also, it will serve admirably those with a small family in search of an efficient, economically built home. The living area, highlighted by the raised hearth fireplace, is spacious. The kitchen features eating space and easy access to the garage and basement. The dining room is adjacent to the kitchen and views the rear yard. Then, there is the basement for recreation and hobby pursuits. The bedroom wing offers three bedrooms and two full baths. Don't miss the sliding doors to the terrace from the living room and the master bedroom. Storage units are plentiful including a pantry cabinet in the eating area of the kitchen. This plan will be efficient and livable.

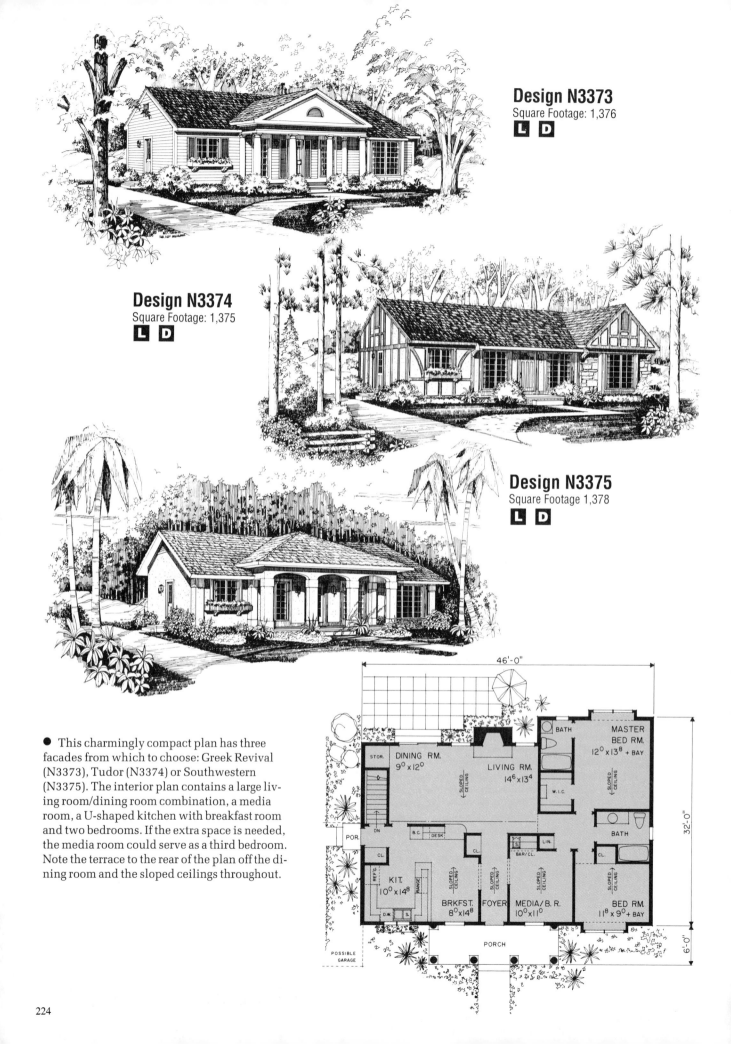

Design N3373
Square Footage: 1,376
L **D**

Design N3374
Square Footage: 1,375
L **D**

Design N3375
Square Footage 1,378
L **D**

● This charmingly compact plan has three facades from which to choose: Greek Revival (N3373), Tudor (N3374) or Southwestern (N3375). The interior plan contains a large living room/dining room combination, a media room, a U-shaped kitchen with breakfast room and two bedrooms. If the extra space is needed, the media room could serve as a third bedroom. Note the terrace to the rear of the plan off the dining room and the sloped ceilings throughout.

46'-0"

STOR.

DINING RM.
9⁰ x 12⁰

LIVING RM.
14⁶ x 13⁴

SLOPED CEILING

BATH

MASTER BED RM.
12⁰ x 13⁸ + BAY

SLOPED CEILING

W.I.C.

POR.

DN

CL.

B.C. DESK

CL.

LIN.

BAR/CL.

S

S

BATH

CL.

32'-0"

REF'G.

KIT.
10⁰ x 14⁸

RANGE

SLOPED CEILING

SLOPED CEILING

SLOPED CEILING

SLOPED CEILING

D.W.

S

BRKFST.
8⁰ x 14⁸

FOYER

MEDIA/B. R.
10⁰ x 11⁰

BED RM.
11⁸ x 9⁰ + BAY

POSSIBLE GARAGE

PORCH

6'-0"

Design N2931
Square Footage: 2,032

● Little details make the difference. Consider these that make this such a charming showplace: master bedroom suite with separate dressing room, private vanities and whirlpool bath; an adjacent study with fireplace; roomy kitchen with breakfast area; spacious gathering room, rear and side terraces, attached two-car garage with storage.

CUSTOMIZABLE

Custom Alterations? See page 349 for customizing this plan to your specifications.

Design N2869
Square Footage: 1,986

● This traditional one-story design offers the benefits of shared living space without sacrificing privacy. The common area (great room, dining room and kitchen) is centrally located between the two private sleeping wings. Separate outdoor entrances lead to each of the sleeping wings. Two bedrooms, a full bath and space for an optional kitchenette are found in each wing. Note the covered porch with skylights and full-width terrace to the back.

225

Design N3350

Square Footage: 1,777

L **D**

● Though smaller in size, this traditional one-story provides a family-oriented floor plan that leaves nothing out. Besides the formal living room (or study if you prefer) and dining room, there's a gathering room with fireplace, snack bar, and sliding glass doors to the rear terrace. The U-shaped kitchen is in close proximity to the handy utility area just off the garage. Of particular note is the grand master bedroom with garden whirlpool tub, walk-in closet and private terrace. The sleeping area is completed with two family bedrooms to the front.

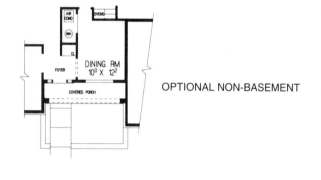

OPTIONAL NON-BASEMENT

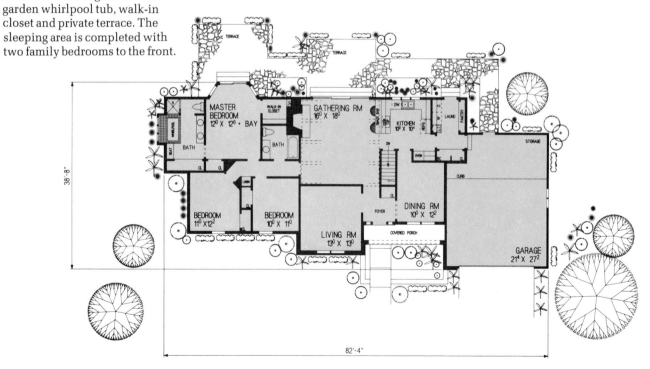

CUSTOMIZABLE

Custom Alterations? See page 349 for customizing this plan to your specifications.

Design N2505

Square Footage: 1,366

L **D**

● This design offers you a choice of three distinctively different exteriors. Which is your favorite? Blueprints show details for all three optional elevations. A study of the floor plan reveals a fine measure of livability. In less than 1,400 square feet there are features galore. An excellent return on your construction dollar. In addition to the two eating areas and the open planning of the gathering room, the indoor-outdoor relationships are of great interest. The basement may be developed for recreational activities. Be sure to note the storage potential, particularly the linen closet, the pantry, the china cabinet and the broom closet.

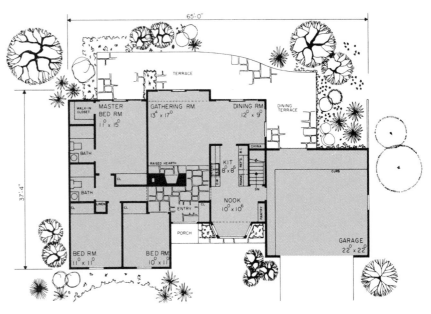

227

Design N1920
Square Footage: 1,600

L

● This home offers a charming exterior with a truly great floor plan. The covered front porch at the entrance heralds outstanding features inside. The sleeping zone has three bedrooms and two full baths. Each of the bedrooms has its own walk-in closet. Note the efficient U-shaped kitchen with the family room and dining room to each side. There is also a laundry with wash room just off the garage. Blueprints for this design include details for both basement and non-basement construction.

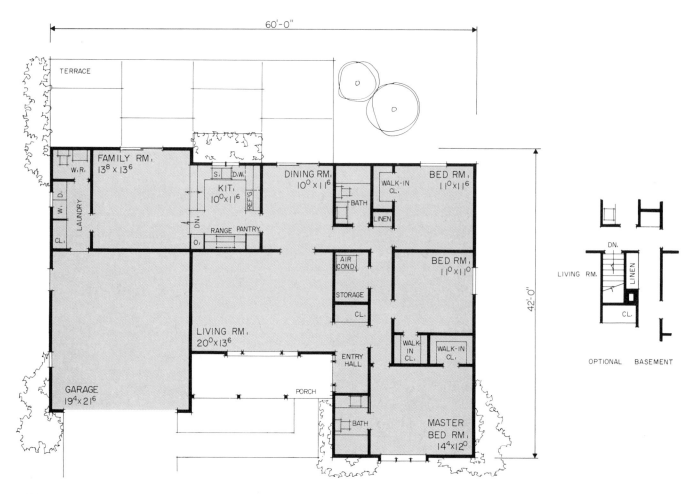

Design N1323

Square Footage: 1,344

L **D**

● Incorporated in the set of blueprints for this design are details for building each of the three charming, traditional exteriors. Each of the three alternate exteriors has a distinction all its own. A study of the floor plan reveals fine livability. There are two full baths, a fine family room, an efficient work center, a formal dining area, bulk storage facilities and sliding glass doors to the quiet and living terraces. The laundry is strategically located near the kitchen.

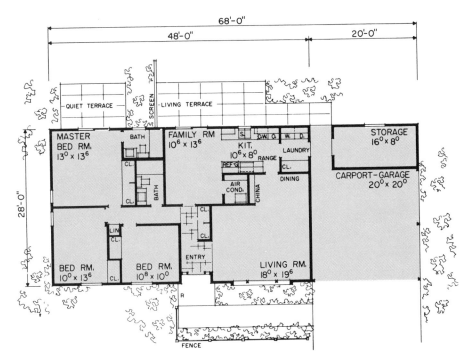

Design N1829
Square Footage: 1,800

L **D**

● All the charm of a traditional heritage is wrapped up in this U-shaped home with its narrow, horizontal siding, delightful window treatment and high-pitched roof. The massive center chimney, the bay window and the double front doors are plus features. Inside, the living potential is outstanding. The sleeping wing is self-contained and has four bedrooms and two baths. The large family and living rooms cater to divergent age groups.

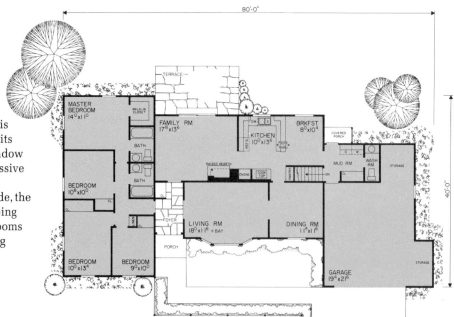

Design N2533
Square Footage: 1,897

● The distinctive appeal of the traditional L-shaped ranch home is hard to beat. Notice the delightful window and door treatment, covered front porch, vertical siding and the fieldstone. The center entrance with slate floor routes traffic effectively. The four-bedroom sleeping wing highlights two full baths. The formal living and dining rooms act as a buffer between the sleeping area and the family room/kitchen area. The family room has sliding glass doors, a fireplace and large bay window.

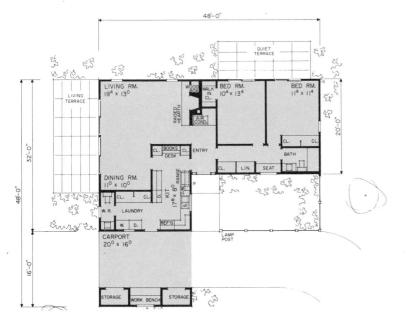

Design N1279

Square Footage: 1,200

● This cozy traditional ranch house is ideal as a starter or retirement home. Its small size and one-story plan make it easy to maintain and enjoy. The house provides large open living spaces, two bedrooms with a full bath, galley kitchen with built-ins and storage in the carport area. Note the two terraces and garden entry court.

BASEMENT OPTION

Width 62'
Depth 50'

Design N1343
Square Footage: 1,620

L

● This traditional L-shaped exterior features a flower court and covered front porch. The formal entry leads to three areas: The sleeping zone with four bedrooms and two full baths; the formal living and dining areas; and a casual family room with snack bar island in the kitchen. A rear terrace enhances outdoor living potential.

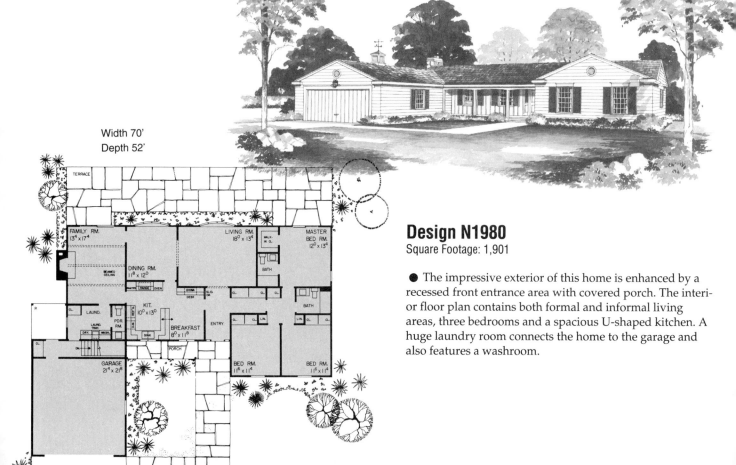

Width 70'
Depth 52'

Design N1980
Square Footage: 1,901

● The impressive exterior of this home is enhanced by a recessed front entrance area with covered porch. The interior floor plan contains both formal and informal living areas, three bedrooms and a spacious U-shaped kitchen. A huge laundry room connects the home to the garage and also features a washroom.

Design N3460

Square Footage: 1,389

L

● A double dose of charm, this special farmhouse plan offers two elevations in its blueprint package—one showcases a delightful wraparound porch. Though rooflines and porch options are different, the floor plan is basically the same and very livable. A formal living room/dining room combination has a warming fireplace and a delightful bay window. The kitchen separates this area from the more casual family room. In the kitchen, you'll find an efficient snack bar that services the family room, as well as a pantry for additional storage space. Three bedrooms include two family bedrooms served by a full bath, and a lovely master suite with its own private bath with separate lavatories. Notice the location of the washer and dryer—convenient to all of the bedrooms.

CUSTOMIZABLE

Custom Alterations? See page 349 for customizing this plan to your specifications.

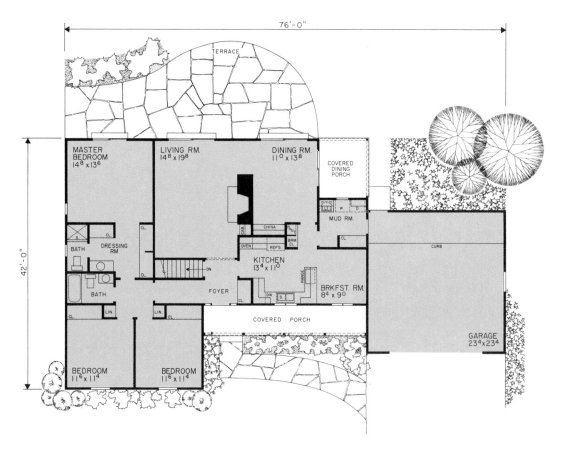

Design N2672

Square Footage: 1,717

L **D**

● The traditional appearance of this one-story is emphasized by its covered porch, multi-paned windows, narrow clapboard and vertical wood siding. Not only is the exterior eye-appealing but the interior has an efficient plan and is very livable. The front U-shaped kitchen will work with the breakfast room and mud room, which houses the laundry facilities. An access to the garage is here. Outdoor dining can be enjoyed on the covered porch adjacent to the dining room. Both of these areas, the porch and dining room, are convenient to the kitchen. Sleeping facilities consist of three bedrooms and two full baths. Note the three sets of sliding glass doors leading to the terrace.

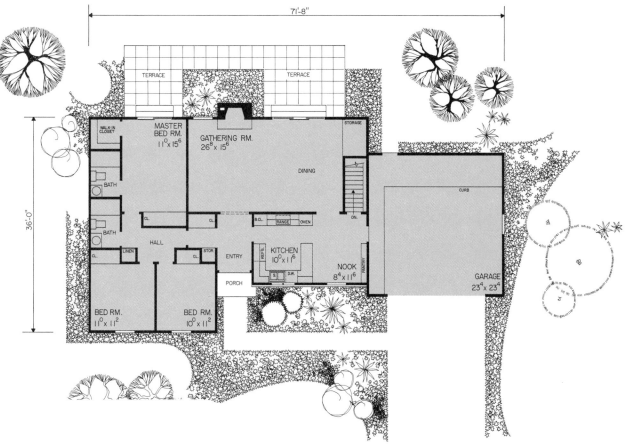

71'-8"

36'-0"

TERRACE   TERRACE

WALK-IN CLOSET

MASTER BED RM.
11⁰ x 15⁶

GATHERING RM.
26⁸ x 15⁶

STORAGE

DINING

CURB

BATH

BATH

CL.   CL.

B.CL.   RANGE   OVEN

DN.

HALL

LINEN   CL.   STOR

CL.   REF'G   KITCHEN
10⁰ x 11⁶

GARAGE
23⁴ x 23⁴

ENTRY

NOOK
8⁴ x 11⁶

PANTRY

PORCH   S   D.W.

BED RM.
11⁰ x 11²

BED RM.
10⁰ x 11²

Design N2597

Square Footage: 1,515

L D

● Whether it be a starter house you are after, or one in which to spend your retirement years, this pleasing frame home will provide a full measure of pride in ownership. The contrast of vertical and horizontal lines, the double front doors and the coach lamp post at the garage create an inviting exterior. Efficiently planned, the floor plan functions in an orderly manner. The 26-foot gathering room has a delightful view of the rear yard and will take care of those formal dining occasions. There are two full baths serving the three bedrooms. Additional features include: plenty of storage facilities, two sets of glass doors to the terraces, a fireplace in the gathering room, a basement and an attached two-car garage to act as a buffer against the wind.

235

Design N1946

Square Footage: 1,632

● This basic exterior may have two different
floor plans. For a three-bedroom home order
blueprints for N1945; for a four-bedroom house
order N1946.

Design N1327

Square Footage: 1,392

● This design overcomes the restrictions of a
narrow building site. It has four bedrooms and
two baths. Notice the efficient traffic patterns
established between the living and family
rooms and the kitchen. An optional basement
plan is included with the blueprint order.

OPTIONAL BASEMENT PLAN

Design N3466

Square Footage: 1,800

L **D**

● Small but inviting, this one-story ranch-style farmhouse is the perfect choice for a small family or empty-nesters. It's loaded with amenities even the most particular homeowner can appreciate. For example, the living room and dining room each have plant shelves, sloped ceilings and built-ins to enhance livability. The living room also sports a warming hearth. The master bedroom contains a well-appointed bath with dual vanity

and walk-in closet. The additional bedroom has its own bath with linen storage. The kitchen is separated from the breakfast nook by a clever bar area. Access to the two-car garage is through a laundry area with washer/dryer hookup space.

CUSTOMIZABLE

Custom Alterations? See page 349 for customizing this plan to your specifications.

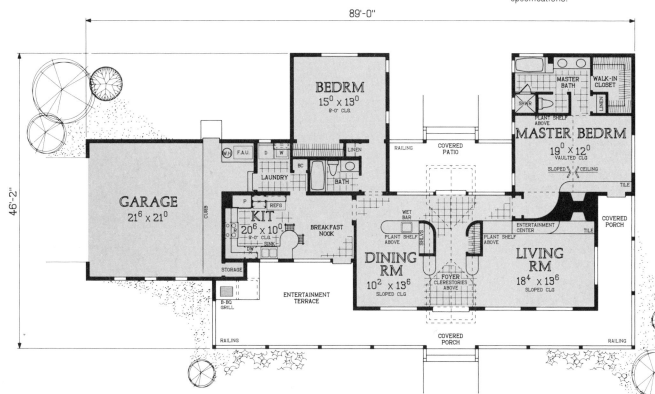

Design N2810
3-Bedroom Plan
Square Footage: 1,536

L **D**

Design N2814
4-Bedroom Plan
Square Footage: 1,536

L **D**

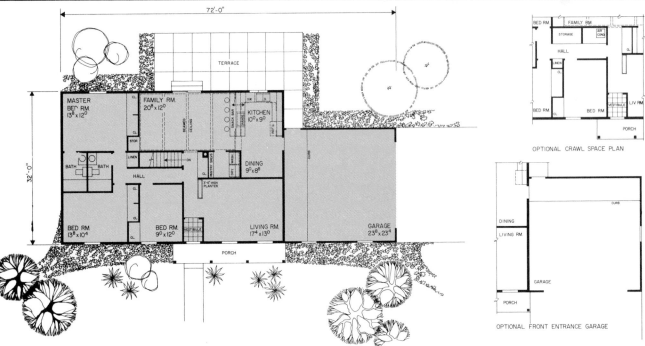

72'-0"

TERRACE

MASTER BED RM
13⁸ x 12⁰

FAMILY RM.
20⁸ x 12⁰

KITCHEN
10⁰ x 9⁰

32'-0"

BATH BATH

LINEN

HALL

DINING
9⁰ x 8⁸

3'-4" HIGH PLANTER

BED RM
13⁸ x 10⁴

BED RM.
9⁰ x 12⁰

VESTIBULE

LIVING RM.
17⁴ x 13⁰

GARAGE
23⁸ x 23⁴

PORCH

BED RM. FAMILY RM.
STORAGE
AIR COND.
HALL
LINEN CL.
BED RM. CL. BED RM. VESTIBULE LIV RM

PORCH

OPTIONAL CRAWL SPACE PLAN

DINING
LIVING RM.

CURB

GARAGE

PORCH

OPTIONAL FRONT ENTRANCE GARAGE

● The designs on these two pages are particularly energy-efficient. All exterior walls employ the use of 2x6 stud construction to permit the installation of extra thick insulation. The high cornice design also allows for more ceiling insulation. Efficiency is also evident at the air-lock vestibule which restricts the flow of outside air to the interior. Also, the basic rectangle shape of the house is very economical to build. Note the back-to-back plumbing plan, centrally located furnace, minimal window and door openings and modest size.

Design N2811
3-Bedroom Plan
Square Footage: 1,581

L **D**

Design N2815
4-Bedroom Plan
Square Footage: 1,581

L **D**

Design N2812
3-Bedroom Plan
Square Footage: 1,581

L **D**

Design N2816
4-Bedroom Plan
Square Footage: 1,581

L **D**

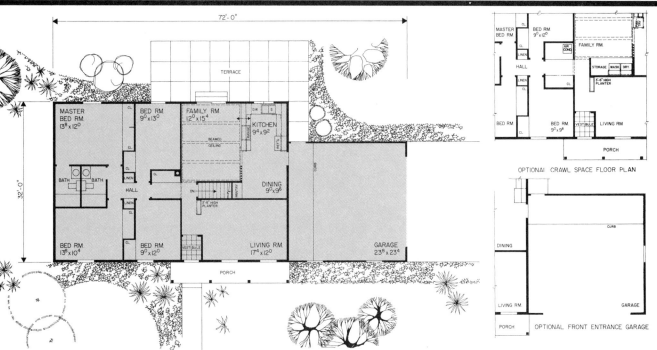

72'-0"

32'-0"

TERRACE

MASTER BED RM. 13⁸×12⁰

BED RM. 9⁰×13⁰

FAMILY RM. 12⁰×15⁴

KITCHEN 9⁴×9²

BEAMED CEILING

BATH BATH

HALL

LINEN

DINING 9⁰×9⁶

5'-6" HIGH PLANTER

BED RM. 13⁸×10⁴

BED RM. 9⁰×12⁰

VESTIBULE

LIVING RM. 17⁴×12⁰

GARAGE 23⁸×23⁴

PORCH

MASTER BED RM.

HALL

LINEN

BED RM.

BED RM. 9⁰×12⁰

AIR COND.

FAMILY RM.

STORAGE WASH-DRY

3'-6" HIGH PLANTER

BED RM. 9⁰×9⁸

VESTIBULE

LIVING RM.

PORCH

OPTIONAL CRAWL SPACE FLOOR PLAN

DINING

CURB

LIVING RM.

GARAGE

PORCH OPTIONAL FRONT ENTRANCE GARAGE

● Within 1,536 square feet there is outstanding livability and a huge variety of options from which to choose: the cozy, front-porch farmhouse adaptation; the pleasing Southern Colonial version, the French creation, or the rugged Western facade. There are also three- or four-bedroom options. If you wish to order blueprints for the hip-roofed design with three bedrooms, specify Design N2812; for the four-bedroom option specify N2816. To order blueprints for the three-bedroom Southern Colonial, request Design N2811, for the four-bedroom, order N2815. The three-bedroom farmhouse is Design N2810; the four-bedroom option is N2814. The three-bedroom Western ranch is Design N2813; the four-bedroom option is N2817.

Design N2813
3-Bedroom Plan
Square Footage: 1,536

L **D**

Design N2817
4-Bedroom Plan
Square Footage: 1,536

L **D**

Design N2911

Square Footage: 1,233

● A low-budget home can be a showplace too! Exquisite proportion, fine detailing, projecting wings and interesting roof lines help provide the appeal of this modest one-story. Each of the bedrooms has excellent wall space and wardrobe storage potential. The master bath features a vanity, twin lavatories, stall shower plus a whirlpool. Another full bath is located near the second bedroom. The spacious gathering room/dining room area has a fireplace and access to outdoor terraces. The design has blueprints for two kitchen plans.

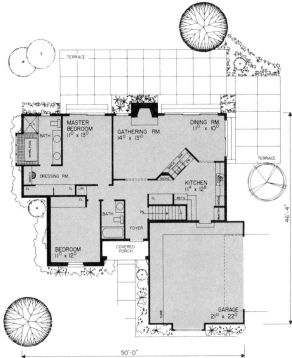

ALTERNATE KITCHEN PLAN

Design N2603
Square Footage: 1,949

L **D**

● Surely it would be difficult to beat the appeal of this traditional one-story home. Its slightly modified U-shape with the two front facing gables, the bay window, the covered front porch and the interesting use of exterior materials all add to the exterior charm. Besides, there are three large bedrooms serviced by two full baths and three walk-in closets. The excellent kitchen is flanked by the formal dining room and the informal family room. Don't miss the pantry, the built-in oven and the pass-thru to the snack bar. The handy first floor laundry is strategically located to act as a mud room. The extra wash room is but a few steps away. The sizable living room highlights a fireplace and a picture window. Note the location of the basement stairs.

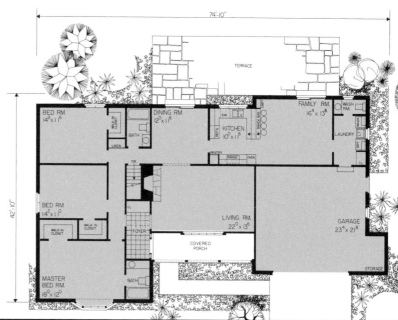

Design N2738
Square Footage: 1,898

● Impressive architecture is apparent in this three-bedroom home. The U-shaped kitchen and breakfast room are located near the formal dining room and hearth-warmed gathering room. Three (or make it two with a study) bedrooms and two baths are in the sleeping wing. Note the dining terrace off the nook and living terrace off the gathering room and master bedroom.

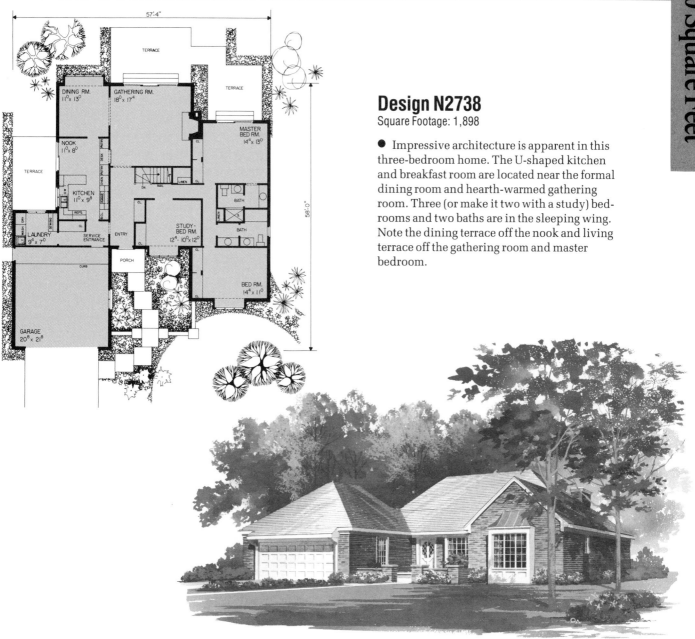

241

Design N3442

Square Footage: 1,273

● This is a superb home-building candidate for those with a narrow, relatively inexpensive building site. Inside, the rounded corners of the foyer add appeal and foster a feeling of spaciousness. Separate formal and informal dining areas are achieved through the incorporation of a breakfast bar. The spacious living room features a sloped ceiling, a central fireplace and cheerful windows. The master suite has a sloped ceiling and a high shelf for plants or other decor items.

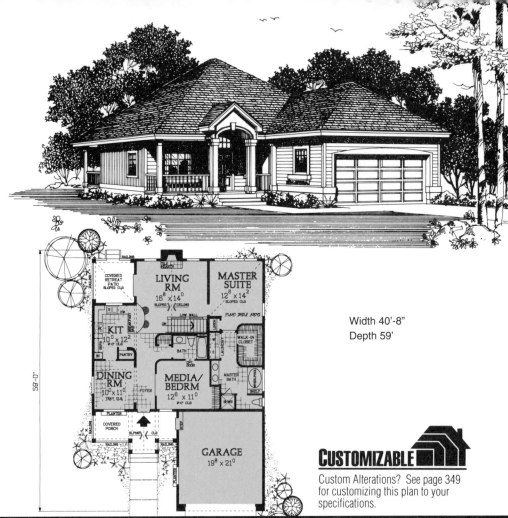

Width 40'-8"
Depth 59'

CUSTOMIZABLE

Custom Alterations? See page 349 for customizing this plan to your specifications.

Design N3465

Square Footage: 1,410

Width 66'-7"
Depth 55'

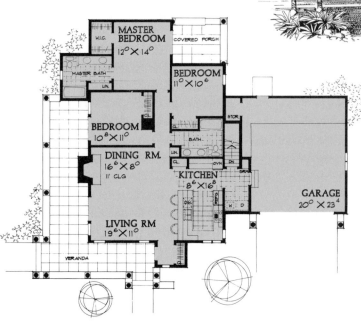

● Horizontal siding with brick accents and multi-paned windows enhance the exterior of this home. A hard-working interior will delight those building within a modest budget. A 36' front room provides plenty of space for both living and family dining activities. A fireplace makes a delightful focal point. The kitchen will be free of annoying cross-room traffic. The centrally located main bath has twin lavatories and a nearby linen closet. One of the two secondary bedrooms has direct access to the veranda. The master bedroom is flanked by the master bath and its own private covered porch.

Design N3481A

Square Footage: 1,901

L

● In just under 2,000 square feet, this pleasing one-story home bears all the livability of houses twice its size. A combined living and dining room offers elegance for entertaining; with two elevations to choose from, the living room can either support an octagonal bay or a bumped-out nook. The U-shaped kitchen finds easy access to the breakfast nook and rear family room; sliding glass doors lead from the family room to a back stoop. The master bedroom has a quaint potshelf and a private bath with a spa tub, a double-bowl vanity, a walk-in closet and a compartmented toilet. With two additional family bedrooms—one may serve as a den if desired—and a hall bath with dual lavatories, this plan offers the best in accommodations. Both elevations come with the blueprint package.

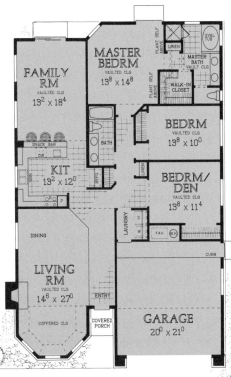

Design N3481B

Square Footage: 1,908

L

Width 42'-4"
Depth 63'-10"

CUSTOMIZABLE

Custom Alterations? See page 349 for customizing this plan to your specifications.

Design N1389
Square Footage: 1,488

D

● Your choice of exterior goes with this outstanding floor plan. If you like French Provincial, Design N1389 is your choice. If you prefer the simple, straightforward lines of contemporary plans, Design N1387 will be your favorite. For the warmth of Colonial adaptations, the charming exterior of Design N1388 is perfect. Note the differences in the three plans: window treatment, roof lines and other details.

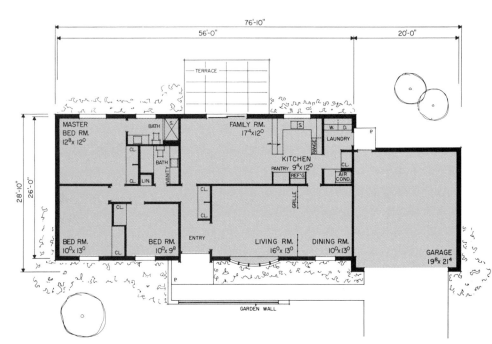

Design N1387
Square Footage: 1,488

D

Design N1388
Square Footage: 1,488

D

Design N1380
Square Footage: 1,399

L **D**

Design N1381
Square Footage: 1,399

L **D**

● These two stylish exteriors have the same practical, L-shaped floor plan. Design N1380 is characterized by the pediment gables and the masses of brick. Design N1381 is captivating because of its hip-roof, panelled shutters and lamp post. Inside, there is an abundance of liva- bility. The formal living and dining area is spacious, and the U-shaped kitchen is efficient. There is informal eating space, a separate laundry and a fine family room. The blueprints include details for building either with or with- out a basement.

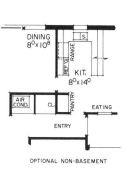

OPTIONAL NON-BASEMENT

Design N1896

Square Footage: 1,690

● Complete family livability is provided by this exceptional floor plan. Further, this design has a truly delightful traditional exterior. The fine layout features a center entrance hall with storage closet in addition to the wardrobe closet. Then, there is the formal, front living room and the adjacent, separate dining room. The U-shaped kitchen has plenty of counter and cupboard space. There is even a pantry. The family room functions with the kitchen and is but a step from the outdoor terrace. The mud room has space for storage and laundry equipment. The extra wash room is nearby. The large family will find those four bedrooms and two full baths just the answer to sleeping and bath accommodations.

Design N1890

Square Footage: 1,628

● The pediment gable and columns help set the charm of this modestly sized home. Here is graciousness normally associated with homes twice its size. The pleasant symmetry of the windows and the double front doors complete the picture. Inside, each square foot is wisely planned to assure years of convenient living. There are three bedrooms, each with twin wardrobe closets. There are two full baths economically grouped with the laundry and heating equipment. A fine feature.

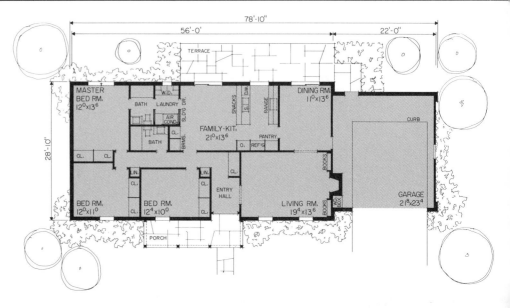

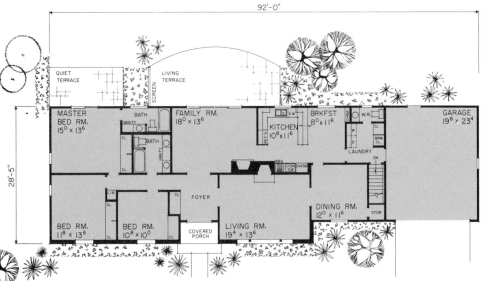

Design N1325

Square Footage: 1,942

L **D**

● The large front entry hall permits direct access to the formal living room, the sleeping area and the informal family room. Both of the living areas have a fireplace. When formal dining is the occasion of the evening the separate dining room is but a step from the living room. The U-shaped kitchen is strategically flanked by the family room and the breakfast areas.

Design N2702
Square Footage: 1,636

● A rear living room with a sloping ceiling, built-in bookcases, a raised-hearth fireplace and sliding glass doors to the rear terrace highlight this design. The kitchen has plenty of cabinet and cupboard space. It features informal eating space and is but a step or two from the separate dining room. Each of the three rooms in the sleeping wing has direct access to outdoor living. The master bedroom has a huge walk-in wardrobe closet, dressing room with built-in vanity and private bath with large towel storage closet.

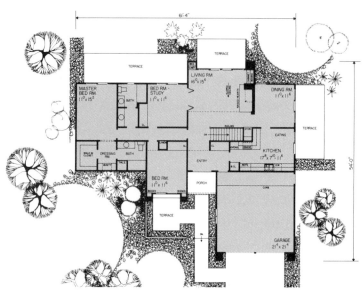

Design N2754
Square Footage: 1,844

● This really is a most dramatic contemporary home. The U-shaped privacy wall of the front entrance area provides an appealing outdoor living spot accessible from the front bedroom. The rectangular floor plan will be economical to build. Two bedrooms and two full baths comprise the sleeping zone. Note the open planning of the L-shaped living and dining rooms and the through-fireplace to the study. The kitchen and breakfast nook function well together.

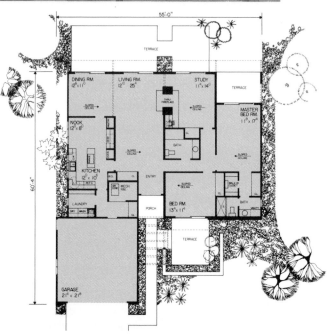

Design N2528
Square Footage: 1,754

D

● This inviting, U-shaped western ranch adaptation offers outstanding living potential behind its double front doors. In only 1,754 square feet there are three bedrooms, 2½ baths, a formal living room and an informal family room, a functional kitchen, an adjacent breakfast nook and good storage facilities. Note the raised-hearth fireplace and sloped ceiling.

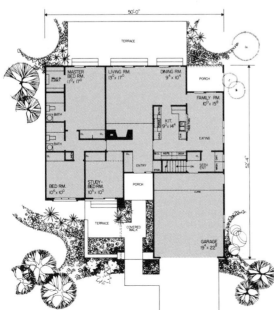

Design N2753
Square Footage: 1,539

D

● Projecting the attached garage from the front line of the house makes a lot of economic sense and leads to interesting roof lines and plan configurations. Here, a pleasing covered walkway to the front door results. A privacy wall adds an extra measure of design appeal and provides a sheltered terrace for the study/bedroom. It would be difficult to find more livability in 1,539 square feet with three bedrooms, two baths, a spacious living/dining area and a family room.

Design N2792

Square Footage: 1,944

● Indoor/outdoor living could hardly be improved upon in this contemporary design. Divide the terrace in three parts and the nook and dining room have access to a dining terrace, the gathering room to a living terrace and two bedrooms to a lounging terrace. Other fine features include the efficient kitchen with plenty of storage space and an island range, a first-floor laundry with stairs to the basement, and a powder room adjacent to the front door.

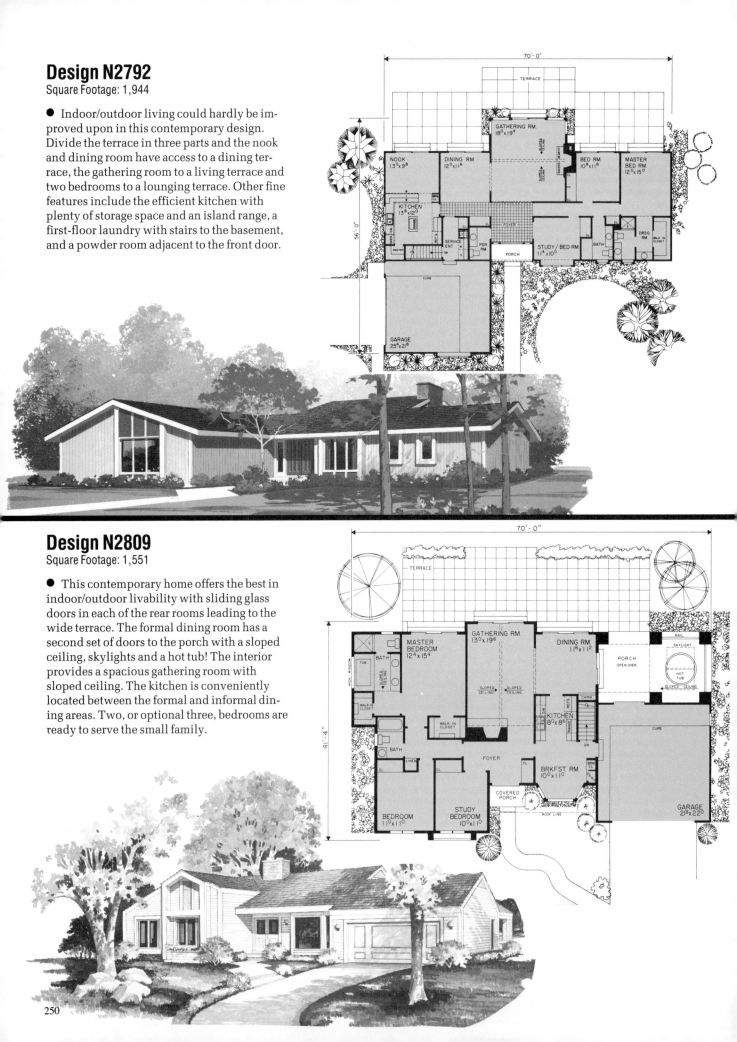

Design N2809

Square Footage: 1,551

● This contemporary home offers the best in indoor/outdoor livability with sliding glass doors in each of the rear rooms leading to the wide terrace. The formal dining room has a second set of doors to the porch with a sloped ceiling, skylights and a hot tub! The interior provides a spacious gathering room with sloped ceiling. The kitchen is conveniently located between the formal and informal dining areas. Two, or optional three, bedrooms are ready to serve the small family.

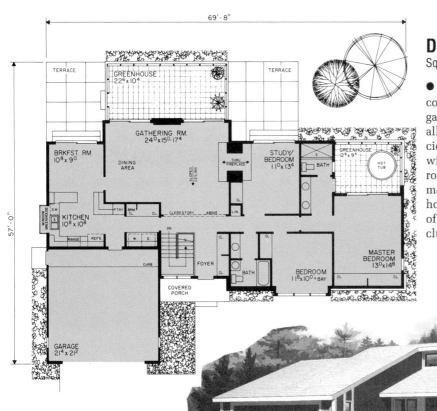

Design N2886
Square Footage: 2,127

● This one-story house is attractive with its contemporary exterior. Note the spacious gathering room with sliding glass doors that allow easy access to the greenhouse. An efficient kitchen has an attached breakfast room with eating terrace. Besides two family bedrooms (one could be a study) there is a roomy master suite with access to a second greenhouse containing a hot tub. The combined area of the greenhouses is 394 square feet, not included in the above total.

Design N2797
Square Footage: 1,791

● The exterior appeal of this delightful one-story is sure to catch the attention of all who pass by. The floor plan is also outstanding. The gathering room has a sloped ceiling, sliding glass doors to a rear terrace and a through-fireplace to the family room. Look for the informal dining area between the kitchen and family room. More formal entertaining can be done in the front dining room. There's also a study with terrace access. Three bedrooms and two baths accommodate sleeping needs.

Design N2917

Square Footage: 1,813

L

● Here's an attractive design with many of today's most-asked-for features: gathering room with fireplace, separate formal dining room, roomy kitchen with equally spacious breakfast area, and three bedrooms including a master suite with huge walk-in closet and two private vanities. One other plus: a great-to-stretch-out-on terrace leading to the backyard.

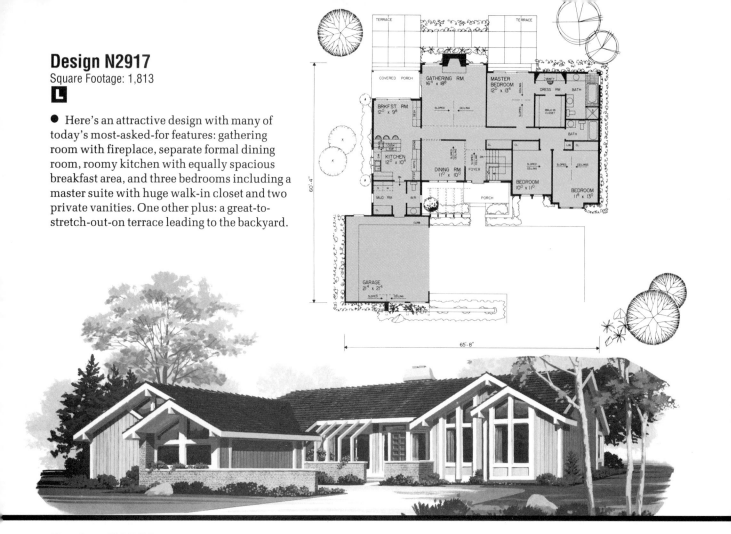

Design N2902

Square Footage: 1,632

L

● A sun space highlights this passive solar design. It has access from the kitchen, dining room and garage. Three skylights illuminate the interior — one in the kitchen, one in the laundry and one in the master bath. The living room/dining room has a sloped ceiling, fireplace and two sets of sliding glass doors to the terrace. Three bedrooms and two baths are found in the sleeping wing. The area of the sunspace is 216 square feet not included in the above total.

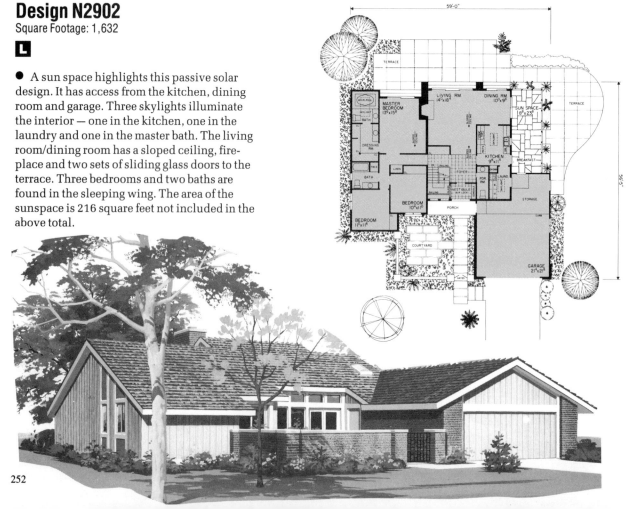

70'-0"

51'-8"

TERRACE

BRKFST RM
11⁰ x 10⁰·BAY

DINING RM
10⁴ x 12⁴

GATHERING RM
17⁰ x 20⁴

SLOPED CEILING

BEDROOM
11⁴ x 10⁸

MASTER BEDROOM
12⁰ x 16⁴

SNACK BAR

KITCHEN
11⁰ x 11⁰

6'-0" FLAT CEILING

LIN

CL

WALK-IN CLOSET

DRSG RM

LAUND
8⁰ x 5⁰

CURIOS

FOYER

RAILING

BATH

CL

BATH

COOK TOP

REFS

CL

SLOPED CEILING

TERRACE

CURB

COVERED PORCH

TV, STEREO, VCR EQUIP, SPEAKERS ETC.

WHIRLPOOL

MEDIA RM

Design N2913
Square Footage: 1,835

D

● This smart design features multi-gabled ends, varied roof lines and vertical windows. A covered porch leads through a foyer to a large central gathering room with fireplace, sloped ceiling and a view of the rear terrace. A modern kitchen with snack bar has a pass-through to a breakfast room; there's also an adjacent dining room. A media room isolated from the rest of the house offers a quiet area. The master bedroom has its own whirlpool.

Design N2864
Square Footage: 1,387

L **D**

● Many characteristics of this design deserve mention. The entrance court and covered porch are a delightful way to enter this home. The foyer leads to an interior kitchen with breakfast room and a snack bar on the gathering room side. A study with wet bar is adjacent (it could also serve as a third bedroom). Sliding glass doors in the master bedroom area open to the rear terrace.

TERRACE

MASTER BEDROOM
13⁸ x 11⁰

SLOPED CEILING

OPEN OVER CLOSET

CL

DRESSING RM.

VANITY

SLOPED CEILING

BATH

LEDGE

SKY-LIGHT

TUB

GARAGE
19⁴ x 21⁸

CUSTOMIZABLE
Custom Alterations? See page 349 for customizing this plan to your specifications.

Design N2871

Square Footage: 1,824

D

● A greenhouse off the dining room and living room provides a cheerful focal point for this comfortable three-bedroom home. The spacious living room features a cozy fireplace and sloped ceiling. In addition to the dining room, there's a less formal breakfast room just off the modern kitchen. Stairs just off the foyer lead down to a recreation room. The master bedroom suite opens to a terrace. The mud room and washroom off the garage allow rear entry to the house during inclement weather.

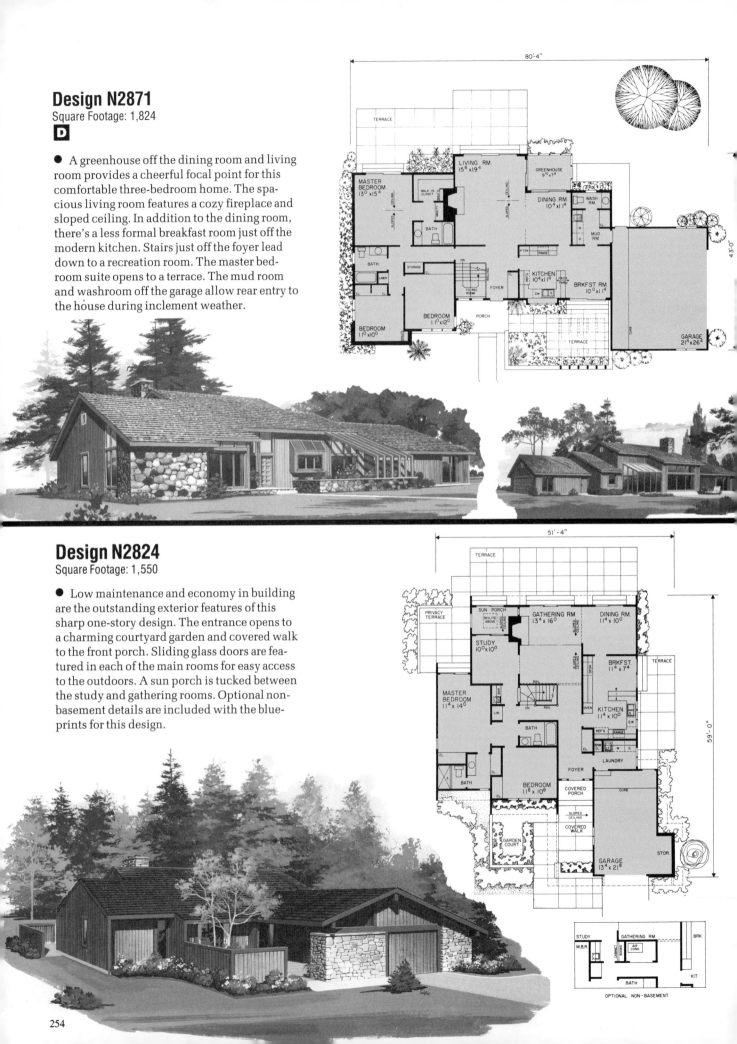

Design N2824

Square Footage: 1,550

● Low maintenance and economy in building are the outstanding exterior features of this sharp one-story design. The entrance opens to a charming courtyard garden and covered walk to the front porch. Sliding glass doors are featured in each of the main rooms for easy access to the outdoors. A sun porch is tucked between the study and gathering rooms. Optional non-basement details are included with the blueprints for this design.

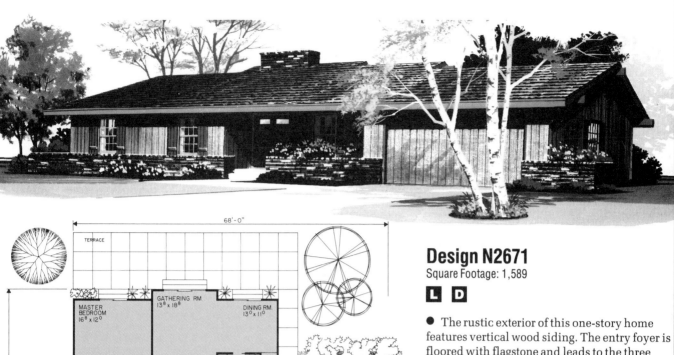

Design N2671
Square Footage: 1,589

L **D**

● The rustic exterior of this one-story home features vertical wood siding. The entry foyer is floored with flagstone and leads to the three areas of the plan: sleeping, living and work center. The sleeping area has three bedrooms including a master with sliding glass doors to the rear terrace. The living area, consisting of gathering and dining rooms, also has access to the terrace. The work center is efficiently planned. It houses the kitchen with snack bar, breakfast room with built-in china cabinet and stairs to the basement.

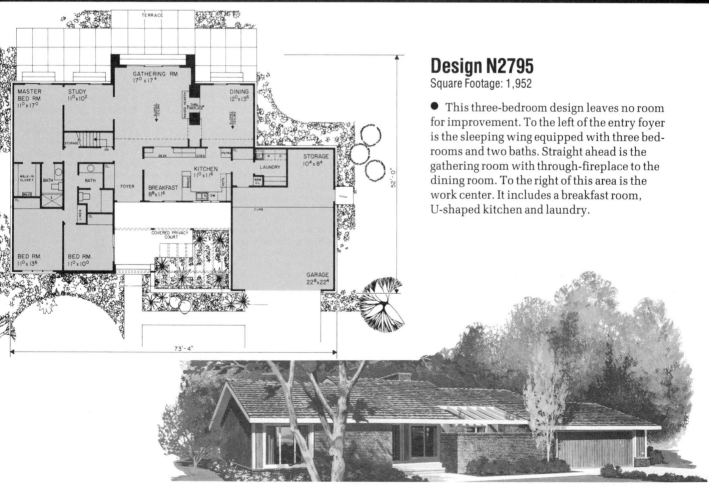

Design N2795
Square Footage: 1,952

● This three-bedroom design leaves no room for improvement. To the left of the entry foyer is the sleeping wing equipped with three bedrooms and two baths. Straight ahead is the gathering room with through-fireplace to the dining room. To the right of this area is the work center. It includes a breakfast room, U-shaped kitchen and laundry.

255

● This is most certainly an outstanding contemporary design. Study the exterior carefully before your journey to inspect the floor plan. The vertical lines are carried from the siding to the paned windows to the garage door. The front entry is recessed so the overhanging roof creates a covered porch.

Note the planter court with privacy wall. The floor plan is just as outstanding. The rear gathering room has a sloped ceiling, raised hearth fireplace, sliding glass doors to the terrace and a snack bar with pass-thru to the kitchen. In addition to the gathering room, there is the living room/study. This

room could be utilized in a variety of ways depending on your family's choice. The formal dining room is convenient to the U-shaped kitchen. Three bedrooms and two closely located baths are in the sleeping wing. This plan includes details for the construction of an optional basement.

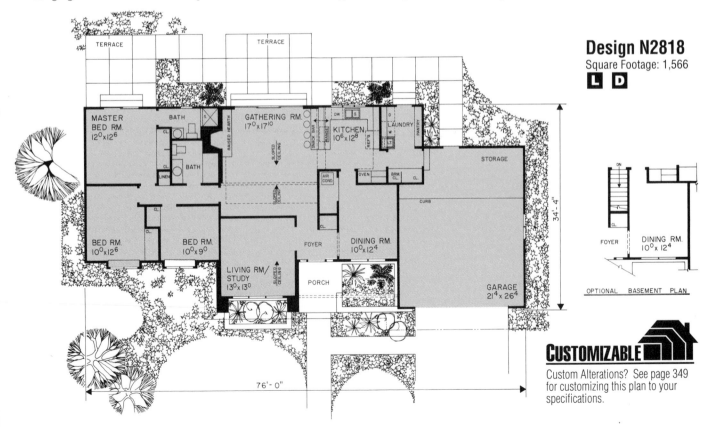

Design N2818
Square Footage: 1,566

L **D**

OPTIONAL BASEMENT PLAN

CUSTOMIZABLE
Custom Alterations? See page 349 for customizing this plan to your specifications.

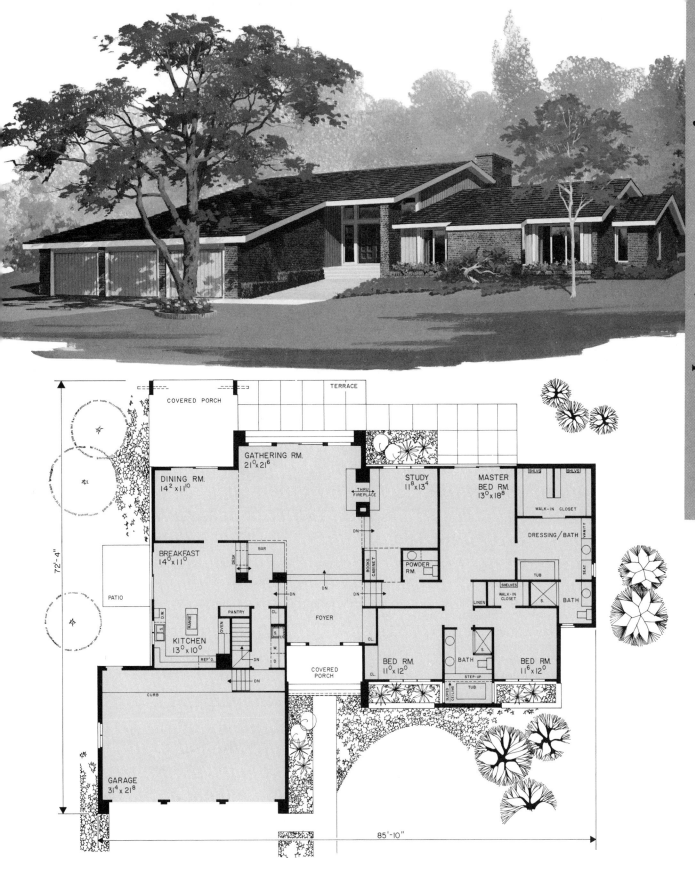

DINING RM.
14²x11¹⁰

GATHERING RM.
21⁰x21⁶

STUDY
11⁸x13⁴

MASTER BED RM.
13⁰x18⁸

BREAKFAST
14⁰x11⁰

KITCHEN
13⁰x10⁰

PANTRY

FOYER

POWDER RM.

BED RM.
11⁰x12⁰

BED RM.
11⁶x12⁰

BATH

GARAGE
31⁴x21⁸

COVERED PORCH

TERRACE

COVERED PORCH

PATIO

72'-4"

85'-10"

Design N2789 Square Footage: 2,732

L D

● An attached three car garage! What a fantastic feature of this three bedroom contemporary design. And there's more. As one walks up the steps to the covered porch and through the double front doors the charm of this design will be overwhelming. Inside, a large foyer greets all visitors and leads them to each of the three areas, each down a few steps. The living area has a large gathering room with fireplace and a study adjacent on one side and the formal dining room on the other. The work center has an efficient kitchen with island range, breakfast room, laundry and built-in desk and bar. Then there is the sleeping area. Note the raised tub with sloped ceiling.

257

Design N2930

Square Footage: 2,032

● The clean lines of this L-shaped contemporary are enhanced by the interesting overhanging roof planes. Horizontal and vertical siding complement one another. The floor plan is made to order for the active small family or empty-nesters: sloping ceilings and plenty of glass areas, an outstanding master bedroom with dressing room and whirlpool, guest room with full bath, study with fireplace, open gathering room and dining room. Note the rear covered porch.

CUSTOMIZABLE

Custom Alterations? See page 349 for customizing this plan to your specifications.

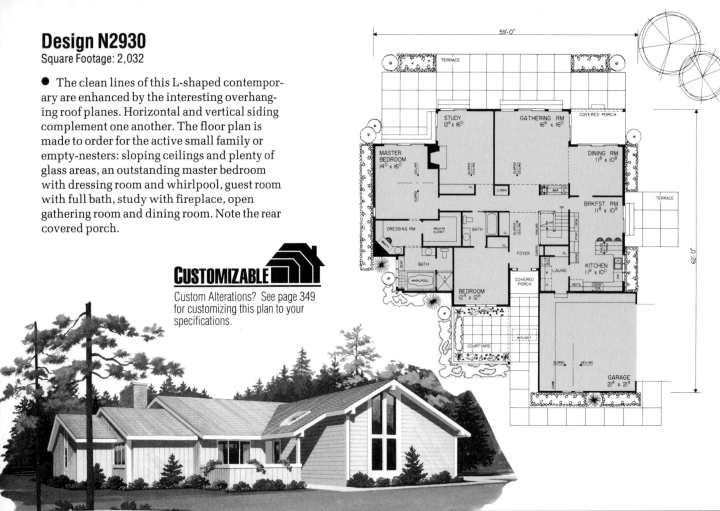

Design N2873

Square Footage: 2,833

● This modern three-bedroom contemporary incorporates many features popular today. A large gathering room with cozy raised-hearth fireplace and sloped ceiling is central focus and centrally located. The dining room has an adjacent bar or butler's pantry. Just off this area is the kitchen with central cooktop island and breakfast room. The master suite is especially luxurious with its own exercise room. There's even a powder room for guests.

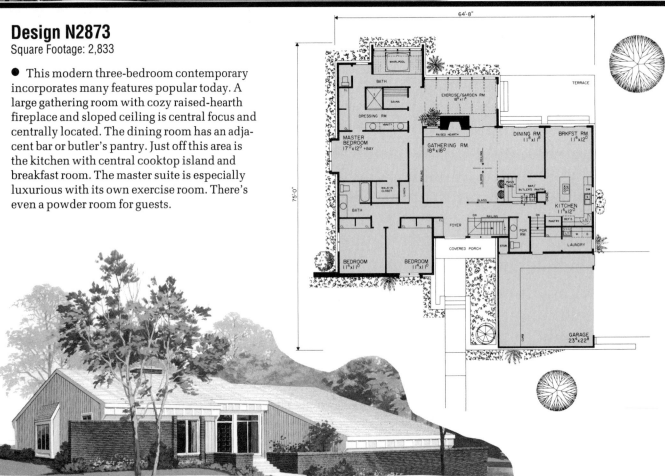

Design N3560
Square Footage: 2,189

L

● Simplicity is the key to the stylish good looks of this home's facade. A walled garden entry and large window areas appeal to outdoor enthusiasts. Inside, the kitchen forms the hub of the plan. It opens directly off the foyer and contains an island counter and a work counter with eating space on the living area side. A sloped ceiling, fireplace, and sliding glass doors to a rear terrace are highlights in living area. The master bedroom also sports sliding glass doors to the terrace. Its dressing area is enhanced with double walk-in closets and lavatories. A whirlpool tub and seated shower are additional amenities. Two family bedrooms are found on the opposite side of the house. They share a full bath with twin lavatories.

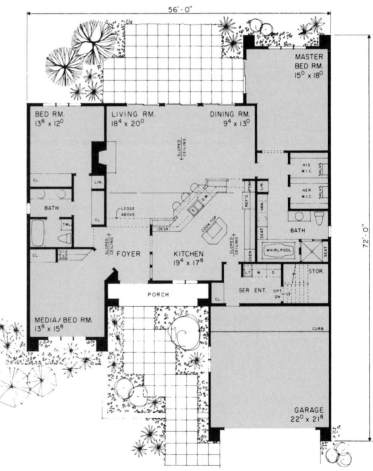

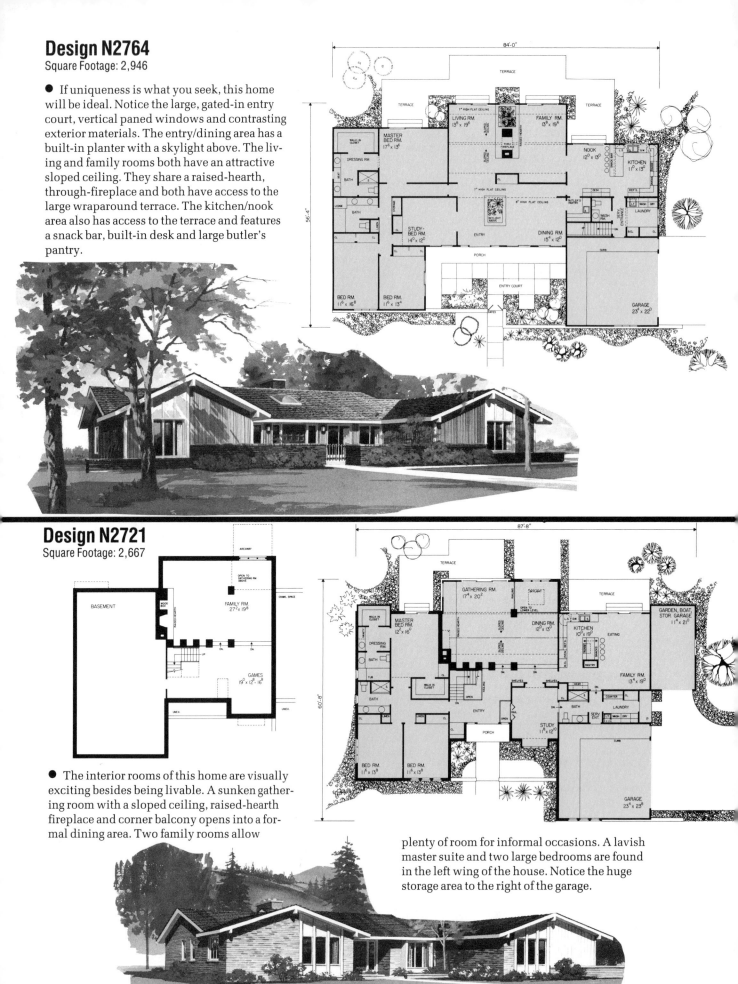

Design N2764

Square Footage: 2,946

- If uniqueness is what you seek, this home will be ideal. Notice the large, gated-in entry court, vertical paned windows and contrasting exterior materials. The entry/dining area has a built-in planter with a skylight above. The living and family rooms both have an attractive sloped ceiling. They share a raised-hearth, through-fireplace and both have access to the large wraparound terrace. The kitchen/nook area also has access to the terrace and features a snack bar, built-in desk and large butler's pantry.

Design N2721

Square Footage: 2,667

- The interior rooms of this home are visually exciting besides being livable. A sunken gathering room with a sloped ceiling, raised-hearth fireplace and corner balcony opens into a formal dining area. Two family rooms allow plenty of room for informal occasions. A lavish master suite and two large bedrooms are found in the left wing of the house. Notice the huge storage area to the right of the garage.

Design N2717
Square Footage: 2,310

● A perfect family plan, this home has a spacious family room in addition to the oversized gathering room. A work-efficient kitchen, featuring a built-in desk and pass-through to the family room, is near to the formal dining room. The three-bedroom sleeping wing contains a master suite and two family bedrooms. Terrace access through sliding glass doors in the master bedroom are a welcome amenity.

Design N2730
Square Footage: 2,490

D

● Here is a basic one-story home loaded with amenities. The central living area of the home includes the gathering room, formal dining room and study. The L-shaped kitchen has an adjacent family room with eating area and an island cooktop. Three bedrooms share space in the sleeping wing of the house. The master has two walk-in closets.

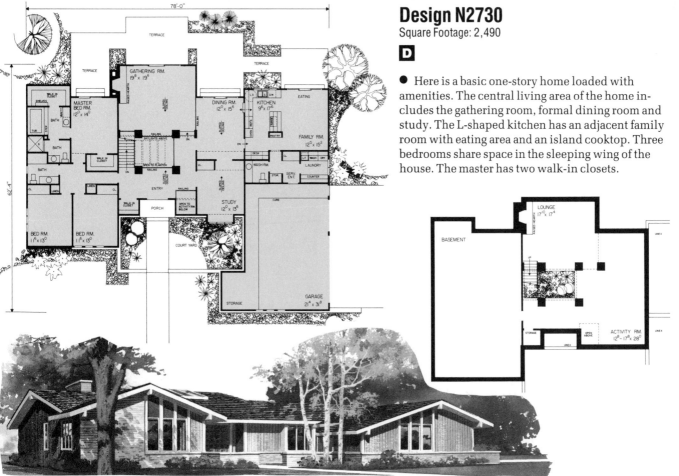

Design N3357
Square Footage: 2,913

L **D**

82'-8"

72'-0"

TERRACE

COUNRTY KITCHEN 14⁰ X 24⁸

GREEN HOUSE

EATING

SNACK BAR

LS T.S. DW

OVEN

LS COOK TOP REF'G

D W LT

CLUTTER RM 14⁴ X 13⁴

WORK ISLAND

WASH RM

PANTRY/ STORAGE

SEWING

DINING RM 11⁰ X 11⁸

LIVING RM 18⁰ X 13⁸   RAISED HEARTH

MASTER BEDROOM 13⁰ X 19⁸

MASTER BATH

WALK-IN CLOSET   WHIRLPOOL

VANITY   BATH

LEDGE ABOVE   SLOPED CEILING

LEDGE ABOVE   SLOPED CEILING   PDR RM   STORAGE LINEN   LIN

FOYER

MEDIA RM/ STUDY 13⁰ X 15⁴   PORCH

BEDROOM 11⁰ X 15⁰   BEDROOM 11⁰ X 15⁰

FREEZER

BC

DN

CURB

GARAGE 23⁶ X 23⁸

● One-story living never had it so good! From the formal living and dining rooms to private media room, this home is designed to be enjoyed. The greenhouse off the kitchen adds 147 square feet to the plan. It offers access to the clutter room where gardening or hobby activities can take place. A the opposite end of the house are a master bedroom with generous bath and two family bedrooms. Notice the wealth of built-ins throughout the house.

Design N3368

Square Footage: 2,720

L **D**

● Roof lines are the key to the interesting exterior of this design. Their configuration allows for sloped ceilings in the gathering room and large foyer. The master bedroom suite has a huge walk-in closet, garden whirlpool and separate shower. Two family bedrooms share a full bath. One of these bedrooms could be used as a media room with pass-through wet bar. Note the large kitchen with conversation bay and the wide terrace to the rear.

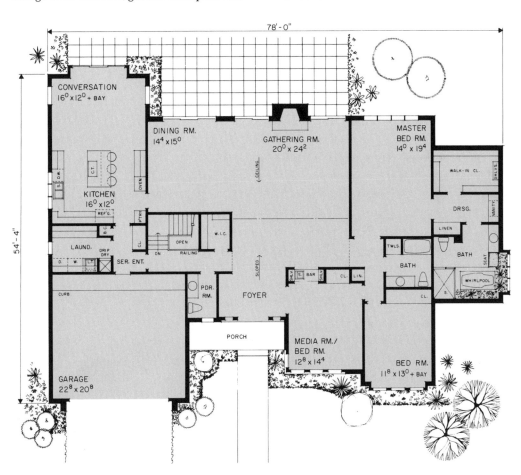

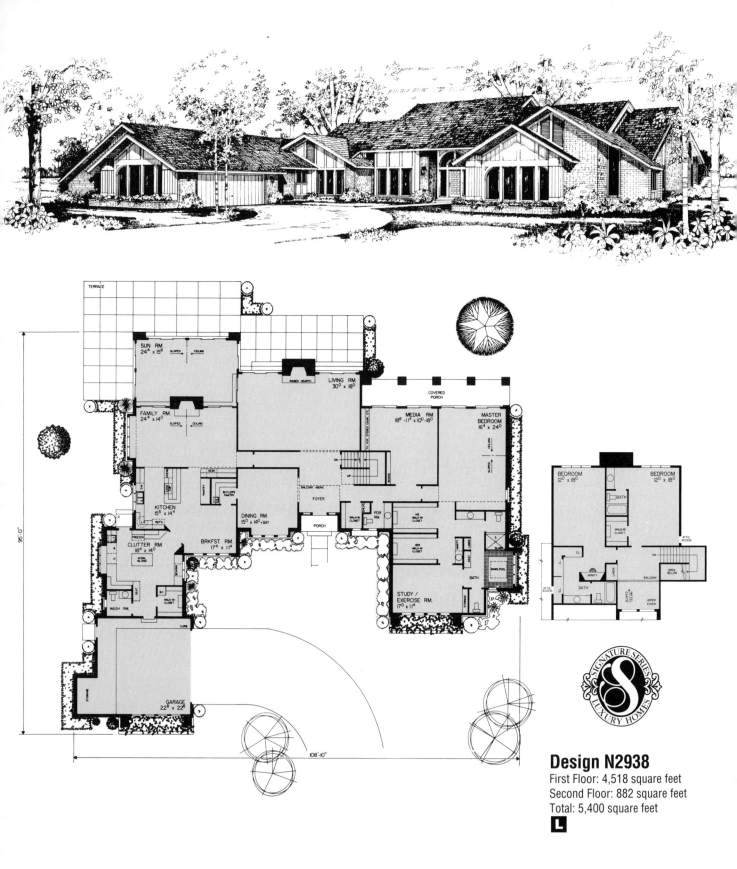

Design N2938
First Floor: 4,518 square feet
Second Floor: 882 square feet
Total: 5,400 square feet

L

● A semi-circular fanlight and side-lights grace the entrance of this striking contemporary. The lofty foyer, with balcony above, leads to an elegant, two-story living room with fireplace. The family room, housing a second fireplace, leads to a glorious sunroom; both have dramatic sloped ceilings.

The kitchen and breakfast room are conveniently located for access to the informal family room or to the formal dining room via the butler's pantry. The large adjoining clutter room with work island offers limitless possibilities for the seamstress, hobbyist, or indoor gardener. An executive-sized, first-

floor master suite offers privacy and relaxation; the bath with whirlpool tub and dressing area with twin walk-in closets open to a study that could dou-ble as an exercise room. Two second-floor bedrooms with private baths and walk-in closets round out the livability in this gracious home.

Design N2791
Square Footage: 3,809

● The use of vertical paned windows and the hipped roof highlight the exterior of this unique design. Upon entrance one will view a charming sunken atrium with skylight above plus a skylight in the dining room and one in the lounge. Formal living will be graciously accommodated in the living room. It features a raised-hearth fireplace, two sets of sliding glass doors to the rear terrace plus two more sliding doors, one to an outdoor dining terrace and the other to an outdoor lounge. Informal living will be enjoyed in the family room with snack bar and in the large library. All will praise the fine planning of the master suite. It features a bay window, His and Hers dressing room with private baths and an abundance of closet space.

Design N2858
Square Footage: 2,231

● This sun oriented design was created to face the south. By doing so, it has minimal northern exposure. It has been designed primarily for the more temperate U.S. latitudes using 2 x 6 wall construction. The morning sun will brighten the living and dining rooms along with the adjacent terrace. Sun enters the garden room by way of the glass roof and walls. In the winter, the solar heat gain from the garden room should provide relief from high energy bills. Solar shades allow you to adjust the amount of light that you want to enter in the warmer months. Interior planning deserves mention, too. The work center is efficient. The kitchen has a snack bar on the garden room side and a serving counter to the dining room. The breakfast room with laundry area is also convenient to the kitchen. Three bedrooms are on the northern wall. The master bedroom has a large tub and a separate shower with a four foot square skylight above. When this design is oriented toward the sun, it should prove to be energy efficient and a joy to live in.

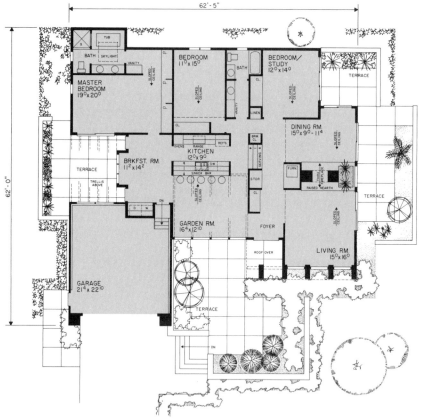

Design N2857

Square Footage: 2,982

L

● You'll applaud the many outstanding features of this home. Notice first the master bedroom. It has His and Hers baths, each with a large walk-in closet, sliding glass doors to a private terrace, and an adjacent study. Two family bedrooms are separate from the master for total privacy. The gathering room is designed for entertaining. It has its own balcony and a fireplace as a focal point. The U-shaped kitchen is efficient and has an attached breakfast room and snack bar pass-through to the dining room.

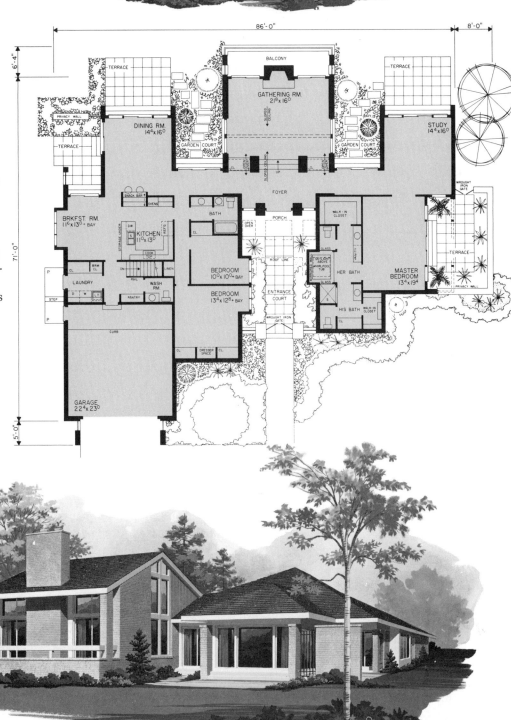

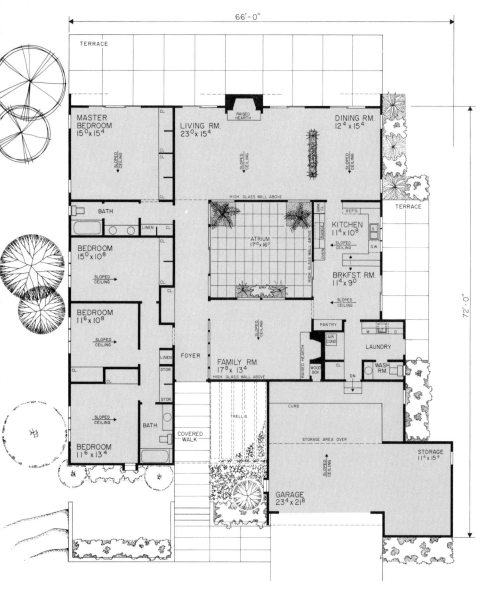

Design N2135

Square Footage: 2,495 (Excluding Atrium)

● For those seeking a new experience in home ownership. The proud occupants of this contemporary home will forever be thrilled at their choice of such a distinguished exterior and such a practical and exciting floor plan. The variety of shed roof planes contrast dramatically with the simplicity of the vertical siding. Inside there is a feeling of spaciousness resulting from the sloping ceilings. The uniqueness of this design is further enhanced by the atrium. Open to the sky, this outdoor area, indoors, can be enjoyed from all parts of the house. The sleeping zone has four bedrooms, two baths and plenty of closets. The informal living zone has a fine kitchen and breakfast room. The formal zone consists of a large living-dining area with fireplace.

OPTIONAL PARTIAL BASEMENT

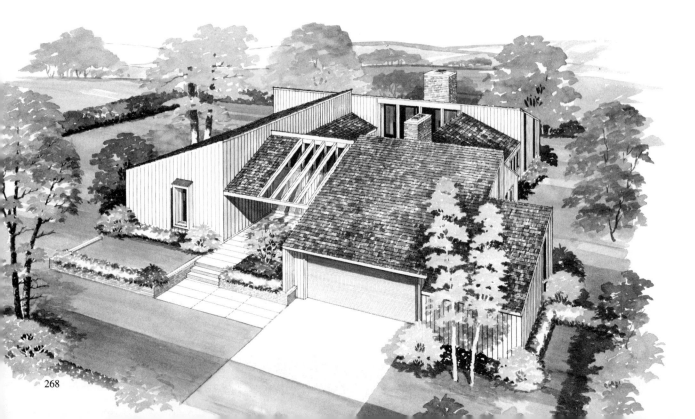

Design N2832

Square Footage: 2,805 (Excluding Atrium)

D

● The advantage of passive solar heating is a significant highlight of this contemporary design. The huge skylight over the atrium provides shelter during inclement weather, while permitting natural light to enter below. The stone floor of this area absorbs an abundance of heat from the sun during the day and permits the circulation of warm air to other areas at night. Sloping ceilings highlight each of the major rooms: three bedrooms, formal living and dining rooms and the study. Broad expanses of roof can accommodate solar panels, if desired, to complement this design.

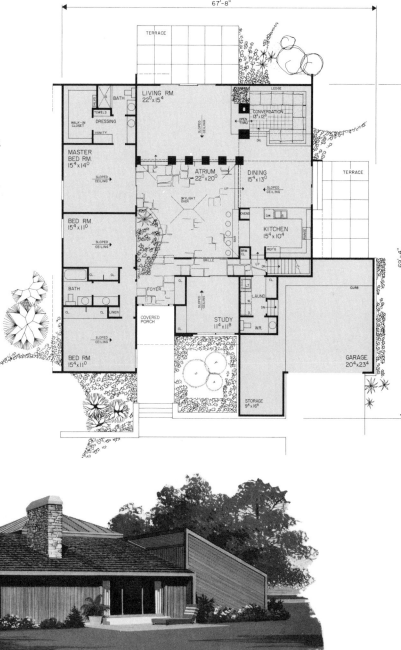

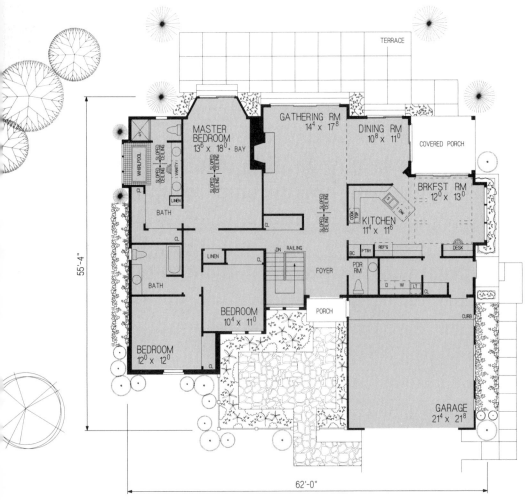

Design N3336

Square Footage: 2,022

L

● Compact and comfortable! This three-bedrooom home is a good consideration for a small family or empty-nester retirees. Of special note are the covered eating porch and sloped ceilings in the gathering room and master bedroom. A well-placed powder room is found at the front entry.

Design N3327

Square Footage: 2,881

L **D**

● The high, massive hipped-roof of this home creates an impressive facade while varying roof planes and projecting gables further enhance appeal. A central, high-ceilinged foyer routes traffic efficiently to the sleeping, formal and informal zones of the house. Note the sliding glass doors that provide access to outdoor living facilities. A built-in china cabinet and planter unit are fine decor features. In the angular kitchen, a high ceiling and efficient work patterning set the pace. The conversation room may act as a multi-purpose room. For TV time, a media room caters to audio-visual activities. Sleeping quarters take off with the spacious master bedroom; here you'll find a tray ceiling and sliding doors to the rear yard. An abundance of wall space for effective and flexible furniture arrangement further characterizes the room. Two sizable bedrooms serve the children or guests.

Width 77'-11"
Depth 73'-11"

CUSTOMIZABLE

Custom Alterations? See page 349 for customizing this plan to your specifications.

271

Design N2882
Square Footage: 2,832

● This plan is designed to be oriented on a west-facing site to take best advantage of energy efficiency. It reflects interesting living patterns and excellent indoor/outdoor relationships. Notice the wide, overhanging roofs, skylights, glass gables, vented walkways, wind-buffering privacy fences and terraces. The 2x6 construction adds to the energy oriented features.

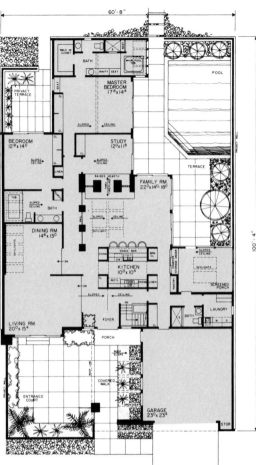

Design N2881
Square Footage: 2,770

● Energy-efficiency was a major consideration in this contemporary design. It was planned for a south-facing lot in temperate zones. Note the variety of outdoor living areas and the centrally located kitchen. Three bedrooms dominate the back of the house, including a master suite with a private terrace. There are two fireplaces: one in the living room and one in the family room.

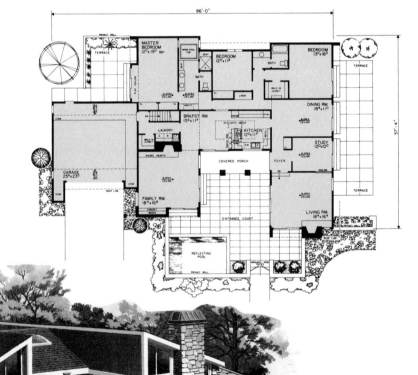

Design N2867 Square Footage: 2,388

L

● A live-in relative would be very comfortable in this home. This design features a self-contained suite (473 sq. ft.) consisting of a bedroom, bath, living room and kitchenette with dining area. This suite is nestled behind the garage away from the main areas of the house. The rest of this traditional, one-story house, faced with fieldstone and vertical wood siding, is also very livable. One whole wing houses the four family bedrooms and bath facilities. The center of the plan has a front, U-shaped kitchen and breakfast room. The formal dining room and large gathering room will enjoy the view, and access to, the backyard. The large, covered porch will receive much use.

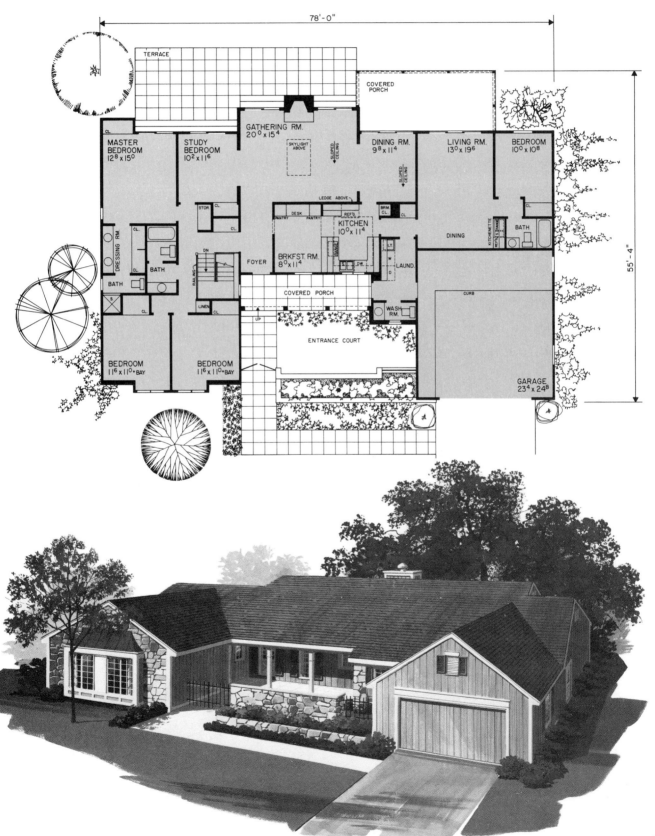

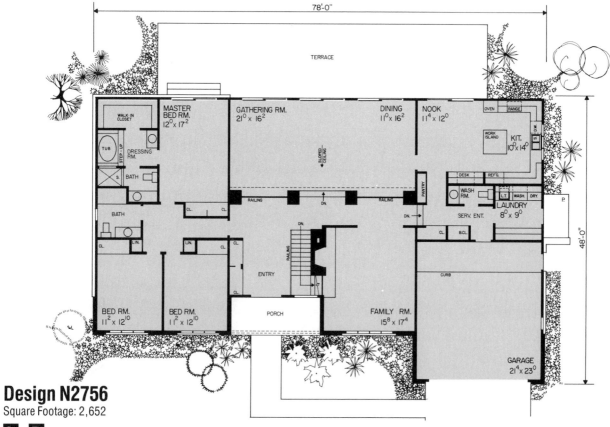

Design N2756

Square Footage: 2,652

L **D**

● This one-story, contemporary design is bound to serve your family well. It will assure the best in contemporary living with its many fine features. Notice the bath with tub and stall shower, dressing room and walk-in closet featured with the master bedroom. Two more family bedrooms are adjacent. The sunken gathering room/dining room is highlighted by the sloped ceiling and sliding glass doors to the large, rear terrace. This formal area is a full 32' x 16'. Imagine the great furniture placement that can be done in this area. In addition to the gathering room, there is an informal family room with a fireplace. You will enjoy the efficient kitchen and get much use out of the work island, pantry and built-in desk. Note the service entrance with washroom and laundry.

Design N2181

Square Footage: 2,612

L **D**

● This home is the complete picture of charm. The interior features are outstanding. It is possible to substitute brick or even siding when building this home.

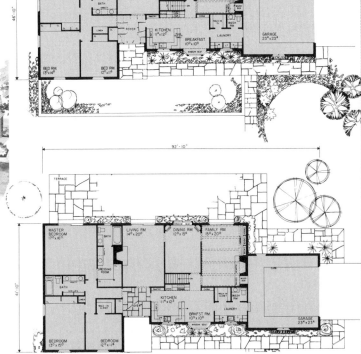

Design N2675

Square Footage: 2,478

D

● Many extra features have been designed into this delightfully traditional home. If you like this design but need a four-bedroom home, order design N2181 above.

Design N2766

Square Footage: 2,711

D

● A sizable master bedroom has a dressing area featuring two walk-in closets, a twin lavatory and compartmented bath. There are also two family bedrooms sharing a full bath. A third bedroom can also be used as a study. Formal living and dining rooms are separated by a through-fireplace. A spacious kitchen/nook is cheerfully informal with a sun room just a step away through sliding glass doors. Be sure to note the number of sizable closets.

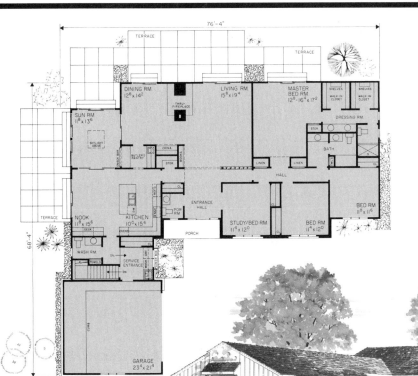

Design N2256

Square Footage: 2,632

● This refreshing contemporary home has a unique exterior that is enhanced by a great floor plan. The central focus is the large living room with raised-hearth fireplace. To the right is the formal dining room and island kitchen with informal eating space. To the left are three family bedrooms — the master has a gigantic walk-in closet. All are tied together with a long hallway. Don't miss the wide terrace at the rear of the plan.

Design N2534

Square Footage: 3,262

L

● The angular wings of this ranch home contribute to its distinctive design. The spacious entrance hall gives way to a large gathering room — the heart of the home. Flanking this all purpose area are a more private study on the right and a formal dining room on the left. The kitchen adjoins the dining room and includes informal eating space. Three bedrooms are found in the right-hand wing. The master bedroom has a private terrace and His and Hers walk-in closets.

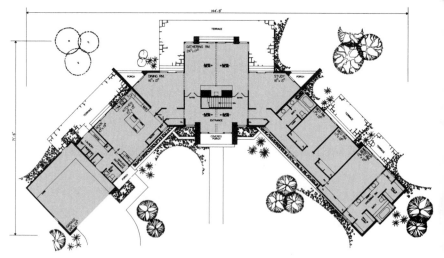

Design N2879 Living Area Including Atrium: 3,173 square feet
Upper Lounge/Balcony: 267 square feet
Total: 3,440 square feet

● This plush modern design seems to have it all, including an upper lounge, upper family room, and upper foyer. There's also an atrium with skylight centrally located downstairs. A modern kitchen with snack bar service to a breakfast room also enjoys its own greenhouse window. A deluxe master bedroom includes its own whirlpool and bay window. Three other bedrooms also are isolated at one end of the house downstairs to allow privacy and quiet. A spacious family room in the rear enjoys its own raised-hearth fireplace and view of a rear covered terrace. A front living room with its own fireplace looks out upon a side garden court and the central atrium. There's also a formal dining room situated between the kitchen and living room, plus a three-car garage, covered porches, and sizable laundry with washroom just off the garage.

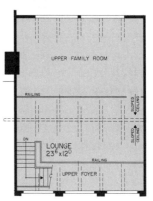

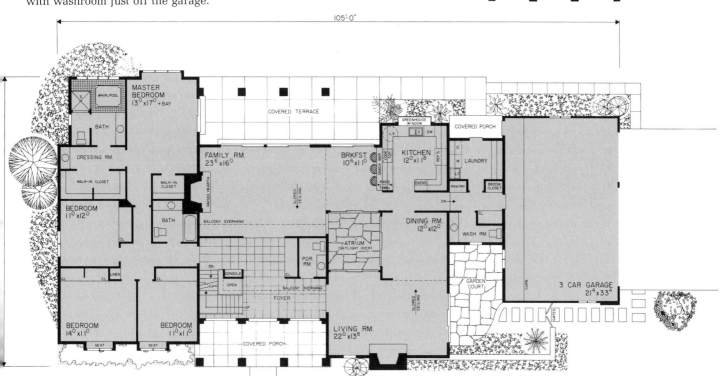

Design N2767
Square Footage: 3,000

D

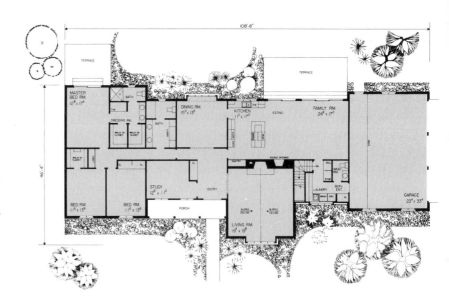

● This home has all the amenities to assure a comfortable lifestyle. Large impressive living areas accommodate both formal and informal occasions. There are three large bedrooms, two full baths with twin lavatories, walk-in closets and a fine study. The kitchen features an island work center with range and desk. The two fireplaces warm their surroundings. Two separate terraces offer a variety of uses. Note the laundry, wash room and three-car garage.

Design N2768
Square Footage: 3,436

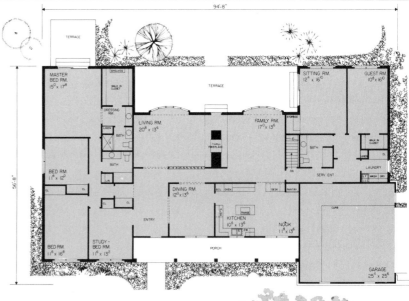

● Besides its elegant traditionally styled exterior with long covered front porch, this home has an exceptionally livable interior. There is an outstanding four-bedroom, two-bath sleeping wing. The efficient kitchen with island range is flanked by the formal dining room and informal breakfast nook. Separated by a through-fireplace are the living and family rooms which overlook the rear yard. There's even a potential live-in facility that could also be used as a hobby room or sewing room.

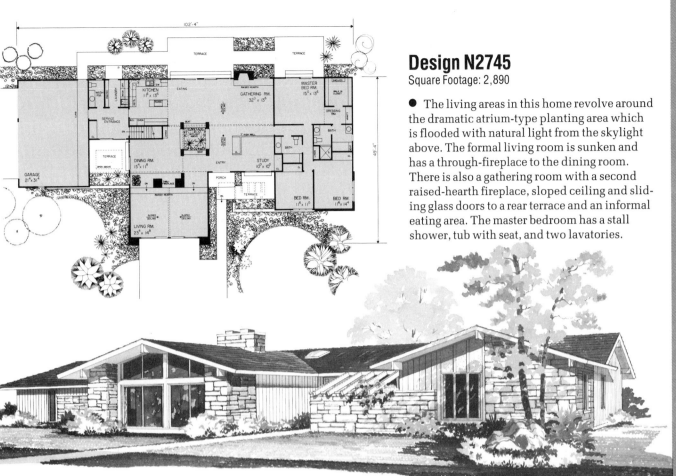

Design N2745
Square Footage: 2,890

● The living areas in this home revolve around the dramatic atrium-type planting area which is flooded with natural light from the skylight above. The formal living room is sunken and has a through-fireplace to the dining room. There is also a gathering room with a second raised-hearth fireplace, sloped ceiling and sliding glass doors to a rear terrace and an informal eating area. The master bedroom has a stall shower, tub with seat, and two lavatories.

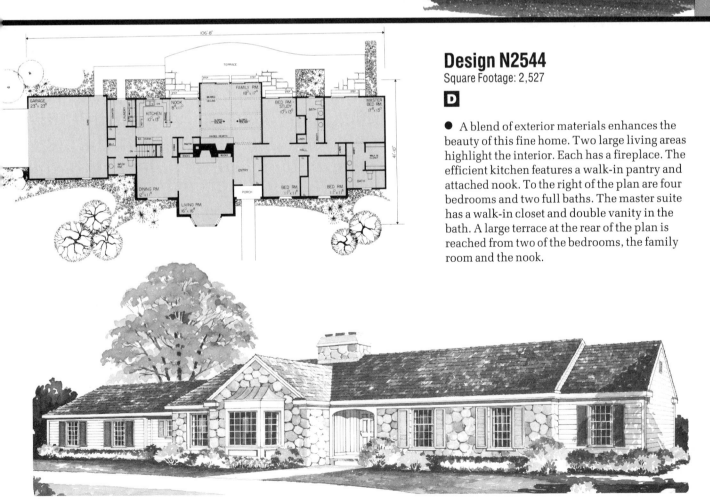

Design N2544
Square Footage: 2,527

D

● A blend of exterior materials enhances the beauty of this fine home. Two large living areas highlight the interior. Each has a fireplace. The efficient kitchen features a walk-in pantry and attached nook. To the right of the plan are four bedrooms and two full baths. The master suite has a walk-in closet and double vanity in the bath. A large terrace at the rear of the plan is reached from two of the bedrooms, the family room and the nook.

Design N2778

Square Footage: 2,761

D

● No matter what the occasion, family and friends alike will enjoy the sizable gathering room in this home. This room has a through-fireplace to the study and two sets of sliding glass doors to the large, rear terrace. Indoor/outdoor living also can be enjoyed from the dining room, study and master bedroom. There is also a covered porch accessible through sliding glass doors in the dining room and breakfast nook.

Design N1786

Square Footage: 2,370

● This is an extremely appealing design, highlighted by its brick masses, its window detailing, its interesting shape and its inviting covered front entrance. The foyer is centrally located and but a step or two from all areas. The bedroom wing is distinctly defined. The quiet, sunken living room is off by itself. There is even a separate formal dining room. The family room has a fireplace and is adjacent to the U-shaped kitchen. Just off the garage is the mud room with washroom for quick clean-ups.

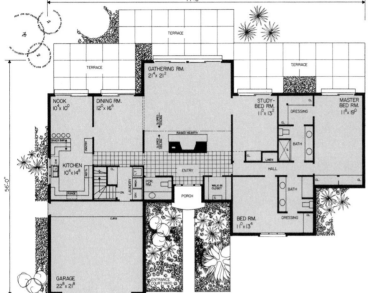

Design N2594

Square Footage: 2,294

D

● A spectacular foyer offers double entry to the heart of this home — a large gathering room complete with raised-hearth fireplace and sliding glass doors onto the terrace. There is also a formal dining room. A well-located study (or third bedroom) offers space for undisturbed work. The kitchen features a snack bar and breakfast nook with sliding glass doors onto the terrace. In the master bedroom suite there are sliding glass doors to the terrace and a dressing room with entry to the bath. Another bedroom is located to the front of the plan.

Design N2784

Square Footage: 2,980

● The projection of the master bedroom and garage create an inviting U-shaped area leading to the covered porch of this delightful traditionally styled design. After entering through the double front doors, the gallery will lead to each of the three living areas: the sleeping wing of two bedrooms, full bath and study; the informal area of the family room with raised-hearth fireplace and sliding glass doors to the terrace; and the formal area consisting of the dining room and the living room. Note the privacy of the master bedroom.

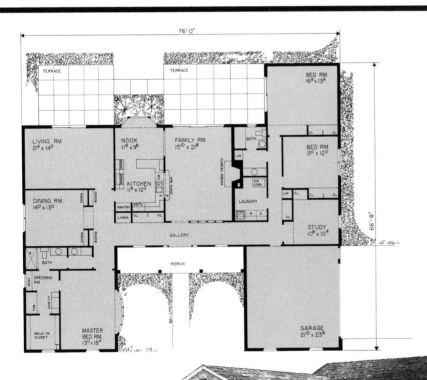

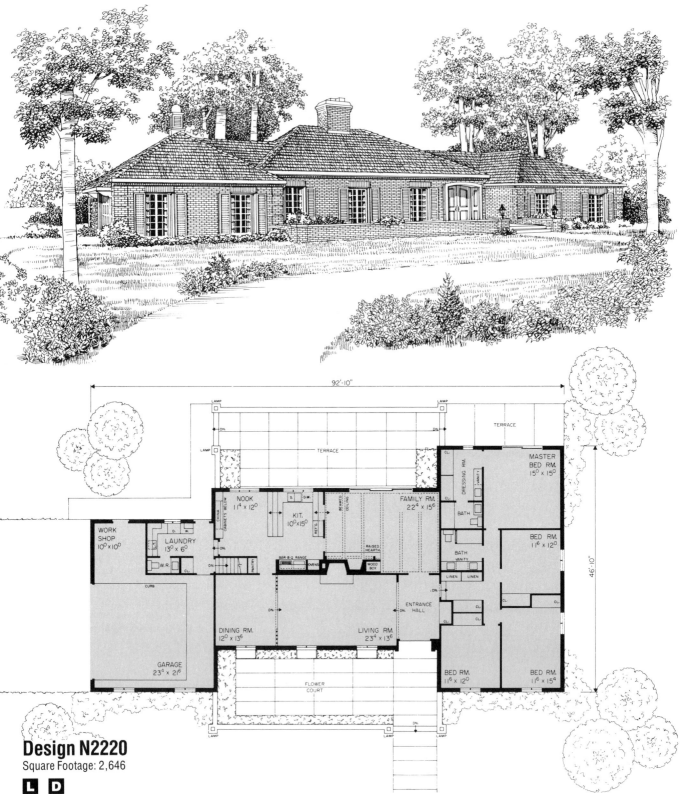

Design N2220

Square Footage: 2,646

L **D**

● The gracious formality of this home is reminiscent of a popularly accepted French styling. The hip-roof, the brick quoins, the cornice details, the arched window heads, the distinctive shutters, the recessed double front door and the massive center chimney, and the delightful flower court are all features which set the dramatic appeal of this home. This floor plan is a favorite of many. The four bedroom, two bath sleeping wing is a zone by itself. Further, the formal living and dining rooms are ideally located. For entertaining they function well together and look out upon the pleasant flower court. Overlooking the raised living terrace at the rear are the family and breakfast rooms and work center. Don't miss the laundry, extra wash room and work shop in garage.

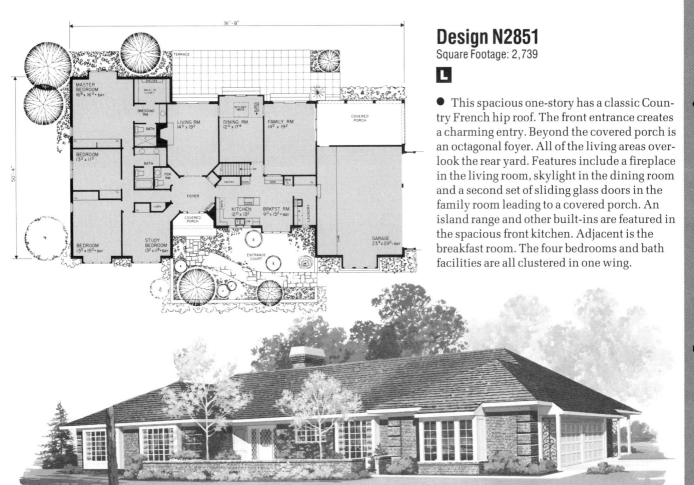

Design N2851
Square Footage: 2,739

L

● This spacious one-story has a classic Country French hip roof. The front entrance creates a charming entry. Beyond the covered porch is an octagonal foyer. All of the living areas overlook the rear yard. Features include a fireplace in the living room, skylight in the dining room and a second set of sliding glass doors in the family room leading to a covered porch. An island range and other built-ins are featured in the spacious front kitchen. Adjacent is the breakfast room. The four bedrooms and bath facilities are all clustered in one wing.

Design N1892
Square Footage: 2,036

L **D**

● Three bedrooms grace one wing of this beautiful one-story design and complement the living areas: formal sunken living room with fireplace, family room with beamed ceiling, formal dining room and U-shaped kitchen. The mud room with attached wash room adds a further measure of convenience.

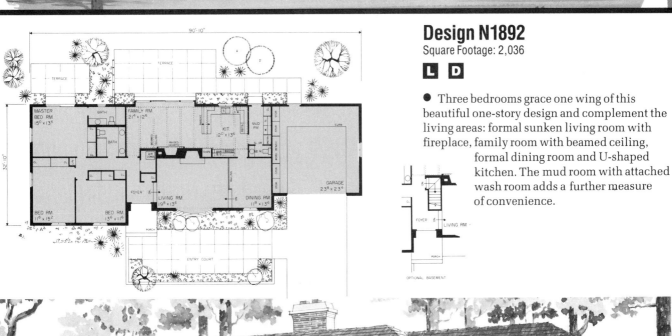

Design N2212
Square Footage: 3,577

L

● From the graceful, curving drive court to the
formal living room, this expansive, hospitable
French country home welcomes the visitor.
Note the spacious terrace area and the many
amenities.

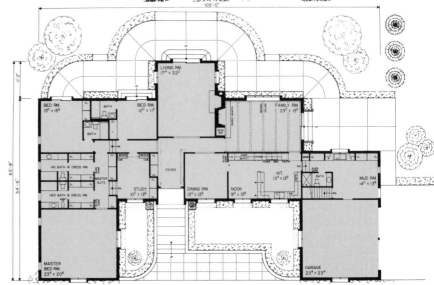

Design N2779
Square Footage: 3,225

L **D**

● This French design is surely impressive. The
exterior is highlighted with a hip roof, paned-
glass windows, brick privacy wall and double
front doors. The inside is just as appealing.
Note the unique placement of rooms and features: formal dining room with butler's pantry,
sizable parlor, gathering room with fireplace
and sliding glass doors, and an adjacent study.
The U-shaped kitchen has an island range,
snack bar, breakfast nook and pantry.

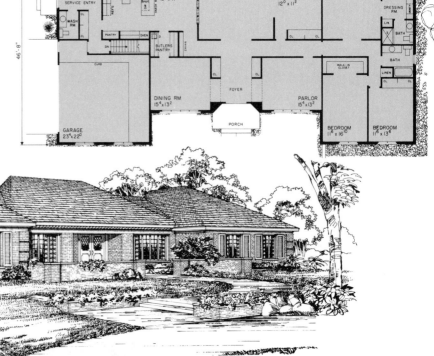

Design N2693

Square Footage: 3,462

● This elegant Georgian manor is reminiscent of historic Rose Hill, built 1818 in Lexington, Kentucky. It is typical of the classic manors with Greek Revival features built in Kentucky as the 19th Century dawned. Note the classical portico of four Ionic columns plus the fine proportions. Also noteworthy is the updated interior, highlighted by a large country kitchen with fireplace and an efficient work center that includes an island cooktop. The country kitchen leads directly into a front formal dining room, just off the foyer. On the other side of the foyer is a front living room. A large library is located in the back of the house. It features built-in bookcases plus a fireplace, one of four fireplaces.

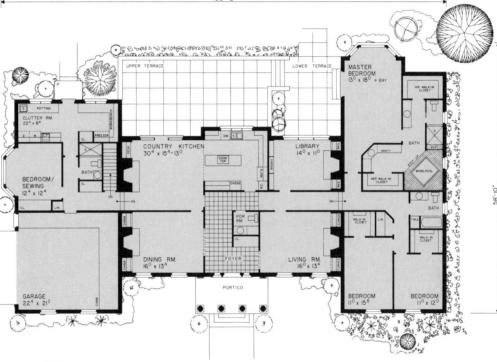

Design N1761

Square Footage: 2,548

L **D**

● Low, strong roof lines and solid, enduring qualities of brick give this house a permanent appearance. The bedroom wing is isolated and the baths and closets deaden noise from the rest of the house. Center fireplaces in the family and living rooms make furniture arrangement easy. There are a number of extras: workshop, large garage, indoor barbecue plus formal and informal eating areas.

Width 92'-10"
Depth 45'-2"

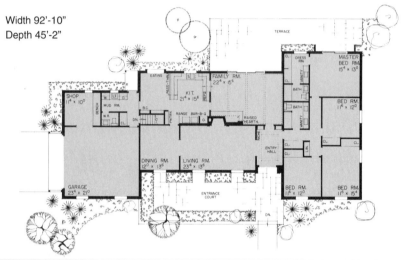

Design N1788

Square Footage: 2,218

L **D**

● In addition to its eye-catching facade, this home has a practical floor plan. The focal point is the formal living room with bay window. It is just a few steps down from the formal dining room and overlooks a terrace. The family room contains a fireplace and sliding glass doors to the same terrace. The bedrooms are located to the left of the plan and include a master suite and two family bedrooms with shared bath.

Width 92'-10"
Depth 32'-10"

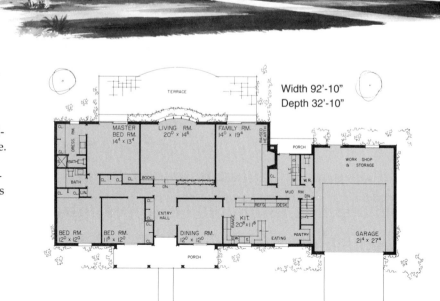

Design N3559

Square Footage: 2,916

● Intricate details make the most of this lovely one-story: high, varied rooflines, circle and half-circle window detailing, multi-pane windows and a solid chimney stack. The floor plan caters to comfortable living. Besides the living room/dining room area to the rear, there is a large conversation area with fireplace and plenty of windows. The kitchen is separated from living areas by an angled snack-bar counter. A media room to the front of the plan provides space for more private activities. Three bedrooms grace the right side of the plan. The master suite features a tray vaulted ceiling and sliding glass doors to the rear terrace. The dressing area is graced by His and Hers walk-in closets, a double-bowl lavatory and a compartmented commode. The shower area is highlighted with glass block and is sunken down one step. A garden whirlpool finishes off the area.

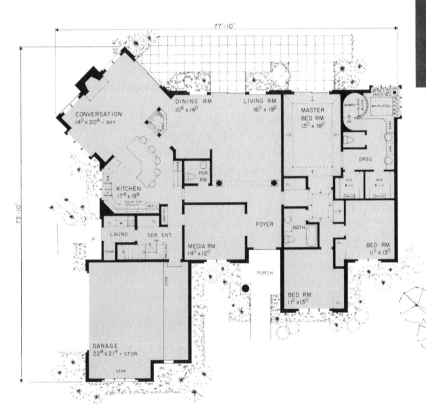

CUSTOMIZABLE

Custom Alterations? See page 349 for customizing this plan to your specifications.

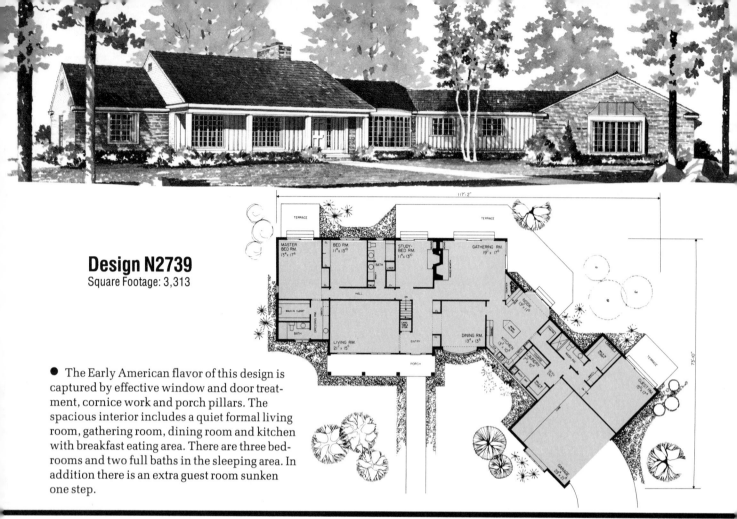

Design N2739
Square Footage: 3,313

● The Early American flavor of this design is captured by effective window and door treatment, cornice work and porch pillars. The spacious interior includes a quiet formal living room, gathering room, dining room and kitchen with breakfast eating area. There are three bedrooms and two full baths in the sleeping area. In addition there is an extra guest room sunken one step.

Design N2783
Square Footage: 3,210

L

● The configuration of this traditional design is outstanding. The garage and bedroom wing on one side and the master bedroom on the other create an inviting U-shaped entry court.

The gathering room has access to the rear terrace along with the dining room, family room and rear bedroom. Note interior kitchen which is adjacent to each of the major rooms.

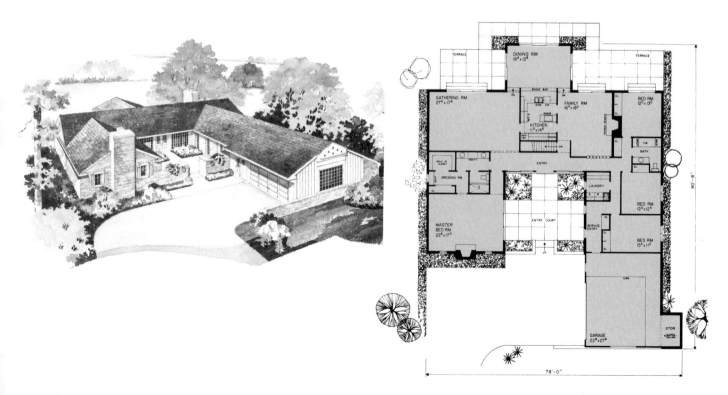

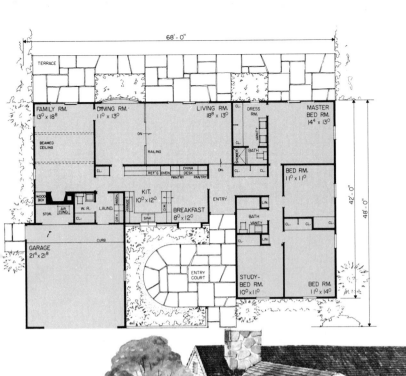

Design N1950
Square Footage: 2,076

● Grace and charm are the key words to describe the exterior of this home. Beyond the delightful entry court and recessed front entry is a grand design. Note the spacious sunken living room, separate dining room, family room with beamed ceiling, excellent kitchen with pass-through to breakfast room, two full baths and a washroom. The outdoor areas are special as well.

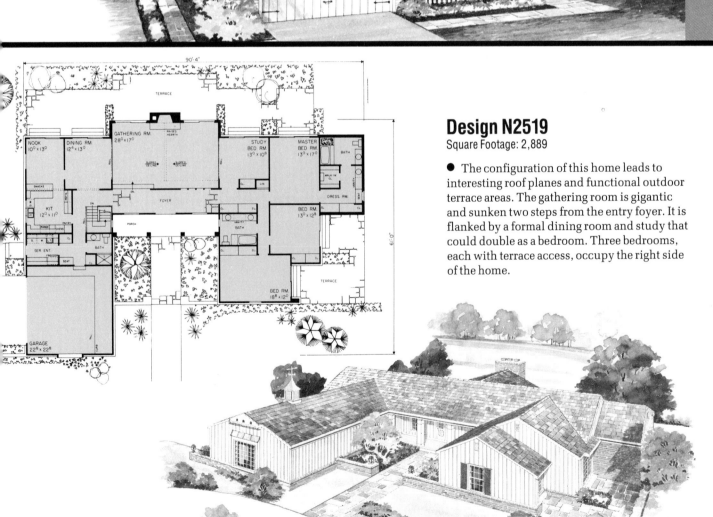

Design N2519
Square Footage: 2,889

● The configuration of this home leads to interesting roof planes and functional outdoor terrace areas. The gathering room is gigantic and sunken two steps from the entry foyer. It is flanked by a formal dining room and study that could double as a bedroom. Three bedrooms, each with terrace access, occupy the right side of the home.

Design N2888
Square Footage: 3,018

L

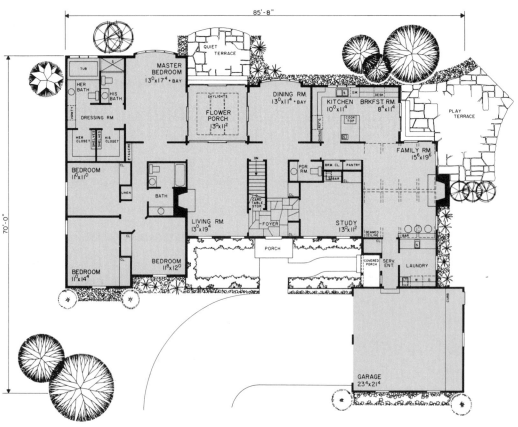

● This is an outstanding Early American design for the 20th-Century. The exterior detailing with narrow clap boards, multi-paned windows and cupola are the features of yesteryear. Interior planning, though, is for today's active family. Formal living room, informal family room plus a study are present. Every activity will have its place in this home. Picture yourself working in the kitchen. There's enough counter space for two or three helpers. Four bedrooms are in the private area. Stop and imagine your daily routine if you occupied the master bedroom. Both you and your spouse would have plenty of space and privacy. The flower porch, accessible from the master bedroom, living and dining rooms, is a very delightful "plus" feature. Study this design's every detail.

Design N2916
Square Footage: 2,129

● The covered front porch of this Early American-styled house, provides a shelter for the inviting panelled front door. Inside, the plan offers wonderful formal and informal living patterns. The country kitchen has a beamed ceiling and a fireplace. The U-shaped work center is most efficient. There are two dining areas — an informal eating space and a formal dining room. The more formal gathering room is spacious and sports a sloped ceiling and two sets of sliding glass doors to the rear terrace.

Design N2880
Living Area: 2,758 square feet
Greenhouse: 149 square feet
Total: 2,907 square feet

● This comfortable traditional home offers plenty of modern livability. A clutter room off the two-car garage is the perfect space for a workbench, sewing and hobbies. Across the hall is a media room and nearby is the country kitchen with attached greenhouse. There are also formal dining and living rooms, a covered porch, and three bedrooms including a master suite.

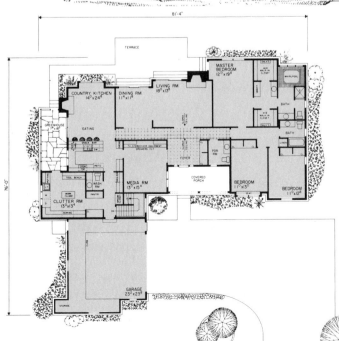

CUSTOMIZABLE

Custom Alterations? See page 349 for customizing this plan to your specifications.

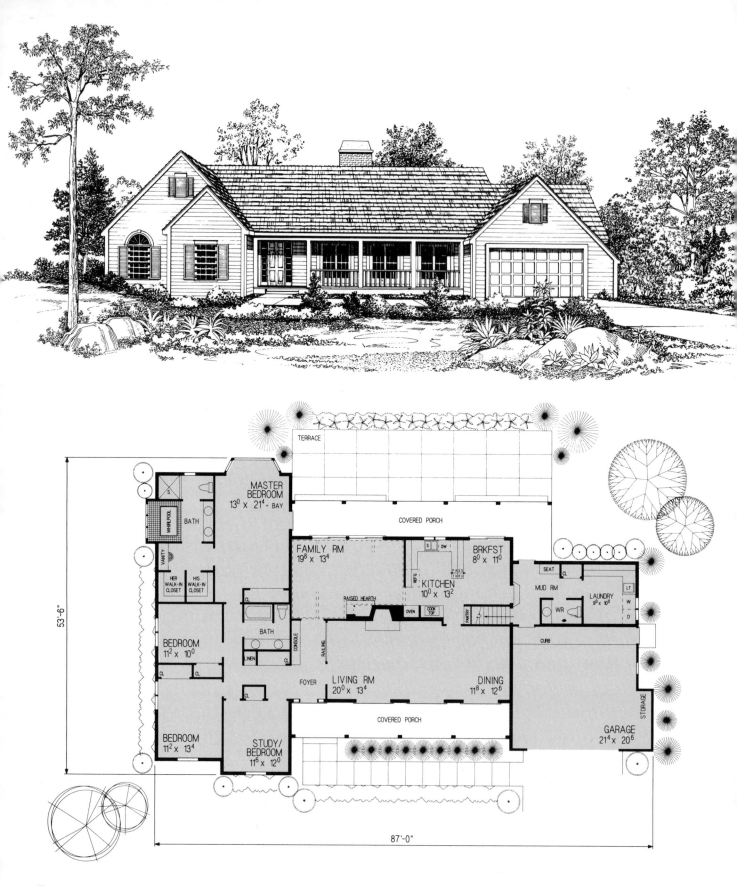

Design N3348 Square Footage: 2,549

L

● Covered porches front and rear will be the envy of the neighborhood when this house is built. The interior plan meets family needs perfectly in well-zoned areas: a sleeping wing with four bedrooms and two baths, a living zone with formal and informal gathering space, and a work zone with U-shaped kitchen and laundry with washroom. The two-car garage has a huge storage area.

Design N3332

Square Footage: 2,168

L

● Nothing completes a traditional-style home quite as well as a country kitchen with fireplace. Notice also the sloped-ceiling living room and well-appointed master suite. A handy washroom is near the laundry, just off the garage.

TERRACE

MASTER BEDROOM
12⁴ x 17⁶

LIVING RM
20⁸ x 17⁴

SLOPED CEILING ← → SLOPED CEILING

PORCH
DN

DINING RM
11⁸ x 11⁴

TERRACE

WALK-IN CLOSET

WHIRLPOOL

BATH

SEAT

S

RAISED HEARTH

WOOD BOX

BC

PANTRY

WASH RM

W D

LAUNDRY
9² x 8⁴

CL

DN

BATH

STOR.

DN

LINEN

CL

PASS THRU

SNACK BAR

DW

RANGE

REFG

CURB

DN

FOYER

COUNTRY KITCHEN
22⁴ x 13⁰

BEDROOM
11⁴ x 11⁴

CL

CL

GARAGE
21⁴ x 21⁴

COVERED PORCH

BEDROOM
11⁴ x 11⁰

DESK

UP

46'-0"

76'-4"

Design N2595

Square Footage: 2,653

● A winged design puts everything in the right place. At the center, formal living and dining rooms with sloped ceiling share one fireplace for added charm. Sliding glass doors in both rooms open onto the main terrace. In the right wing, there is a spacious family room with another raised-hearth fireplace, built-in desk, dining area and adjoining smaller terrace. A study, the master suite and family bedrooms (all bedrooms having access to a third terrace) plus baths are in the left wing. Notice the open staircase leading to the basement.

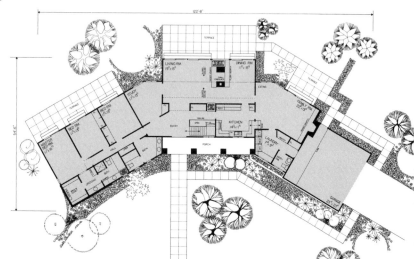

Design N2720

Square Footage: 3,130

● A raised-hearth fireplace lights up the sunken gathering room at the center of this home. For more living space, a well-located study and formal dining room each have direct access to the gathering room. The kitchen boasts all the right features: island range, pantry, built-in desk and separate breakfast nook. Bedrooms include a master suite with double closets, dressing room and private bath. Don't miss the extra curb area in the garage.

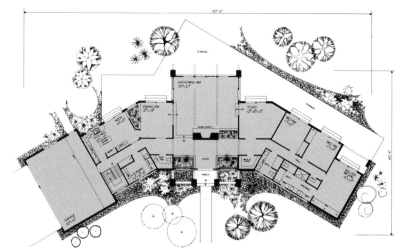

Design N2746
Square Footage: 2,790

D

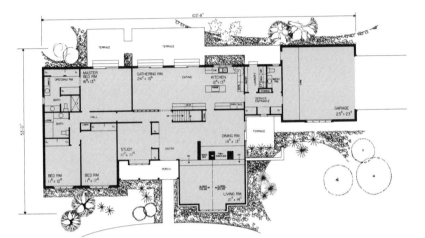

● This impressive one-story is the embodiment of sound investment. The projecting living room with stucco, simulated wood beams and effective window treatment is sunken by two steps. The large rear gathering room has adjacent eating space, near the island kitchen. A study is also part of the plan. Three bedrooms dominate the left wing of the design. The master has a fine bath with dressing area.

Design N2317
Square Footage: 3,161

● Here's a rambling English manor with a full measure of individuality. The formal living room with sloping beamed ceiling and fireplace flanked by bookshelves and cabinets is offset by an informal family room. The kitchen separates this room from the formal dining room. Three bedrooms include a large master suite with private terrace. Don't miss the huge main terrace and the three full baths.

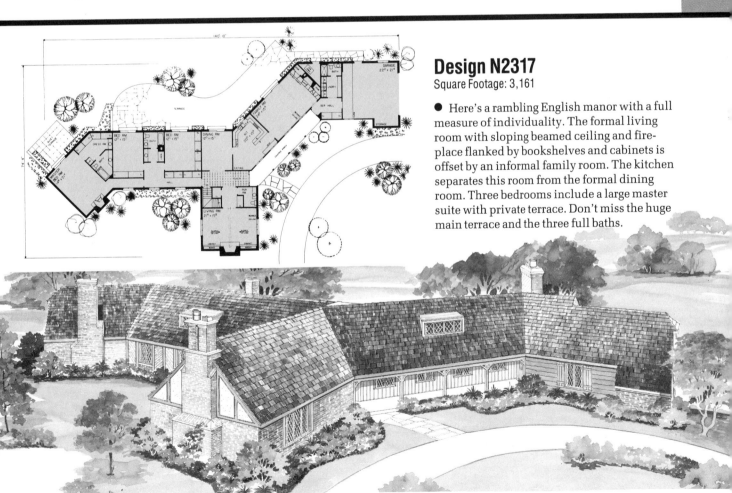

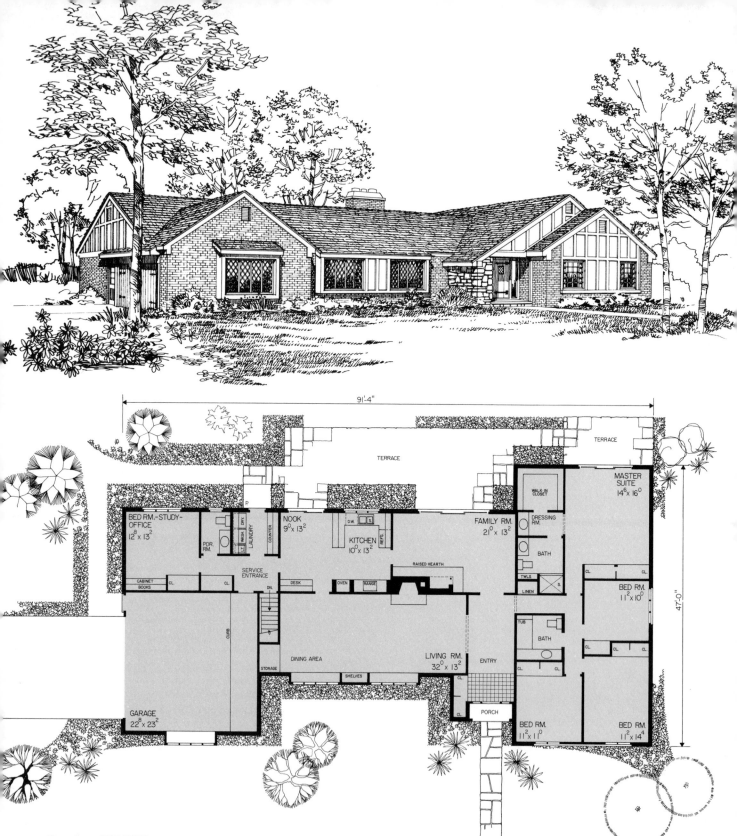

TERRACE

TERRACE

MASTER
SUITE
14⁶ x 16⁰

WALK-IN
CLOSET

DRESSING
RM.

BED RM.-STUDY-
OFFICE
12⁸ x 13²

FAMILY RM.
21⁰ x 13²

BATH

BED RM.
11² x 10⁰

PDR.
RM.

DRY.
WASH

LT.

LAUNDRY

COUNTER

NOOK
9⁰ x 13²

DW.

S

KITCHEN
10⁰ x 13²

REFG.

TWLS

SERVICE
ENTRANCE

RAISED HEARTH

LINEN

S

CABINET
BOOKS

CL.

CL.

DESK

OVEN

RANGE

TUB

BATH

DN.

CL.

CL.

CURB

DINING AREA

LIVING RM.
32⁰ x 13²

ENTRY

CL.

CL.

STORAGE

SHELVES

CL.

GARAGE
22⁸ x 23²

PORCH

BED RM.
11² x 11⁰

BED RM.
11² x 14⁴

91'-4"

47'-0"

Design N2573
Square Footage: 2,747

L **D**

● A Tudor ranch! Combining brick
and wood for an elegant look. It has a
living/dining room measuring 32' by
13', large indeed. It is fully appointed
with a traditional fireplace and built-in
shelves, flanked by diagonally paned
windows. There's much more! There is

a family room with a raised hearth
fireplace and sliding glass doors that
open onto the terrace. A U-shaped
kitchen has lots of built-ins . . . a
range, an oven, a desk. Plus a separate
breakfast nook. The sleeping facilities
consist of three family bedrooms plus

an elegant master bedroom suite. A
conveniently located laundry with a
folding counter is in the service entrance. Adjacent to the laundry is a
washroom. The corner of the plan has
a study or make it a fifth bedroom if
you prefer.

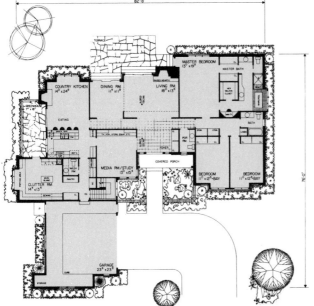

Design N2961
Square Footage: 2,919

● This is an interesting and charming one-story. Contributing to the appeal: varying roof planes, cornice detailing, brick exterior and accents of stucco and beam-work. Inside, the spacious foyer with slate floor routes traffic effectively. Highlights here include a media room, clutter room, country kitchen, formal living room, dining room and large master bedroom with its luxurious master bath. Be sure to notice the glass-walled greenhouse.

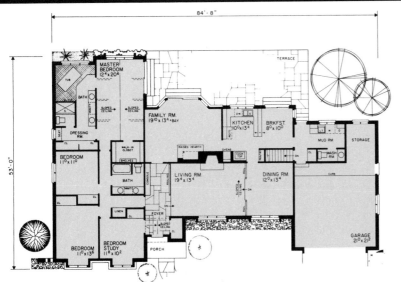

Design N2877
Square Footage: 2,612
L **D**

● Here's a dramatic Post-Modern exterior with a popular plan featuring an outstanding master bedroom suite. The bedroom itself is spacious, has a sloped ceiling, a large walk-in closet and sliding glass doors to the terrace. Along with this bedroom, there are three more served by a full bath. The living area of this plan has the formal areas in the front and informal areas in the rear. Both have a fireplace. The roomy work center is efficiently planned.

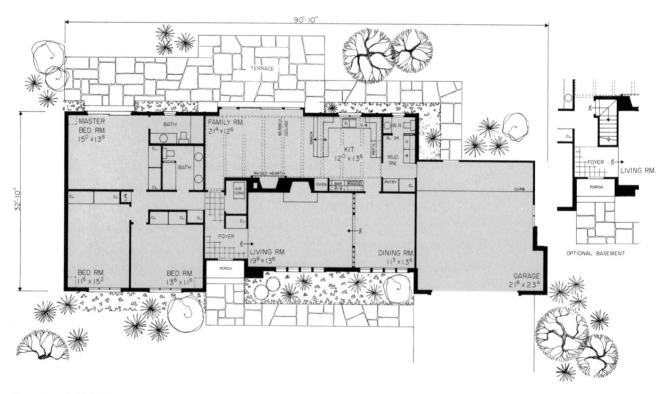

Design N2318
Square Footage: 2,029

L **D**

● Warmth and charm are characteristics of Tudor adaptations. This modest sized home with its twin front-facing gabled roofs represents a great investment. While it will be an exciting and refreshing addition to any neighborhood, its appeal will never grow old.

The covered, front entrance opens to the center foyer. Traffic patterns flow in an orderly and efficient manner to the three main zones — the formal dining zone, the sleeping zone and the informal living zone. The sunken living room with its fireplace is separated

from the dining room by an attractive trellis divider. A second fireplace, along with beamed ceiling and sliding glass doors, highlights the family room. Note snack bar, mud room, cooking facilities, two full baths and optional basement.

Design N2962
Square Footage: 2,112

● A Tudor exterior with an efficient floor plan is favored by many. Each of the three main living zones in this plan are within a few steps of the foyer for easy traffic flow. Open planning and plenty of glass create a nice environment for the living/dining area. The L-shaped kitchen with island range and work surface is delightfully open to the large breakfast room. Nearby is the step-saving laundry. The sleeping zone has the flexibility of functioning as a two- or three-bedroom area. Notice the economical back-to-back plumbing.

CUSTOMIZABLE

Custom Alterations? See page 349 for customizing this plan to your specifications.

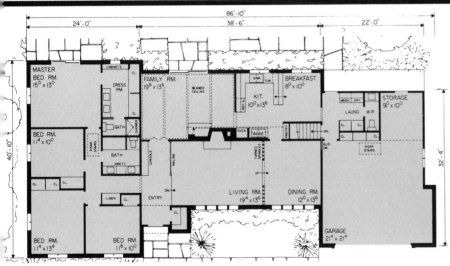

Design N1989
Square Footage: 2,282

L D

● High style abounds in this picturesque, ground-hugging design. The plan calls for a sunken living room and separate dining room. Overlooking the rear yard is an informal family room with beamed ceiling. Note the proximity of the kitchen and breakfast room. A master bedroom suite is one of four bedrooms found to the left of the entry foyer.

299

 CUSTOMIZABLE

Custom Alterations? See page 349 for customizing this plan to your specifications.

Design N3346

Square Footage: 2,032

L

● This home boasts a delightful Tudor exterior with a terrific interior floor plan. Though compact, there's plenty of living space: large study with fireplace, gathering room, dining room, and breakfast room. The master bedroom has an attached bath with whirlpool tub. Note the double walk-in closets.

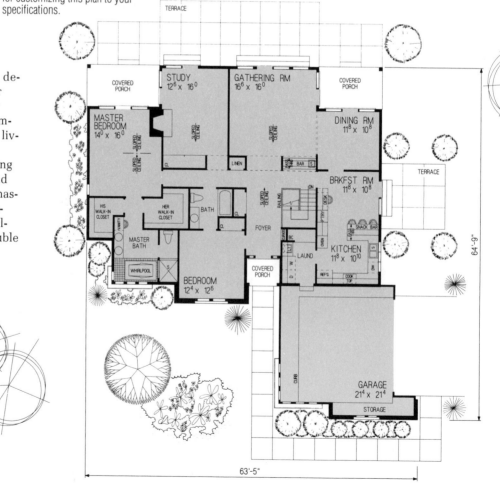

TERRACE

STUDY
12⁶ x 16⁰

GATHERING RM
16⁶ x 16⁰

COVERED PORCH

COVERED PORCH

MASTER BEDROOM
14⁰ x 16⁰

DINING RM
11⁸ x 10⁸

LINEN

BAR

TERRACE

HIS WALK-IN CLOSET

HER WALK-IN CLOSET

BATH

BRKFST RM
11⁸ x 10⁸

RAILING

MASTER BATH

FOYER

SNACK BAR

WHIRLPOOL

KITCHEN
11⁸ x 10¹⁰

BEDROOM
12⁴ x 12⁶

COVERED PORCH

LAUND

REF'G

COOK TOP

GARAGE
21⁴ x 21⁴

STORAGE

64'-9"

63'-5"

Design N3600

Square Footage: 2,258

● This unique, one-story plan is tailor-made for a small family or for empty-nesters. Formal areas are situated well for entertaining—living room to the right and formal dining room to the left. A large family room is found to the rear. It has access to a rear wood deck and is warmed in the cold months by a welcoming hearth. The U-shaped kitchen features an attached morning room for casual meals. It is near the laundry room and a wash room. Bedrooms are split. The master suite sits to the right of the plan and has a walk-in closet and a fine bath. A nearby study has a private porch. One family bedroom is on the other side of the home and also has a private bath.

Width 68'
Depth 64'

CUSTOMIZABLE

Custom Alterations? See page 349 for customizing this plan to your specifications.

Design N3602

Square Footage: 2,312

● This lovely one-story home fits right into sunny regions—or any area of the country. The floor plan includes both formal and informal living spaces, a dining room and a morning room. A study or media room provides a getaway for quiet pursuits. The master bedroom and bath occupy space to the rear of the plan, while a secondary bedroom is to the left of the plan. A third bedroom can be built if extra room is needed.

Width 68'
Depth 64'

CUSTOMIZABLE

Custom Alterations? See page 349 for customizing this plan to your specifications.

Design N2142

Square Footage: 2,450

D

● Adaptations of Old English homes have enjoyed great popularity. This design is no exception. Notice the up-to-date floor planning inside: formal living and dining rooms to the right, family room and kitchen/breakfast room at center, sleeping wing to the left. Notice the two terrace areas, raised-hearth fireplace, and conveniently located powder room.

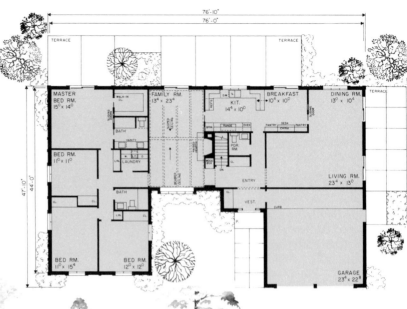

Design N2515

Square Footage: 2,363

D

● The brick veneer of this house is effectively complemented by beam work, stucco and window treatment. The interior plan is equally engaging. The kitchen, nook and dining room overlook the front yard. The laundry is around the corner. A sloping, beamed ceiling and raised-hearth fireplace are highlights of the family room. Like the living room and master bedroom, it functions with the rear terrace. Wood posts separate the living room and hall.

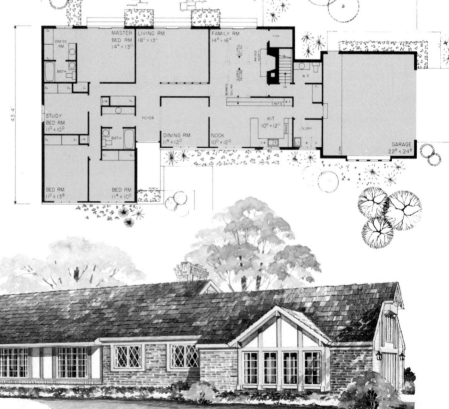

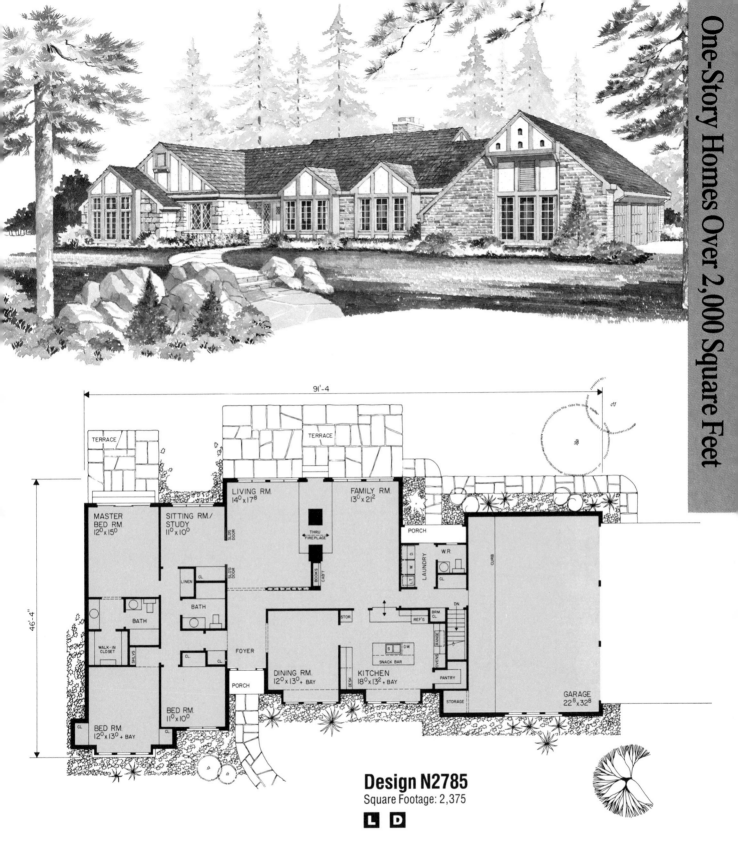

91'-4

46'-4"

TERRACE

TERRACE

LIVING RM.
14⁰ x 17⁸

FAMILY RM.
13⁰ x 21²

MASTER
BED RM.
12⁰ x 15⁰

SITTING RM./
STUDY
11⁰ x 10⁰

THRU
FIREPLACE

PORCH

LAUNDRY

W.R.

LINEN

CL.

BOOKS

CAB'T

CL.

BATH

BATH

BRM.
CL.

DN.

REF'G

RANGE

STOR.

WALK-IN
CLOSET

SHLVS

CL.

FOYER

CL.

SNACK BAR

S

DW

OVENS

PANTRY

PORCH

DINING RM.
12⁰ x 13⁰ + BAY

KITCHEN
18⁰ x 13² + BAY

STORAGE

GARAGE
22⁸ x 32⁸

BED RM.
12⁰ x 13⁰ + BAY

CL.

BED RM.
11⁰ x 10⁰

CL.

Design N2785
Square Footage: 2,375

L **D**

Exceptional Tudor design! Passersby will take a second glance at this fine home wherever it may be located. And the interior is just as pleasing. As one enters the foyer and looks around, the plan will speak for itself in the areas of convenience and efficiency.

Cross room traffic will be avoided. There is a hall leading to each of the three bedrooms and study of the sleeping wing and another leading to the living room, family room, kitchen and laundry with washroom. The formal dining room can be entered from both

the foyer and the kitchen. Efficiency will be the by-word when describing the kitchen. Note the fine features: a built-in desk, pantry, island snack bar with sink and pass-thru to the family room. The fireplace will be enjoyed in the living and family rooms.

303

Design N2966
Square Footage: 3,687

● This Tudor adaptation is as dramatic inside as it is outside. As a visitor approaches the front courtyard there is much that catches the eye. The interesting roof lines, the appealing window treatment, the contrasting exterior materials and their textures, the inviting panelled front door and the massive twin chimneys with their protruding clay pots. Inside, the spacious foyer with its sloping ceiling looks up into the balcony-type lounge. It also looks down the open stairwell to the lower level area. From the foyer, traffic flows conveniently to other areas. The focal point of the living zone is the delightful atrium. Both the formal living room and the informal family room feature a fireplace. Each of the full baths highlights a tub and shower, a vanity and twin lavatories. Note the secondary access to the basement adjacent to the door to three car garage. Lounge adds an additional 284 sq. ft.

Design N2926

First Floor: 1,570 square feet; Second Floor: 598 square feet
Lower Level: 1,080 square feet; Total: 3,248 square feet

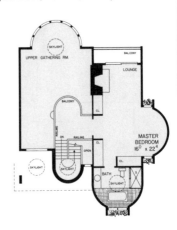

● This striking Contemporary design offers plenty of leisure living on three levels including an activities room with bar, exercise room with sauna, two gathering rooms, circular glass windows, and skylights. Note the outstanding master bedroom suite with skylight over the bath, adjoining lounge, and adjacent upper gathering room.

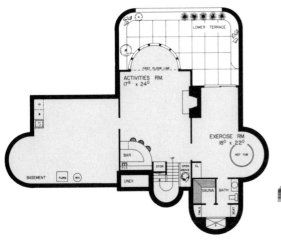

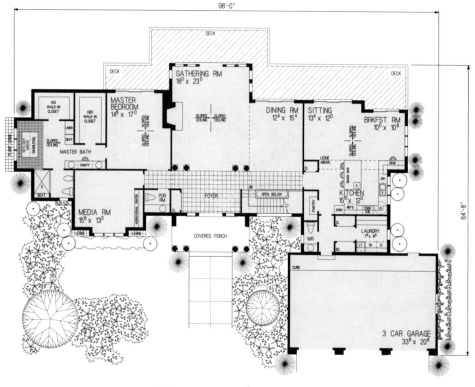

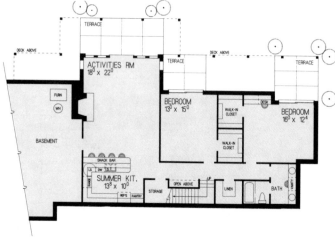

Design N3311

Main Level: 2,662 square feet
Lower Level: 1,548 square feet
Total: 4,210 square feet

L **D**

● Here's a hillside haven
for family living with plenty
of room to entertain in style.
Enter the main level from a
dramatic columned portico
that leads to a large entry
hall. The gathering room is
straight back and adjoins a
formal dining area. A true
gourmet kitchen with plenty
of room for casual eating
and conversation is nearby.
The abundantly appointed
master suite on this level is
complemented by a luxuri-
ous bath. Note the media
room to the front of the
house. On the lower level
are two more bedrooms, a
full bath, a large activity
area with fireplace and a
convenient summer kitchen.

Design 3361

Main Level: 3,548 square feet
Lower Level: 1,036 square feet
Total: 4,584 square feet

L

● Here's a dandy hillside home that can easily accommodate the largest of families and is perfect for both formal and informal entertaining. Straight back from the entry foyer is a grand gathering room/dining room combination. It is complemented by the breakfast room and a front-facing media room. The sleeping wing contains three bedrooms and two full baths. On the lower level is an activities room with summer kitchen and a fourth bedroom that makes the perfect guest room.

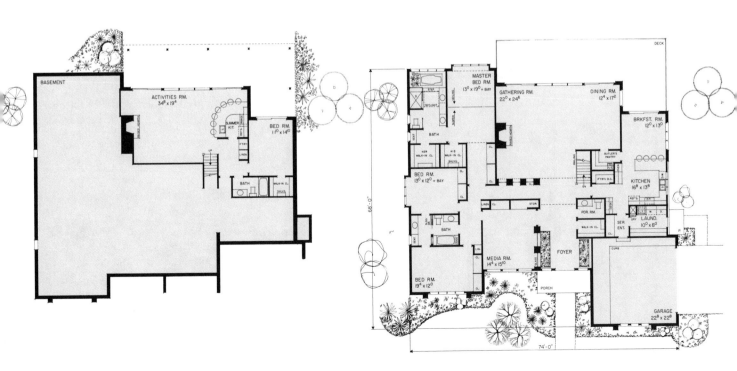

Design N2841

Main Level: 1,044 square feet
Upper Level: 851 square feet
Lower Level: 753 square feet
Total: 2,648 square feet

D

● This spacious tri-level with traditional stone exterior offers excellent comfort and zoning for the modern family. A main-floor gathering area is continued above with two-story appeal. The lower level offers an activities room with raised-hearth in addition to an optional bunk room with bath. A modern kitchen on the main level features a handy snack bar in addition to a dining room. A study on the main level could be used as a bedroom. The master bedroom is located on the upper level along with a rectangular bunk room with its own balcony.

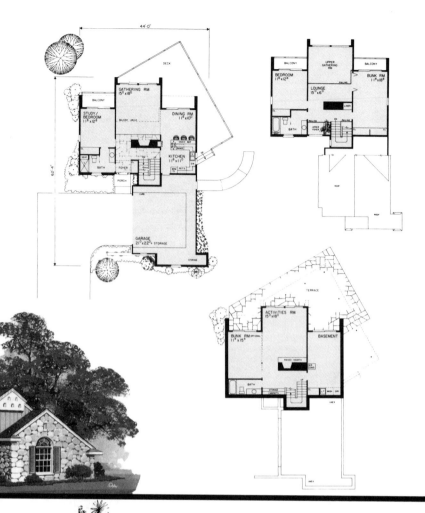

Design N3360

Upper Level: 2,673 square feet
Lower Level: 1,389 square feet
Total: 4,062 square feet

L

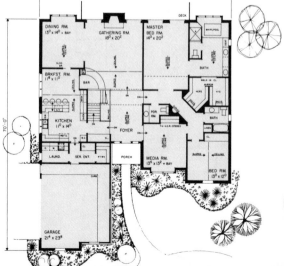

● This plan has the best of both worlds — a traditional exterior and a modern multi-level floor plan. The central foyer routes traffic effectively to all areas: the kitchen, gathering room, sleeping area, media room and the stairs leading to the lower level. Highlights include a master bedroom suite with luxurious bath and a lower-level activities room with fireplace and kitchen. Also note the bedroom on this level.

Design N3366

Main Level: 1,638 square feet
Upper Level: 650 square feet
Lower Level: 934 square feet
Total: 3,222 square feet

L

● There is much more to this design than meets the eye. While it may look like a 1½-story plan, bonus recreation and hobby space in the walk-out basement adds almost 1,000 square feet. The first floor holds living and dining areas as well as the master bedroom suite. Two family bedrooms on the second floor are connected by a balcony area that overlooks the gathering room below. Notice the covered porch beyond the breakfast and dining rooms.

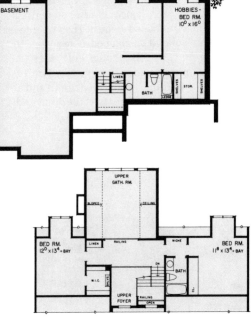

Design N2944

Main Level: 1,545 square feet
Upper Level: 977 square feet
Lower Level: 933 square feet
Total: 3,455 square feet

● This eye-catching contemporary features three stacked levels of livability. The main level has a fine U-shaped kitchen which is flanked by the informal breakfast room and formal dining room. The living room is dramatic with a sloped ceiling that extends through the upper level. A two-way fireplace can be enjoyed from the dining room, living room and media room. Upstairs, the balcony serves as the connecting link for the three bedrooms. The lower level offers a huge activities room plus lounge. Note the bar and fireplace.

Design N2679

Main Level: 1,179 square feet
Upper Level: 681 square feet
Family Room Level: 643 square feet
Lower Level: 680 square feet
Total: 3,183 square feet

● This spacious contemporary offers space for the large or growing family. The main level includes a breakfast room in addition to a formal dining room. Adjacent is a sloped-ceiling living room with raised-hearth. The upper level features an isolated master bedroom suite with adjoining study or sitting room and balcony. The family-room level includes a long family room with adjoining terrace on one end and an adjoining bar with washroom at the other end. Two other bedrooms are positioned in the lower level, each with its own terrace.

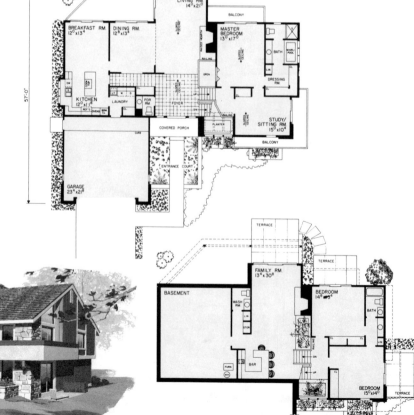

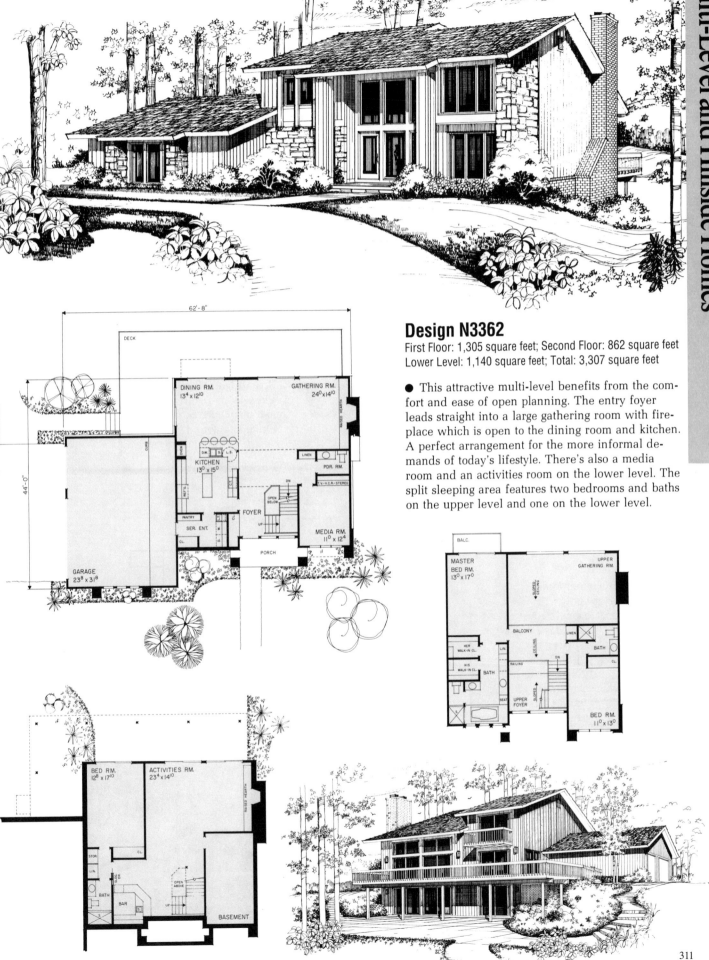

Design N3362

First Floor: 1,305 square feet; Second Floor: 862 square feet
Lower Level: 1,140 square feet; Total: 3,307 square feet

● This attractive multi-level benefits from the comfort and ease of open planning. The entry foyer leads straight into a large gathering room with fireplace which is open to the dining room and kitchen. A perfect arrangement for the more informal demands of today's lifestyle. There's also a media room and an activities room on the lower level. The split sleeping area features two bedrooms and baths on the upper level and one on the lower level.

Design N2901

Main Level: 1,449 square feet
Upper Level: 665 square feet
Master Bedroom Level: 448 square feet
Activities Room Level: 419 square feet
Total: 2,981 square feet

L

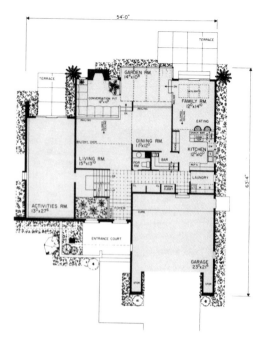

● This luxurious three-bedroom offers comfort on many levels. Its modern design incorporates a rear garden room and conversation pit in the living room/dining room area. There are skylights brightening the adjacent family room with a high sloped ceiling. Other features include an entrance court, activities room, modern kitchen, upper lounge and master bedroom.

Design N2936

Main Level: 1,980 square feet
Lower Level: 1,475 square feet
Total: 3,455 square feet

L

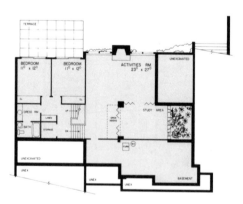

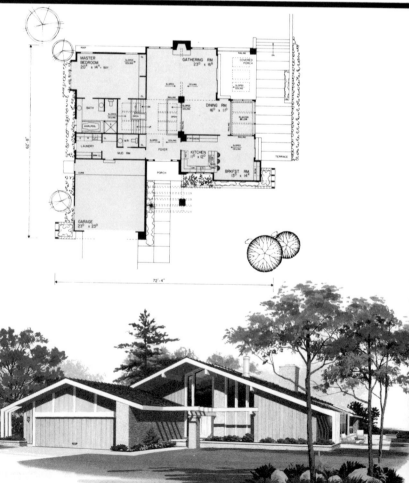

● This dramatic contemporary multi-level offers the active family great new lifestyle options. The main level is spacious. Sloping ceilings and easy access to the outdoor living areas contribute to that feeling of openness. The dining room overlooks the planting area in the activities room. Notice that the master suite is conveniently separated from family bedrooms. Also of note are the laundry, covered porch and basement utility area.

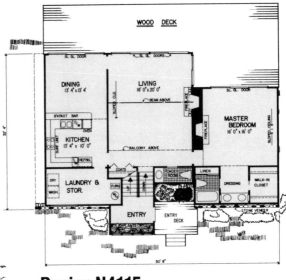

Design N4115

Main Level: 1,494 square feet
Upper Level: 597 square feet
Total: 2,091 square feet

● Here is a home that's moderately sized without sacrificing livability. Just off the entry is a large, two-story living room. There's also a dining room with a breakfast bar/pass-through to the kitchen. To the rear is an enormous deck for sunning and relaxing. A split-sleeping area features two upper-level bedrooms and a main-level master bedroom. Notice the fireplace and sloped ceilings.

Design N4308

Main Level: 1,494 square feet
Upper Level: 597 square feet
Lower Level: 1,035 square feet
Total: 3,126 square feet

● You can't help but feel spoiled by this design. Downstairs from the entry is the large living room with sloped ceiling and fireplace. Nearby is the U-shaped kitchen with a pass-through to the dining room. Also on this level, the master suite boasts a fireplace and a sliding glass door onto the deck. The living and dining rooms also feature deck access. Upstairs are two bedrooms and shared bath. A balcony sitting area overlooks the living room. The enormous lower-level playroom includes a fireplace, a large bar and sliding glass doors to the patio.

313

Design N2511

Main Level: 1,043 square feet
Upper Level: 703 square feet
Lower Level: 794 square feet
Total: 2,540 square feet

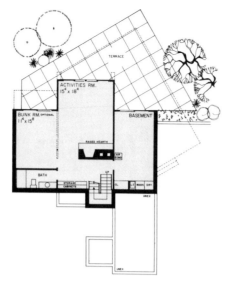

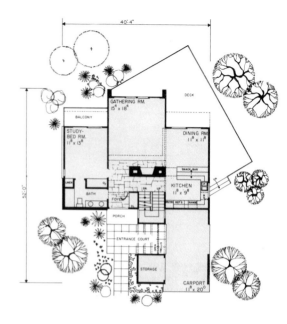

● Rustic yet contemporary, this design on three levels is a real beauty. Living areas include a gathering room, study (or optional bedroom), dining room and activities room in the basement. There are two bunk rooms — upper level and lower level — and terrace space for any outdoor activity.

Design N2716

Main Level: 1,013 square feet
Upper Level: 885 square feet
Lower Level: 1,074 square feet
Total: 2,972 square feet

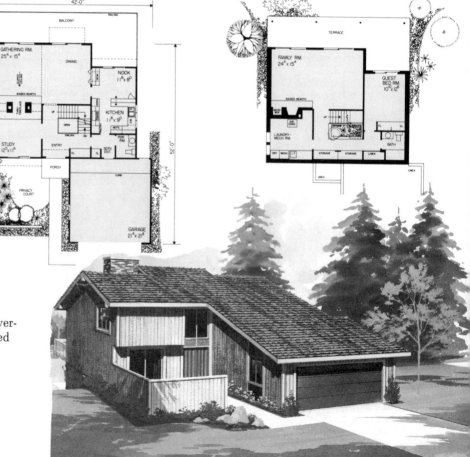

● This plan has a genuine master suite — overlooking the gathering room through shuttered windows. The gathering room has a raised-hearth fireplace, sloped ceiling and sliding glass doors onto the main balcony. A family room and study also have fireplaces. The kitchen features plenty of built-ins and a separate dining nook.

314

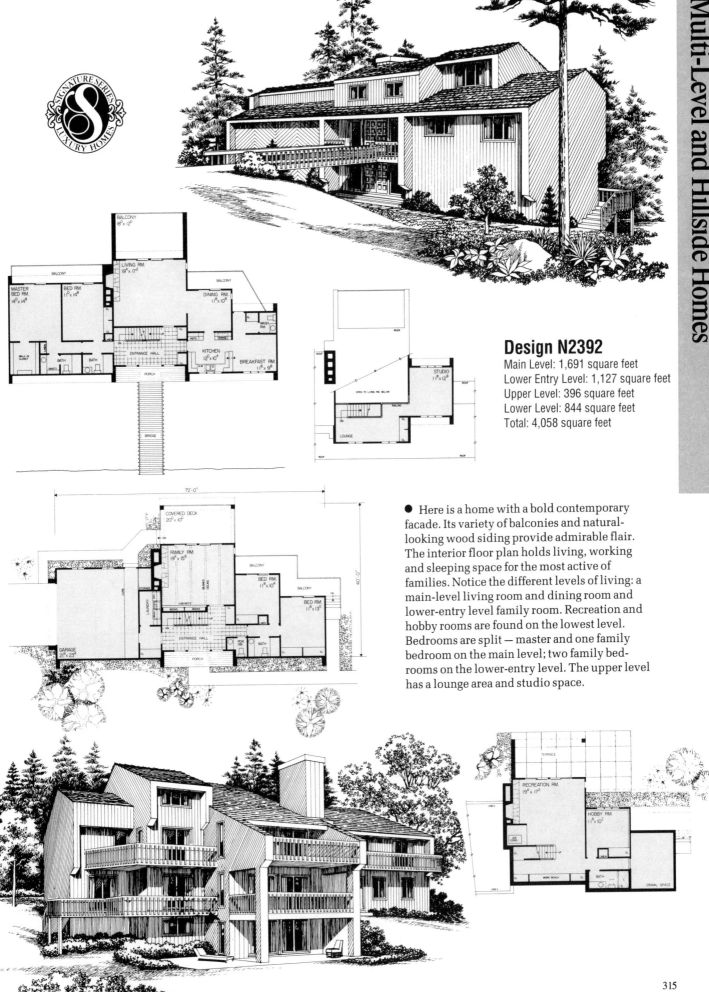

Design N2392
Main Level: 1,691 square feet
Lower Entry Level: 1,127 square feet
Upper Level: 396 square feet
Lower Level: 844 square feet
Total: 4,058 square feet

● Here is a home with a bold contemporary facade. Its variety of balconies and natural-looking wood siding provide admirable flair. The interior floor plan holds living, working and sleeping space for the most active of families. Notice the different levels of living: a main-level living room and dining room and lower-entry level family room. Recreation and hobby rooms are found on the lowest level. Bedrooms are split — master and one family bedroom on the main level; two family bedrooms on the lower-entry level. The upper level has a lounge area and studio space.

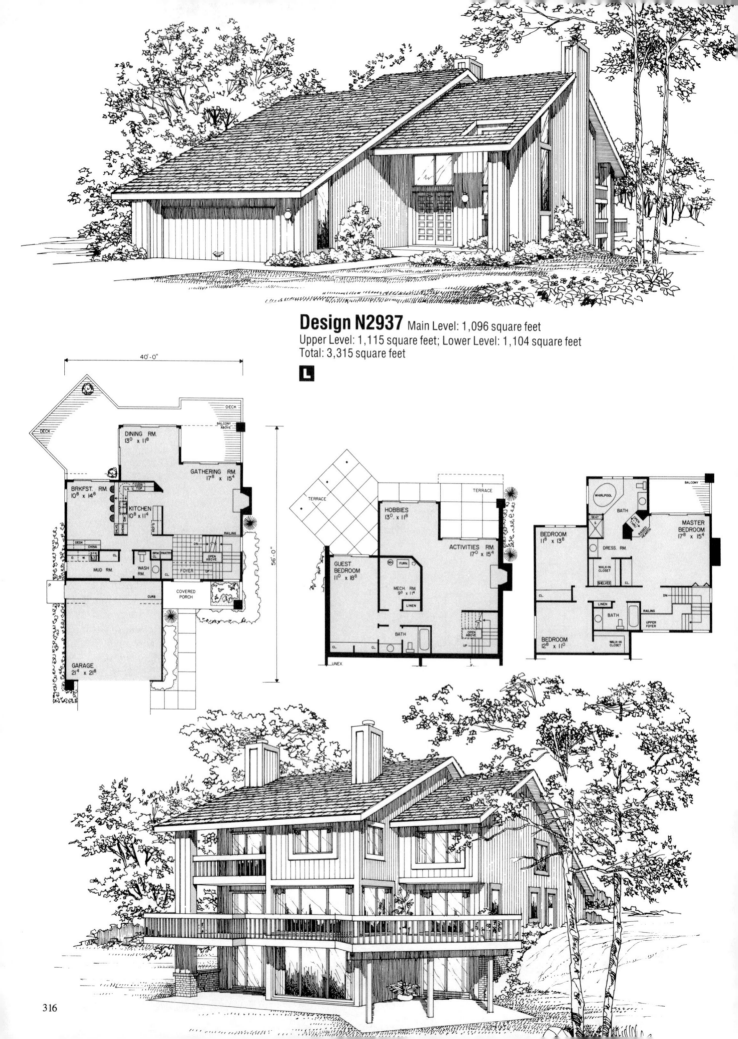

Design N2937 Main Level: 1,096 square feet
Upper Level: 1,115 square feet; Lower Level: 1,104 square feet
Total: 3,315 square feet

L

40'-0"

DECK

DECK

BALCONY ABOVE

DINING RM.
13⁰ x 11⁸

GATHERING RM.
17⁸ x 15⁴

BRKFST. RM.
10⁸ x 14⁸

KITCHEN
10⁸ x 11⁴

DESK CHINA

DN

RAILING

MUD RM.

WASH RM.

FOYER

OPEN ABOVE

UP

COVERED PORCH

CURB

56'-0"

GARAGE
21⁴ x 21⁸

TERRACE

TERRACE

HOBBIES
13⁰ x 11⁸

ACTIVITIES RM.
17⁰ x 15⁴

GUEST BEDROOM
11⁰ x 18⁸

FURN.

MECH. RM.
9⁰ x 11⁴

LINEN

OPEN ABOVE

UP

BATH

UNEX.

WHIRLPOOL

BATH

SEAT

BEDROOM
11⁸ x 13⁸

DRESS. RM.

BALCONY

MASTER BEDROOM
17⁸ x 15⁴

WALK-IN CLOSET

SHELVES

CL.

LINEN

DN

BATH

RAILING

UPPER FOYER

BEDROOM
12⁸ x 11⁰

WALK-IN CLOSET

STORAGE
12⁸ x 8⁰

FUTURE BAR

ACTIVITIES RM.
23⁰ x 24⁸

STORAGE
12⁸ x 10⁰

FURN.

FURN.

UP

CL.

WASH RM.

UNEX.

UNEXCAVATED

BASEMENT PLAN

Design N2828
First Floor: 817 square feet–Living Area; Foyer & Laundry: 261 square feet
Second Floor: 852 square feet–Living Area; Foyer & Storage: 214 square feet; Total: 2,144 square feet

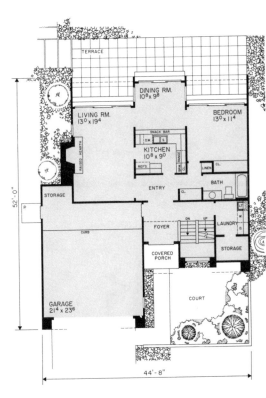

TERRACE

DINING RM.
10⁸ x 9⁸

LIVING RM.
13⁰ x 19⁴

BEDROOM
13⁰ x 11⁴

SNACK BAR

KITCHEN
10⁸ x 9⁰

REF'G.

RANGE

LINEN

CL.

RAISED HEARTH

ENTRY

BATH

STORAGE

CL.

52'-0"

P

CURB

DN

UP

LAUNDRY

FOYER

STORAGE

COVERED PORCH

COURT

GARAGE
21⁴ x 23⁶

44'-8"

● A fine contemporary design in two stories, this home also extends its livability to the basement where bonus space could be converted later to an activities or hobby room. On the first floor, living areas revolve around a central kitchen with snack bar in the dining room. The first-floor bedroom could also serve as a study, family room or library. Note the raised-hearth fireplace in the living room. Upstairs are three bedrooms, or two and a lounge, and a sewing or hobby room. Two long balconies here overlook the terrace below.

BALCONY

BEDROOM/ LOUNGE
10⁸ x 10⁴

BALCONY

SLOPED CEILING

MASTER BEDROOM
13⁰ x 21⁸

SLOPED CEILING

BEDROOM
13⁰ x 11⁴

SLOPED CEILING

OPTIONAL FIREPLACE

BATH

CL.

LINEN

SKYLIGHT

BATH

CL.

CL.

LINEN

SLOPED CEILING

SKYLIGHTS

DN

SEWING/ HOBBIES

UPPER FOYER

SLOPED CEILING

SLOPED CEILING

Design N2786

Main Level: 871 square feet
Upper Level: 1,132 square feet
Lower Level: 528 square feet
Total: 2,531 square feet

● Bay windows in both the formal living room and formal dining room add much appeal to this traditional tri-level. The interior livability is outstanding. An abundance of built-ins in the kitchen create an efficient work center. Features include an island range, pantry, broom closet, desk and breakfast room with sliding glass doors to the rear terrace. The lower level houses an informal family room, wash room and laundry. Note the walk-in closet in the master bedroom suite.

Design N2787

Main Level: 976 square feet
Upper Level: 1,118 square feet
Lower Level: 524 square feet
Total: 2,618 square feet

L **D**

● Main, upper and lower levels serve the residents of this home. The family room with raised-hearth fireplace, laundry and wash room are on the lower level. Formal living and dining rooms, a kitchen and breakfast room are on the main level. The upper level holds three bedrooms and a study (or four bedrooms, if desired) and two baths.

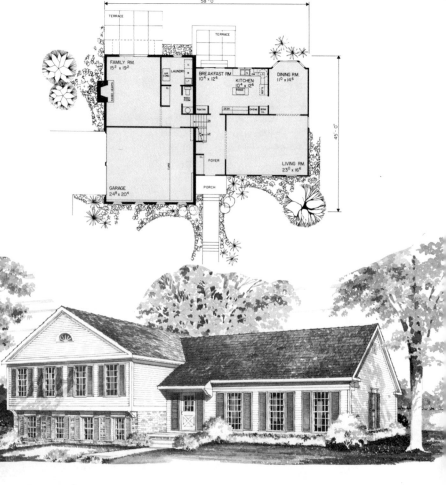

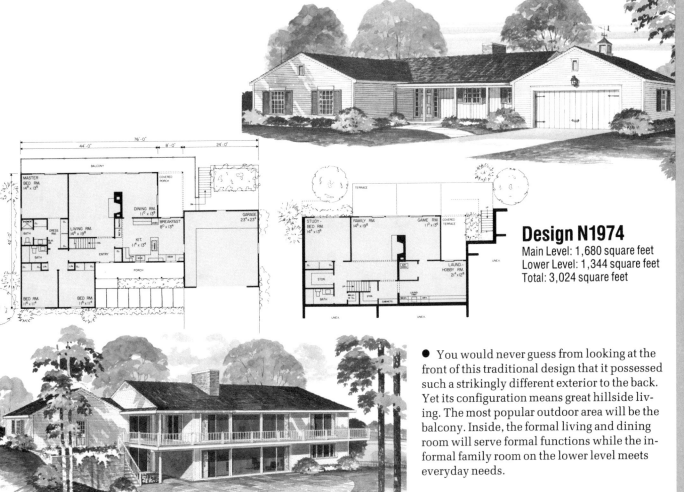

Design N1974

Main Level: 1,680 square feet
Lower Level: 1,344 square feet
Total: 3,024 square feet

● You would never guess from looking at the front of this traditional design that it possessed such a strikingly different exterior to the back. Yet its configuration means great hillside living. The most popular outdoor area will be the balcony. Inside, the formal living and dining room will serve formal functions while the informal family room on the lower level meets everyday needs.

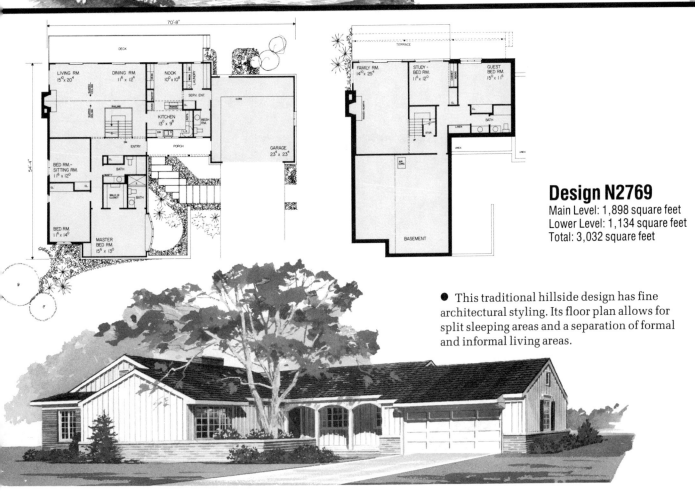

Design N2769

Main Level: 1,898 square feet
Lower Level: 1,134 square feet
Total: 3,032 square feet

● This traditional hillside design has fine architectural styling. Its floor plan allows for split sleeping areas and a separation of formal and informal living areas.

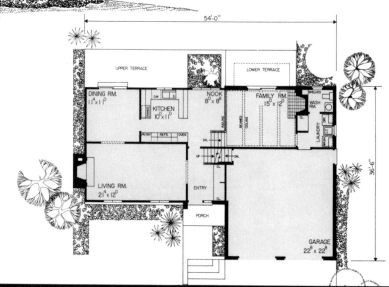

Design N2608

Main Level: 728 square feet; Upper Level: 874 square feet
Lower Level: 310 square feet; Total: 1,912 square feet

L **D**

● Here is tri-level livability with a fourth
basement level for bulk storage and, per-
haps, a shop area. There are four bedrooms,
a handy laundry, two eating areas, formal
and informal living areas and two fireplaces.
Sliding glass doors in the formal dining room
and the family room open to a terrace. The
U-shaped kitchen has a built-in range/oven
and storage pantry. The breakfast nook overlooks the family room.

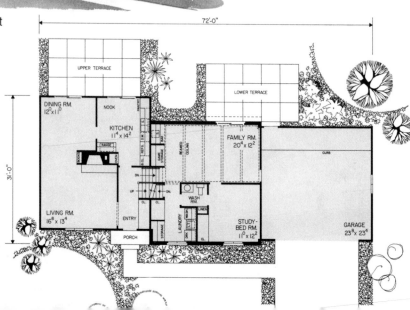

Design N2628

Main Level: 649 square feet; Upper Level: 672 square feet
Lower Level: 624 square feet; Total: 1,945 square feet

L **D**

● Traditional, yet contemporary! With lots of
extras, too. Like a wet bar and game storage in
the family room. A beamed ceiling, too, and a
sliding glass door onto the terrace. In short, a
family room designed to make your life easy
and enjoyable. There's more. A living room
with a traditionally styled fireplace and built-
in bookshelves. And a dining room with a sliding glass door that opens to a second terrace.
Here's the appropriate setting for those times
when you want a touch of elegance.

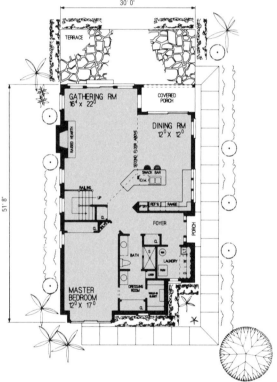

Design N2493

First Floor: 1,387 square feet
Second Floor: 929 square feet
Total: 2,316 square feet

● Perfect for a narrow lot, this shingle-and-stone-sided Nantucket Cape caters to the casual lifestyle. The side entrance gives direct access to the wonderfully open living areas: gathering room with fireplace, kitchen with angled, pass-through snack bar, dining area with sliding glass doors to a covered eating area. Note also the large deck that further extends the living potential. Also on this floor is a large master suite. Upstairs is a convenient guest suite with private balcony. It is complemented by two smaller bedrooms.

Custom Alterations? See page 349 for customizing this plan to your specifications.

Design N2488 First Floor: 1,113 square feet; Second Floor: 543 square feet; Total: 1,656 square feet

D

CUSTOMIZABLE

Custom Alterations? See page 349 for customizing this plan to your specifications.

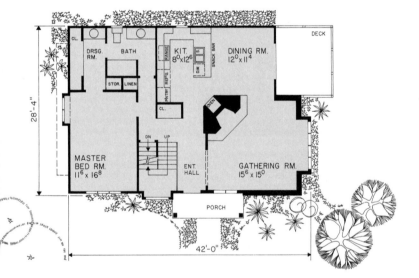

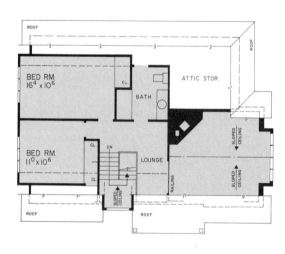

● A cozy cottage for the young at heart! Whether called upon to serve the young active family as a leisure-time retreat at the lake, or the retired couple as a quiet haven in later years, this charming design will perform well. As a year round second home, the up-stairs with its two sizable bedrooms, full bath and lounge area looking down into the gathering room below, will ideally accommodate the younger generation. When called upon to function as a retirement home, the second floor will cater to the visiting family members and friends. Also, it will be available for use as a home office, study, sewing room, music area, the pursuit of hobbies, etc. Of course, as an efficient, economical home for the young, growing family, this design will function well.

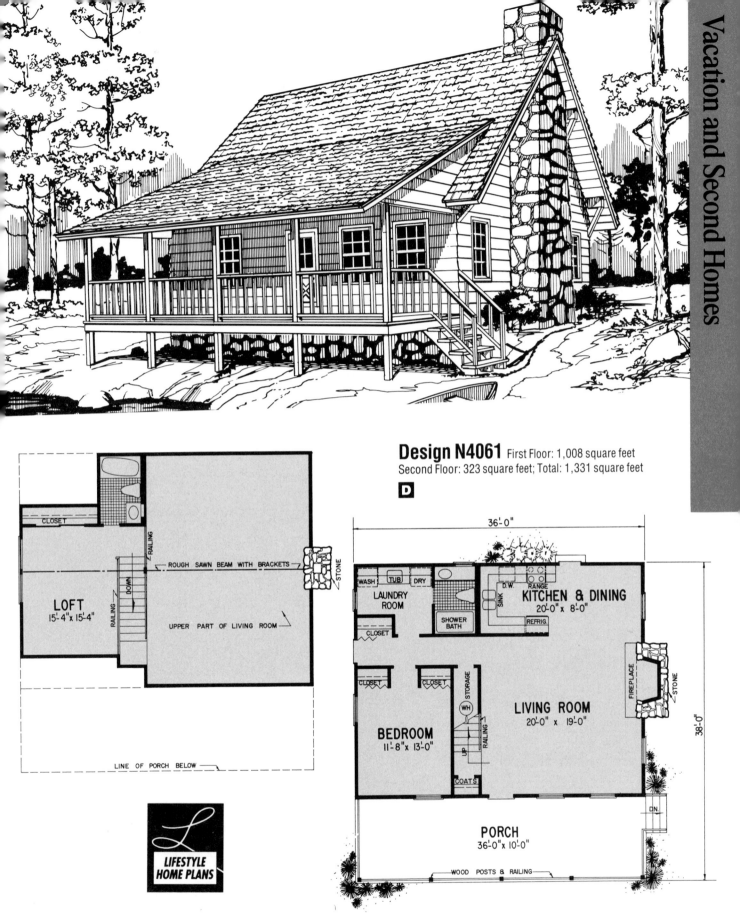

Design N4061 First Floor: 1,008 square feet
Second Floor: 323 square feet; Total: 1,331 square feet

D

LOFT
15'-4" x 15'-4"

ROUGH SAWN BEAM WITH BRACKETS

STONE

RAILING

DOWN

RAILING

UPPER PART OF LIVING ROOM

CLOSET

LINE OF PORCH BELOW

LIFESTYLE HOME PLANS

36'-0"

WASH TUB DRY

LAUNDRY ROOM

D.W. RANGE

SINK

KITCHEN & DINING
20'-0" x 8'-0"

REFRIG.

SHOWER BATH

CLOSET

CLOSET CLOSET

WH STORAGE

UP

RAILING

FIREPLACE

STONE

BEDROOM
11'-8" x 13'-0"

LIVING ROOM
20'-0" x 19'-0"

38'-8"

COATS

DN.

PORCH
36'-0" x 10'-0"

WOOD POSTS & RAILING

● This charming farmhouse design will be economical to build and a pleasure to occupy. Like most vacation homes, this design features an open plan. The large living area includes a living room and dining room and a massive stone fireplace. A partition separates the kitchen from the living room. Also downstairs are a bedroom, full bath, and laundry room. Upstairs is a spacious sleeping loft overlooking the living room. Don't miss the large front porch — this will be a favorite spot for relaxing.

Design N4124

Square Footage: 1,772

● What an unusual entrance this home has! A wooden footbridge leads across a sunken garden for a dramatically different approach. The spacious great room will be a favorite gathering spot. The dining room is open to the great room, yet is contained within its own distinct space. Three sliding glass doors provide access to the L-shaped deck and allow nice views of the back yard. Three good-sized bedrooms comprise a private sleeping wing away from the living and working areas.

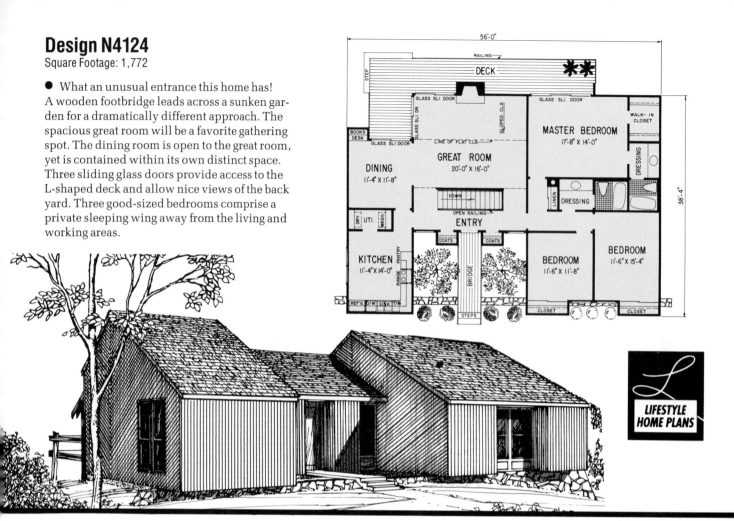

Design N4114

Main Level: 852 square feet
Upper Level: 146 square feet
Total: 998 square feet

● This home was designed with the outdoors in mind. A large, wraparound deck provides ample space for sunning and relaxing. Huge windows and sliding glass doors open up the interior with lots of sunlight and great views — a must in a vacation home. Open planning makes for relaxed living patterns: the kitchen, living and eating area flow together into one large working and living space. An upstairs loft provides space for a lounge or an extra sleeping area.

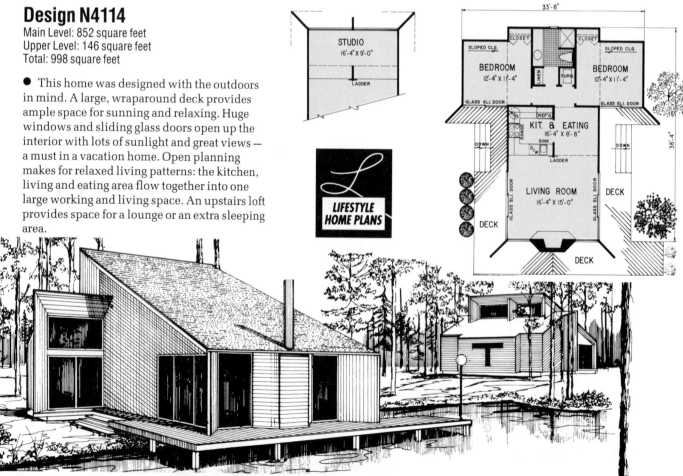

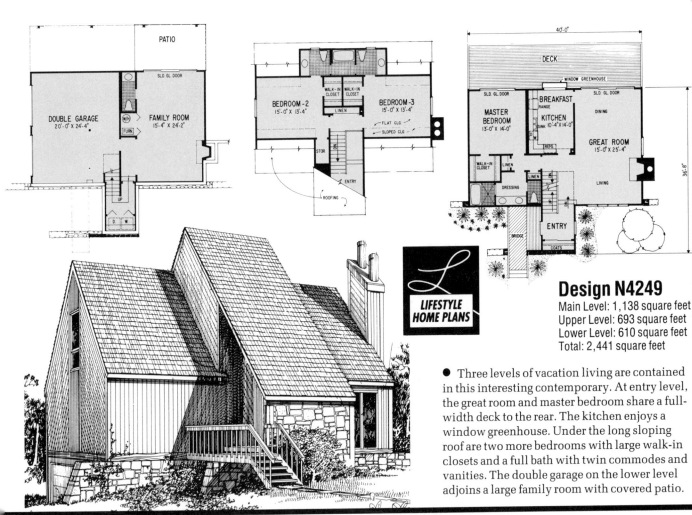

PATIO

SLD. GL. DOOR

DOUBLE GARAGE
20'-0" X 24'-4"

FAMILY ROOM
15'-4" X 24'-2"

W/H

FURN

UP

D. W.

BEDROOM-2
15'-0" X 13'-4"

WALK-IN CLOSET   WALK-IN CLOSET

LINEN

BEDROOM-3
15'-0" X 13'-4"

FLAT CLG.

SLOPED CLG.

STOR

DN

ENTRY

ROOFING

40'-0"

DECK

WINDOW GREENHOUSE

SLD. GL. DOOR

MASTER BEDROOM
13'-0" X 14'-0"

BREAKFAST

RANGE

KITCHEN
SINK 10'-4" X 14'-0"

SLD. GL. DOOR

DINING

DW

CHMS.

GREAT ROOM
15'-0" X 25'-4"

WALK-IN CLOSET

LINEN

LINEN

LIVING

DRESSING

DN

ENTRY

BRIDGE

COATS

36'-8"

LIFESTYLE HOME PLANS

Design N4249

Main Level: 1,138 square feet
Upper Level: 693 square feet
Lower Level: 610 square feet
Total: 2,441 square feet

● Three levels of vacation living are contained in this interesting contemporary. At entry level, the great room and master bedroom share a full-width deck to the rear. The kitchen enjoys a window greenhouse. Under the long sloping roof are two more bedrooms with large walk-in closets and a full bath with twin commodes and vanities. The double garage on the lower level adjoins a large family room with covered patio.

LIFESTYLE HOME PLANS

Design N4153

First Floor: 893 square feet
Second Floor: 549 square feet
Total: 1,442 square feet

L **D**

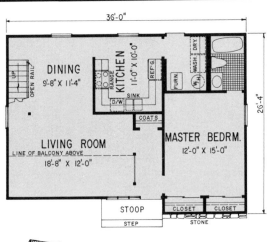

36'-0"

UP

OPEN RAIL

DINING
9'-8" X 11'-4"

RANGE

KITCHEN
11'-0" X 10'-0"

REF'G

SINK

D/W

WASH DRY.

FURN.

W.H.

COATS

LIVING ROOM
LINE OF BALCONY ABOVE
18'-8" X 12'-0"

MASTER BEDRM.
12'-0" X 15'-0"

26'-4"

STOOP

CLOSET   CLOSET

STEP

STONE

BEDROOM
12'-0" X 11'-4"

CLG.

DOWN

CLOSET

LIN.

CLOSET

BEDROOM
12'-0" X 15'-4"

SLOPED

BALCONY
OPEN RAIL

CLOSET

SKYLIGHTS

● The rectangular shape of this design will make it an economical and easy-to-build choice for those wary of high construction costs. The first floor benefits from the informality of open planning: the living room and dining room combine to make one large living space. The partitioned kitchen is convenient. Also down-stairs is the master bedroom and bath. The second floor houses two large bedrooms, a full bath and a balcony over the living room. Notice the skylights.

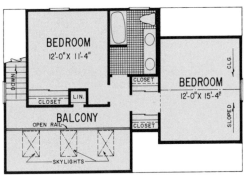

Design N4125 Entry Level: 1,089 square feet
Upper Level: 508 square feet; Total: 1,597 square feet

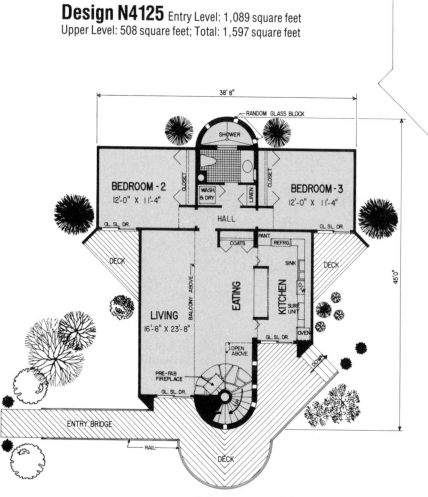

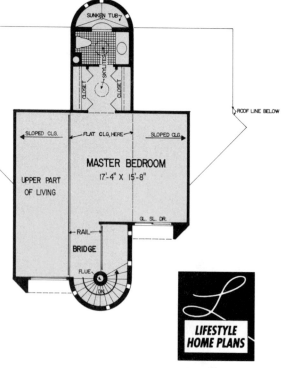

LIFESTYLE
HOME PLANS

● Geometrical design elements are used to
striking effect in this appealing contemporary. Several entrances lead into the
open living and eating area. A pass-through
to the kitchen saves steps in serving and
cleaning up. Two rear bedrooms each have
a private deck. A large circular tower en-
closes a spiral staircase leading up to the
balcony master suite. Notice the semicircu-
lar sunken tub in the bath.

Design N4132

First Floor: 1,233 square feet
Second Floor: 915 square feet
Total: 2,148 square feet

● This home is designed to take full advantage of a spectacular view. Each room enjoys views and access to a deck through a sliding glass door. There's plenty of living space on the entry level with both a family room and living room. Notice the corner fireplace in the living room. The three-bedroom second level includes a large deck and an alcove which could accommodate a small sitting area.

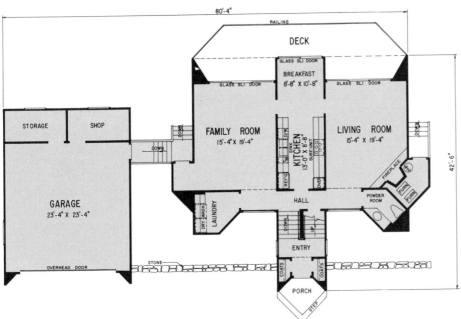

Design N4010

Main Level: 1,664 square feet
Lower Level: 1,150 square feet
Total: 2,814 square feet

LIFESTYLE HOME PLANS

● With the relaxed lifestyle of vacationers in mind, this design features plenty of living and leisure space. A large, wraparound deck accommodates sun worshippers. The carefully planned interior includes an open living room and dining room. The kitchen features a pass-through to the dining room to facilitate serving and clearing. Also on the main level are two bedrooms and a laundry room. The lower level boasts an enormous game room with fireplace and wet bar, a bunk room and a hobby room. Don't miss the patio.

LIFESTYLE HOME PLANS

Design N4015

Square Footage: 1,420

● The perfect vacation home combines open, formal living spaces with lots of sleeping space. Study this plan carefully. The spacious living room has a warming fireplace and sliding glass doors onto the deck. Convenient to the dining room, the efficient kitchen is carefully placed so as not to interfere with the living room. Notice the four spacious bedrooms — there is plenty of room for accommodating guests. Two of the bedrooms boast private porches.

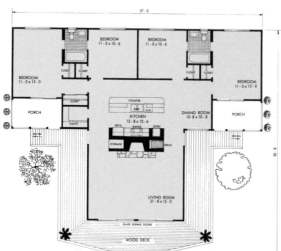

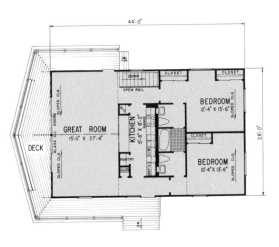

Optional Basement

Design N4027
Square Footage: 1,232

LIFESTYLE HOME PLANS

● Good things come in small packages, too! The size and shape of this design will help hold down construction costs without sacrificing livability. The enormous great room is a multi-purpose living space with room for a dining area and several seating areas. Also notice the sloped ceilings. Sliding glass doors provide access to the wraparound deck and sweeping views of the outdoors. The well-equipped kitchen includes a pass-through and pantry. Two bedrooms, each with sloped ceiling and compartmented bath, round out the plan.

Design N4012
Main Level: 1,250 square feet
Lower Level: 740 square feet
Total: 1,990 square feet

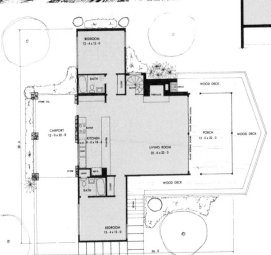

LIFESTYLE HOME PLANS

● This plan features the kind of indoor/outdoor relationship found in vacation homes. Sliding glass doors in the living room open onto a screened porch which, in turn, leads to a large deck. Note the built-in grille. The large living room with welcoming fireplace has enough space to accommodate an eating area. The sleeping quarters are split with two private bedrooms and baths on the entry level and a spacious dormitory with fireplace on the lower level. Just steps away is a covered patio.

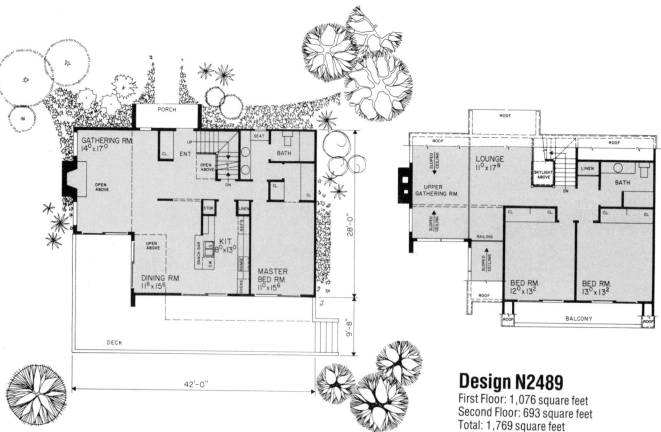

Design N2489
First Floor: 1,076 square feet
Second Floor: 693 square feet
Total: 1,769 square feet

● Outdoors-oriented families will appreciate the dramatic sliding glass doors and the sweeping decks that make this contemporary perfect. The plan of the first floor features a spacious two-story gathering room with sloping ceiling, a large fireplace and access to the large deck which runs the full length of the house. Also having direct access to the deck is the dining room which is half-open to the second floor above. A snack bar divides the dining room from the compact kitchen. The master bedroom is outstanding with its private bath, walk-in closet and sliding glass door. The second floor is brightened by a skylight and houses two bedrooms, lounge and full bath.

Design N2485 Main Level: 1,108 square feet
Lower Level: 983 square feet; Total: 2,091 square feet

● This hillside vacation home gives the appearance of being a one-story from the road. However, since it is built off the edge of a slope, the rear exterior is a full two-story structure. Notice the projecting deck and how it shelters the terrace. Each of the generous glass areas is protected from the summer sun by the overhangs and the extended walls. The clerestory windows of the front exterior provide natural light to the center of the plan.

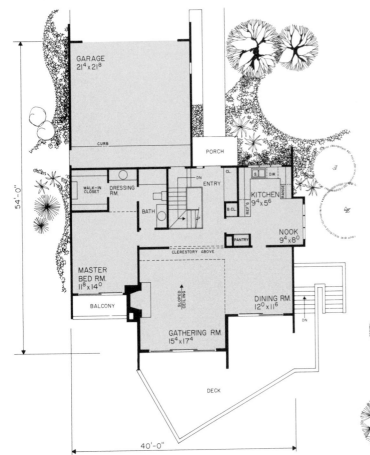

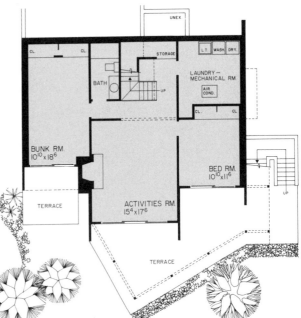

331

Design N1482

First Floor: 1,008 square feet
Second Floor: 637 square feet
Total: 1,645 square feet

● Here is a chalet right from the pages of travel folders. In addition to the big bedrooms on the first floor, there are three more upstairs. The large master bedroom has a balcony which overlooks the lower wood deck. There are two full baths. The first-floor bath is directly accessible from the outdoors. Note snack bar and pantry. A laundry area is adjacent to the side door.

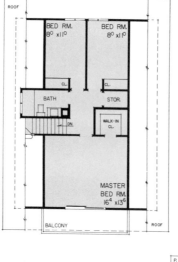

Design N2427

First Floor: 784 square feet
Second Floor: 504 square feet
Total: 1,288 square feet

● If ever a design had "vacation home" written all over it, this one does. The most carefree characteristic is the second-floor balcony which looks down onto the wood deck. Also on the second floor is the three-bunk dormitory. Panels through the knee walls give access to an abundant storage area. Downstairs there is yet another bedroom, a full bath and long living room.

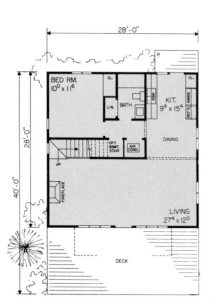

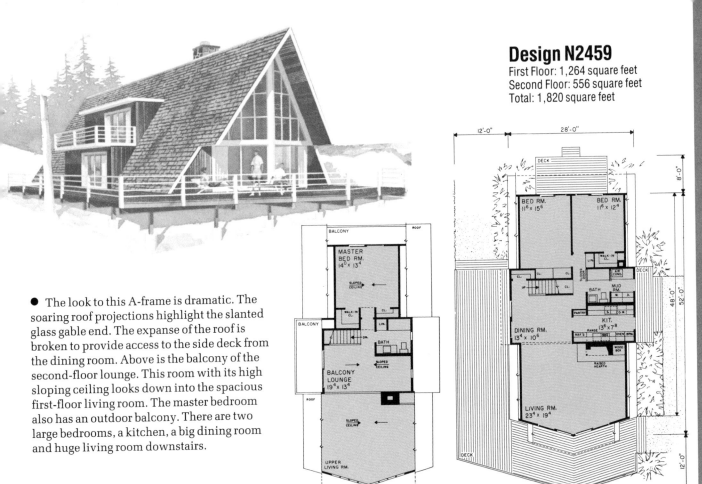

Design N2459

First Floor: 1,264 square feet
Second Floor: 556 square feet
Total: 1,820 square feet

● The look to this A-frame is dramatic. The soaring roof projections highlight the slanted glass gable end. The expanse of the roof is broken to provide access to the side deck from the dining room. Above is the balcony of the second-floor lounge. This room with its high sloping ceiling looks down into the spacious first-floor living room. The master bedroom also has an outdoor balcony. There are two large bedrooms, a kitchen, a big dining room and huge living room downstairs.

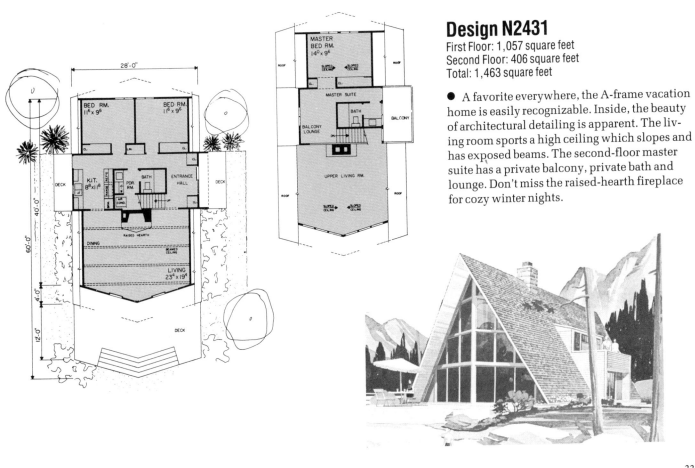

Design N2431

First Floor: 1,057 square feet
Second Floor: 406 square feet
Total: 1,463 square feet

● A favorite everywhere, the A-frame vacation home is easily recognizable. Inside, the beauty of architectural detailing is apparent. The living room sports a high ceiling which slopes and has exposed beams. The second-floor master suite has a private balcony, private bath and lounge. Don't miss the raised-hearth fireplace for cozy winter nights.

When You're Ready To Order . . .

Let Us Show You Our Home Blueprint Package.

Building a home? Planning a home? Our Blueprint Package has nearly everything you need to get the job done right, whether you're working on your own or with help from an architect, designer, builder or subcontractors. Each Blueprint Package is the result of many hours of work by licensed architects or professional designers.

QUALITY

Hundreds of hours of painstaking effort have gone into the development of your blueprint set. Each home has been quality-checked by professionals to insure accuracy and buildability.

VALUE

Because we sell in volume, you can buy professional-quality blueprints at a fraction of their development cost. With our plans, your dream home design costs only a few hundred dollars, not the thousands of dollars that custom architects charge.

SERVICE

Once you've chosen your favorite home plan, you'll receive fast, efficient service whether you choose to mail or fax your order to us or call us toll free at 1-888-299-5229.

SATISFACTION

Over 50 years of service to satisfied home plan buyers provide us unparalleled experience and knowledge in producing quality blueprints. What this means to you is satisfaction with our product and performance.

ORDER TOLL FREE 1-888-299-5229

After you've looked over our Blueprint Package and Important Extras on the following pages, simply mail the order form on page 349 or call toll free on our Blueprint Hotline: 1-888-299-5229. We're ready and eager to serve you.

Each set of blueprints is an interrelated collection of detail sheets which includes components such as floor plans, interior and exterior elevations, dimensions, cross-sections, diagrams and notations. These sheets show exactly how your house is to be built.

Among the sheets included may be:

Frontal Sheet
This artist's sketch of the exterior of the house gives you an idea of how the house will look when built and landscaped. Large ink-line floor plans show all levels of the house and provide an overview of your new home's livability, as well as a handy reference for deciding on furniture placement.

Foundation Plan
This sheet shows the foundation layout includ-

SAMPLE PACKAGE

ing support walls, excavated and unexcavated areas, if any, and foundation notes. If slab construction rather than basement, the plan shows footings and details for a monolithic slab. This page, or another in the set, may include a sample plot plan for locating your house on a building site.

Detailed Floor Plans

These plans show the layout of each floor of the house. Rooms and interior spaces are carefully dimensioned and keys are given for cross-section details provided later in the plans. The positions of electrical outlets and switches are shown.

House Cross-Sections

Large-scale views show sections or cut-aways of the foundation, interior walls, exterior walls, floors, stairways and roof details. Additional cross-sections may show important changes in

floor, ceiling or roof heights or the relationship of one level to another. Extremely valuable for construction, these sections show exactly how the various parts of the house fit together.

Interior Elevations

Many of our drawings show the design and placement of kitchen and bathroom cabinets, laundry areas, fireplaces, bookcases and other built-ins. Little "extras," such as mantelpiece and wainscoting drawings, plus moulding sections, provide details that give your home that custom touch.

Exterior Elevations

These drawings show the front, rear and sides of your house and give necessary notes on exterior materials and finishes. Particular attention is given to cornice detail, brick and stone accents or other finish items that make your home unique.

Frontal Sheet

Foundation Plans

Detailed Floor Plans

Exterior Elevations

Interior Elevations

House Cross-Sections

*I*ntroducing nine important planning and construction aids

NEW

CUSTOM ENGINEERING

Our Custom Engineering Service Package provides an engineering seal for the structural elements of any Home Planners plan. This new Package provides complete calculations (except foundation engineering) from a registered professional, and offers many options invaluable to anyone planning to build. The Package includes: Structural framing plans for each horizontal framing area; Individual, certified truss designs; Specifications for all framing members; Calculation sheets detailing engineering problems and solutions concerning shear, bending, and deflections for all key framing members; Structural details for all key situations; Hanger and special connections specifications; Load and geometry information that may be used by a foundation design engineer and a Registered Professional Engineer's Seal for all of the above services. Home Planners also offers 3 Optional Engineering Services: Lateral load calculations and specifications for both wind and seismic considerations; Secondary Framing information for roofs, floors and walls; Light-gauge steel framing, providing details and cost comparisons for steel and wood.

SPECIFICATION OUTLINE

This valuable 16-page document is critical to building your house correctly. Designed to be filled in by you or your builder, this book lists 166 stages or items crucial to the building process. It provides a comprehensive review of the construction process and helps in making choices of materials. When combined with the blueprints, a signed contract, and a schedule, it becomes a legal document and record for the building of your home.

MATERIALS LIST

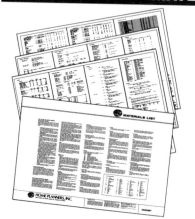

(Note: Because of the diversity of local building codes, our Materials List does not include mechanical materials.)

For many of the designs in our portfolio, we offer a customized materials take-off that is invaluable in planning and estimating the cost of your new home. This Materials List outlines the quantity, type and size of materials needed to build your house (with the exception of mechanical system items). Included are framing lumber, windows and doors, kitchen and bath cabinetry, rough and finish hardware, and much more. This handy list helps you or your builder cost out materials and serves as a reference sheet when you're compiling bids.

QUOTE ONE®

Summary Cost Report / Materials Cost Report

A new service for estimating the cost of building select designs, the Quote One® system is available in two separate stages: The Summary Cost Report and the Materials Cost Report.

The Summary Cost Report is the first stage in the package and shows the total cost per square foot for your chosen home in your zip-code area and then breaks that cost down into ten categories showing the costs for building materials, labor and installation. The total cost for the report (which includes three grades: Budget, Standard and Custom) is just $19.95 for one home, and additionals are only $14.95. These reports allow you to evaluate your building budget and compare the costs of building a variety of homes in your area.

Make even more informed decisions about your home-building project with the second phase of our package, our Materials Cost Report. This tool is invaluable in planning and estimating the cost of your new home. The material and installation (labor and equipment) cost is shown for each of over 1,000 line items provided in the Materials List (Standard grade) which is included when you purchase this estimating tool. It allows you to determine building costs for your specific zip-code area and for your chosen home design. Space is allowed for additional estimates from contractors and subcontractors, such as for mechanical materials, which are not included in our packages. This invaluable tool is available for a price of $110 ($120 for a Schedule E plan) which includes a Materials List.

To order these invaluable reports, use the order form on page 349 or call 1-888-299-5229.

Plan-A-Home®

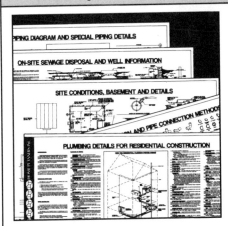

PLUMBING

The Blueprint Package includes locations for all the plumbing fixtures in your new house, including sinks, lavatories, tubs, showers, toilets, laundry trays and water heaters. However, if you want to know more about the complete plumbing system, these 24x36-inch detail sheets will prove very useful. Prepared to meet requirements of the National Plumbing Code, these six fact-filled sheets give general information on pipe schedules, fittings, sump-pump details, water-softener hookups, septic system details and much more. Color-coded sheets include a glossary of terms.

ELECTRICAL

The locations for every electrical switch, plug and outlet are shown in your Blueprint Package. However, these Electrical Details go further to take the mystery out of household electrical systems. Prepared to meet requirements of the National Electrical Code, these comprehensive 24x36-inch drawings come packed with helpful information, including wire sizing, switch-installation schematics, cable-routing details, appliance wattage, door-bell hookups, typical service panel circuitry and much more. Six sheets are bound together and color-coded for easy reference. A glossary of terms is also included.

Plan-A-Home® is an easy-to-use tool that helps you design a new home, arrange furniture in a new or existing home, or plan a remodeling project. Each package contains:

- **More than 700 reusable peel-off planning symbols** on a self-stick vinyl sheet, including walls, windows, doors, all types of furniture, kitchen components, bath fixtures and many more.

- **A reusable, transparent, 1/4-inch scale planning grid** that matches the scale of actual working drawings (1/4-inch equals 1 foot). This grid provides the basis for house layouts of up to 140x92 feet.

- **Tracing paper** and a protective sheet for copying or transferring your completed plan.

- **A felt-tip pen,** with water-soluble ink that wipes away quickly.

Plan-A-Home® lets you lay out areas as large as a 7,500 square foot, six-bedroom, seven-bath house.

CONSTRUCTION

The Blueprint Package contains everything an experienced builder needs to construct a particular house. However, it doesn't show all the ways that houses can be built, nor does it explain alternate construction methods. To help you understand how your house will be built—and offer additional techniques—this set of drawings depicts the materials and methods used to build foundations, fireplaces, walls, floors and roofs. Where appropriate, the drawings show acceptable alternatives. These six sheets will answer questions for the advanced do-it-yourselfer or home planner.

MECHANICAL

This package contains fundamental principles and useful data that will help you make informed decisions and communicate with subcontractors about heating and cooling systems. The 24x36-inch drawings contain instructions and samples that allow you to make simple load calculations and preliminary sizing and costing analysis. Covered are today's most commonly used systems from heat pumps to solar fuel systems. The package is packed full of illustrations and diagrams to help you visualize components and how they relate to one another.

To Order,
Call Toll Free
1-888-299-5229

To add these important extras to your Blueprint Package, simply indicate your choices on the order form on page 349 or call us Toll Free 1-888-299-5229 and we'll tell you more about these exciting products.

◨ *The Deck Blueprint Package*

Many of the homes in this book can be enhanced with a professionally designed Deck Plan. Those home plans highlighted with a ◨ have a matching or corresponding deck plan available which includes a Deck Plan Frontal Sheet, Deck Framing and Floor Plans, Deck Elevations and a Deck Materials List. A Standard Deck Details Package, also available, provides all the how-to information necessary for building *any* deck. Our Complete Deck Building Package contains 1 set of Custom Deck Plans of your choice, plus 1 set of Standard Deck Building Details all for one low price. Our plans and details are carefully prepared in an easy-to-understand format that will guide you through every stage of your deck-building project. See these pages for 25 different Deck layouts to match your favorite house.

SPLIT–LEVEL SUN DECK
Deck Plan D100

BI–LEVEL DECK WITH COVERED DINING
Deck Plan D101

FRESH–AIR CORNER DECK
Deck Plan D102

BACK–YARD EXTENDER DECK
Deck Plan D103

WRAP–AROUND FAMILY DECK
Deck Plan D104

DRAMATIC DECK WITH BARBECUE
Deck Plan D105

SPLIT–PLAN COUNTRY DECK
Deck Plan D106

DECK FOR DINING AND VIEWS
Deck Plan D107

BOLD, ANGLED CORNER DECK
Deck Plan D108

SPECTACULAR "RESORT–STYLE" DECK
Deck Plan D109

TREND–SETTER DECK
Deck Plan D110

TURN–OF–THE–CENTURY DECK
Deck Plan D111

WEEKEND ENTERTAINER DECK
Deck Plan D112

STRIKING "DELTA" DECK
Deck Plan D113

CENTER–VIEW DECK
Deck Plan D114

KITCHEN–EXTENDER DECK
Deck Plan D115

BI–LEVEL RETREAT DECK
Deck Plan D116

SPLIT–LEVEL ACTIVITY DECK
Deck Plan D117

OUTDOOR LIFESTYLE DECK
Deck Plan D118

TRI–LEVEL DECK WITH GRILL
Deck Plan D119

CONTEMPORARY LEISURE DECK
Deck Plan D120

ANGULAR WINGED DECK
Deck Plan D121

DECK FOR A SPLIT–LEVEL HOME
Deck Plan D122

GRACIOUS GARDEN DECK
Deck Plan D123

TERRACED DECK FOR ENTERTAINING
Deck Plan D124

For Deck Plan prices and ordering information, see pages 344-349.

 Or call **Toll Free,**
1-888-299-5229.

◨ *The Landscape Blueprint Package*

For the homes marked with an ◨ in this book, we have created a front-yard landscape plan that matches or is complementary in design to the house plan. These comprehensive blueprint packages include a Frontal Sheet, Plan View, Regionalized Plant & Materials List, a sheet on Planting and Maintaining Your Landscape, Zone Maps and Plant Size and Description Guide. These plans will help you achieve professional results, adding value and enjoyment to your property for years to come. Each set of blueprints is a full 18" x 24" in size with clear, complete instructions and easy-to-read type. See the following pages for 40-different front-yard Landscape Plans to match your favorite house.

Regional Order Map

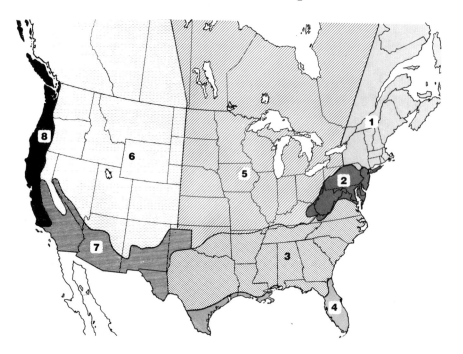

Most of the Landscape Plans shown on these pages are available with a Plant & Materials List adapted by horticultural experts to 8 different regions of the country. Please specify Geographic Region when ordering your plan. See pages 344-349 for prices, ordering information and regional availability.

Region	1	Northeast
Region	2	Mid-Atlantic
Region	3	Deep South
Region	4	Florida & Gulf Coast
Region	5	Midwest
Region	6	Rocky Mountains
Region	7	Southern California & Desert Southwest
Region	8	Northern California & Pacific Northwest

CAPE COD TRADITIONAL
Landscape Plan L200

WILLIAMSBURG CAPE
Landscape Plan L201

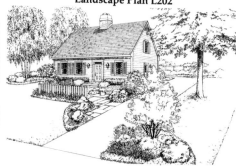

CAPE COD COTTAGE
Landscape Plan L202

GAMBREL–ROOF COLONIAL
Landscape Plan L203

CENTER–HALL COLONIAL
Landscape Plan L204

CLASSIC NEW ENGLAND COLONIAL
Landscape Plan L205

SOUTHERN COLONIAL
Landscape Plan L206

COUNTRY–STYLE FARMHOUSE
Landscape Plan L207

PENNSYLVANIA STONE FARMHOUSE
Landscape Plan L208

RAISED–PORCH FARMHOUSE
Landscape Plan L209

NEW ENGLAND BARN–STYLE HOUSE
Landscape Plan L210

NEW ENGLAND COUNTRY HOUSE
Landscape Plan L211

TRADITIONAL COUNTRY ESTATE
Landscape Plan L212

FRENCH PROVINCIAL ESTATE
Landscape Plan L213

GEORGIAN MANOR
Landscape Plan L214

GRAND–PORTICO GEORGIAN
Landscape Plan L215

BRICK FEDERAL
Landscape Plan L216

COUNTRY FRENCH RAMBLER
Landscape Plan L217

FRENCH MANOR HOUSE
Landscape Plan L218

ELIZABETHAN TUDOR
Landscape Plan L219

TUDOR ONE–STORY
Landscape Plan L220

ENGLISH–STYLE COTTAGE
Landscape Plan L221

MEDIEVAL GARRISON
Landscape Plan L222

QUEEN ANNE VICTORIAN
Landscape Plan L223

GOTHIC VICTORIAN
Landscape Plan L224

BASIC RANCH
Landscape Plan L225

L–SHAPED RANCH
Landscape Plan L226

SPRAWLING RANCH
Landscape Plan L227

TRADITIONAL SPLIT–LEVEL
Landscape Plan L228

SHED–ROOF CONTEMPORARY
Landscape Plan L229

WOOD–SIDED CONTEMPORARY
Landscape Plan L230

HILLSIDE CONTEMPORARY
Landscape Plan L231

FLORIDA RAMBLER
Landscape Plan L232

CALIFORNIA STUCCO
Landscape Plan L233

LOW–GABLE CONTEMPORARY
Landscape Plan L234

NORTHERN BRICK CHATEAU
Landscape Plan L235

MISSION–TILE RANCH
Landscape Plan L236

ADOBE–BLOCK HACIENDA
Landscape Plan L237

COURTYARD PATIO HOME
Landscape Plan L238

CENTER–COURT CONTEMPORARY
Landscape Plan L239

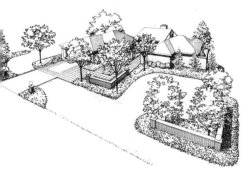

For Landscape Plan prices and ordering
information, see pages 344-349.

 Or call **Toll Free,**
1-888-299-5229.

Price Schedule & Plans Index

House Blueprint Price Schedule
(Prices guaranteed through December 31, 1998)

Tier	1-set Study Package	4-set Building Package	8-set Building Package	1-set Reproducible Sepias	Home Customizer® Package
A	$350	$395	$455	$555	$605
B	$390	$435	$495	$615	$665
C	$430	$475	$535	$675	$725
D	$470	$515	$575	$735	$785
E	$590	$635	$695	$795	$845

Prices for 4-or 8-set Building Packages honored only at time of original order.

Additional Identical Blueprints in same order ....$50 per set
Reverse Blueprints (mirror image) ....$50 per set
Specification Outlines ....$10 each
Materials Lists:
      Schedule A-D $50
      Schedule E $60
Exchanges ....$50 exchange fee for the first set; $10 for each
      additional set
      $70 total exchange fee for 4 sets
      $100 total exchange fee for 8 sets

Deck Plans Price Schedule

CUSTOM DECK PLANS

Price Group	Q	R	S
1 Set Custom Plans	$25	$30	$35

   Additional identical sets:..$10 each
   Reverse sets (mirror image):...$10 each

STANDARD DECK DETAILS
1 Set Generic Construction Details....................................$14.95 each

COMPLETE DECK BUILDING PACKAGE

Price Group	Q	R	S
1 Set Custom Plans 1 Set Standard Deck Details	$35	$40	$45

Landscape Plans Price Schedule

Price Group	X	Y	Z
1 set	$35	$45	$55
3 sets	$50	$60	$70
6 sets	$65	$75	$85

Additional Identical Sets ....$10 each
Reverse Sets (mirror image) ....$10 each

These pages contain all the information you need to price your blueprints. In general the larger and more complicated the house, the more it costs to design and thus the higher the price we must charge for the blueprints. Remember, however, that these prices are far less than you would normally pay for the services of a licensed architect or professional designer.

Custom home designs and related architectural services often cost thousands of dollars, ranging from 5% to 15% of the cost of construction. By ordering our blueprints you are potentially saving enough money to afford a larger house, or to add those "extra" amenities such as a patio, deck, swimming pool or even an upgraded kitchen or luxurious master suite.

Index

To use the Index below, refer to the design number listed in numerical order (a helpful page reference is also given). Note the price index letter and refer to the House Blueprint Price Schedule above for the cost of one, four or eight sets of blueprints or the cost of a reproducible sepia. Additional prices are shown for identical and reverse blueprint sets, as well as a very useful Materials List for some of the plans. Also note in the Index below those plans that have matching or complementary Deck Plans or Landscape Plans. Refer to the schedules above for prices of these plans. All of our plans can be customized with our Home Customizer® Package. See page 349 for more information.

To Order: Fill in and send the order form on page 349—or call toll free 1-800-848-2550 or 520-297-8200.

DESIGN	PRICE	PAGE	CUSTOMIZABLE	DECK	DECK PRICE	LANDSCAPE	LANDSCAPE PRICE	REGIONS
N1228	D	36		D124	S	L217	Y	1-8
N1279	A	231						
N1285	B	82		D117	S	L205	Y	1-3,5,6,8
N1305	A	222		D106	S			
N1323	A	229		D117	S	L225	X	1-3,5,6,8
N1325	B	247		D106	S	L225	X	1-3,5,6,8
N1327	A	236						
N1343	B	232				L226	X	1-8
N1371	B	84		D101	R	L207	Z	1-6,8
N1380	A	245		D114	R	L226	X	1-8
N1381	A	245		D114	R	L226	X	1-8
N1382	A	222		D106	S			
N1383	A	222		D106	S			
N1387	A	244		D101	R			
N1388	A	244		D101	R			
N1389	A	244		D101	R			
N1482	A	332						
N1718	B	58		D114	R	L210	Y	1-3,5,6,8
N1719	A	43		D105	R	L203	Y	1-3,5,6,8
N1761	C	286		D117	S	L217	Y	1-8
N1786	C	280						
N1787	C	81						
N1788	C	286		D101	R	L206	Z	1-6,8
N1791	B	60		D114	R	L205	Y	1-3,5,6,8
N1829	B	230		D113	R	L226	X	1-8
N1858	C	28		D101	R			
N1870	B	60						
N1890	B	246						
N1892	B	283		D106	S	L225	X	1-3,5,6,8
N1896	B	246						
N1920	B	228				L225	X	1-3,5,6,8
N1946	B	236						
N1950	B	289						
N1956	A	82	🏠	D117	S			
N1957	A	85		D100	Q	L228	Y	1-8
N1974	C	319						
N1980	B	232						
N1987	B	59		D101	R	L203	Y	1-3,5,6,8
N1989	C	299		D100	Q	L220	Y	1-3,5,6,8
N1993	D	37				L213	Z	1-8
N2131	B	59		D117	S	L203	Y	1-3,5,6,8
N2133	D	24		D106	S			

DESIGN	PRICE	PAGE	CUSTOMIZABLE	QUOTE ONE®	DECK	DECK PRICE	LANDSCAPE	LANDSCAPE PRICE	REGIONS
N2131	B	59	✓		D117	S	L203	Y	1-3,5,6,8
N2133	D	24	✓		D106	S			
N2135	C	268	✓						
N2142	C	302	✓		D106	S			
N2145	A	196	✓	✓			L209	Y	1-6,8
N2146	A	197	✓		D114	R	L203	Y	1-3,5,6,8
N2170	B	213	✓				L221	X	1-3,5,6,8
N2176	B	32	✓		D112	R	L206	Z	1-6,8
N2181	C	275	✓				L226	X	1-8
N2192	D	27	✓		D117	S	L218	Z	1-6,8
N2206	B	216	✓	✓	D100	Q	L220	Y	1-3,5,6,8
N2211	B	42	✓		D117	S	L201	Y	1-3,5,6,8
N2212	C	284	✓				L217	Y	1-8
N2220	C	282	✓		D114	R	L217	Y	1-8
N2245	D	80	✓		D100	Q	L208	Z	1,2,5,6,8
N2256	C	276	✓						
N2283	C	29	✓		D114	R	L206	Z	1-6,8
N2317	D	295	✓						
N2318	B	298	✓		D117	S	L220	Y	1-3,5,6,8
N2356	D	79	✓		D119	S	L219	Z	1-3,5,6,8
N2391	C	74	✓						
N2392	D	315	✓						
N2395	B	198	✓				L201	Y	1-3,5,6,8
N2396	B	60	✓		D100	Q			
N2399	B	39	✓						
N2427	A	332	✓						
N2431	A	333	✓						
N2459	A	333	✓						
N2485	C	331	✓						
N2488	A	322	✓	✓	D102	Q			
N2489	A	330	✓						
N2490	A	103	✓	✓					
N2491	A	67	✓	✓					
N2493	C	321	✓						
N2500	B	202	✓		D100	Q	L204	Y	1-3,5,6,8
N2505	A	227	✓	✓	D113	R	L226	X	1-8
N2510	A	202	✓		D105	R	L200	X	1-3,5,6,8
N2511	B	314	✓		D108	R	L229	Y	1-8
N2515	C	302	✓	✓	D101	R			
N2519	C	289	✓						
N2520	B	4	✓		D105	R	L201	Y	1-3,5,6,8
N2528	B	249	✓		D100	Q			
N2533	B	230	✓						
N2534	D	276	✓	✓			L227	Z	1-8
N2538	B	45	✓		D113	R	L201	Y	1-3,5,6,8
N2540	B	83	✓		D113	R	L205	Y	1-3,5,6,8
N2543	D	35	✓		D107	S	L218	Z	1-6,8
N2544	C	279	✓		D124	S			
N2559	B	203	✓		D112	R			
N2562	D	100	✓		D122	S			
N2563	B	5	✓	✓	D114	R	L201	Y	1-3,5,6,8
N2565	B	221	✓	✓	D101	R	L225	X	1-3,5,6,8
N2569	A	198	✓		D112	R	L200	X	1-3,5,6,8
N2570	A	212	✓		D113	R	L225	X	1-3,5,6,8
N2573	C	296	✓		D114	R	L220	Y	1-3,5,6,8
N2587	A	32	✓						
N2594	C	281	✓		D120	R			
N2595	C	294	✓						
N2596	B	197	✓		D114	R	L201	Y	1-3,5,6,8
N2597	B	235	✓		D114	R	L226	X	1-8
N2599	C	90	✓		D100	Q			
N2603	B	241	✓		D106	S	L220	Y	1-3,5,6,8
N2604	B	214	✓				L220	Y	1-3,5,6,8
N2606	A	216	✓	✓			L221	X	1-3,5,6,8
N2607	A	215	✓				L220	Y	1-3,5,6,8
N2608	A	320	✓	✓	D112	R	L228	Y	1-8
N2610	C	38	✓	✓	D114	R	L204	Y	1-3,5,6,8
N2615	D	201	✓	✓	D106	S	L211	Y	1-8
N2622	A	45	✓	✓	D103	R	L200	X	1-3,5,6,8
N2628	A	320	✓		D105	R	L234	Y	1-8
N2631	B	62	✓		D112	R	L201	Y	1-3,5,6,8
N2633	C	28	✓						
N2640	B	39	✓		D114	R	L205	Y	1-3,5,6,8
N2658	A	196	✓						
N2659	B	41	✓	✓	D113	R	L205	Y	1-3,5,6,8
N2661	A	56	✓	✓	D113	R	L202	X	1-3,5,6,8
N2662	C	31	✓	✓			L216	Y	1-3,5,6,8
N2664	B	47	✓		D113	R			
N2665	D	51	✓	✓					
N2667	B	49	✓				L216	Y	1-3,5,6,8
N2668	B	48	✓				L214	X	1-3,5,6,8
N2671	B	255	✓	✓	D114	R	L234	Y	1-8
N2672	B	234	✓	✓	D112	R	L226	X	1-8
N2675	C	275	✓		D106	S			
N2678	C	215	✓		D117	S	L220	Y	1-3,5,6,8
N2679	C	310	✓						
N2680	C	56	✓		D114	R	L224	Y	1-3,5,6,8
N2682	A	194	✓	✓	D115	Q	L200	X	1-3,5,6,8
N2683	D	3	✓	✓	D101	R	L214	Z	1-3,5,6,8
N2684	C	57	✓		D114	R	L204	Y	1-3,5,6,8
N2693	D	285	✓						
N2694	C	150	✓	✓			L209	Y	1-6,8
N2699	C	200	✓	✓			L211	Y	1-8
N2702	B	248	✓						
N2707	A	223	✓	✓	D117	S	L226	X	1-8
N2711	B	108	✓	✓	D105	R	L229	Y	1-8
N2716	C	314	✓				L229	Y	1-8
N2717	C	261	✓						
N2718	C	204	✓		D105	R			
N2720	D	294	✓						
N2721	C	260	✓						
N2728	B	214	✓		D112	R	L221	X	1-3,5,6,8
N2729	B	109	✓				L234	Y	1-8
N2730	C	261	✓		D124	S			
N2731	B	42	✓		D114	R	L205	Y	1-3,5,6,8
N2733	B	44	✓	✓	D100	Q	L205	Y	1-3,5,6,8
N2737	B	217	✓				L220	Y	1-3,5,6,8
N2738	B	241	✓						
N2739	D	288	✓				L211	Y	1-8
N2745	C	279	✓						
N2746	C	295	✓		D101	R			
N2753	B	249	✓		D112	R			
N2754	B	248	✓						
N2756	C	274	✓		D101	R	L234	Y	1-8
N2764	C	260	✓						
N2766	C	275	✓		D101	R			
N2767	D	278	✓		D106	S			
N2768	D	278	✓						
N2769	C	319	✓						
N2774	B	2	✓	✓	D100	Q	L207	Z	1-6,8
N2776	B	158	✓	✓	D113	R	L207	Z	1-6,8
N2778	C	280	✓		D120	R			
N2779	D	284	✓	✓	D100	Q	L217	Y	1-8
N2781	C	106	✓	✓	D121	S	L230	Z	1-8
N2783	D	288	✓				L211	Y	1-8
N2784	C	281	✓						
N2785	C	303	✓		D100	Q	L220	Y	1-3,5,6,8
N2786	B	318	✓						
N2787	B	318	✓		D105	R	L228	Y	1-8
N2789	C	257	✓		D117	S	L228	Y	1-8
N2791	D	265	✓						
N2792	B	250	✓						
N2795	B	255	✓						
N2797	B	251	✓						
N2798	A	34	✓		D100	Q	L200	X	1-3,5,6,8
N2800	B	69	✓	✓	D113	R	L220	Y	1-3,5,6,8
N2802	B	218	✓	✓	D118	R	L220	Y	1-3,5,6,8
N2803	B	218	✓		D118	R	L225	X	1-3,5,6,8
N2804	B	218	✓		D118	R	L232	Y	4,7
N2805	B	219	✓	✓	D113	R	L220	Y	1-3,5,6,8
N2806	B	219	✓		D113	R	L220	Y	1-3,5,6,8
N2807	B	219	✓		D113	R	L220	Y	1-3,5,6,8
N2809	B	250	✓						
N2810	B	238	✓	✓	D112	R	L204	Y	1-3,5,6,8
N2811	B	238	✓		D112	R	L204	Y	1-3,5,6,8
N2812	B	239	✓		D112	R	L204	Y	1-3,5,6,8
N2813	B	239	✓		D112	R	L204	Y	1-3,5,6,8
N2814	B	238	✓		D112	R	L204	Y	1-3,5,6,8

DESIGN	PRICE	PAGE	CUSTOMIZABLE	QUOTE ONE®	DECK	DECK PRICE	LANDSCAPE	LANDSCAPE PRICE	REGIONS
N2815	B	238	✓						
N2816	B	239	✓		D112	R	L204	Y	1-3,5,6,8
N2817	B	239	✓		D112	R	L204	Y	1-3,5,6,8
N2818	B	256	✓	✓	D101	R	L234	Y	1-8
N2822	A	104	✓	✓			L229	Y	1-8
N2824	B	254	✓						
N2826	B	92	✓	✓	D116	R			
N2828	B	317	✓						
N2832	C	269	✓		D113	R			
N2841	B	308	✓				L228	Y	1-8
N2843	C	182	✓				L228	Y	1-8
N2846	C	183	✓						
N2850	C	182	✓	✓	D122	S	L236	Z	3,4,7
N2851	C	283	✓	✓			L217	Y	1-8
N2854	B	69	✓	✓	D112	R	L220	Y	1-3,5,6,8
N2855	B	77	✓	✓	D103	R	L219	Z	1-3,5,6,8
N2857	D	267	✓				L239	Z	1-8
N2858	C	266	✓						
N2864	A	253	✓	✓	D100	Q	L225	X	1-3,5,6,8
N2865	C	158	✓		D114	R	L207	Z	1-6,8
N2867	C	273	✓				L220	Y	1-3,5,6,8
N2869	B	225	✓						
N2871	B	254	✓	✓	D117	S			
N2873	C	258	✓						
N2875	B	185	✓	✓	D113	R	L236	Z	3,4,7
N2877	C	297	✓		D114	R	L220	Y	1-3,5,6,8
N2878	B	15	✓	✓	D112	R	L200	X	1-3,5,6,8
N2879	D	277	✓	✓					
N2880	C	291	✓		D114	R	L212	Z	1-8
N2881	C	272	✓						
N2882	C	272	✓				L234	Y	1-8
N2883	C	205	✓						
N2884	B	207	✓				L228	Y	1-8
N2886	B	251	✓						
N2887	A	207	✓						
N2888	D	290	✓				L211	Y	1-8
N2889	D	17	✓	✓	D107	S	L215	Z	1-6,8
N2892	B	206	✓						
N2894	C	7	✓				L229	Y	1-8
N2899	C	20	✓				L214	Z	1-3,5,6,8
N2901	C	312	✓				L229	Y	1-8
N2902	B	252	✓	✓			L234	Y	1-8
N2905	B	100	✓	✓	D121	S	L229	Y	1-8
N2907	B	152	✓				L224	Y	1-3,5,6,8
N2908	B	149	✓	✓	D117	S	L205	Y	1-3,5,6,8
N2911	A	240	✓						
N2912	B	191	✓	✓					
N2913	B	253	✓		D124	S			
N2914	B	72	✓				L230	Z	1-8
N2915	C	9	✓	✓	D114	R	L212	Z	1-8
N2916	B	291	✓				L221	X	1-3,5,6,8
N2917	B	252	✓				L221	X	1-3,5,6,8
N2920	D	8	✓	✓	D104	S	L212	Z	1-8
N2921	D	6	✓	✓	D104	S	L212	Z	1-8
N2922	D	188	✓	✓					
N2925	B	108	✓						
N2926	D	305	✓						
N2927	B	90	✓	✓	D100	Q			
N2929	B	212	✓						
N2930	B	258	✓						
N2931	B	225	✓						
N2936	C	312	✓				L228	Y	1-8
N2937	C	316	✓	✓			L229	Y	1-8
N2938	E	264	✓				L221	X	1-3,5,6,8
N2940	E	118	✓	✓	D114	R	L230	Z	1-8
N2941	B	220	✓		D112	R			
N2942	B	220	✓		D112	R			
N2943	B	220	✓	✓	D112	R			
N2944	B	310	✓						
N2945	B	151	✓						
N2946	C	16	✓	✓	D114	R	L207	Z	1-6,8
N2947	B	14	✓	✓	D112	R	L200	X	1-3,5,6,8
N2948	B	166	✓						
N2949	C	161	✓	✓					
N2950	C	167	✓	✓					
N2951	E	122	✓						
N2952	E	116	✓				L235	Z	1-3,5,6,8
N2953	E	115	✓	✓	D111	S	L223	Z	1-3,5,6,8
N2954	E	114	✓				L223	Z	1-3,5,6,8
N2955	E	123	✓						
N2956	E	117	✓						
N2957	D	73	✓		D107	S	L218	Z	1-6,8
N2959	B	72	✓	✓					
N2961	D	297	✓						
N2962	B	299	✓	✓					
N2963	D	30	✓						
N2966	D	304	✓						
N2967	B	66	✓				L217	Y	1-8
N2968	E	119	✓	✓			L227	Z	1-8
N2969	C	140	✓		D110	R	L223	Z	1-3,5,6,8
N2970	D	141	✓	✓			L223	Z	1-3,5,6,8
N2971	C	134	✓	✓			L223	Z	1-3,5,6,8
N2972	B	136	✓				L223	Z	1-3,5,6,8
N2973	B	136	✓				L223	Z	1-3,5,6,8
N2974	A	133	✓				L223	Z	1-3,5,6,8
N2975	D	30	✓						
N2977	D	25	✓	✓			L214	Z	1-3,5,6,8
N2979	C	49	✓						
N2981	D	153	✓				L224	Y	1-3,5,6,8
N2984	E	18	✓				L214	Z	1-3,5,6,8
N2987	D	23	✓	✓					
N2988	B	159	✓	✓	D120	R	L201	Y	1-3,5,6,8
N2989	D	128	✓	✓			L215	Z	1-6,8
N2990	D	126	✓	✓			L209	Y	1-6,8
N2992	E	127	✓	✓	D103	R	L203	Y	1-3,5,6,8
N2993	D	125	✓	✓	D115	Q	L214	Z	1-3,5,6,8
N3126	A	199	✓		D114	R	L203	Y	1-3,5,6,8
N3300	E	120	✓				L230	Z	1-8
N3301	E	124	✓	✓					
N3302	A	68	✓				L205	Y	1-3,5,6,8
N3303	D	19	✓	✓			L215	Z	1-6,8
N3304	E	144	✓				L209	Y	1-6,8
N3305	E	121	✓						
N3308	E	145	✓	✓			L207	Z	1-6,8
N3309	B	137	✓	✓			L209	Y	1-6,8
N3310	C	33	✓	✓	D111	S	L227	Z	1-8
N3311	D	306	✓	✓	D109	S	L220	Y	1-3,5,6,8
N3313	B	208	✓	✓			L200	X	1-3,5,6,8
N3314	B	12	✓	✓			L200	X	1-3,5,6,8
N3315	D	13	✓	✓			L200	X	1-3,5,6,8
N3316	A	193	✓	✓			L202	X	1-3,5,6,8
N3320	D	20	✓	✓			L215	Z	1-6,8
N3323	C	175	✓	✓			L223	Z	1-3,5,6,8
N3325	C	152	✓	✓	D100	Q	L238	Y	3,4,7,8
N3326	C	93	✓	✓			L217	Y	1-8
N3327	C	271	✓	✓	D110	R	L217	Y	1-8
N3330	A	95	✓	✓					
N3331	A	67	✓	✓			L203	Y	1-3,5,6,8
N3332	B	293	✓	✓			L200	X	1-3,5,6,8
N3334	C	64	✓	✓			L207	Z	1-6,8
N3335	C	75	✓	✓			L201	Y	1-3,5,6,8
N3336	B	270	✓	✓			L200	X	1-3,5,6,8
N3337	D	22	✓	✓			L214	Z	1-3,5,6,8
N3338	B	102	✓	✓			L204	Y	1-3,5,6,8
N3339	B	21	✓	✓			L215	Z	1-6,8
N3340	B	11	✓	✓			L224	Y	1-3,5,6,8
N3342	B	66	✓	✓			L217	Y	1-8
N3343	C	63	✓	✓			L202	X	1-3,5,6,8
N3344	D	184	✓	✓			L211	Y	1-8
N3345	B	209	✓	✓			L220	Y	1-3,5,6,8
N3346	B	300	✓	✓			L204	Y	1-3,5,6,8
N3347	D	102	✓	✓			L230	Z	1-8
N3348	C	292	✓	✓			L200	X	1-3,5,6,8
N3349	E	26	✓	✓	D107	S	L216	Y	1-3,5,6,8
N3350	B	226	✓	✓	D115	Q	L205	Y	1-3,5,6,8
N3351	B	203	✓	✓	D115	Q	L209	Y	1-6,8
N3352	B	98	✓	✓	D108	R	L229	Y	1-8
N3353	C	204	✓	✓	D113	R	L206	Z	1-6,8
N3354	E	75	✓	✓	D104	S	L212	Z	1-8
N3355	A	10	✓	✓	D117	S	L220	Y	1-3,5,6,8

DESIGN	PRICE	PAGE	CUSTOMIZABLE	QUOTE ONE®	DECK	DECK PRICE	LANDSCAPE	LANDSCAPE PRICE	REGIONS
N3356	C	91	●	●	D103	R	L217	Y	1-8
N3357	D	262	●	●	D115	Q	L211	Y	1-8
N3360	D	308	●	●			L207	Z	1-6,8
N3361	D	307	●	●			L230	Z	1-8
N3362	D	311	●	●					
N3366	D	309	●	●			L220	Y	1-3,5,6,8
N3367	D	64	●	●			L220	Y	1-3,5,6,8
N3368	C	263	●	●	D104	S	L220	Y	1-3,5,6,8
N3369	E	74	●	●	D121	S	L206	Z	1-6,8
N3370	D	91	●	●	D119	S	L235	Z	1-3,5,6,8
N3372	C	62	●	●	D102	Q	L200	X	1-3,5,6,8
N3373	A	224	●		D110	R	L202	X	1-3,5,6,8
N3374	A	224	●		D110	R	L202	X	1-3,5,6,8
N3375	A	224	●		D110	R	L202	X	1-3,5,6,8
N3376	B	210	●		D114	R	L205	Y	1-3,5,6,8
N3381	E	76	●	●	D106	S	L204	Y	1-3,5,6,8
N3382	C	129	●	●	D110	R	L202	X	1-3,5,6,8
N3383	C	131	●	●	D111	S	L205	Y	1-3,5,6,8
N3384	C	131	●	●	D115	Q	L207	Z	1-6,8
N3385	C	132	●	●	D100	Q	L207	Z	1-6,8
N3386	E	139	●	●	D111	S	L216	Y	1-3,5,6,8
N3387	E	143	●		D110	R	L224	Y	1-3,5,6,8
N3388	D	138	●	●	D111	S	L207	Z	1-6,8
N3389	C	135	●	●	D115	Q	L205	Y	1-3,5,6,8
N3390	C	132	●	●	D106	S	L207	Z	1-6,8
N3391	C	130	●	●	D116	R	L207	Z	1-6,8
N3392	D	142	●	●	D110	R	L223	Z	1-3,5,6,8
N3393	C	135	●	●	D115	Q	L207	Z	1-6,8
N3394	D	138	●	●	D111	S	L207	Z	1-6,8
N3395	E	113	●	●	D111	S	L223	Z	1-3,5,6,8
N3396	C	154	●	●	D111	S	L207	Z	1-6,8
N3397	C	156	●	●	D110	R	L209	Y	1-6,8
N3398	C	155	●	●	D111	S	L224	Y	1-3,5,6,8
N3399	D	157	●	●	D110	R	L224	Y	1-3,5,6,8
N3403	C	192	●	●	D115	Q	L237	Y	7
N3404	D	97	●	●	D106	S	L230	Z	1-8
N3405	D	161	●	●			L236	Z	3,4,7
N3408	C	168	●	●			L230	Z	1-8
N3409	C	101	●	●			L230	Z	1-8
N3412	B	173	●	●			L233	Y	3,4,7
N3413	C	165	●	●			L238	Y	3,4,7,8
N3414	C	176	●	●			L233	Y	3,4,7
N3419	B	168	●	●			L239	Z	1-8
N3420	B	178	●	●			L233	Y	3,4,7
N3421	B	164	●	●			L238	Y	3,4,7,8
N3422	B	169	●	●			L239	Z	1-8
N3423	C	171	●	●					
N3424	B	174	●	●			L233	Y	3,4,7
N3425	C	176	●	●					
N3427	C	170	●	●			L239	Z	1-8
N3429	C	181	●	●			L233	Y	3,4,7
N3430	C	173	●	●			L233	Y	3,4,7
N3431	B	187	●	●					
N3432	C	179	●	●			L233	Y	3,4,7
N3433	C	187	●	●			L213	Z	1-8
N3434	D	186	●	●			L233	Y	3,4,7
N3435	D	177	●	●			L227	Z	1-8
N3436	C	190	●	●			L227	Z	1-8
N3437	C	177	●	●			L212	Z	1-8
N3438	C	112	●	●			L209	Y	1-6,8
N3439	C	107	●	●			L205	Y	1-3,5,6,8
N3440	C	172	●	●	D120	R	L233	Y	3,4,7
N3441	C	180	●	●			L239	Z	1-8
N3442	A	242	●	●	D115	Q	L200	X	1-3,5,6,8
N3443	B	146	●	●	D110	R	L220	Y	1-3,5,6,8
N3444	B	86	●	●	D105	R	L220	Y	1-3,5,6,8
N3445	B	89	●	●	D114	R	L205	Y	1-3,5,6,8
N3446	C	110	●	●	D115	Q	L220	Y	1-3,5,6,8
N3447	D	180	●	●	D120	R	L237	Y	7
N3449	C	175	●	●			L236	Z	3,4,7
N3450	C	65	●	●	D106	S	L229	Y	1-8
N3451	B	211	●	●			L220	Y	1-3,5,6,8
N3452	C	71	●	●			L220	Y	1-3,5,6,8
N3454	B	210	●	●	D110	R	L220	Y	1-3,5,5,8
N3455	B	55	●	●	D105	R	L238	Y	3,4,7,8
N3456	C	110	●	●			L238	Y	3,4,7,8
N3457	B	52	●	●			L217	Y	1-8
N3458	C	70	●	●	D105	R	L222	Y	1-3,5,6,8
N3459	C	53	●	●			L220	Y	1-3,5,6,8
N3460	A	233	●	●			L200	X	1-3,5,6,8
N3461	B	147	●	●			L204	Y	1-3,5,6,8
N3462	B	146	●	●			L207	Z	1-6,8
N3463	C	54	●	●			L238	Y	3,4,7,8
N3464	C	54	●	●	D110	R	L233	Y	3,4,7
N3465	A	242	●	●			L205	Y	1-3,5,6,8
N3466	B	237	●	●	D110	R	L207	Z	1-6,8
N3467	B	148	●	●			L203	Y	1-3,5,6,8
N3468	B	160	●	●			L209	Y	1-6,8
N3469	B	148	●	●			L204	Y	1-3,5,6,8
N3471	E	96	●	●			L236	Z	3,4,7
N3476	B	94	●	●			L205	Y	1-3,5,6,8
N3479	B	88	●	●	D111	S	L200	X	1-3,5,6,8
N3480	B	189	●	●	D112	R	L238	Y	3,4,7,8
N3481	B	243	●	●					
N3484	B	87	●	●	D105	R	L200	X	1-3,5,6,8
N3485	C	46	●	●			L238	Y	3,4,7,8
N3495	C	89	●	●					
N3503	E	40	●	●	D108	R	L210	Y	1-3,5,6,8
N3558	C	78	●	●	D105	R	L203	Y	1-3,5,6,8
N3559	C	287	●	●	D111	S	L217	Y	1-8
N3560	B	259	●	●			L234	Y	1-8
N3562	B	105	●	●	D110	R	L238	Y	3,4,7,8
N3563	B	99	●	●	D115	Q	L233	Y	3,4,7
N3565	C	162	●	●	D110	R	L233	Y	3,4,7
N3569	C	163	●	●	D105	R	L238	Y	3,4,7,8
N3600	C	301	●	●					
N3602	C	301	●	●					
N4010	C	328	●						
N4012	A	329	●						
N4015	A	328	●						
N4027	A	329	●						
N4061	A	323	●	●	D115	Q			
N4114	A	324	●						
N4115	B	313	●						
N4124	B	324	●						
N4125	A	326	●						
N4132	C	327	●						
N4153	A	325	●		D115	Q	L202	X	1-3,5,6,8
N4249	B	325	●						
N4287	B	111	●		D111	S	L230	Z	1-8
N4308	C	313	●				L231	Z	1-8
N4334	B	111	●				L231	Z	1-8

Before You Order . . .

Before completing the coupon at right or calling us on our Toll-Free Blueprint Hotline, you may be interested to learn more about our service and products. Here's some information you will find helpful.

Quick Turnaround
We process and ship every blueprint order from our office within 48 hours. Because of this quick turnaround, we won't send a formal notice acknowledging receipt of your order.

Our Exchange Policy
Since blueprints are printed in response to your order, we cannot honor requests for refunds. However, we will exchange your entire first order for an equal number of blueprints at a price of $50 for the first set and $10 for each additional set;
$70 total exchange fee for 4 sets: $100 total exchanged fee for 8 sets...*plus* the difference in cost if exchanging for a design in a higher price bracket or *less* the difference in cost if exchanging for a design in a lower price bracket. One exchange is allowed within a year of purchase date. **(Sepias are not exchangeable.)** All sets from the first order must be returned before the exchange can take place. Please add $18 for postage and handling via ground service; $30 via 2nd Day Air; $40 via Next Day Air.

About Reverse Blueprints
If you want to build in reverse of the plan as shown, we will include an extra set of reversed blueprints (mirror image) for an additional fee of $50. Although lettering and dimensions appear backward, reverses will be a useful visual aid if you deside to flop the plan

Modifying or Customizing Our Plans
With such a great selection of homes, you are bound to find the one that suits you. However, if you need to make alterations to a design that is customizable, you need only order our Home Customizer® Package to get you started.

Architectural and Engineering Seals
Some cities and states are now requiring that a licensed architect or engineer review and "seal" your blueprints prior to construction. This is often due to local or regional concerns over energy consumption, safety codes, seismic ratings, or other factors. For this reason, it may be necessary to consult with a local professional to have your plans reviewed.

Compliance with Local Codes and Regulations
At the time of creation, our plans are drawn to specifications published by the Building Officials and Code Administrators (BOCA) International, Inc.; the Southern Building Code Congress (SBCCI) International, Inc.; the International Conference of Building Officials; or the Council of American Building Officials (CABO). Our plans are designed to meet or exceed national building standards. Some states, counties and municipalities have their own codes, zoning requirements and building regulations. Before building, contact your local building authorities to make sure you comply with local ordinances and codes, including obtaining any necessary permits or inspections as building progresses. In some cases, minor modifications to your plans by your builder, architect or designer may be required to meet local conditions and requirements.

Notice: Plans for homes to be built in Nevada must be re-drawn by a Nevada-registered professional. Consult your building official for more information on this subject.

Foundation and Exterior Wall Changes
Most of our plans are drawn with either a full or partial basement foundation. Depending upon your specific climate or regional building practices, you may wish to convert this basement to a slab or crawlspace. Most professional contractors and builders can easily adapt your plans to alternate foundation types. Likewise, most can easily convert 2x4 wall construction to 2x6, or vice versa.

Terms and Conditions
These designs are protected under the terms of United States Copyright Law and may not be copied or reproduced in any way, by any means, unless you have purchased Sepias or Reproducibles which clearly indicate your right to copy or reproduce. We authorize the use of your chosen design as an aid in the construction of one single-family home only. You may not use this design to build a second or multiple dwellings without purchasing another blueprint or blueprints or paying additional design fees.

Disclaimer
We and the designers we work with have put substantial care and effort into the creation of our blueprints. However, because we cannot provide on-site consultation, supervision and control over actual construction, and because of the great variance in local building requirements, building practices and soil, seismic, weather and other conditions, WE CANNOT MAKE ANY WARRANTY, EXPRESS OR IMPLIED, WITH RESPECT TO THE CONTENT OR USE OF OUR BLUEPRINTS, INCLUDING BUT NOT LIMITED TO ANY WARRANTY OF MERCHANTABILITY OR OF FITNESS FOR A PARTICULAR PURPOSE.

How Many Blueprints Do You Need?
A single set of blueprints is sufficient to study a home in greater detail. However, if you are planning to obtain cost estimates from a contractor or subcontractors—or if you are planning to build immediately—you will need more sets. Because additional sets are cheaper when ordered in quantity with the original order, make sure you order enough blueprints to satisfy all requirements. The following checklist will help you determine how many you need:

_____Owner

_____Builder (generally requires at least three sets; one as a legal document, one to use during inspections, and at least one to give to subcontractors)

_____Local Building Department (often requires two sets)

_____Mortgage Lender (usually one set for a conventional loan; three sets for FHA or VA loans)

_____TOTAL NUMBER OF SETS

Toll Free 1-800-848-2550
Regular Office Hours:
8:00 a.m. to 8:00 p.m. Eastern Time, Monday through Friday Our staff will gladly answer any questions during normal office hours. Our answering service can place orders after hours or on weekends.

If we receive your order by 4:00 p.m. Eastern Time, Monday through Friday, we'll process it the same day and ship within 48 hours. When ordering by phone, please have your charge card ready. We'll also ask you for the Order Form Key Number at the bottom of the coupon.

By FAX: Copy the Order Form on the next page and send it on our FAX line: 1-800-224-6699. or 1-520-544-3086

Canadian Customers
Order Toll-Free 1-800-561-4169
For faster service and plans that are modified for building in Canada, customers may now call in orders directly to our Canadian supplier of plans and charge the purchase to a charge card. Or, you may complete the order form at right, adding 40% to all prices and mail in Canadian funds to:

The Plan Centre 60 Baffin Place
Unit 5
Waterloo, Ontario N2V 1Z7

OR: Copy the Order Form and send it via our Canadian Faxline: 1-800-719-3291.

The Home Customizer®

"This house is perfect...if only the family room were two feet wider." Sound familiar? In response to the numerous requests for this type of modification, Home Planners has developed **The Home Customizer® Package**. This exclusive package offers our top-of-the-line materials to make it easy for anyone, anywhere to customize any Home Planners design to fit their needs. Check the index on page 344 for those plans which are customizable.

Some of the changes you can make to any of our plans include:

- exterior elevation changes
- kitchen and bath modifications
- roof, wall and foundation changes
- room additions and more!

The Home Customizer® Package includes everything you'll need to make the necessary changes to your favorite Home Planners design. The package includes:

- instruction book with examples
- architectural scale and clear work film
- erasable red marker and removable correction tape
- ¼"-scale furniture cutouts
- 1 set reproducible, erasable Sepias
- 1 set study blueprints for communicating changes to your design professional
- a copyright release letter so you can make copies as you need them
- referral letter with the name, address and telephone number of the professional in your region who is trained in modifying Home Planners designs efficiently and inexpensively.

The price of the **Home Customizer® Package** ranges from $605 to $845, depending on the price schedule of the design you have chosen. **The Home Customizer® Package** will not only save you 25% to 75% of the cost of drawing the plans from scratch with a custom architect or engineer, it will also give you the flexibility to have your changes and modifications made by our referral network or by the professional of your choice. Now it's even easier and more affordable to have the custom home you've always wanted.

 For information about The Home Customizer® Package, or to order call 1-800-521-6797.

BLUEPRINTS ARE NOT RETURNABLE

For Customer Service
call toll free 1-888-690-1116.

ORDER FORM

HOME PLANS, 3275 WEST INA ROAD
SUITE 110, TUCSON, ARIZONA 85741

THE BASIC BLUEPRINT PACKAGE
Rush me the following (please refer to the Plans Index and Price Schedule in this section):

_____ Set(s) of blueprints for plan number(s) _____.	$_____
_____ Set(s) of sepias for plan number(s) _____.	$_____
_____ Additional identical blueprints in same order @ $50 per set.	$_____
_____ Reverse blueprints @ $50 per set.	$_____
_____ Home Customizer® Package for Plan(s)_____.	$_____

IMPORTANT EXTRAS
Rush me the following:

_____ Materials List @ $40 Schedule A-D; $50 Schedule E	$_____
_____ Specification Outlines @ $10 each.	$_____
_____ Detail Sets @ $14.95 each; any two for $22.95; three for $29.95; all four for $39.95 (save $19.85).	$_____

❑ Plumbing ❑ Electrical ❑ Construction ❑ Mechanical
(These helpful details provide general construction advice and are not specific to any single plan.)

DECK BLUEPRINTS

_____ Set(s) of Deck Plan _____.	$_____
_____ Additional identical blueprints in same order @ $10 per set.	$_____
_____ Reverse blueprints @ $10 per set.	$_____
_____ Set of Standard Deck Details @ $14.95 per set.	$_____
_____ Complete Deck Building Package (Best Buy!) Includes Custom Deck Plan _____ (see Index and Price Schedule) Plus Standard Deck Details.	$_____

LANDSCAPE BLUEPRINTS

_____ Set(s) of Landscape Plan _____.	$_____
_____ Additional identical blueprints in same order @ $10 per set.	$_____
_____ Reverse blueprints @ $10 per set.	$_____

Please indicate the appropriate region of the country for Plant & Material List. (See Map on page 340): Region _____

POSTAGE AND HANDLING	1-3 sets	4+ sets
DELIVERY (Requires street address - No P.O. Boxes)		
•Regular Service (Allow 7-10 days delivery)	❑ $15.00	❑ $18.00
•Priority (Allow 4-5 days delivery)	❑ $20.00	❑ $30.00
•Express (Allow 3 days delivery)	❑ $30.00	❑ $40.00
CERTIFIED MAIL (Requires signature) If no street address available. (Allow 7-10 days delivery)	❑ $20.00	❑ $30.00
OVERSEAS DELIVERY Note: All delivery times are from date Blueprint Package is shipped.	fax, phone or mail for quote	

POSTAGE (From box above) $_____
SUB-TOTAL $_____

SALES TAX: (AZ, CA, DC, IL, MI, MN, NY & WA residents, please add appropriate state and local sales tax.)

TOTAL (Sub-total and tax) $_____
$_____

YOUR ADDRESS (please print)

Name _____
Street _____
City _____ State _____ Zip _____
Daytime telephone number (_____) _____

FOR CREDIT CARD ORDERS ONLY
Please fill in the information below:

Credit card number _____

Exp. Date: Month/Year _____

Check one ❑ Visa ❑ MasterCard ❑ Discover Card

Signature _____

Please check appropriate box: Order Form Key
❑ Licensed Builder-Contractor   [CHPEBP]
❑ Homeowner

 ORDER TOLL FREE
1-800-848-2250 or 1- 520-297-8200

CREATIVE HOMEOWNER PRESS®
How-To Books for...

ADDING SPACE WITHOUT ADDING ON

Cramped for space? This book, which replaces our old book of the same title, shows you how to find space you may not know you had and convert it into useful living areas. 40 colorful photographs and 530 full-color drawings.

BOOK #: 277680   192pp.   8½"x10⅞"

BASIC WIRING
(Third Edition, Conforms to latest National Electrical Code)

Included are 350 large, clear, full-color illustrations and no-nonsense step-by-step instructions. Shows how to replace receptacles and switches; repair a lamp; install ceiling and attic fans; and more.

BOOK #: 277048   160pp.   8½"x10⅞"

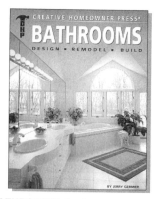

BATHROOMS: Design, Remodel, Build

Shows how to plan, construct, and finish a bathroom. Remodel floors; rebuild walls and ceilings; and install windows, skylights, and plumbing fixtures. Specific tools and materials are given for each project.

BOOK #: 277053   192pp.   8½"x10⅞"

Designing and Planning BATHROOMS

From the planning stage to final decorating, this book includes innovative and dramatic ideas for master baths, fitness bathrooms, powder rooms, and more. 200 inspirational color illustrations and photographs.

Book #: 287627   96 pp.   8½"x10⅞"

BUILD A KIDS' PLAY YARD

Here are detailed plans and step-by-step instructions for building the play structures that kids love most: swing set, monkey bars, balance beam, playhouse, teeter-totter, sandboxes, kid-sized picnic table, and a play tower that supports a slide. 200 color photographs and illustrations.

BOOK #: 277622   144 pp.   8½"x10⅞"

CABINETS & BUILT-INS

26 custom cabinetry projects are included for every room in the house, from kitchen cabinets to a bedroom wall unit, a bunk bed, computer workstation, and more. Also included are chapters on tools, techniques, finishing, and materials.

BOOK #: 277079   160 pp.   8½"x10⅞"

DECKS: Plan, Design, Build

With this book, even the novice builder can build a deck that perfectly fits his yard. The step-by-step instructions lead the reader from laying out footings to adding railings. Includes three deck projects, 500 color drawings, and photographs.

BOOK #: 277180   176pp.   8½"x10⅞"

FURNITURE REPAIR & REFINISHING

From structural repairs to restoring older finishes or entirely refinishing furniture: a hands-on step-by-step approach to furniture repair and restoration. More than 430 color photographs and 60 full-color drawings.

BOOK #: 277335   240pp.   8½"x10⅞"

HOUSE FRAMING

Written for those with beginning to intermediate building skills, this book is designed to walk you through the framing basics, from assembling simple partitions to cutting compound angles on dormer rafters. More than 400 full-color drawings.

BOOK #: 277655   240pp.   8½"x10⅞"

the Home Planner, Builder & Owner

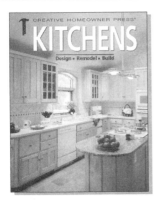

KITCHENS: Design, Remodel, Build

This is the reference book for modern kitchen design, with more than 100 full-color photos to help homeowners plan the layout. Step-by-step instructions illustrate basic plumbing and wiring techniques; how to finish walls and ceilings; and more.

BOOK #: 277065   192pp.   8½"x10⅞"

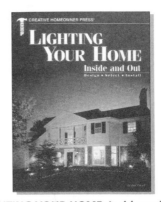

LIGHTING YOUR HOME: Inside and Out

Lighting should be selected with care. This book thoroughly explains lighting design for every room as well as outdoors. It is also a step-by-step manual that shows how to install the fixtures. More than 125 photos and 400 drawings.

BOOK #: 277583   160pp.   8½"x10⅞"

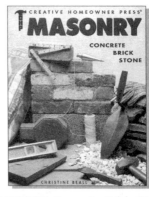

MASONRY: Concrete, Brick, Stone

Concrete, brick, and stone choices are detailed with step-by-step instructions and over 35 color photographs and 460 illustrations. Projects include a brick or stone garden wall, steps and patios, a concrete-block retaining wall, a concrete sidewalk.

BOOK #: 277106   176pp.   8½"x10⅞"

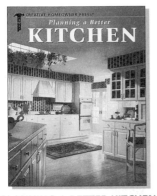

PLANNING A BETTER KITCHEN

From layout to design, no detail of efficient and functional kitchen planning is overlooked. Covers everything from built-in ovens and ranges to sinks and faucets. Over 260 color illustrations and photographs.

Book #: 287495   96 pp.   8½"x10⅞"

PLANNING YOUR ADDITION

Planning an addition to your home involves a daunting number of choices, from choosing a contractor to selecting bathroom tile. Using 280 color drawings and photographs, architect/author Jerry Germer helps you make the right decision.

BOOK #: 277004   192pp.   8½"x10⅞"

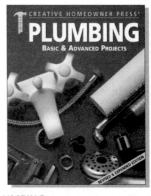

PLUMBING: Basic & Advanced Projects

Take the guesswork out of plumbing repair and installation for old and new systems. Projects include replacing faucets, unclogging drains, installing a tub, replacing a water heater, and much more. 500 illustrations and diagrams.

BOOK #: 277620   176pp.   8½"x10⅞"

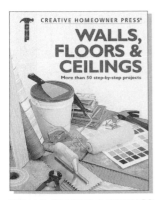

WALLS, FLOORS & CEILINGS

Here's the definitive guide to interiors. It shows you how to replace old surfaces with new professional-looking ones. Projects include installing molding, skylights, insulation, flooring, carpeting, and more. Over 500 color photos and drawings.

BOOK #: 277697   176pp.   8½"x10⅞"

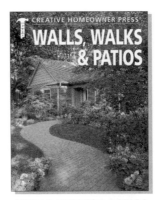

WALLS, WALKS & PATIOS

Learn how to build a patio from concrete, stone, or brick and complement it with one of a dozen walks. Learn about simple mortarless walls, landscape timber walls, and hefty brick and stone walls. A special design section helps turn your dreams into reality. 50 photographs and 320 illustrations.

Book #: 277994   192 pp.   8½"x10⅞"

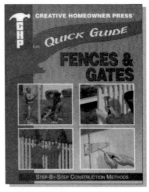

QUICK GUIDE: FENCES & GATES

Learn how to build and install all kinds of fences and gates for your yard, from hand-built wood privacy and picket fences to newer prefabricated vinyl and chain-link types. Over 200 two-color drawings illustrate step-by-step procedures.

BOOK #: 287732   80pp.   8½"x10⅞"

Place your Order ...

The Smart Approach to [...]

Everything you need to know [...]
bathroom like a professional is [...]
book. Creative solutions and pra[...]
space, the latest in fixtures and [...]
features accompany over 150 ph[...]

BOOK #: 287225   176pp.   9"x10[...]

[...]OLOR SCHEME

[...]tive decorating schemes for
[...]e and flair of a professional in-
[...]rn how color, light, pattern, and
[...]her. Over 170 full-color illustrations
[...]ns of wallcovering, paint, fabric, and
[...] design schemes.

287531   96pp.   8½"x10⅞"

BOOK ORDER FORM   *Please Print*
SHIP TO:

Name: _____

Address: _____

City: _____ State: _____ Zip: _____ Phone Number: _____

(Should there be a problem with your order)

Quantity	Title	Price	CHP #	Cost
_____	Adding Space without Adding On	14.95	277680	_____
_____	Basic Wiring	14.95	277048	_____
_____	Bathrooms: Design, Remodel, Build	14.95	277053	_____
_____	Build a Kids' Play Yard	14.95	277662	_____
_____	Cabinets & Built-Ins	14.95	277079	_____
_____	Choosing a Color Scheme	9.95	287531	_____
_____	Color in the American Home	16.95	287264	_____
_____	Decks: Plan, Design, Build	14.95	277180	_____
_____	Designing and Planning Bathrooms	9.95	287627	_____
_____	Furniture Repair & Refinishing	19.95	277335	_____
_____	House Framing	19.95	277655	_____
_____	Kitchens: Design, Remodel, Build (New Ed.)	14.95	277065	_____
_____	Lighting Your Home Inside & Out	14.95	277583	_____
_____	Masonry: Concrete, Brick, Stone	14.95	277106	_____
_____	Planning a Better Kitchen	9.95	287495	_____
_____	Planning Your Addition	14.95	277004	_____
_____	Plumbing: Basic & Advanced Projects	14.95	277620	_____
_____	The Smart Approach to Bath Design	16.95	287225	_____
_____	Walls, Floors & Ceilings	14.95	277697	_____
_____	Walls, Walks & Patios	14.95	277994	_____
_____	Quick Guide - Attics	7.95	287711	_____
_____	Quick Guide - Basements	7.95	287242	_____
_____	Quick Guide - Ceramic Tile	7.95	287730	_____
_____	Quick Guide - Decks	7.95	277344	_____
_____	Quick Guide - Fences & Gates	7.95	287732	_____
_____	Quick Guide - Floors	7.95	287734	_____

Quantity	Title	Price	CHP #	Cost
_____	Quick Guide - Garages & Carports	7.95	287785	_____
_____	Quick Guide - Gazebos	7.95	287757	_____
_____	Quick Guide - Insulation & Ventilation	7.95	287367	_____
_____	Quick Guide - Interior & Exterior Painting	7.95	287784	_____
_____	Quick Guide - Masonry Walls	7.95	287741	_____
_____	Quick Guide - Patios & Walks	7.95	287778	_____
_____	Quick Guide - Plumbing	7.95	287863	_____
_____	Quick Guide - Ponds & Fountains	7.95	287804	_____
_____	Quick Guide - Roofing	7.95	287807	_____
_____	Quick Guide - Shelving & Storage	7.95	287763	_____
_____	Quick Guide - Siding	7.95	287892	_____
_____	Quick Guide - Stairs & Railings	7.95	287755	_____
_____	Quick Guide - Storage Sheds	7.95	287815	_____
_____	Quick Guide - Swimming Pools & Spas	7.95	287901	_____
_____	Quick Guide - Trim & Molding	7.95	287745	_____
_____	Quick Guide - Walls & Ceilings	7.95	287792	_____
_____	Quick Guide - Windows & Doors	7.95	287812	_____
_____	Quick Guide - Wiring, Second Edition	7.95	287884	_____

Number of Books Ordered _____ Total for Books _____

NJ Residents add 6% tax _____

Prices subject to change without notice.   Subtotal _____

Postage/Handling Charges _____
$2.50 for first book / $1.00 for each additional book

Make checks (in U.S. currency only) payable to: **Total** _____
CREATIVE HOMEOWNER PRESS®
P.O. BOX 38, 24 Park Way
Upper Saddle River, New Jersey 07458-9960